AMAZINGLY STUPID MAD®

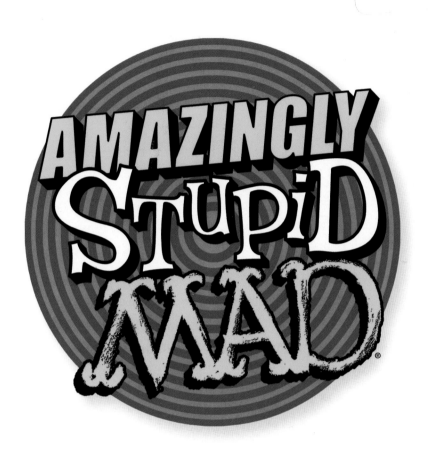

Also Available from MAD Books

Insanely Awesome MAD

Epic MAD

Spy vs. Spy Omnibus

MAD About Super Heroes Vol. 2

Spy vs. Spy: The Top Secret Files!

Plus

Planet Tad (HarperCollins)

MAD's Greatest Artists: Sergio Aragonés (Running Press)

The MAD Fold-In Collection 1964–2010 (Chronicle Books)

Spy vs. Spy 2: The Joke and Dagger Files (Watson-Guptill Publications)

MAD About *Star Wars* (Ballantine Books – Del Rey)

MAD Archives Volume 3 (DC Comics)

MAD Kindle Fire eBooks

MAD About Super Heroes Vol. 1

MAD About Super Heroes Vol. 2

MAD About the 50s

MAD About the 60s

MAD About the Oscars

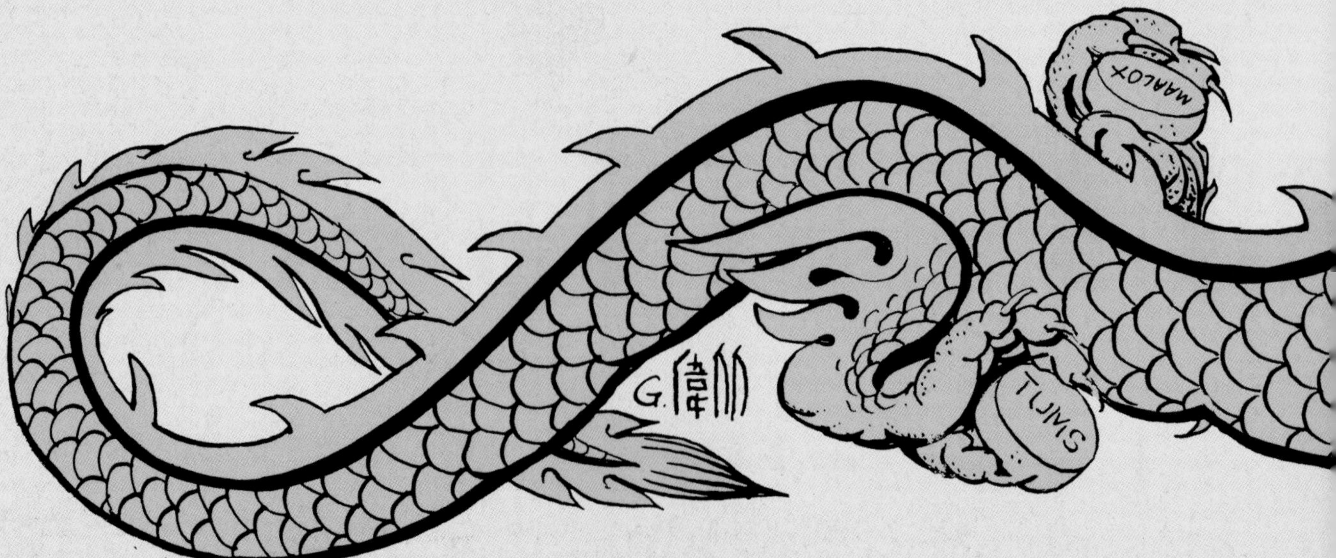
MAALOX
TUMS

AMAZINGLY STUPID MAD

By
"The Usual Gang of Idiots"

MAD
NEW YORK
BOOKS™

MAD BOOKS

William Gaines FOUNDER

John Ficarra EDITOR

Charlie Kadau, Joe Raiola SENIOR EDITORS

Dave Croatto, Jacob Lambert ASSOCIATE EDITORS

Sam Viviano ART DIRECTOR

Ryan Flanders ASSISTANT ART DIRECTOR

Doug Thomson PRODUCTION ARTIST

CONTRIBUTING WRITERS AND ARTISTS:
"The Usual Gang of Idiots"

ADMINISTRATION

Diane Nelson PRESIDENT
Dan DiDio and Jim Lee CO-PUBLISHERS
Geoff Johns CHIEF CREATIVE OFFICER
John Rood EXECUTIVE VP – SALES, MARKETING AND BUSINESS DEVELOPMENT
Amy Genkins SENIOR VP – BUSINESS AND LEGAL AFFAIRS
Nairi Gardiner SENIOR VP – FINANCE
Jeff Boison VP – PUBLISHING OPERATIONS
John Cunningham VP – MARKETING
Terri Cunningham VP – TALENT RELATIONS AND SERVICES
Anne DePies VP – STRATEGY PLANNING AND REPORTING
Amit Desai SENIOR VP – FRANCHISE MANAGEMENT
Alison Gill SENIOR VP – MANUFACTURING AND OPERATIONS
Bob Harras VP – EDITOR-IN-CHIEF
Jason James VP – INTERACTIVE MARKETING
Hank Kanalz SENIOR VP – DIGITAL
Jay Kogan VP – BUSINESS AND LEGAL AFFAIRS, PUBLISHING
Jack Mahan VP – BUSINESS AFFAIRS, TALENT
Nick Napolitano VP – MANUFACTURING ADMINISTRATION
Rich Palermo VP – BUSINESS AFFAIRS, MEDIA
Sue Pohja VP – BOOK SALES
Courtney Simmons SENIOR VP – PUBLICITY
Bob Wayne SENIOR VP – SALES

SUSTAINABLE FORESTRY INITIATIVE
Certified Chain of Custody
At Least 25% Certified Forest Content
www.sfiprogram.org
SFI-01042
APPLIES TO TEXT STOCK ONLY

Visit MAD online at: www.madmagazine.com

Though Alfred E. Neuman wasn't the first to say "a fool and his money are soon parted," here's
your chance to prove the old adage right — subscribe to MAD! Simply call 1-800-4-MADMAG
and mention code AWFMDIA. Operators are standing by (the water cooler).

CONTENTS

"Drawn Out Dramas" Throughout by Sergio Aragonés

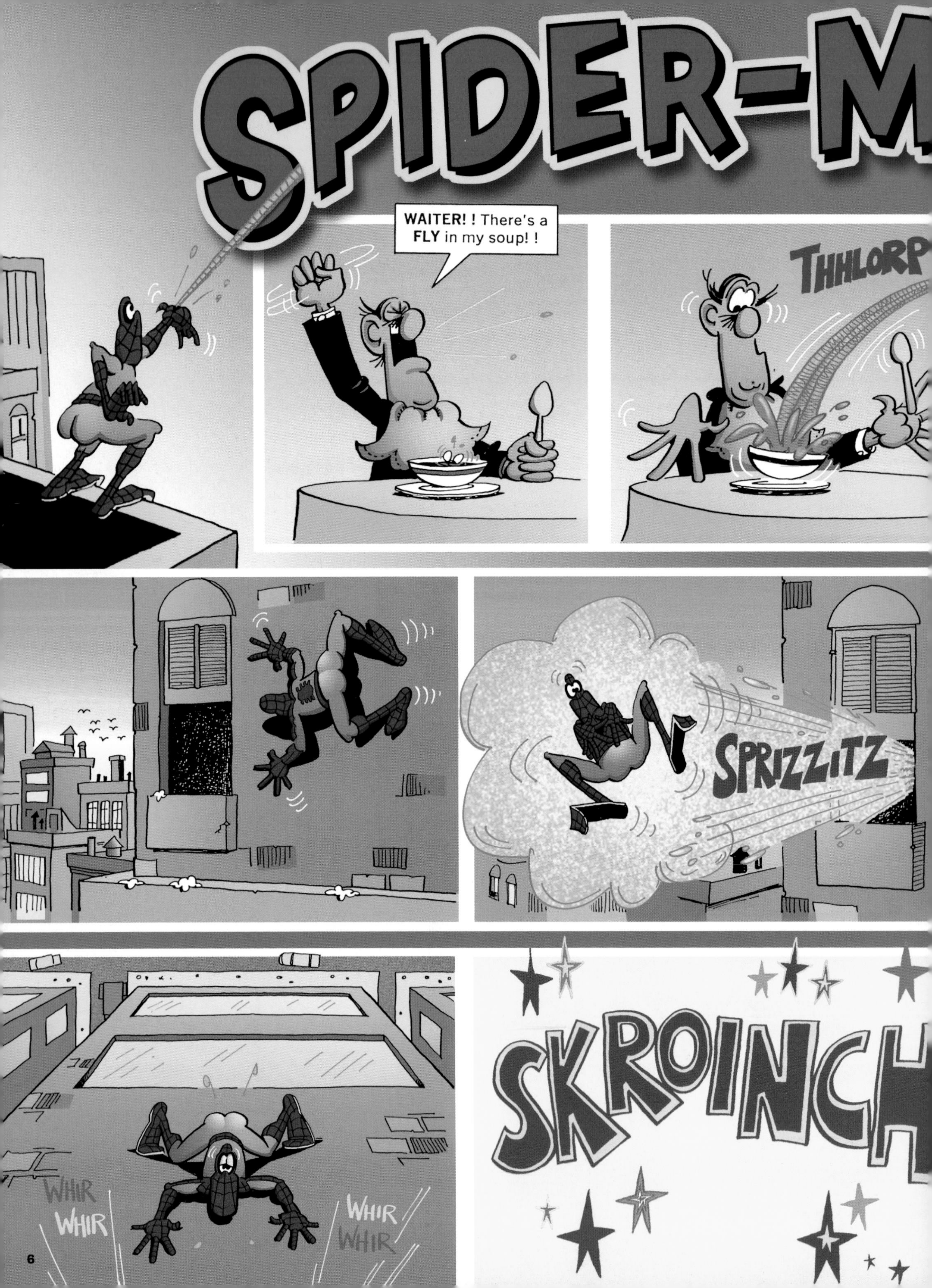

SPIDER-M
WAITER! ! There's a FLY in my soup! !
THHLORP
SPRIZZITZ
WHIR WHIR
WHIR WHIR
SKROINCH

AN FUNNIES

WRITER AND ARTIST: DON MARTIN

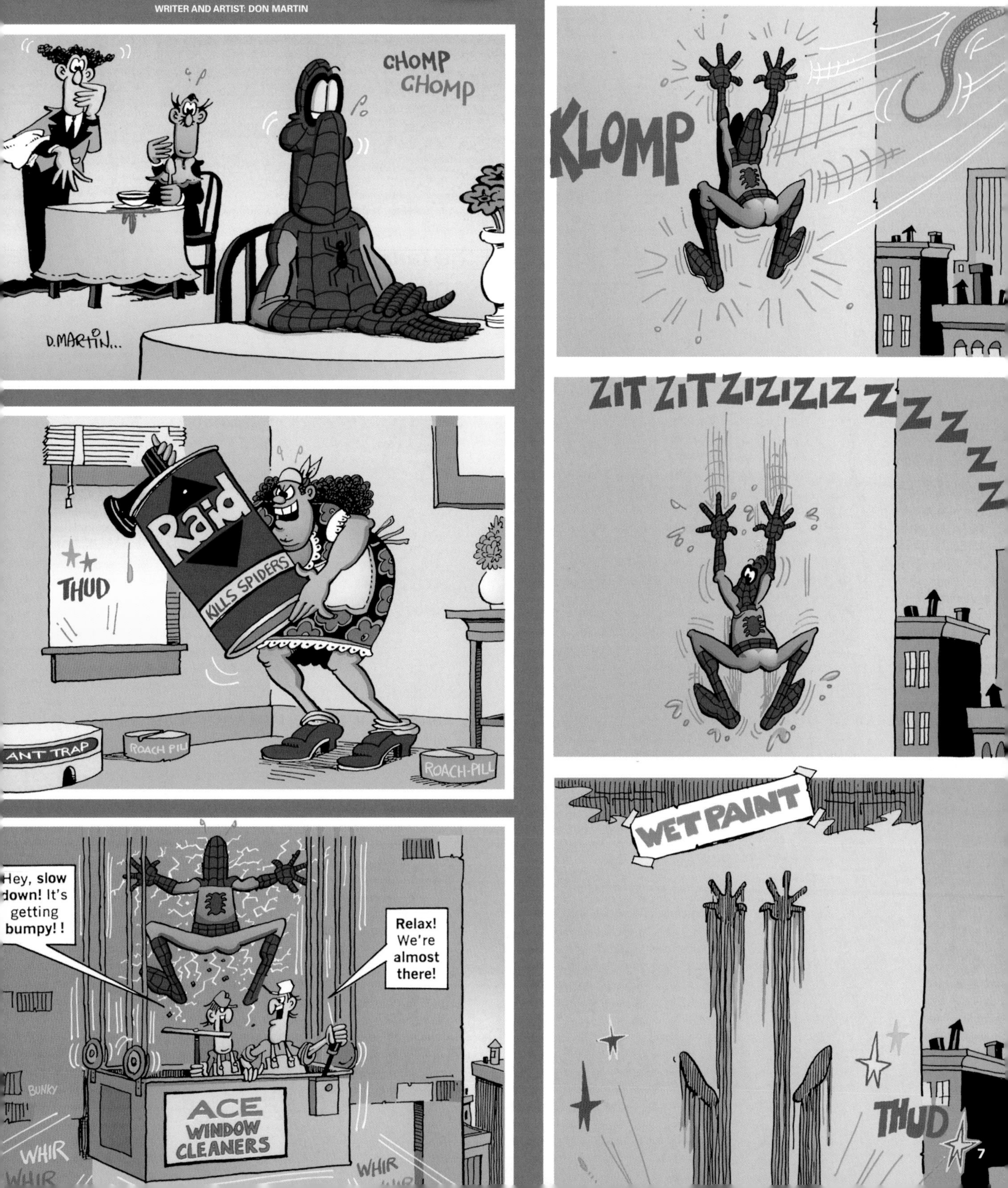
CHOMP
CHOMP
D.MARTIN...
Raid
KILLS SPIDERS
THUD
ANT TRAP
ROACH PILL
ROACH-PILL
Hey, slow down! It's getting bumpy!!
Relax! We're almost there!
ACE WINDOW CLEANERS
BUNKY
WHIR
WHIR
WHIR
KLOMP
ZIT ZIT ZIZIZIZ ZZZZZ
WET PAINT
THUD

A COLLECTION OF VITAL TEMPERATURE READINGS

95°

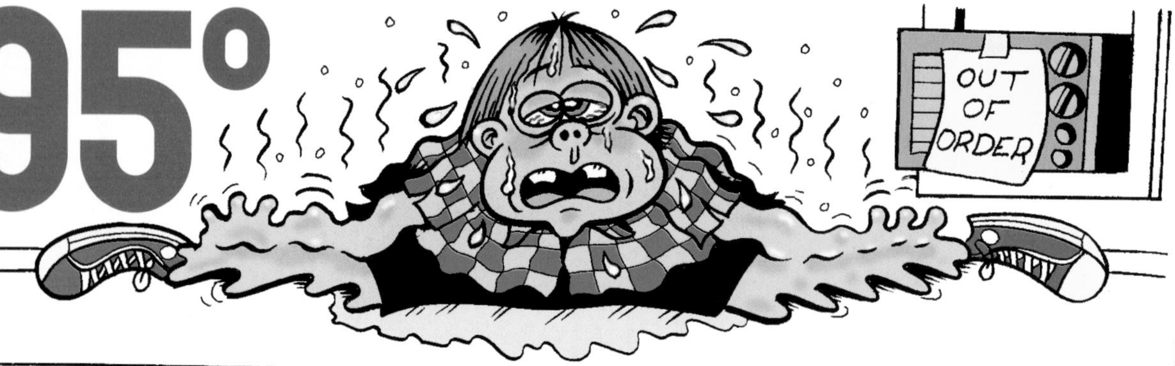
OUT OF ORDER

...is the lowest the temperature is when your air conditioner konks out.

12°

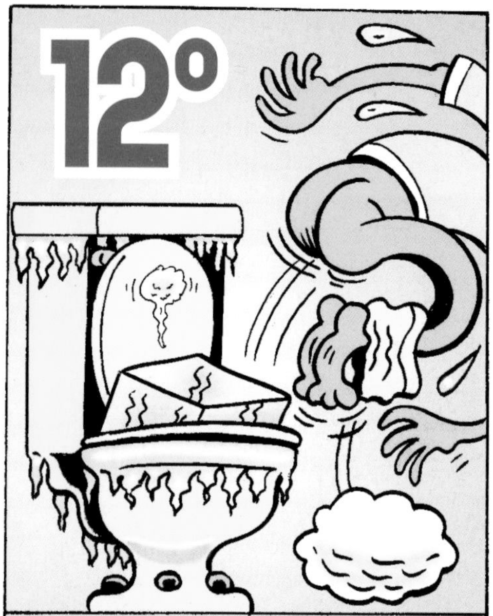

...is the temperature of the average toilet seat on the average Winter morning.

23.7°

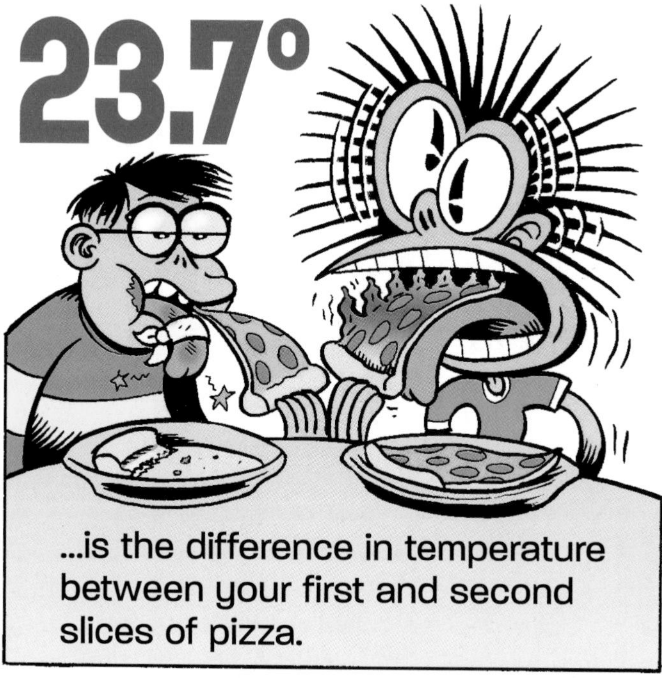

...is the difference in temperature between your first and second slices of pizza.

52°

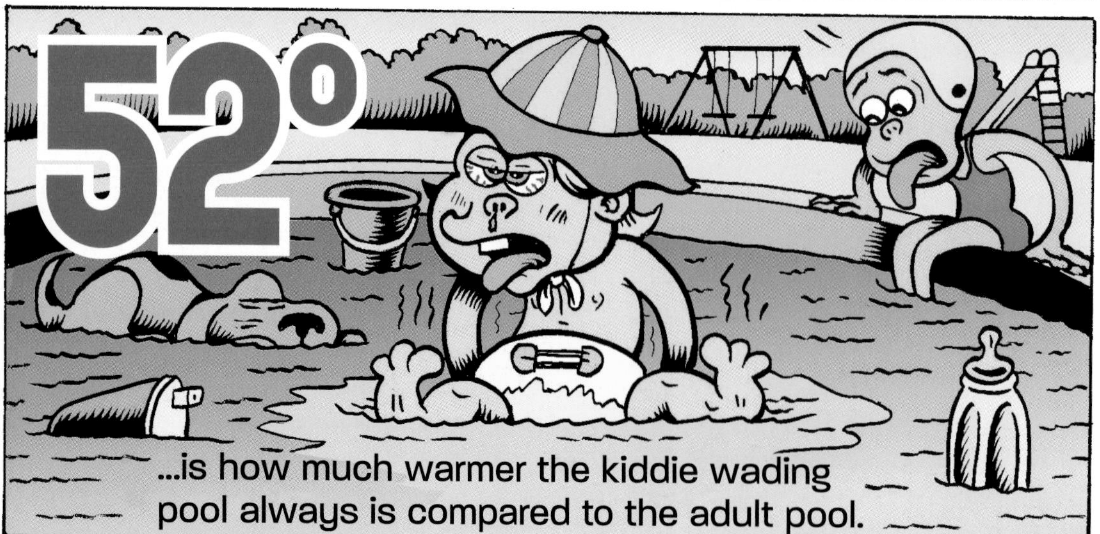

...is how much warmer the kiddie wading pool always is compared to the adult pool.

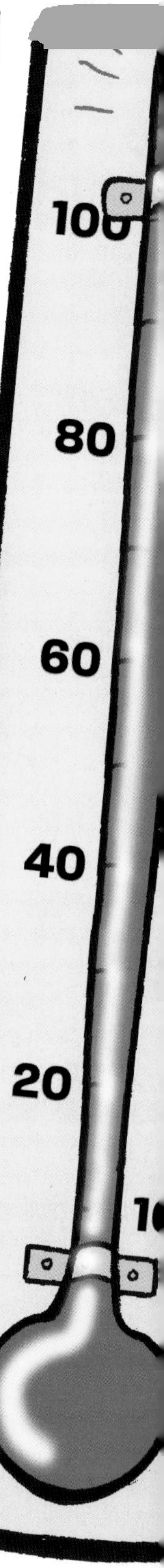
100
80
60
40
20
10

WRITER: J. PRETE ARTIST: PETER BAGGE

FOUND ON THE MAD THERMOMETER

103.7°

...is your temperature when your Mother finally announces to the world, "I think it's time we called the Doctor!"

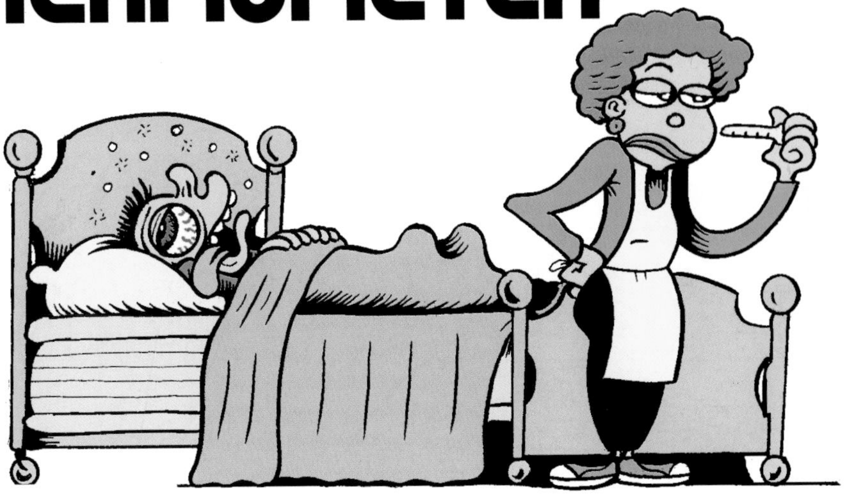

110°

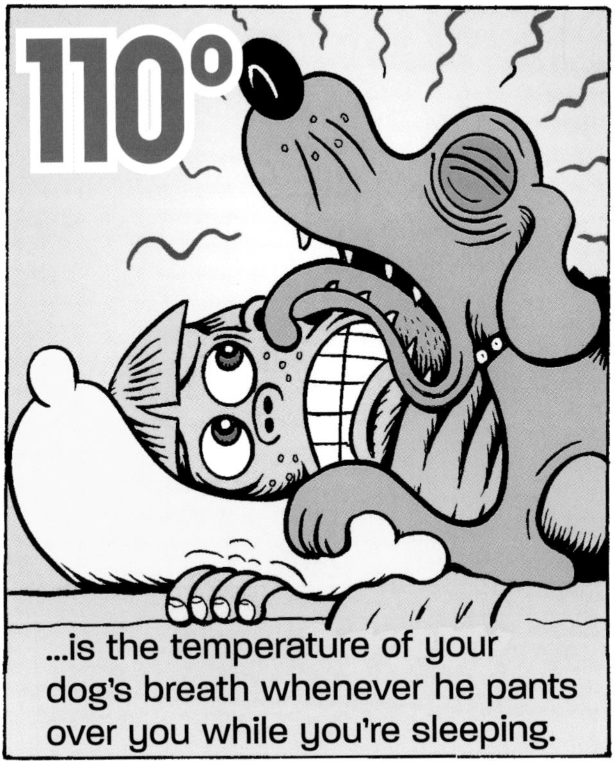

...is the temperature of your dog's breath whenever he pants over you while you're sleeping.

9°

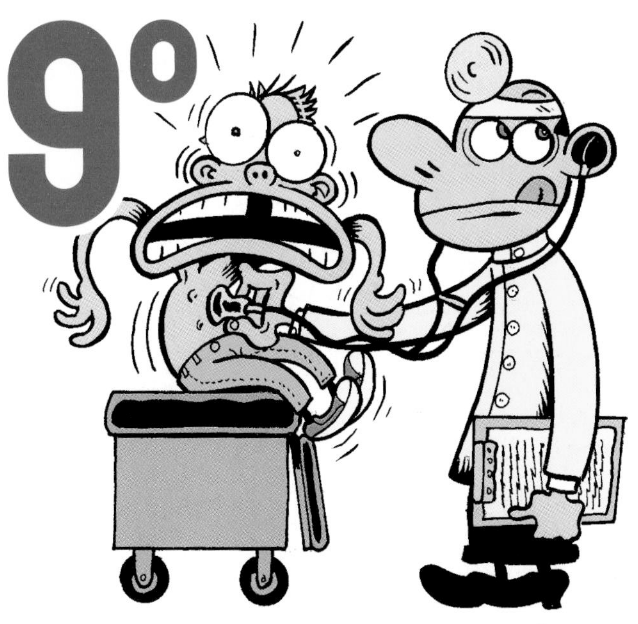

...is the average temperature of your Doctor's stethoscope when he tries to examine you.

75.5°

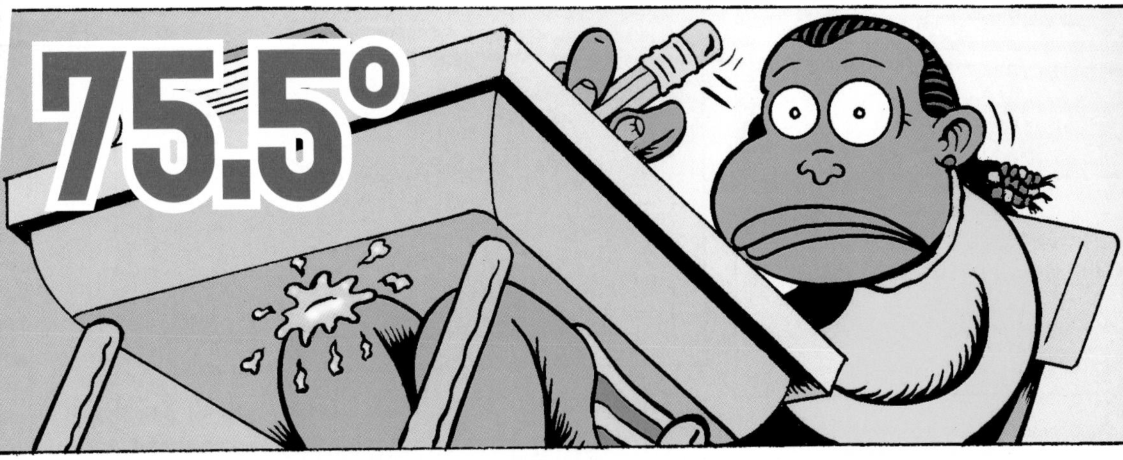

...is the temperature when the chewing gum stuck to the bottom of your school desk starts to get yecchy again.

34.4°

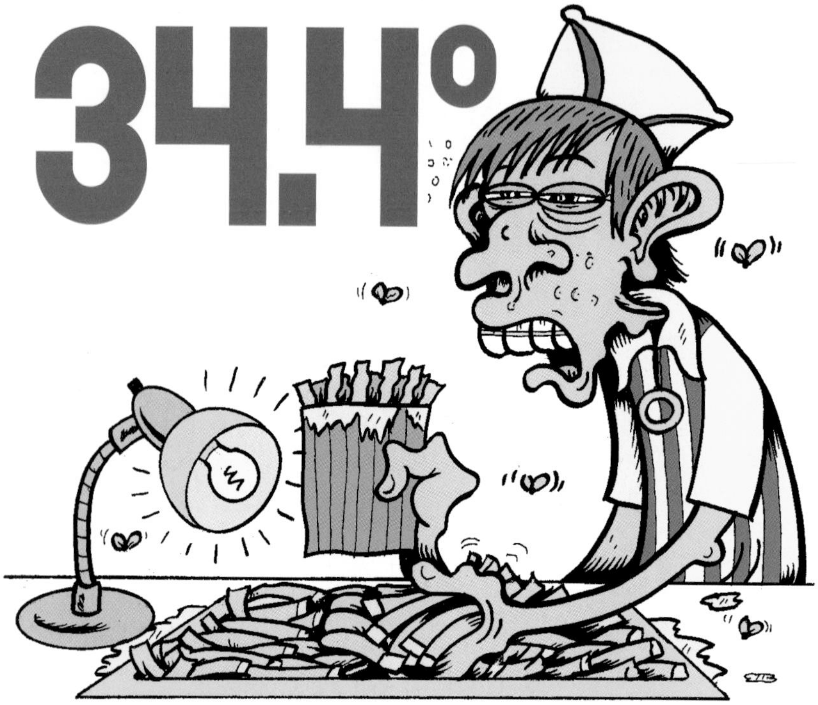

...is the hottest those artificial heating lamps will ever keep fast-food French fries.

104.5°

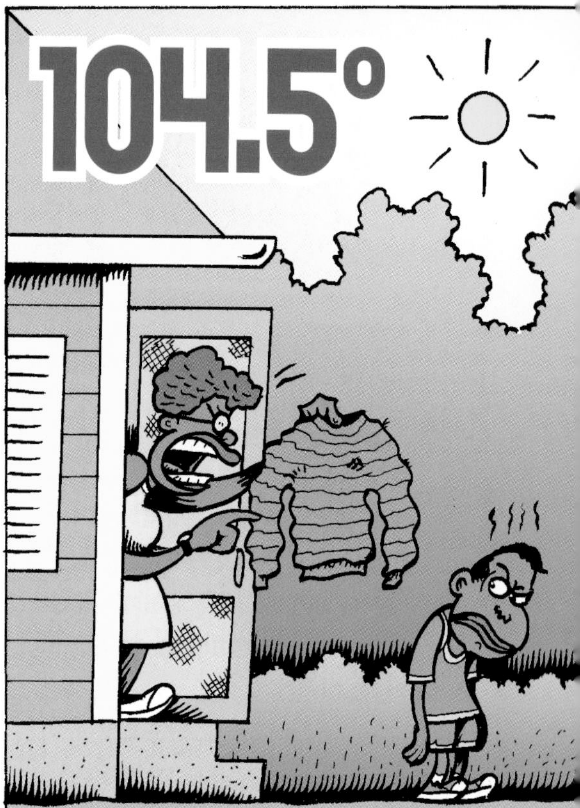

...is the minimum the temperature must be for your Mother to let you step foot out of the house without saying, "Take a sweater for later on!"

92.6°

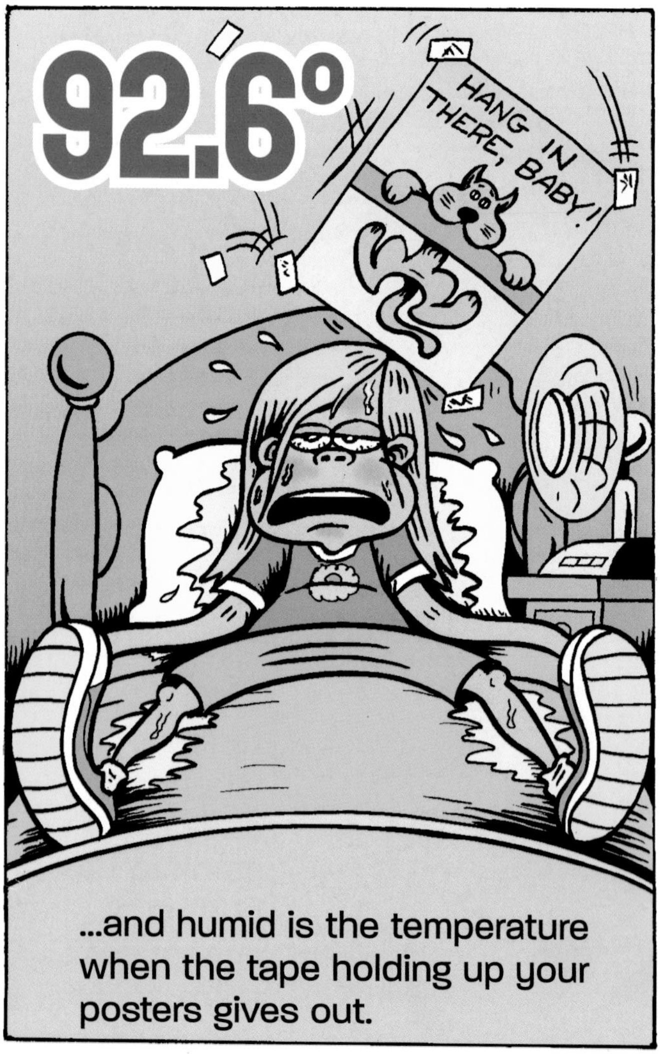

HANG IN THERE, BABY!

...and humid is the temperature when the tape holding up your posters gives out.

212°

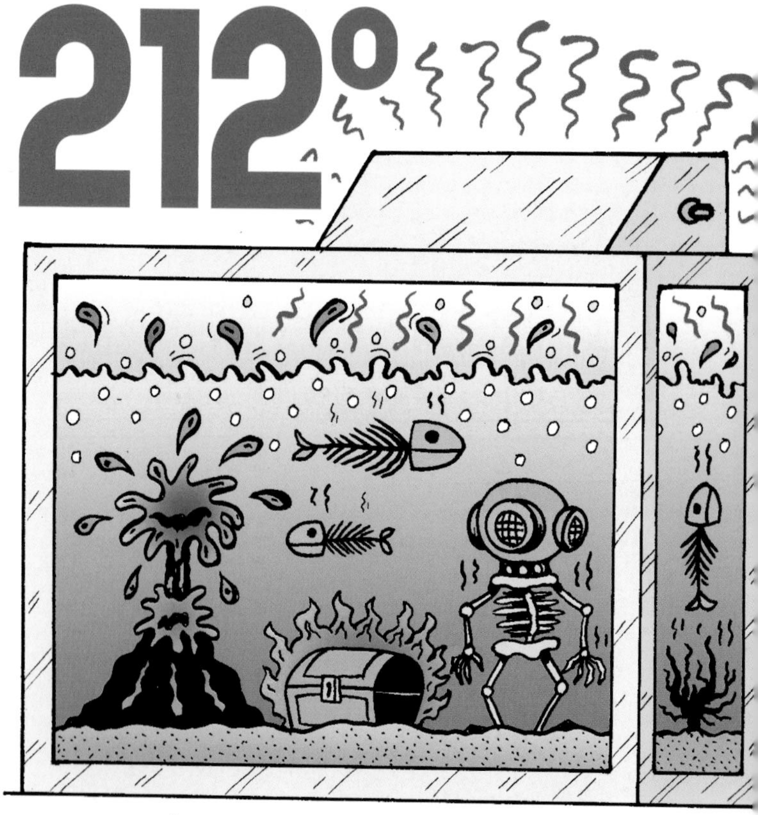

...was the temperature in your fish tank the night the electric heater went haywire.

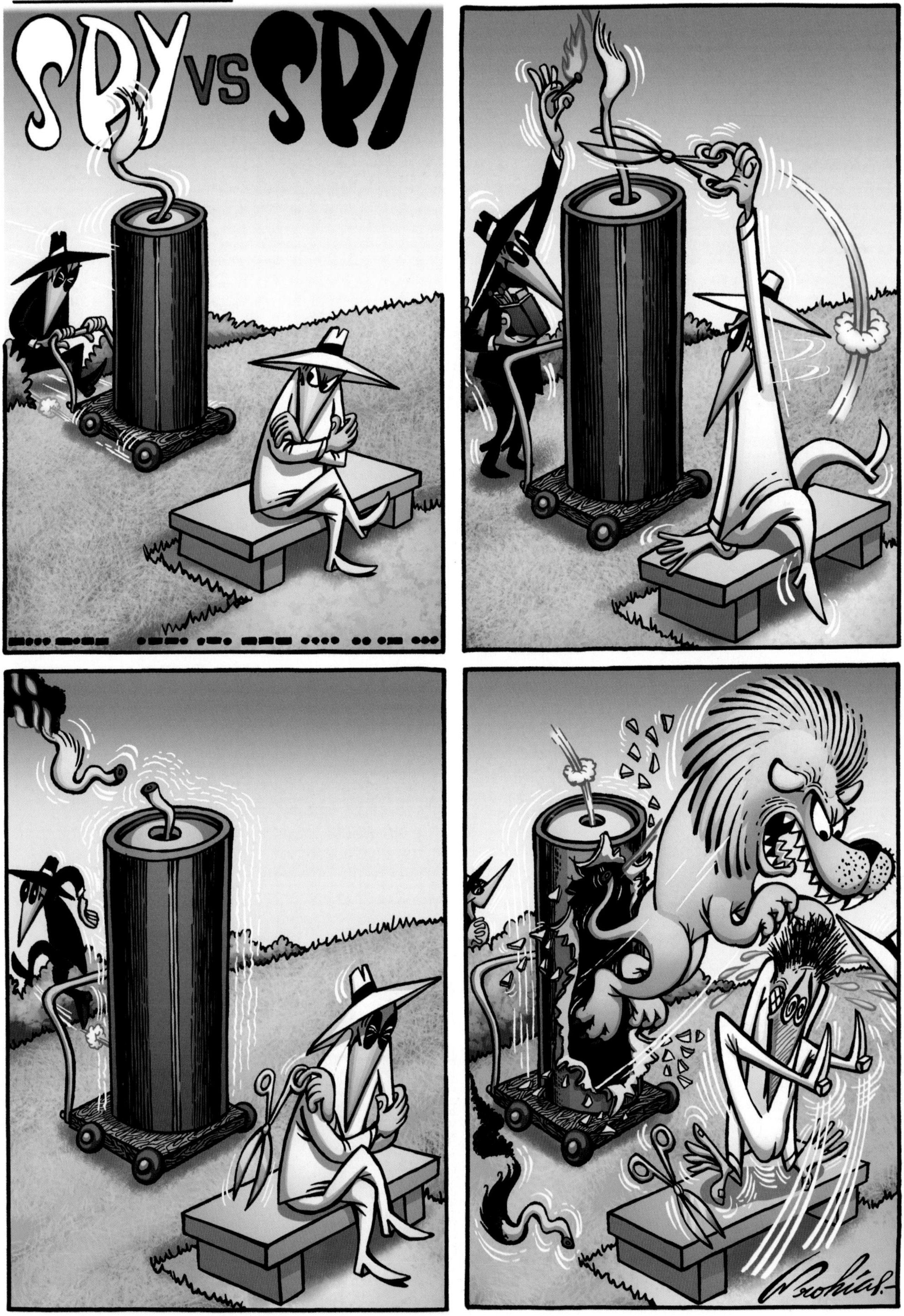
SPY VS SPY

WRITER AND ARTIST: ANTONIO PROHIAS COLORIST: CARRIE STRACHAN

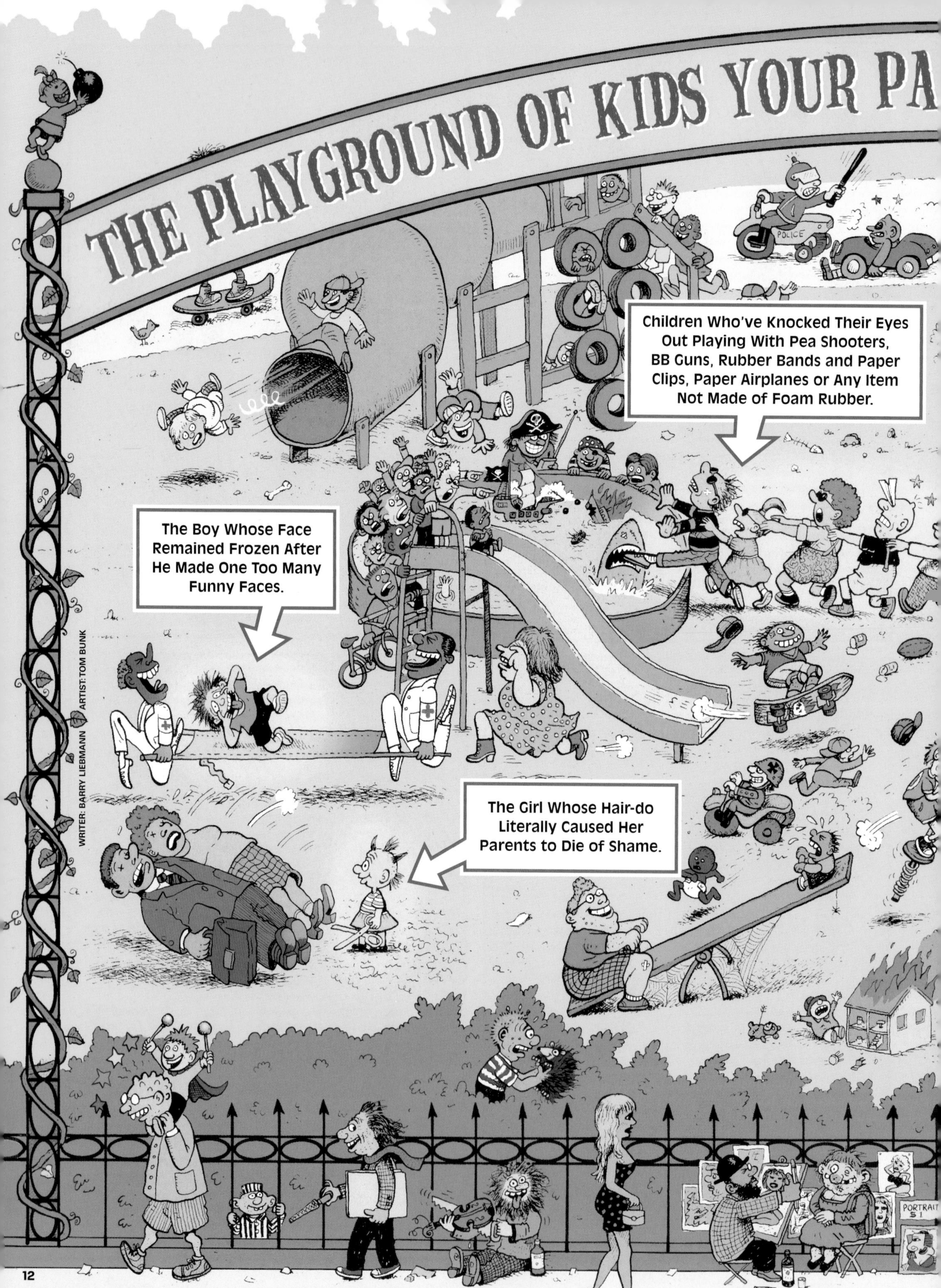
THE PLAYGROUND OF KIDS YOUR PA
Children Who've Knocked Their Eyes Out Playing With Pea Shooters, BB Guns, Rubber Bands and Paper Clips, Paper Airplanes or Any Item Not Made of Foam Rubber.
The Boy Whose Face Remained Frozen After He Made One Too Many Funny Faces.
The Girl Whose Hair-do Literally Caused Her Parents to Die of Shame.
POLICE
PORTRAIT $1
WRITER: BARRY LIEBMANN ARTIST: TOM BUNK

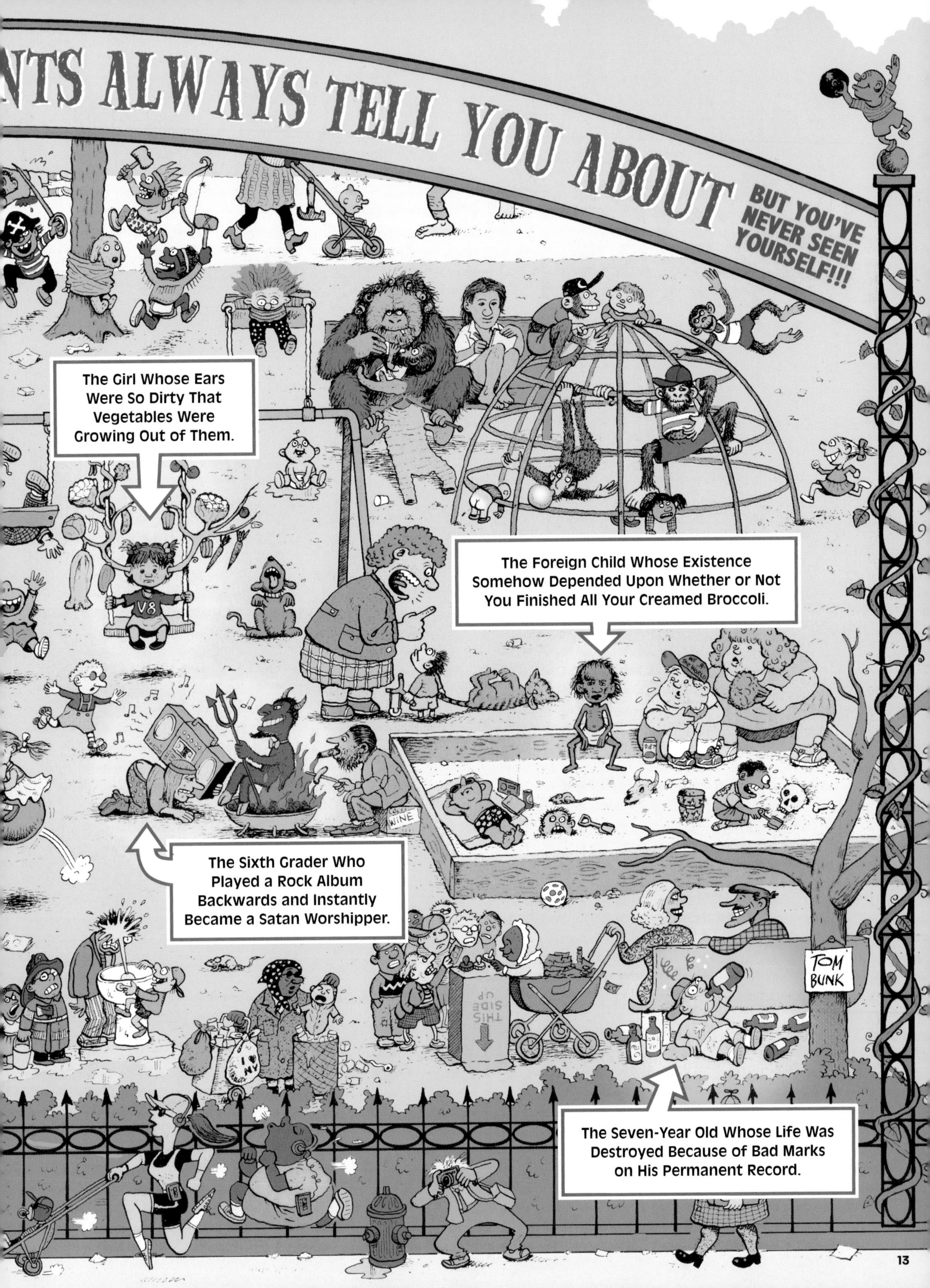

NTS ALWAYS TELL YOU ABOUT
BUT YOU'VE NEVER SEEN YOURSELF!!!
The Girl Whose Ears Were So Dirty That Vegetables Were Growing Out of Them.
V8
The Foreign Child Whose Existence Somehow Depended Upon Whether or Not You Finished All Your Creamed Broccoli.
DIET
WINE
The Sixth Grader Who Played a Rock Album Backwards and Instantly Became a Satan Worshipper.
THIS SIDE UP
TOM BUNK
The Seven-Year Old Whose Life Was Destroyed Because of Bad Marks on His Permanent Record.

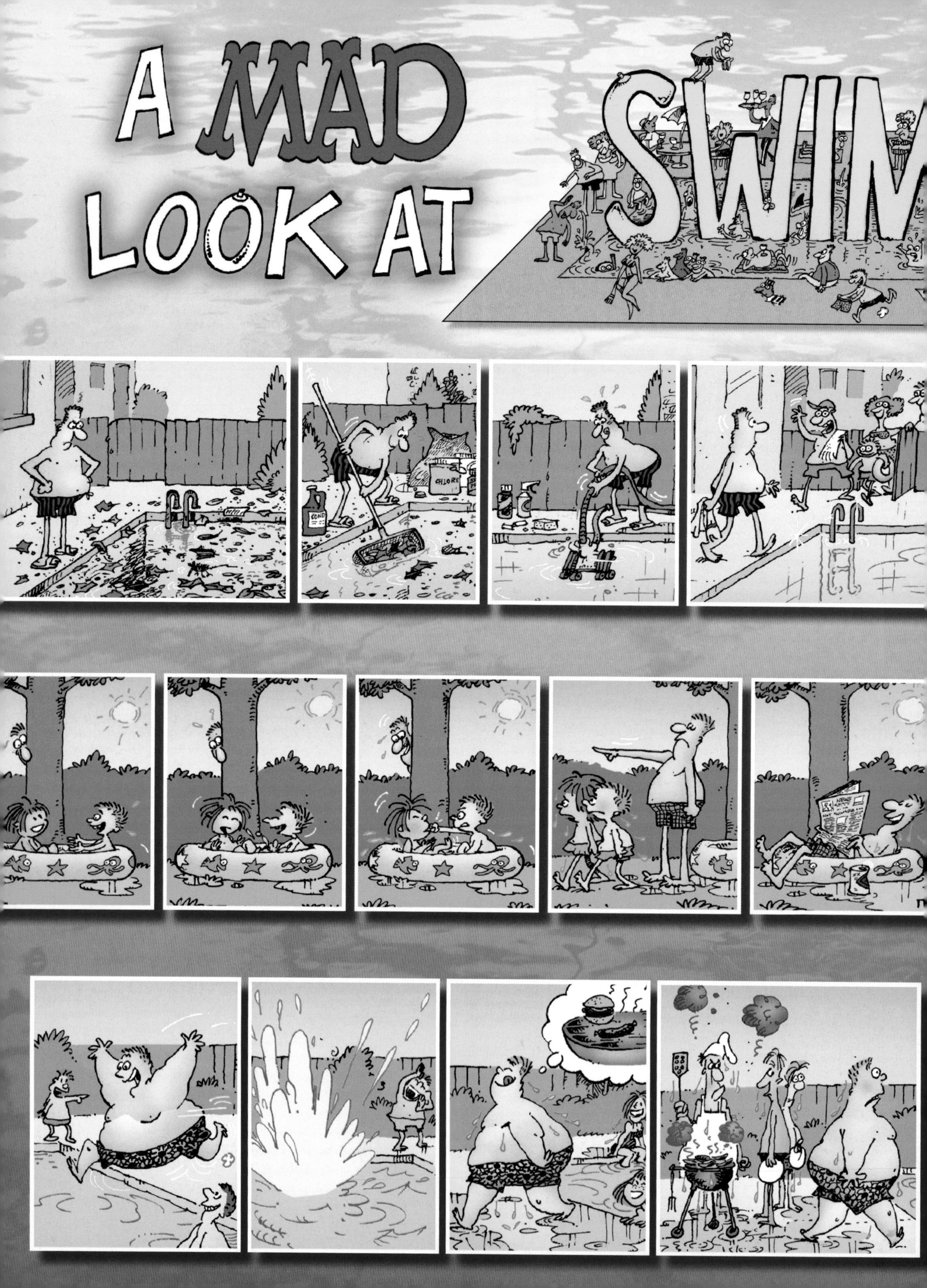
A MAD LOOK AT
SWIM

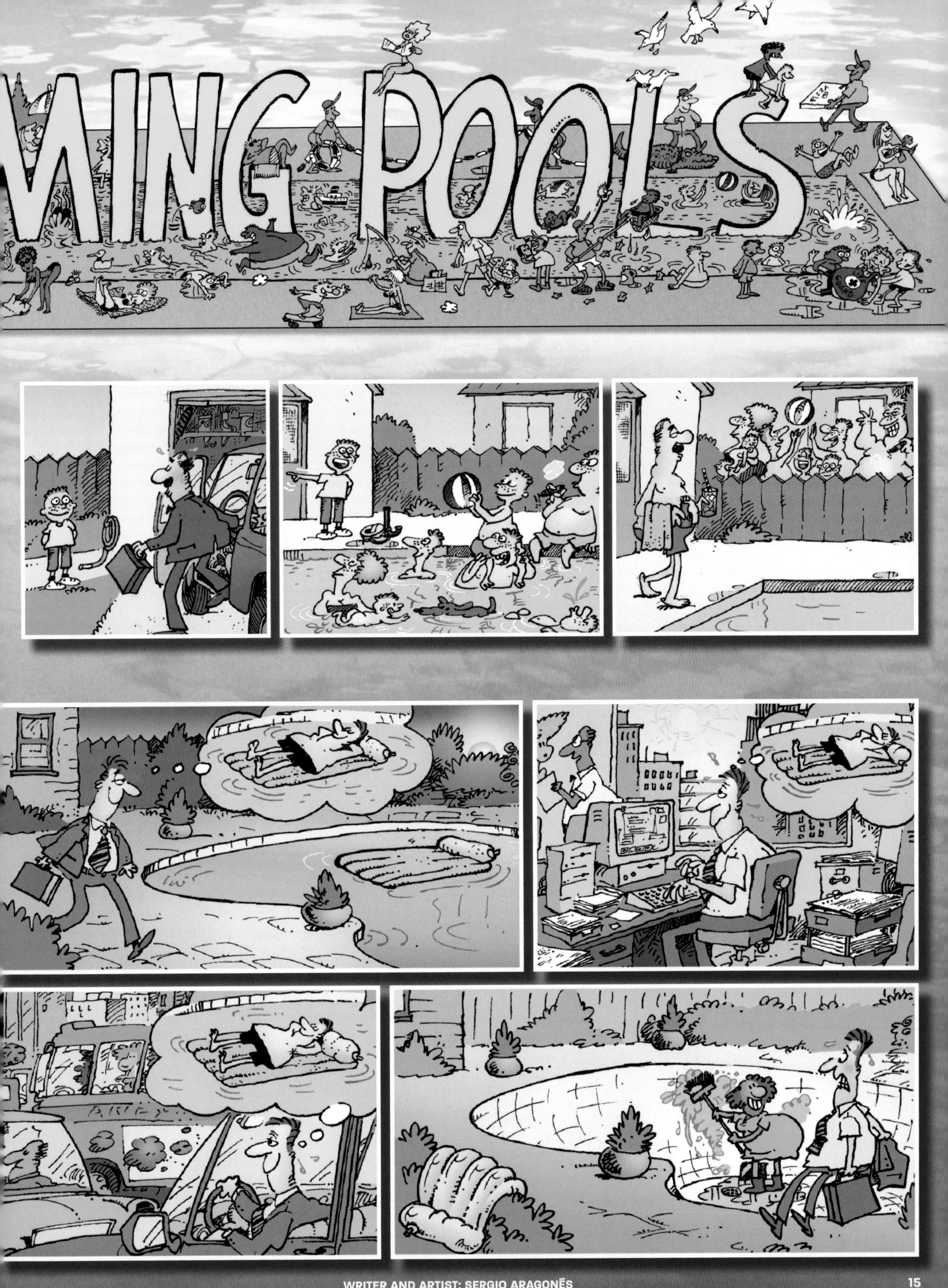
WING POOLS

WRITER AND ARTIST: SERGIO ARAGONÉS

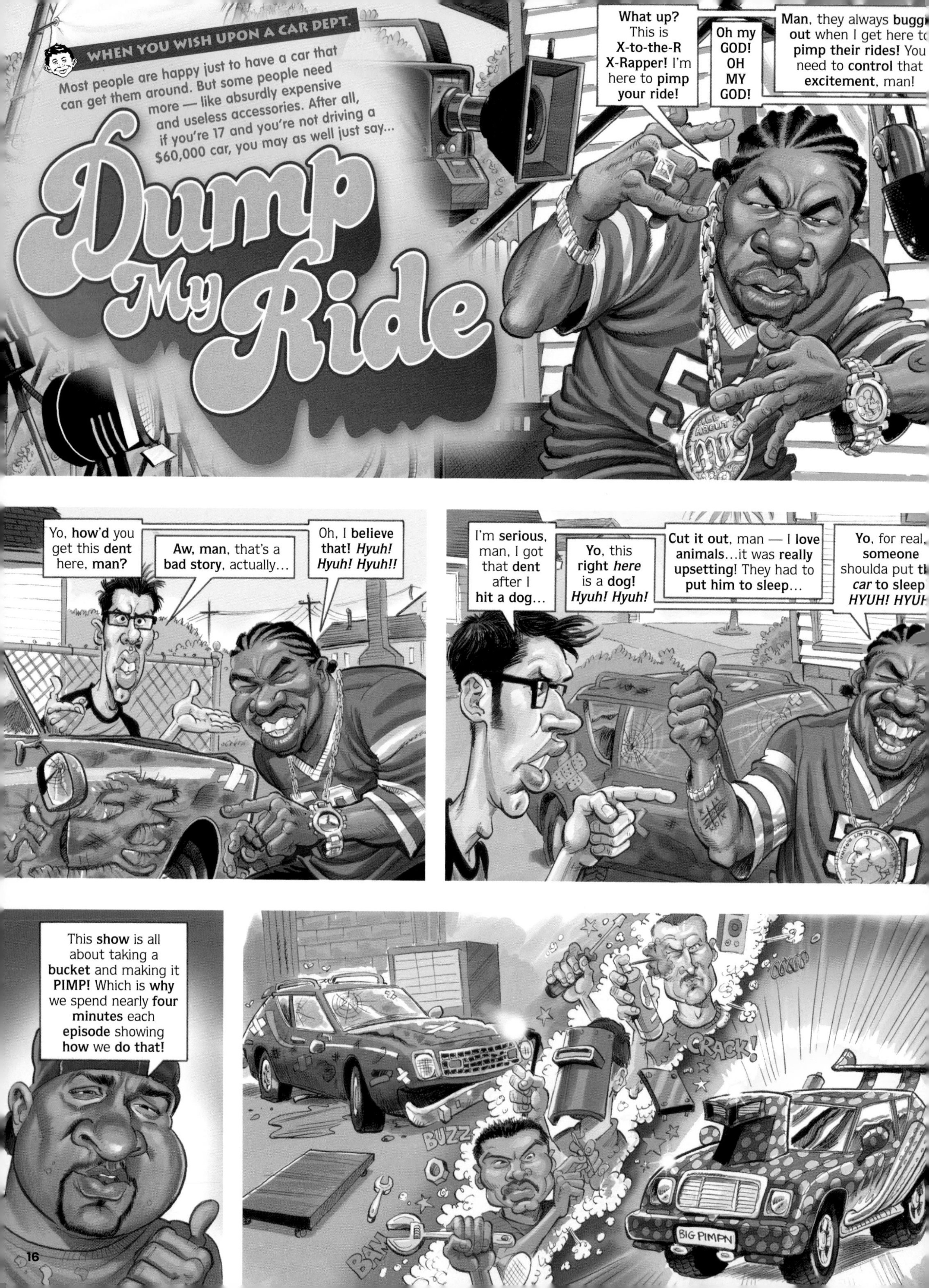
WHEN YOU WISH UPON A CAR DEPT.
Most people are happy just to have a car that can get them around. But some people need more — like absurdly expensive and useless accessories. After all, if you're 17 and you're not driving a $60,000 car, you may as well just say...
Dump My Ride
What up? This is X-to-the-R X-Rapper! I'm here to pimp your ride!
Oh my GOD! OH MY GOD!
Man, they always bugg out when I get here to pimp their rides! You need to control that excitement, man!
Yo, how'd you get this dent here, man?
Aw, man, that's a bad story, actually...
Oh, I believe that! Hyuh! Hyuh! Hyuh!!
I'm serious, man, I got that dent after I hit a dog...
Yo, this right here is a dog! Hyuh! Hyuh!
Cut it out, man — I love animals...it was really upsetting! They had to put him to sleep...
Yo, for real, someone shoulda put th car to sleep HYUH! HYUH
This show is all about taking a bucket and making it PIMP! Which is why we spend nearly four minutes each episode showing how we do that!
CRACK!
BUZZ
BAM
BIG PIMPN

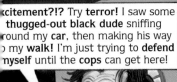

citement?!? Try **terror!** I saw some thugged-out black dude sniffing round my **car**, then making his way o my **walk!** I'm just trying to **defend** myself until the **cops** can get here!

Aw, **quit frontin'**, man! **Everyone** acts so **shocked** — like you **didn't notice** me and my **camera crew** setting up on your **front lawn** for the **last two hours!**

Ok, man, I **already** made **fun** of your **car** before I **knocked** on your **door!** I'm just gonna **make fun** of it with **you here**, before I **drive** it off to **Messed-Up Customs** and **make fun** of it **again** with **those guys**.

That's not exactly **biting satire**, man! The whole **point** of the **show** is that I **realize** my **ride** is beat! Hey, **maybe** you can get a **job** hosting *The Swan* so you can point out to the **contestants** that they're **fugly!**

ARTIST: TOM RICHMOND   WRITER: DAVE CROATTO

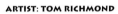

What are you even **laughing** at? And can you **at least** make **eye contact** with me?

I **laugh** at **all** my own **lame** cracks! *Hyuh! Hyuh!* It's either **that** or my **deadpan** look of **disbelief!**

This **better?**

Just **take** the **car** and go!

Good work, guys! Now we ve **time** to give the **viewers** hat they **really** want to **see:** me **prop comedy** that would ake even **Carrot Top** cringe!

That's **BULL!**

When you brought your **wheels** in here, your **trunk** was **cluttered** with all kinds of **junk** — a spare tire, a jack, flares... so we decided to **convert** your **trunk** into a **slot car track!**

Your **solution** to my **messy trunk** was to give me a **useless trunk?**

No — 'cause check **this out!** The geniuses at Messed-Up Customs also gave you a **trailer hitch** and this **U-Haul! Problem solved!**

17

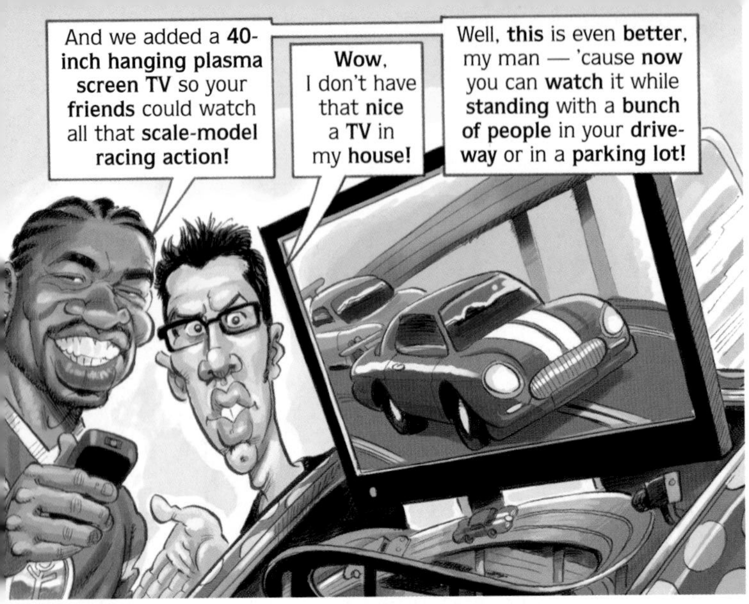
And we added a 40-inch hanging plasma screen TV so your friends could watch all that scale-model racing action!
Wow, I don't have that nice a TV in my house!
Well, this is even better, my man — 'cause now you can watch it while standing with a bunch of people in your drive-way or in a parking lot!

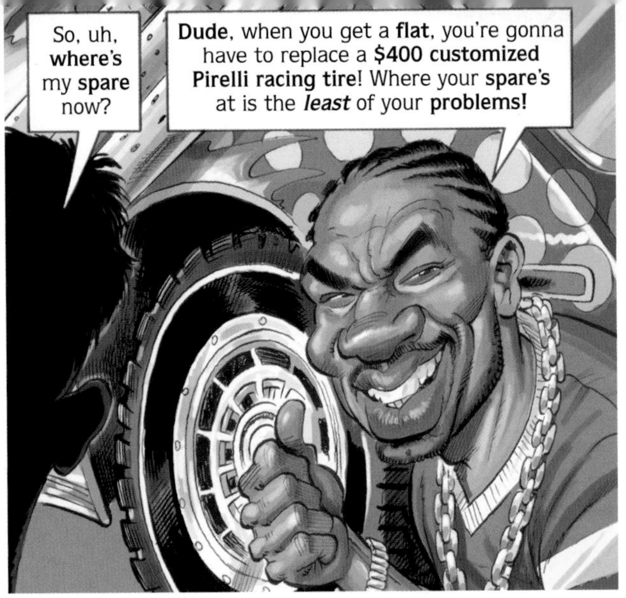
So, uh, where's my spare now?
Dude, when you get a flat, you're gonna have to replace a $400 customized Pirelli racing tire! Where your spare's at is the least of your problems!

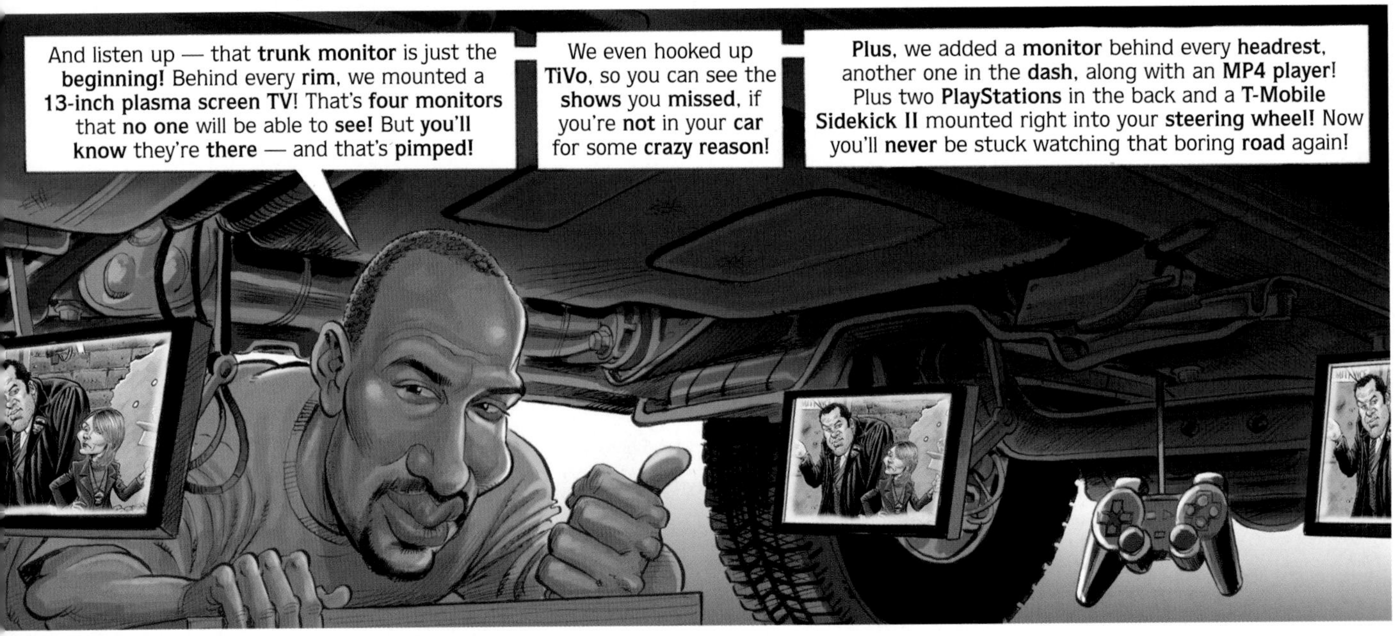
And listen up — that trunk monitor is just the beginning! Behind every rim, we mounted a 13-inch plasma screen TV! That's four monitors that no one will be able to see! But you'll know they're there — and that's pimped!
We even hooked up TiVo, so you can see the shows you missed, if you're not in your car for some crazy reason!
Plus, we added a monitor behind every headrest, another one in the dash, along with an MP4 player! Plus two PlayStations in the back and a T-Mobile Sidekick II mounted right into your steering wheel! Now you'll never be stuck watching that boring road again!

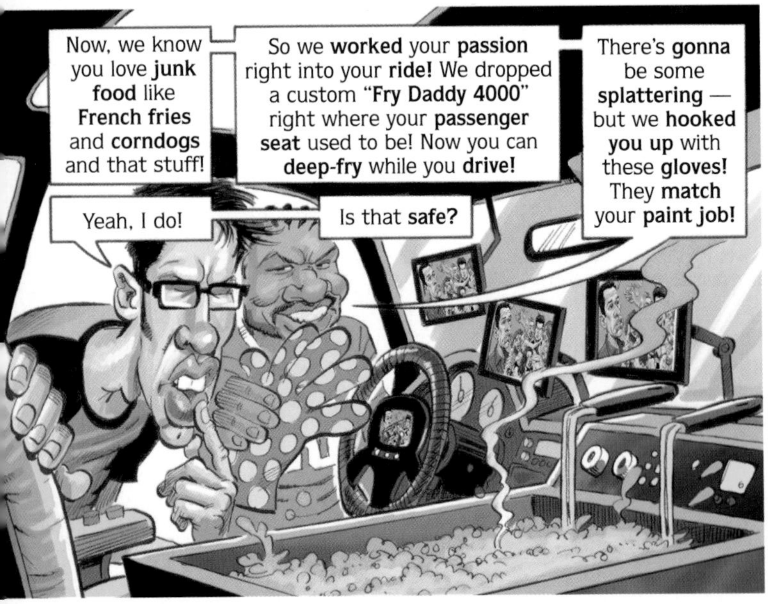
Now, we know you love junk food like French fries and corndogs and that stuff!
Yeah, I do!
So we worked your passion right into your ride! We dropped a custom "Fry Daddy 4000" right where your passenger seat used to be! Now you can deep-fry while you drive!
Is that safe?
There's gonna be some splattering — but we hooked you up with these gloves! They match your paint job!

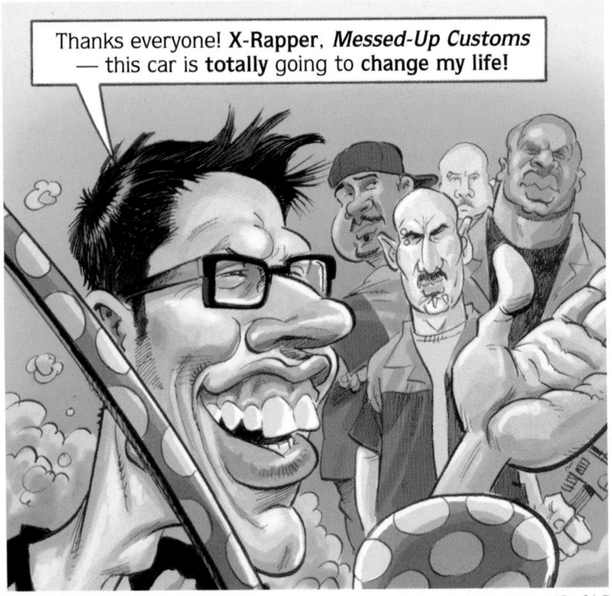
Thanks everyone! X-Rapper, Messed-Up Customs — this car is totally going to change my life!

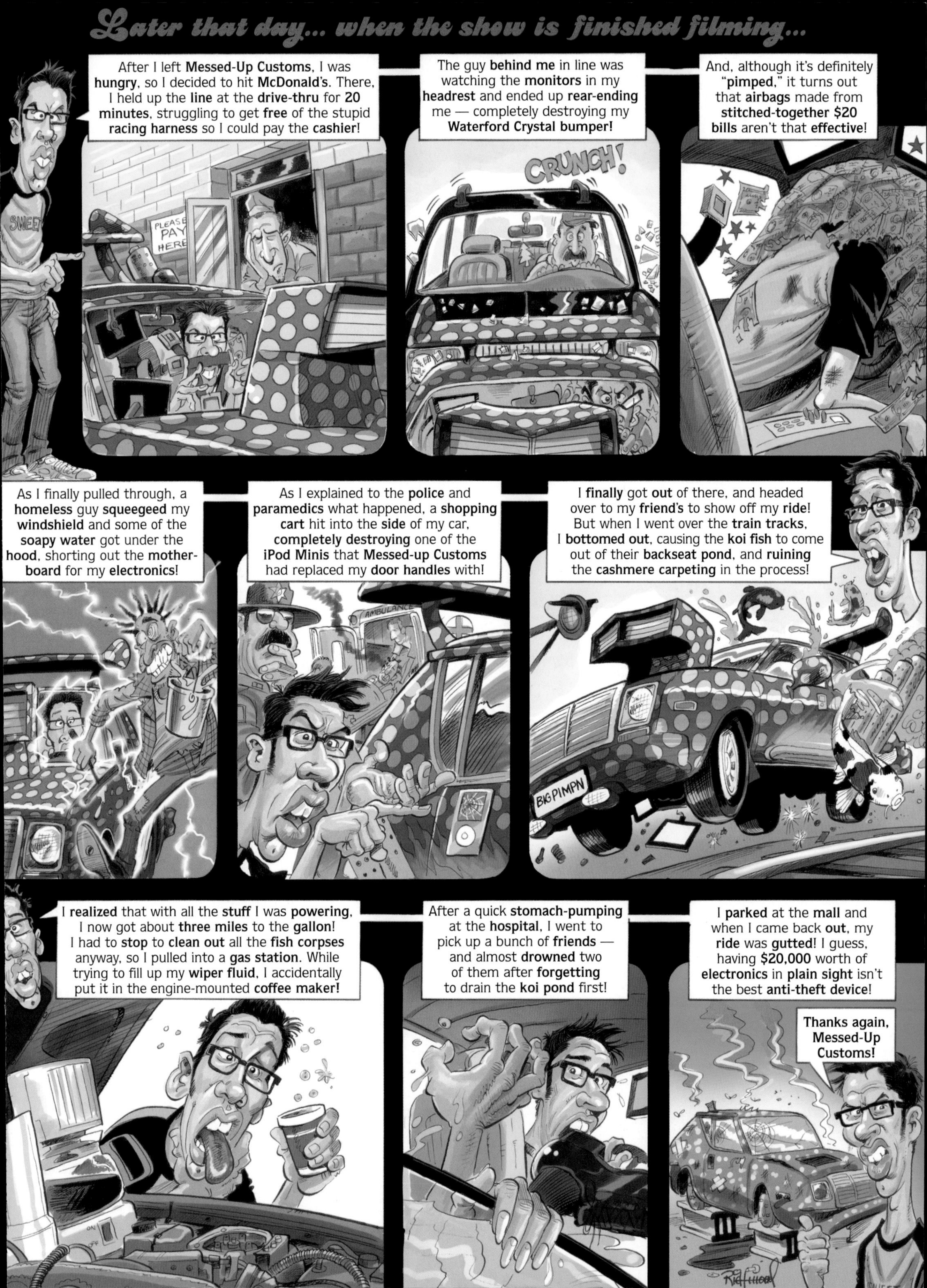

Later that day... when the show is finished filming...
After I left Messed-Up Customs, I was hungry, so I decided to hit McDonald's. There, I held up the line at the drive-thru for 20 minutes, struggling to get free of the stupid racing harness so I could pay the cashier!
SWEET
PLEASE PAY HERE
The guy behind me in line was watching the monitors in my headrest and ended up rear-ending me — completely destroying my Waterford Crystal bumper!
CRUNCH!
And, although it's definitely "pimped," it turns out that airbags made from stitched-together $20 bills aren't that effective!
As I finally pulled through, a homeless guy squeegeed my windshield and some of the soapy water got under the hood, shorting out the mother-board for my electronics!
As I explained to the police and paramedics what happened, a shopping cart hit into the side of my car, completely destroying one of the iPod Minis that Messed-up Customs had replaced my door handles with!
AMBULANCE
I finally got out of there, and headed over to my friend's to show off my ride! But when I went over the train tracks, I bottomed out, causing the koi fish to come out of their backseat pond, and ruining the cashmere carpeting in the process!
BIG PIMPN
I realized that with all the stuff I was powering, I now got about three miles to the gallon! I had to stop to clean out all the fish corpses anyway, so I pulled into a gas station. While trying to fill up my wiper fluid, I accidentally put it in the engine-mounted coffee maker!
After a quick stomach-pumping at the hospital, I went to pick up a bunch of friends — and almost drowned two of them after forgetting to drain the koi pond first!
I parked at the mall and when I came back out, my ride was gutted! I guess, having $20,000 worth of electronics in plain sight isn't the best anti-theft device!
Thanks again, Messed-Up Customs!

CARDS for SOMEONE who's having a BAD DAY

Sharing the Pain You're Feeling

You bragged about how tough you are
And thought that it was cool;
And soon your mighty fighting words
Were heard throughout the school;
If only you had been concerned
By what you said more fully,
You might have saved yourself from getting
Creamed by the school bully.

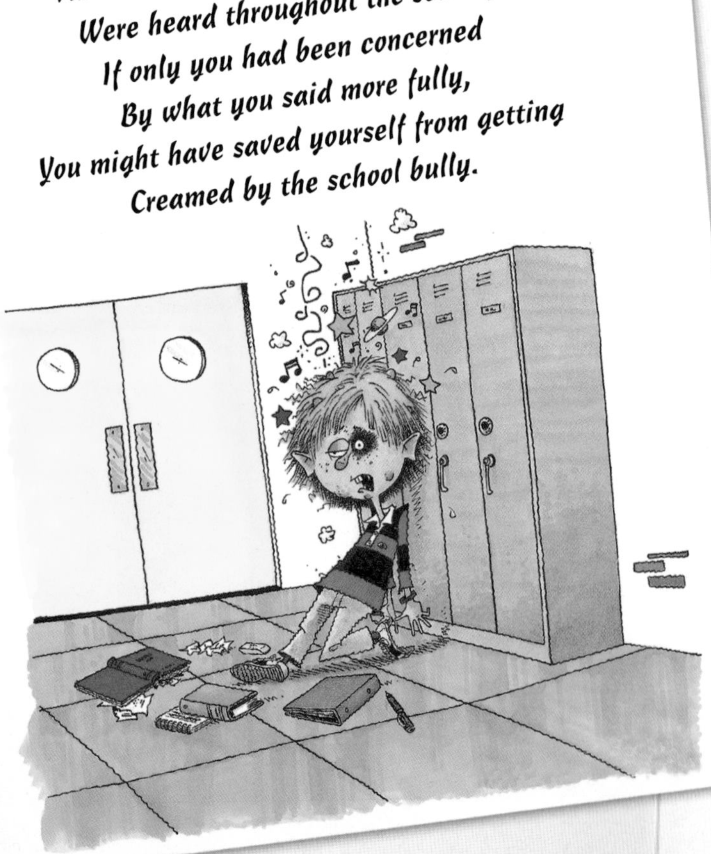

ARTIST: JOHN CALDWELL

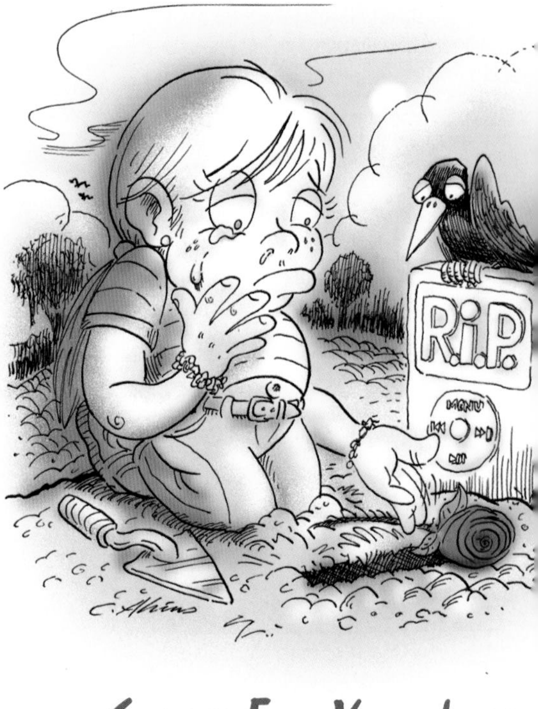

R.I.P.

ARTIST: CHARLES AKINS

Sorry For Your Loss

Your life's an endless struggle
And the world does not seem fair,
And often you're tormented by
The darkness of despair;
Deep sorrows fill your heart with grie
This cannot be denied;
But none can match your sadness
When your iPod crashed and died.

Such a Pity

At school you felt the urge to poop,
But as all students know,
The bathrooms are a filthy mess
And so you didn't go;
But then the urge grew stronger
And you prayed that you could shake it;
Your house is just a block away—
Next time we hope you'll make it.

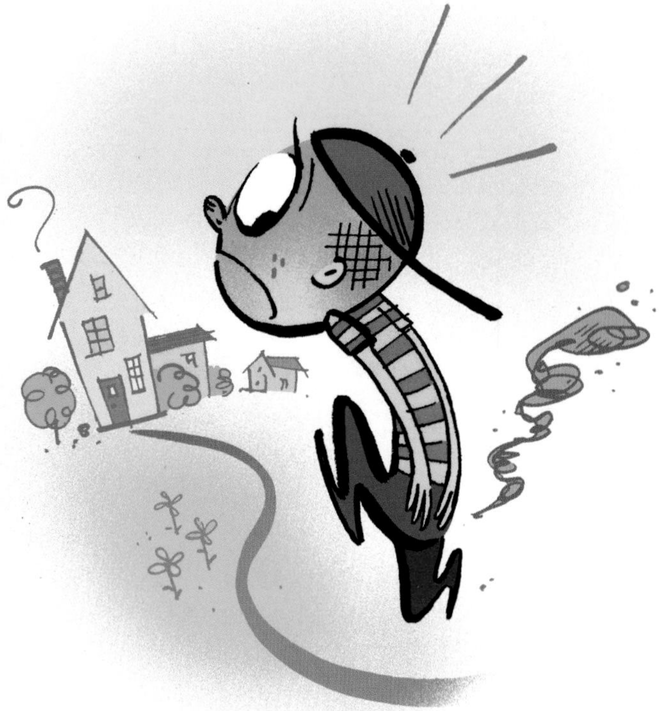

ARTIST: BOB STAAKE

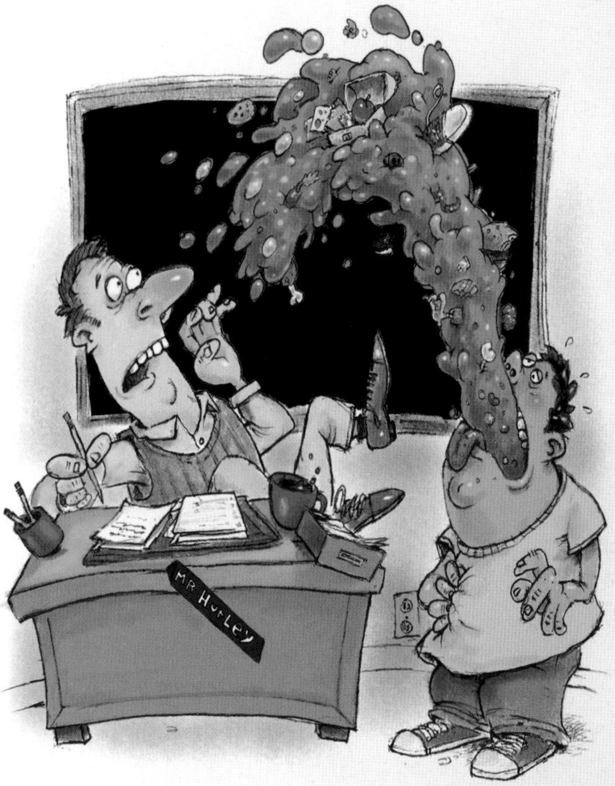
MR HURLEY

ARTIST: RICH POWELL

Thinking of You

You wolf down hot dogs by the ton,
Pig out on shakes and fries;
They know you well at Burger King,
Which comes as no surprise;
But yesterday you went too far
And now must take the rap;
Not only did you barf in class
But in the teacher's lap.

In Your Time of Embarrassment

The sound of farting fills the room;
The stink no one can bear;
And now it's you your classmates blame;
They point at you and stare;
You sit there while they shout your name;
"You farted!" they remind you;
Which really stinks, because it was
The kid who sits behind you!

ARTIST: TIM HAMILTON

In This Time of Sadness

You once enjoyed those hearty meals
Of chicken, ham and beef,
But now each night at supper time
Your life is filled with grief;
Your mom's turned vegetarian,
Small wonder that you're sad;
Thank goodness that you own a dog —
Hey, Alpo ain't half-bad!

ARTIST: PAUL GILLIGAN

Understanding During This Difficult Period

Your friends are looking closely
At your recent dental work;
We're sure it's not a pleasure
When you see them laugh and smirk;
Most sadly, you cannot forget
Those looks upon their faces,
When yesterday you tried to eat
Spaghetti — wearing braces.

A VISIT TO THE COUNTRY

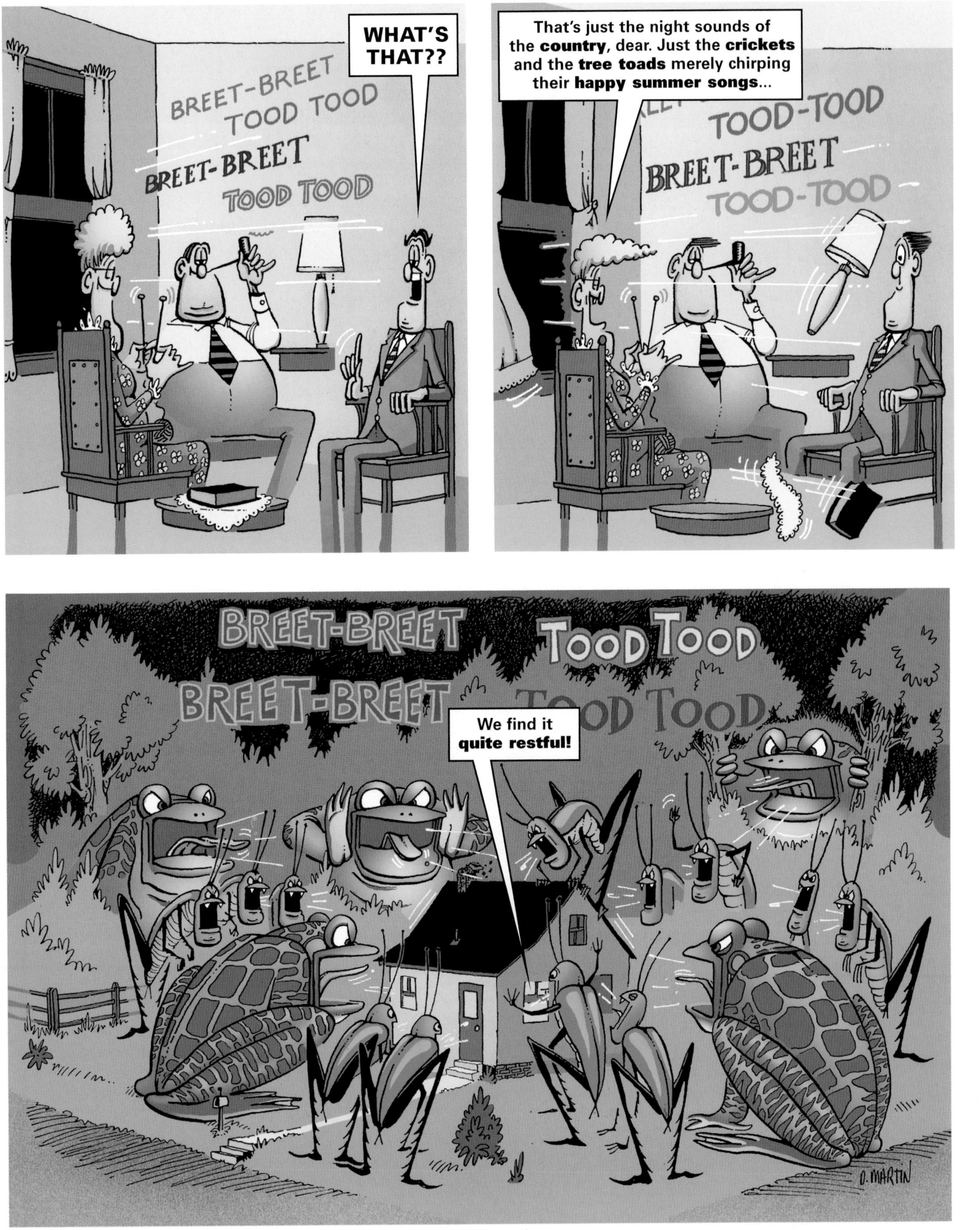
BREET-BREET
TOOD TOOD
BREET-BREET
TOOD TOOD
WHAT'S THAT??
That's just the night sounds of the **country**, dear. Just the **crickets** and the **tree toads** merely chirping their **happy summer songs**...
TOOD-TOOD
BREET-BREET
TOOD-TOOD
BREET-BREET
TOOD TOOD
BREET-BREET
We find it **quite restful!**
D. MARTIN

WRITER AND ARTIST: DON MARTIN

DEVICE AGE DEPT.

WHAT IF TECHNOLOGY

What if Moses had a Fax Machine!

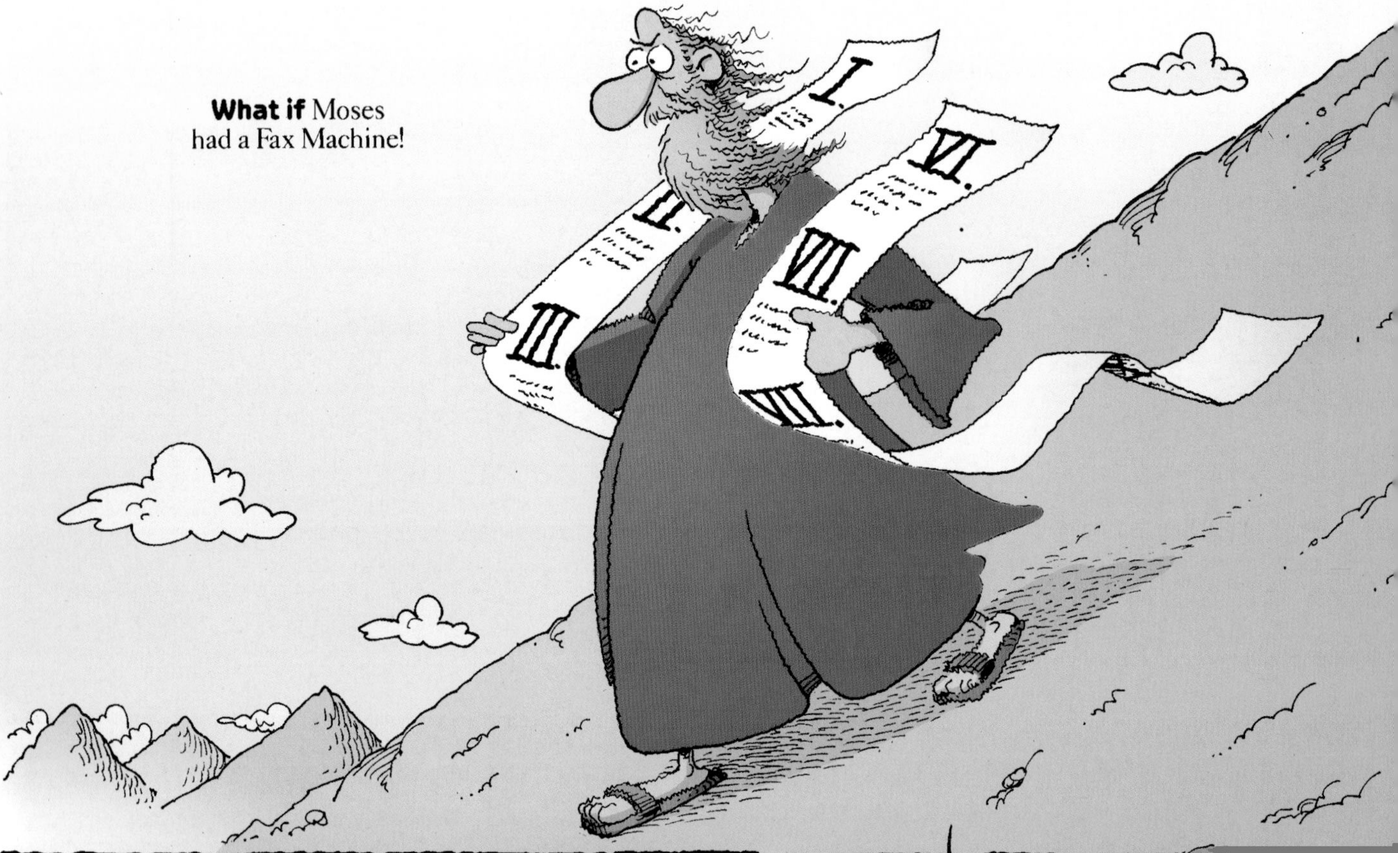
I.
VI.
II.
VII.
III.
VIII.

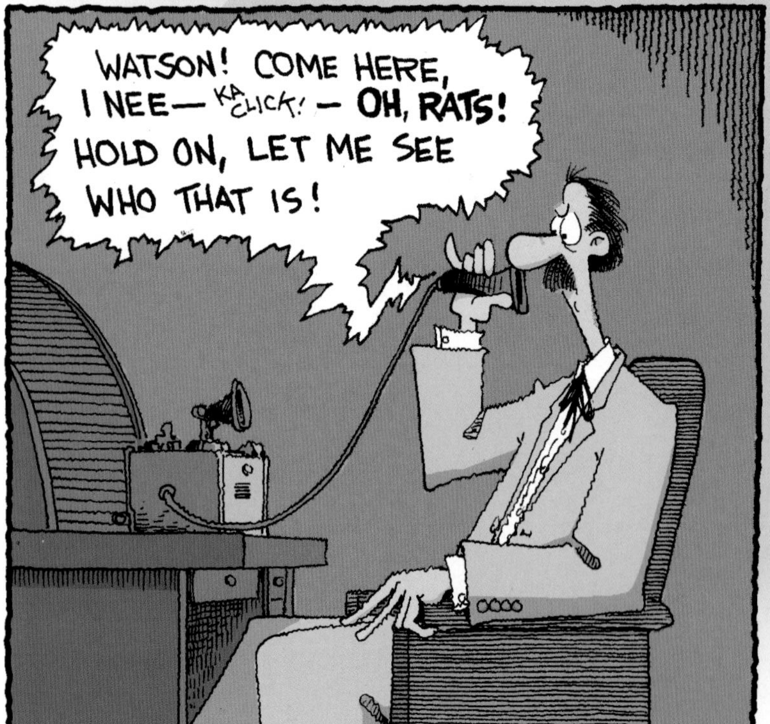
WATSON! COME HERE, I NEE— KA CLICK! – OH, RATS! HOLD ON, LET ME SEE WHO THAT IS!

What if Alexander Graham Bell had Call Waiting!

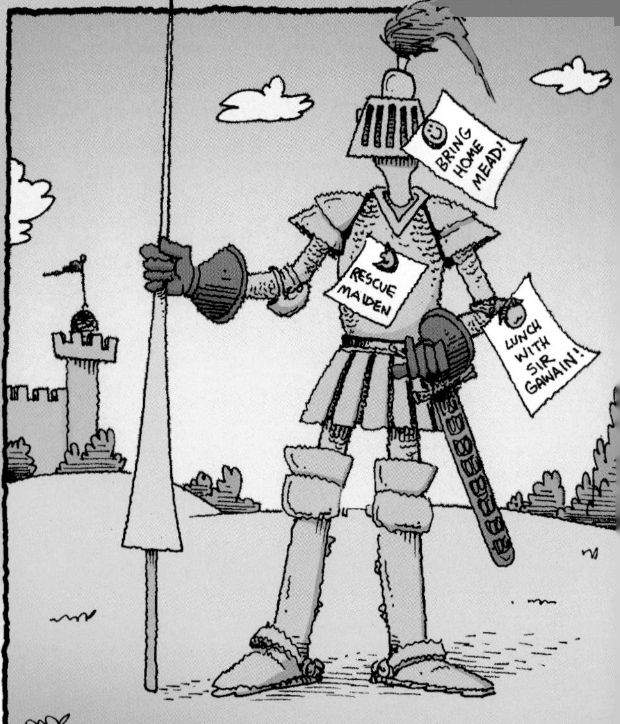
BRING HOME MEAD!
RESCUE MAIDEN
LUNCH WITH SIR GAWAIN!

What if Medieval Knights had Refrigerator Magnets!

VADED **HISTORY?!?**

ARTIST AND WRITER: JOHN CALDWELL

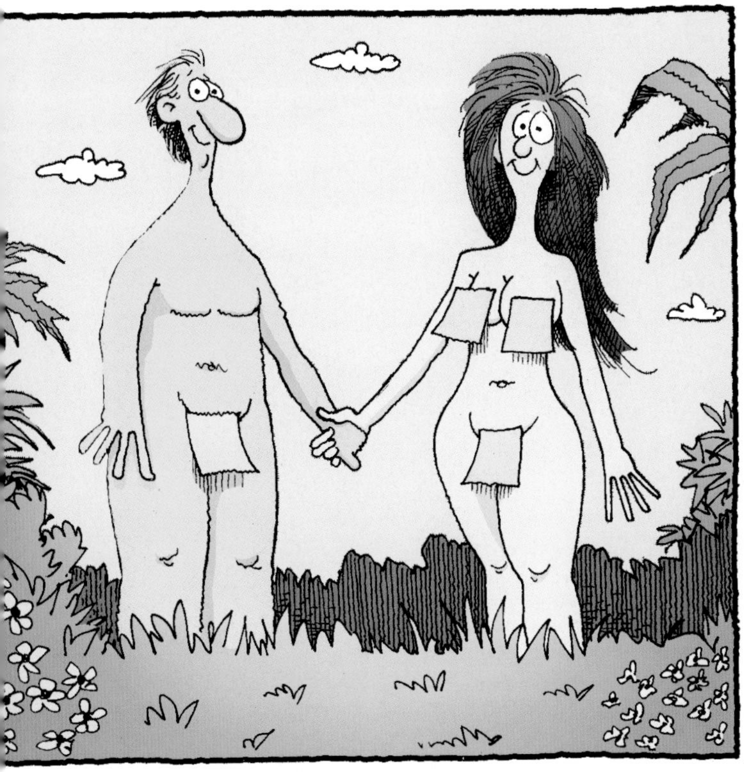

What if Adam and Eve had Post-It Notes!

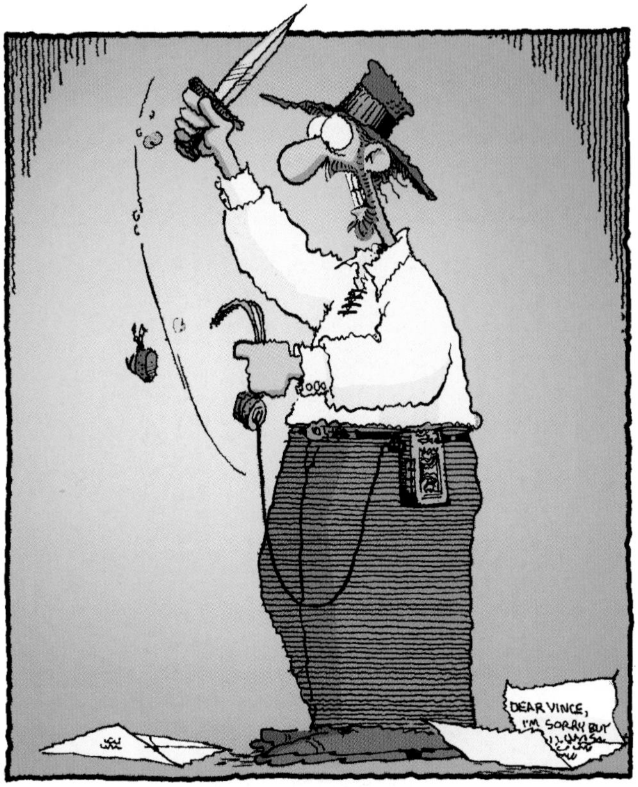
DEAR VINCE,
I'M SORRY BUT

What if Vincent Van Gogh had a Walkman!

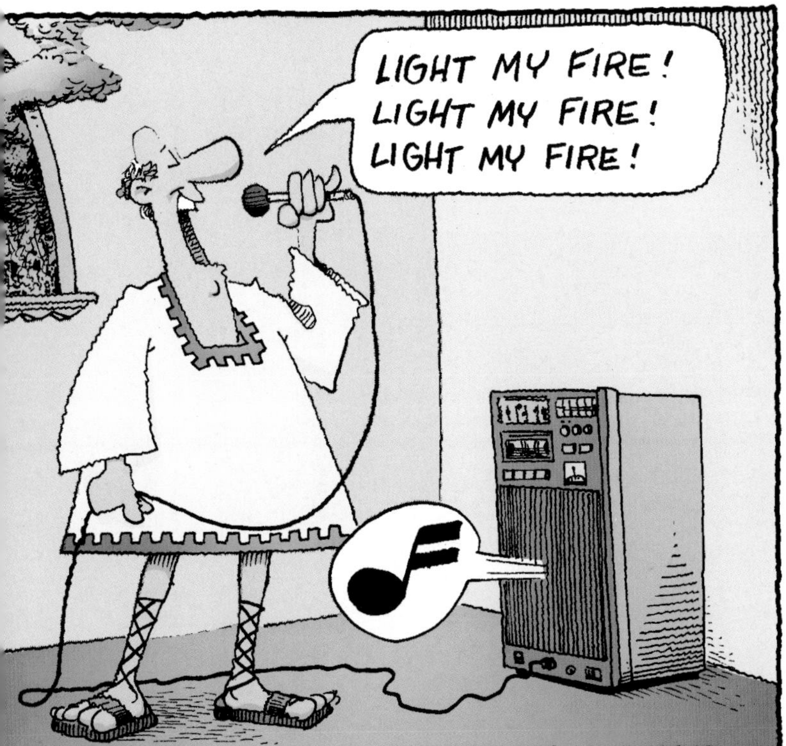
LIGHT MY FIRE! LIGHT MY FIRE! LIGHT MY FIRE!

What if Nero had a Karaoke Machine!

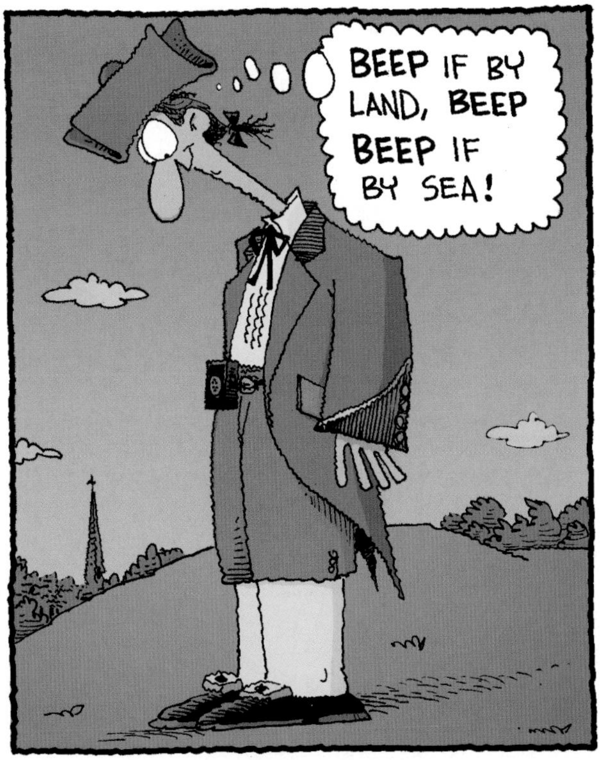
BEEP IF BY LAND, BEEP BEEP IF BY SEA!

What if Paul Revere had a Pager!

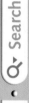

Planet TAD!!!!!

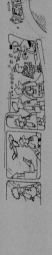

http://www.galaxyo'blogs.com/planettad

Search

Planet TAD!!!!!

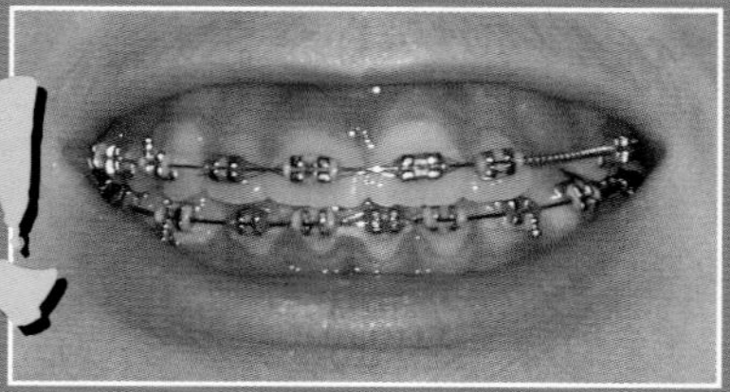

[**About Me**]

[**Name**|Tad]
[**Age**|14]
[**Middle name**|
None of your business]

[31 October|**08:41pm**]

[**mood**| full of tiny Snickers bars]

Tonight was Halloween, and my little sister Sophie decided to go as an angel. When I saw her downstairs in the hallway, I pointed out that "angel" is one possible name for her costume. Another is "dead kid." And then Sophie started crying and went to her room and wouldn't come out, and Mom and Dad made me go to my room.

HALLOWEEEEE!
BOOoooo

[2 November|**07:34pm**]

I just finished the sixth Harry Potter book, and here's what I don't understand about Hogwarts: Okay, so, the school has a sorting hat that can figure out each student's true nature, and assign him to the appropriate house, right? But there are four houses. Three of them — Gryffindor, Hufflepuff, and Ravenclaw — are full of normal people. And then there's Slytherin, which is NOTHING BUT EVIL PEOPLE. If I ran Hogwarts, when the sorting hat assigned a student to Slytherin, I'd send him home, or maybe to, like, wizard reform school. I mean, duh.

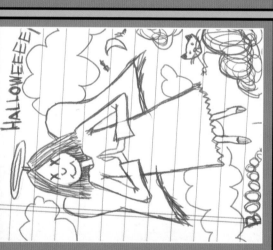

[4 November|**04:15pm**]

At school today, the signs went up for the fall dance, Pilgrimfest '05. (It's called Pilgrimfest because it happens around Thanksgiving. They decorate the gym with leaves and cutouts of turkeys.) I've decided to ask Katie Zembla from my geometry class. She seems really friendly and pretty, and she's always really nice to me after I let her copy my homework.

[7 November|**03:37pm**]

[**mood**| feeling dorky]

I tried asking Katie to the dance today, but I got all nervous and wound up asking to borrow her eraser instead. And then I had to erase some stuff so it wouldn't look weird, so I wound up erasing a couple of answers on my homework right before I had to hand it in.

[**mood**| feeling completely dorky]

I tried asking Katie again, but I wound up asking her to borrow her protractor. It's getting embarrassing.

[9 November|**05:05pm**]

[**mood**| very happy]

Good news! I finally asked her, and she said she'd go with me! Well, actually, she said she'd go if this person she's waiting to ask her doesn't by Friday. So I'm her second choice!

[11 November|**03:36pm**]

It's Friday, and I caught up with Katie after class, and she says he still hasn't asked her, but she wants to give him until Monday.

[14 November|**04:10pm**]

[**mood**| very very very very happy]

Hooray! Katie said she'd go with me! Pilgrimfest is four days away, so I have until then to find out stuff like what to wear and how to dance.

[16 November|**06:51pm**]

Mom took me to the mall today to look for a new tie. I like the one I have, but she says girls don't like boys who like ties that look like fish.

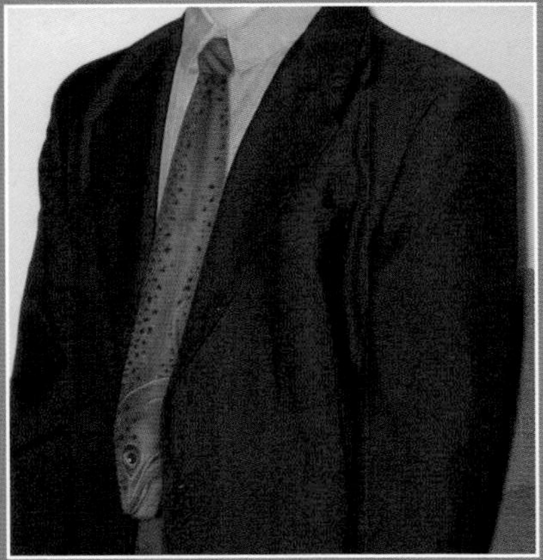

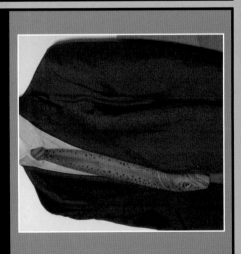

[17 November|**07:18pm**]

Tomorrow's the big dance! I went to the Dollar Depot today and bought some cK One cologne. Well, actually, it's called dB Two, but it smells just like cK One, and it only costs a buck! It's pretty good — my dad noticed it right when he came home, and I was all the way up in my room. He asked how much I paid for it, and when I told him, he said, "That's a bargain for cologne that strong!" And then he opened all the windows.

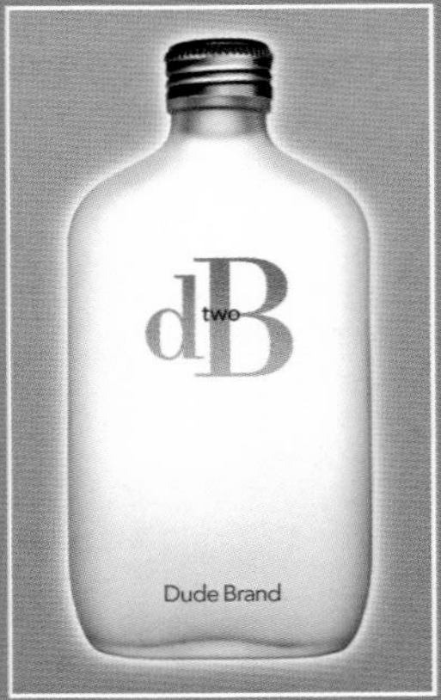
dB two
Dude Brand

[19 November|**11:26am**]

[**mood**| itchy]

Ugh. I didn't wind up going to the dance after all. I woke up yesterday morning covered in hives. Mom took me to Dr. Bauer, who tested me and told me that I'm probably allergic to the artificial musk in the dB Two, which I guess is good to know. He gave me some Benadryl, and I spent the night at home, recovering, watching TV with my parents. They tried to be nice about it, but every once in a while, my dad would look over at me and start laughing, and then he'd try to pretend that he was laughing at the TV, but we were watching Law & Order SVU, which isn't really all that funny.

ARTIST: BRIAN DURNIAK WRITER: TIM CARVELL

A MAD LOOK AT THE MOMENT BEFORE THE DISASTER

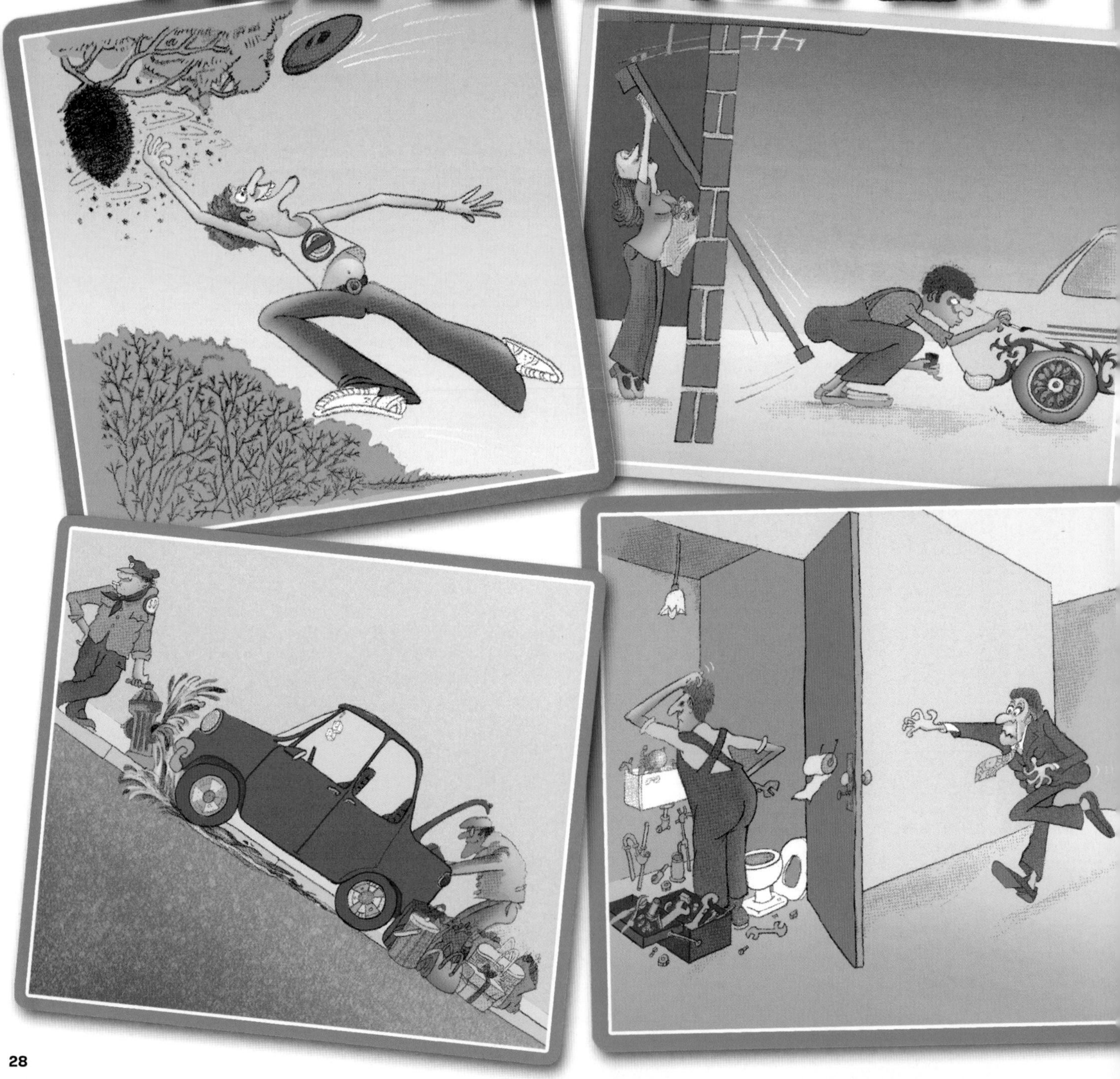

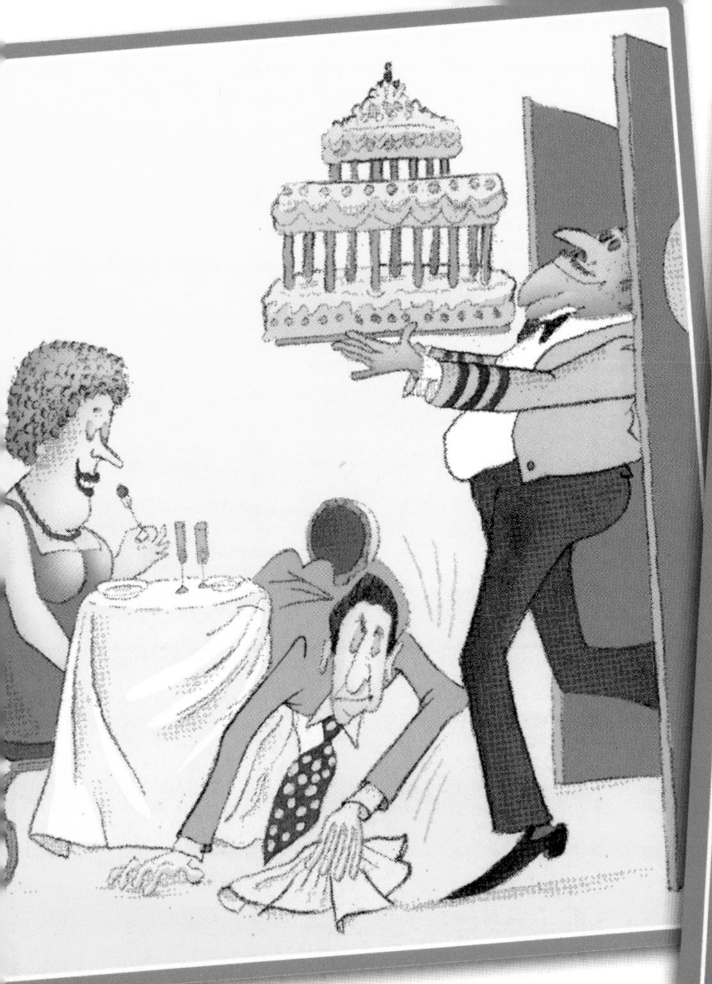

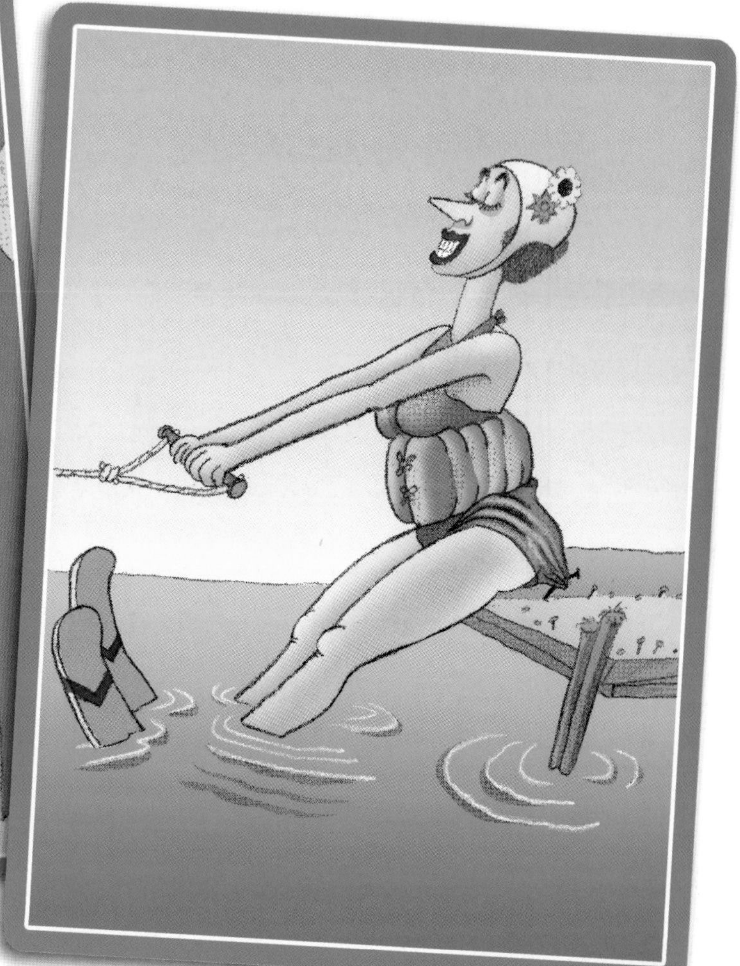

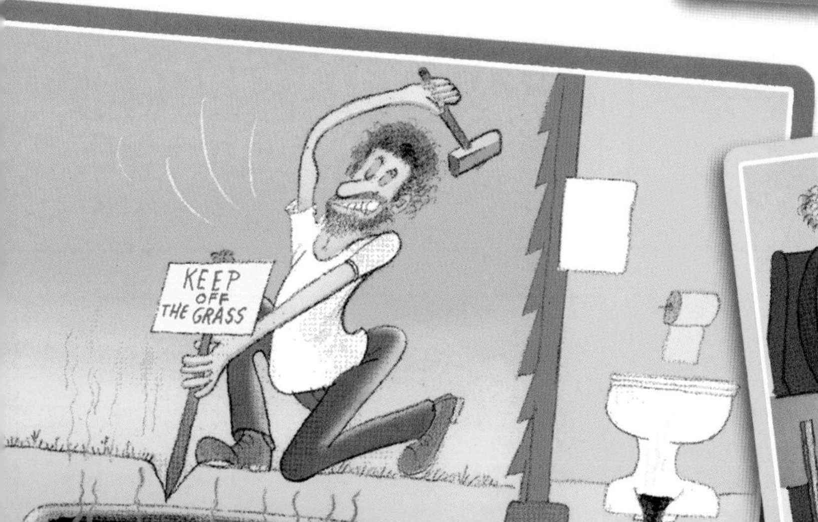
KEEP OFF THE GRASS

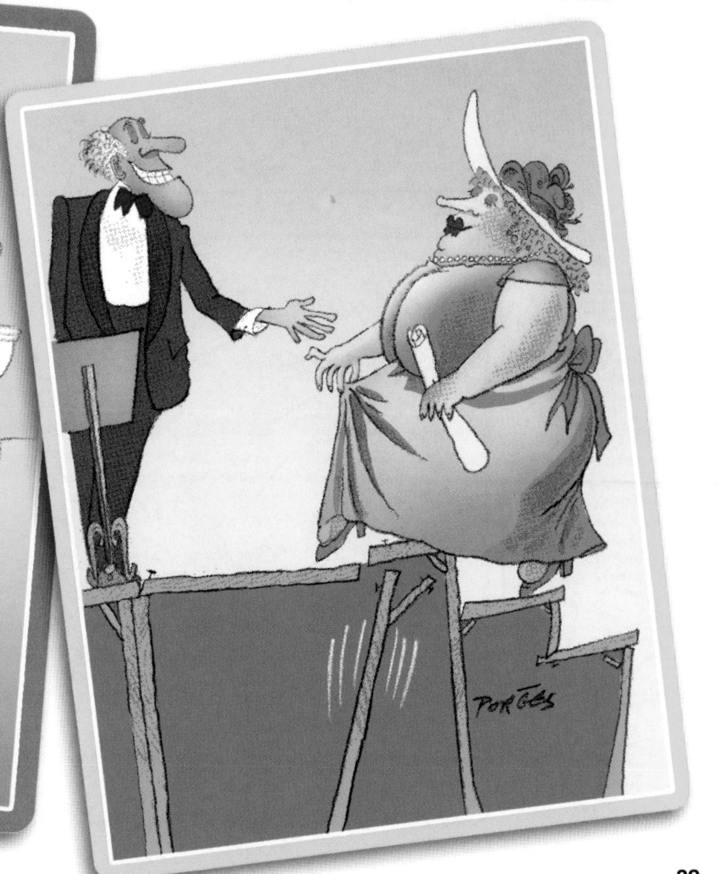
PORGES

THE CONTINUING ADVENTURES OF WILLY NILLY

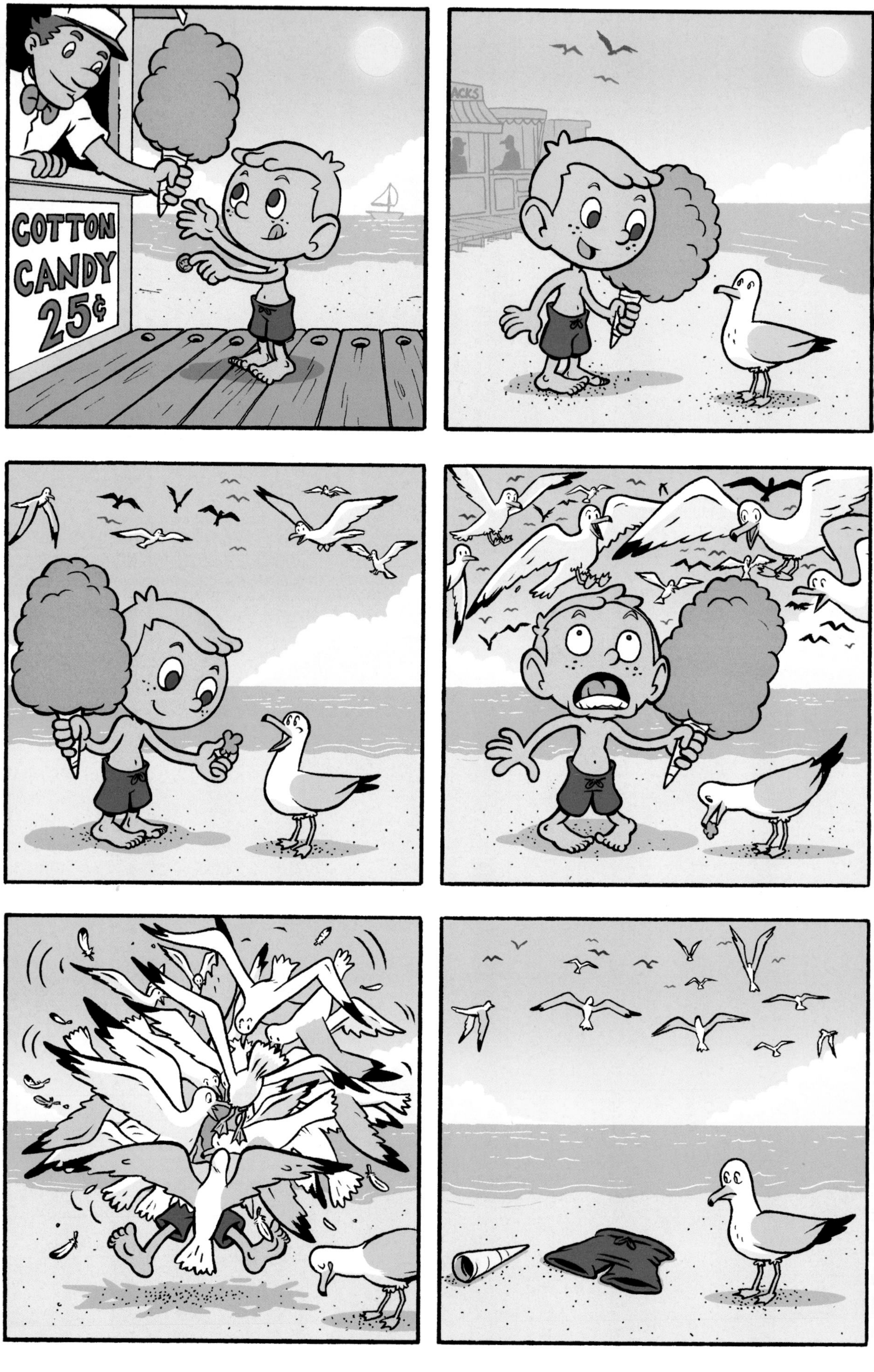
COTTON
CANDY
25¢
ACKS

Surprise! That's NOT Meat! It's Mulch, Mulch More.

Taste familiar? It should.
Your old comic books are in there. So's your baseball card collection. (Thanks, Mom!) Grass clippings, too. And so's the oak that came down in that storm last March and blocked the street until a road crew could get out with a chainsaw and a wood chipper! It's *all* in there, plus a lot more. With Fiber Burger, a meatless patty made from recycled materials isn't pulp fiction anymore.

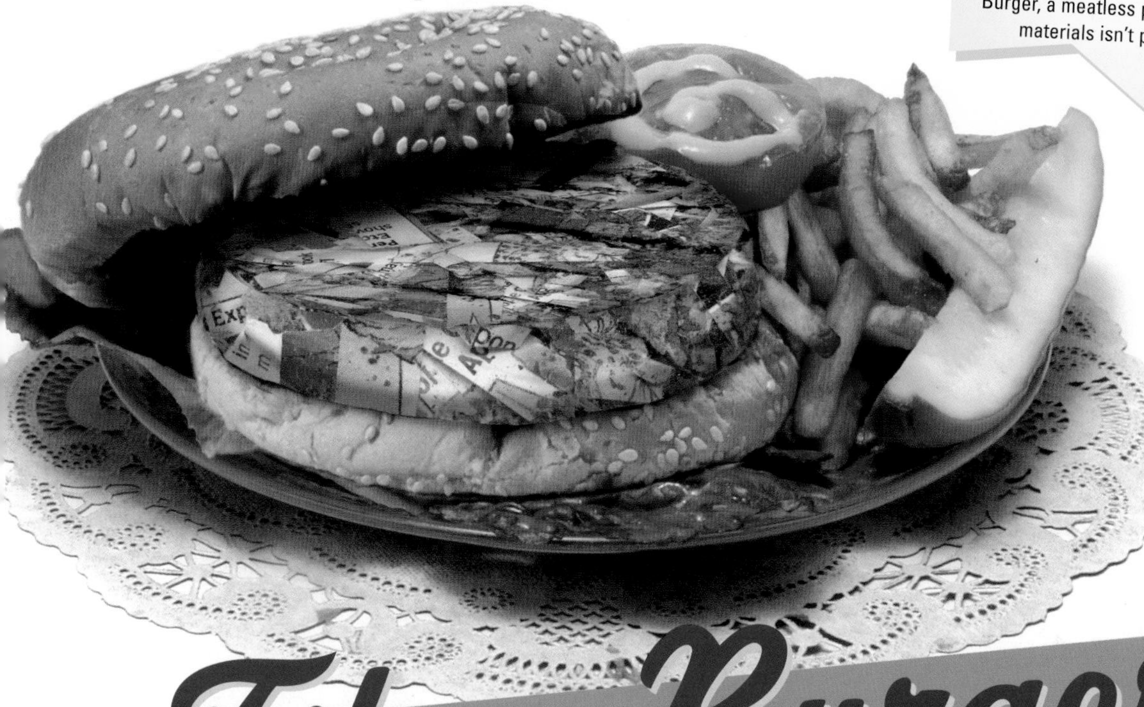

Fiber Burger

85% Post-Consumer Content 100% Delicious

TRY ALL 4 VARIETIES!

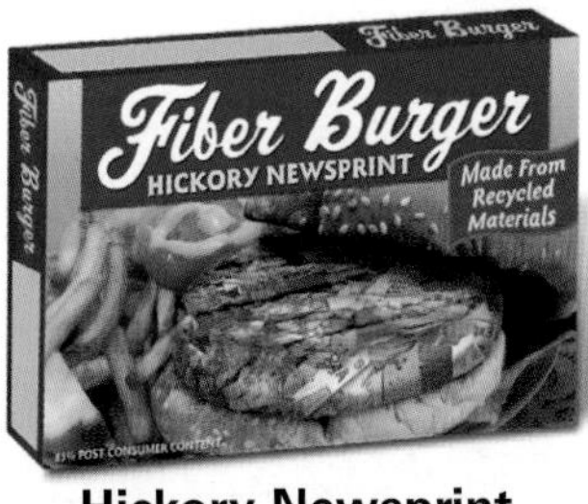

Fiber Burger
HICKORY NEWSPRINT
Made From Recycled Materials

Hickory Newsprint

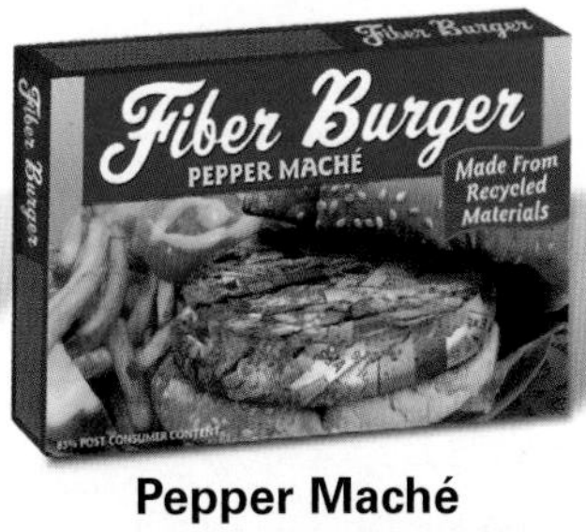

Fiber Burger
PEPPER MACHÉ
Made From Recycled Materials

Pepper Maché

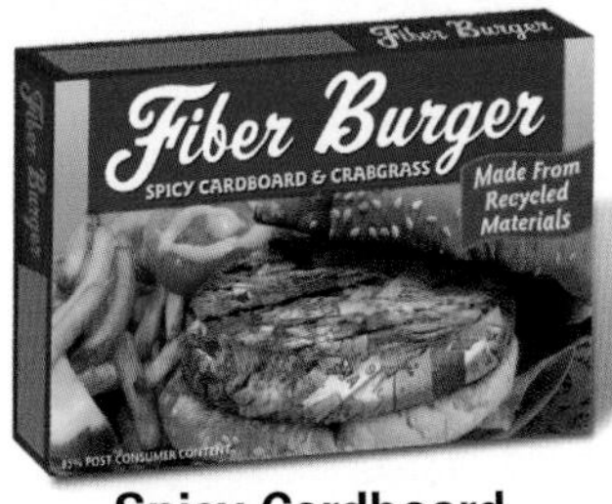

Fiber Burger
SPICY CARDBOARD & CRABGRASS
Made From Recycled Materials

Spicy Cardboard & Crabgrass

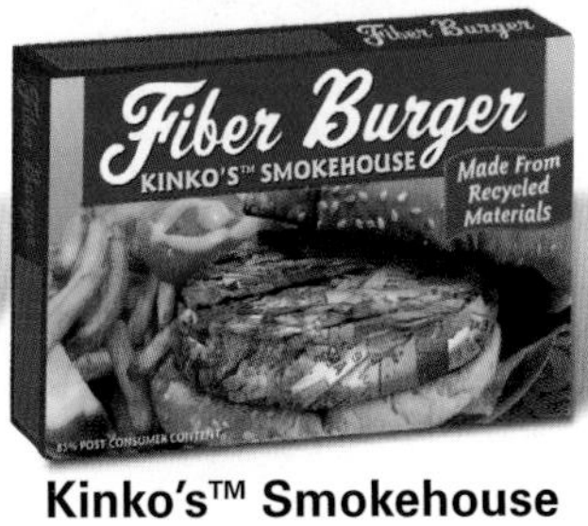

Fiber Burger
KINKO'S™ SMOKEHOUSE
Made From Recycled Materials

Kinko's™ Smokehouse

MANUFACTURER'S COUPON	NOT REDEEMABLE

Save $1.00

on any variety of Fiber Burger

TO THE CONSUMER: This coupon is good on any purchase of FIBER BURGER Recycled Meal Patties. Any other use constitutes fraud. It's a lousy coupon! What else are you going to do with it?! Pay off a gambling debt? Re-paper the bedroom? Collect your dry-cleaning? Listen, pal, it's not worth it. You've worked too hard to get where you are to throw it all away like this. Think of your family, man! There's people out there who care about you! It doesn't have to end this way. C'mon, now, drop the coupon. That's it. Nice and slowly...Okay, Becker, MOVE IN NOW! GO GO GO!

PHOTOGRAPHER: IRVING SCHILD WRITER: SCOTT MAIKO

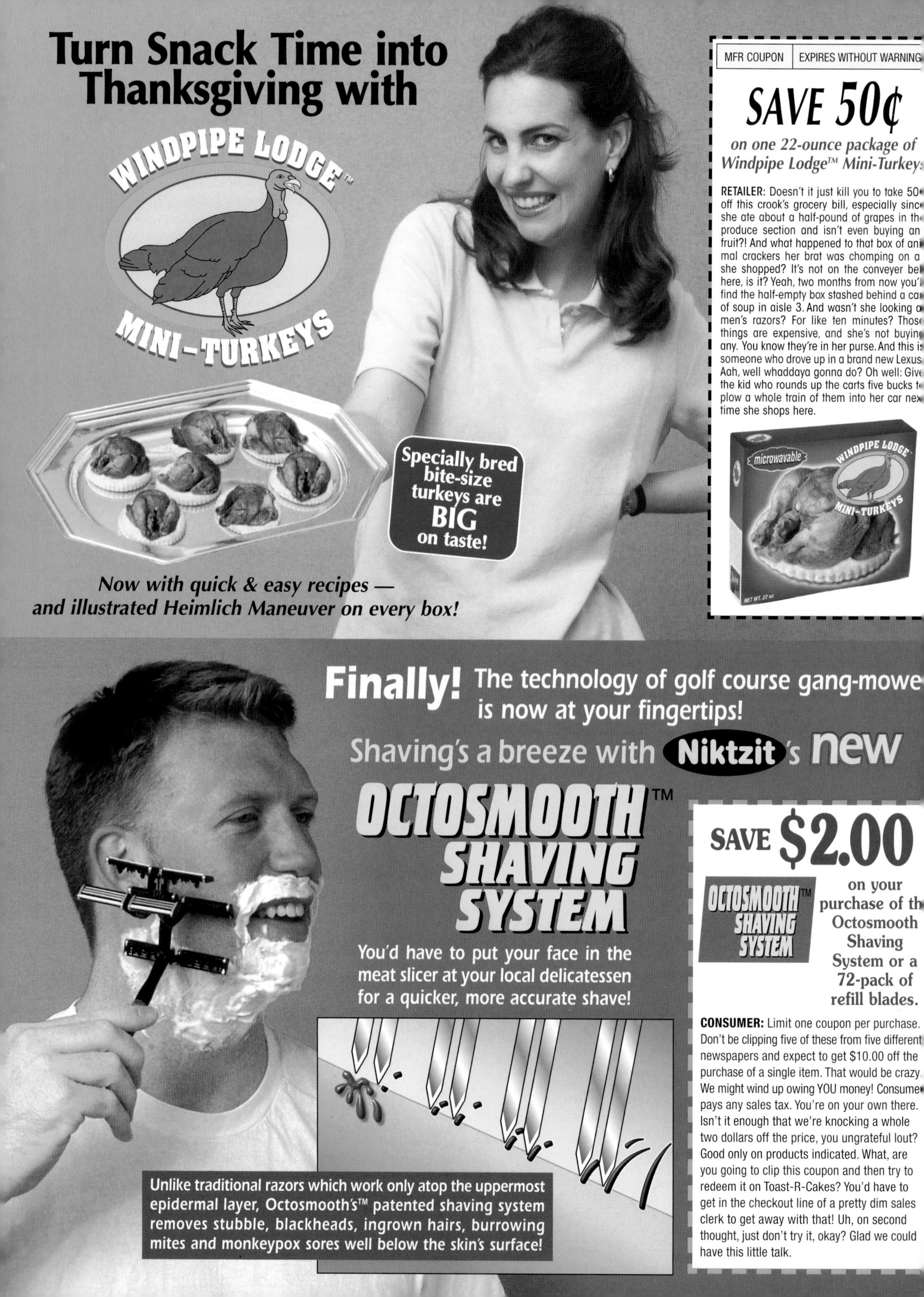
Turn Snack Time into Thanksgiving with
WINDPIPE LODGE™
MINI-TURKEYS
Specially bred bite-size turkeys are BIG on taste!
Now with quick & easy recipes — and illustrated Heimlich Maneuver on every box!
MFR COUPON
EXPIRES WITHOUT WARNING
SAVE 50¢
on one 22-ounce package of Windpipe Lodge™ Mini-Turkey
RETAILER: Doesn't it just kill you to take 50 off this crook's grocery bill, especially sinc she ate about a half-pound of grapes in th produce section and isn't even buying an fruit?! And what happened to that box of ani mal crackers her brat was chomping on a she shopped? It's not on the conveyer bel here, is it? Yeah, two months from now you' find the half-empty box stashed behind a ca of soup in aisle 3. And wasn't she looking a men's razors? For like ten minutes? Those things are expensive, and she's not buying any. You know they're in her purse. And this is someone who drove up in a brand new Lexus Aah, well whaddaya gonna do? Oh well: Give the kid who rounds up the carts five bucks t plow a whole train of them into her car nex time she shops here.
microwavable
WINDPIPE LODGE
MINI-TURKEYS
NET WT. 22 oz.
Finally! The technology of golf course gang-mowe is now at your fingertips!
Shaving's a breeze with Niktzit's new
OCTOSMOOTH™ SHAVING SYSTEM
You'd have to put your face in the meat slicer at your local delicatessen for a quicker, more accurate shave!
Unlike traditional razors which work only atop the uppermost epidermal layer, Octosmooth's™ patented shaving system removes stubble, blackheads, ingrown hairs, burrowing mites and monkeypox sores well below the skin's surface!
SAVE $2.00
OCTOSMOOTH™ SHAVING SYSTEM
on your purchase of th Octosmooth Shaving System or a 72-pack of refill blades.
CONSUMER: Limit one coupon per purchase. Don't be clipping five of these from five different newspapers and expect to get $10.00 off the purchase of a single item. That would be crazy We might wind up owing YOU money! Consume pays any sales tax. You're on your own there. Isn't it enough that we're knocking a whole two dollars off the price, you ungrateful lout? Good only on products indicated. What, are you going to clip this coupon and then try to redeem it on Toast-R-Cakes? You'd have to get in the checkout line of a pretty dim sales clerk to get away with that! Uh, on second thought, just don't try it, okay? Glad we could have this little talk.

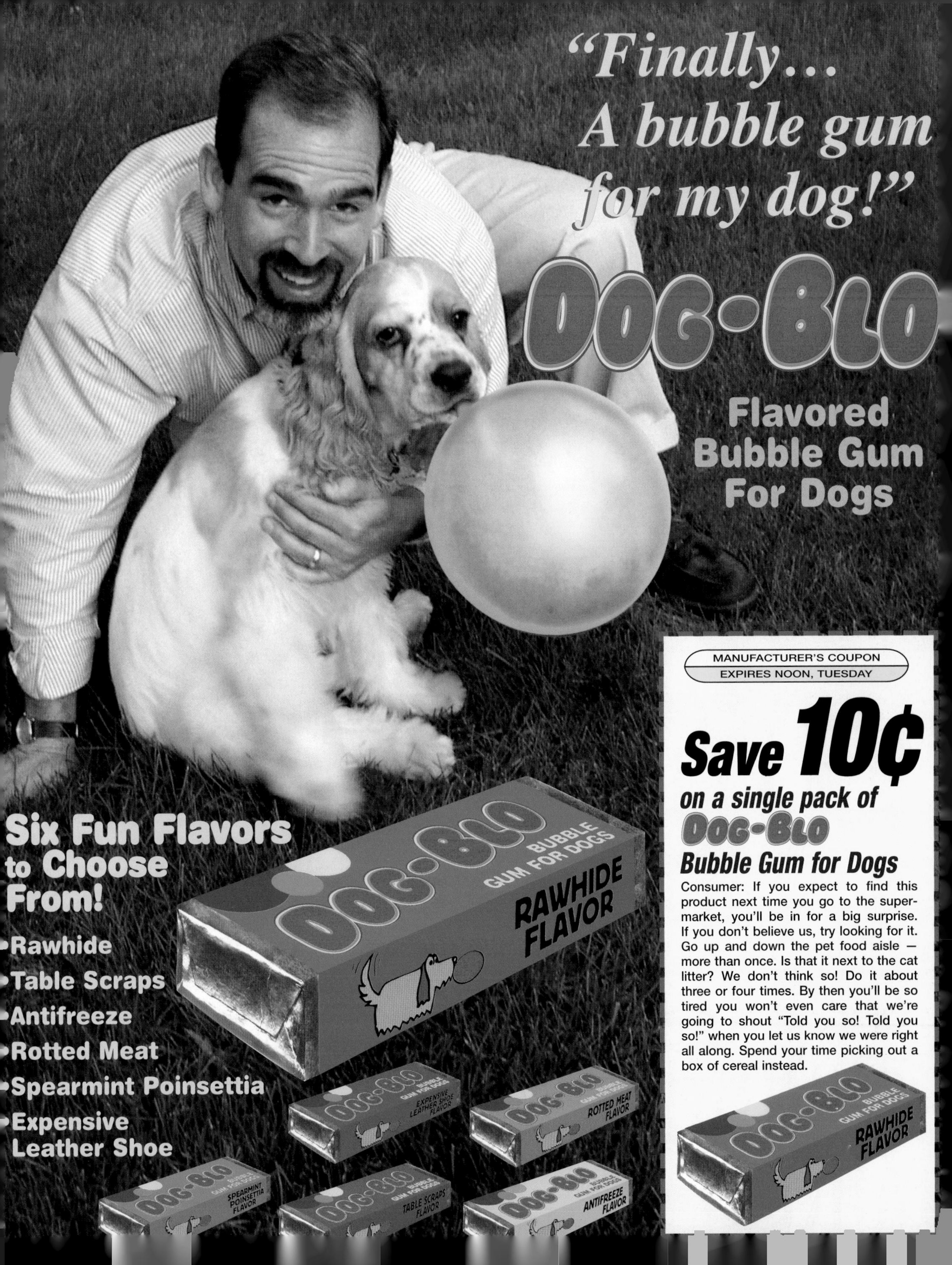
"Finally... A bubble gum for my dog!"
DOG-BLO
Flavored Bubble Gum For Dogs
Six Fun Flavors to Choose From!
•Rawhide
•Table Scraps
•Antifreeze
•Rotted Meat
•Spearmint Poinsettia
•Expensive Leather Shoe
DOG-BLO BUBBLE GUM FOR DOGS
RAWHIDE FLAVOR
EXPENSIVE LEATHER SHOE FLAVOR
ROTTED MEAT FLAVOR
SPEARMINT POINSETTIA FLAVOR
TABLE SCRAPS FLAVOR
ANTIFREEZE FLAVOR
MANUFACTURER'S COUPON
EXPIRES NOON, TUESDAY
Save 10¢
on a single pack of
DOG-BLO
Bubble Gum for Dogs
Consumer: If you expect to find this product next time you go to the supermarket, you'll be in for a big surprise. If you don't believe us, try looking for it. Go up and down the pet food aisle — more than once. Is that it next to the cat litter? We don't think so! Do it about three or four times. By then you'll be so tired you won't even care that we're going to shout "Told you so! Told you so!" when you let us know we were right all along. Spend your time picking out a box of cereal instead.
DOG-BLO BUBBLE GUM FOR DOGS
RAWHIDE FLAVOR

ROAMING WASN'T BILLED IN A DAY DEPT.

Consider a cell phone plan that gives you 500 free minutes a month. 500 minutes! Not 300, not 400...500!! That's sooo many minutes! That is, until you start using them the way a lot of cell phone owners do — then 500 isn't so many minutes! Need proof? Just review the findings of our exhaustively researched and lavishly illustrated study we call...

MAD'S FEARLESS BREAK-DOWN OF 500 FREE CELL PHONE MINUTES

15 minutes:

Hello?
Hey, Nick, it's me, Bob. How's things over on the couch?

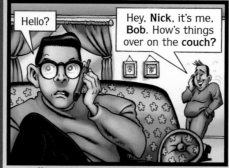

Calling someone you're in the same room with as a joke.

26 minutes:

Okay, I got the goat cheese, the Clamato Juice and the plastic hanger. Did you say we needed fabric softener or stool softener?
CLAMATO
CHÈVRE

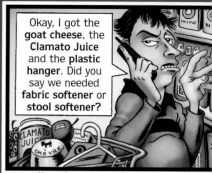

Calling home to ask what you were sent to the store for.

8 minutes:

I don't know why everybody's looking at me funny!

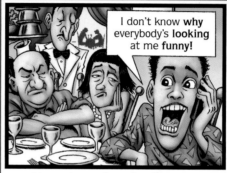

At a restaurant, saying the same nine words over and over again...

18 minutes:

But nurse, it's swelling and throbbing. Can't you squeeze me in?

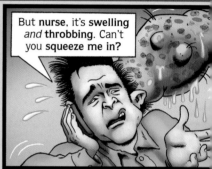

Calling around for a good brain tumor doctor.

33 minutes:

I was just thinking, how's my good friend Steve in Dubuque?
Who the hell is this?

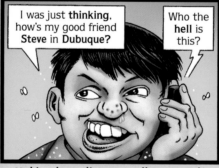

Making long distance calls to people you wouldn't otherwise talk to if you had to pay long distance charges.

16 minutes:

Hi Steve, glad I reached you. I need to speak with you about...
This is John. I'm not home right now. But if you leave...

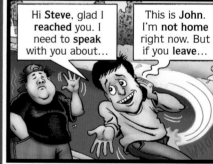

Calling your own number and pretendir to be talking to someone to avoid havir to talk to someone who's with you.

3 minutes:

AM'S PIZZA
Yeah, I'd like to order a slice, please.

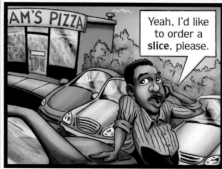

Calling in your pizza order from the parking lot after determining that the line was too long to wait on.

21 minutes:

You say there's a Wendy's on the right? Uh, then I don't know where the heck I am.

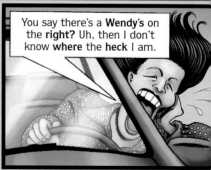

Getting or giving "real time" driving directions.

ARTIST: RICK TULKA
COLORIST: CARRIE STRACHAN
WRITER: BUTCH D'AMBROSIO

minutes:

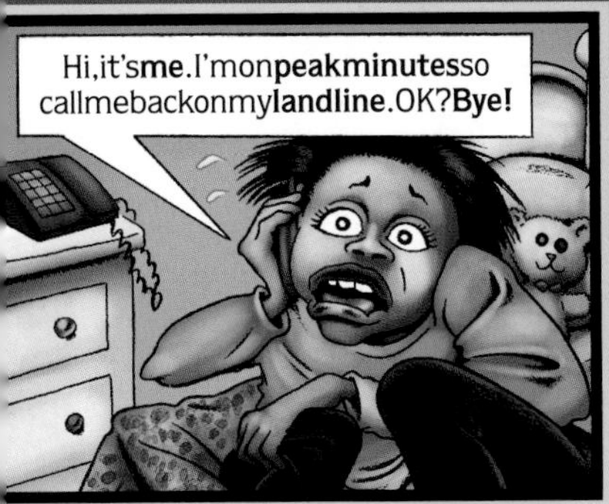
Hi,it'sme.I'monpeakminutesso callmebackonmylandline.OK?Bye!

elling your boyfriend or girlfriend to :all you at home so you don't use up all of your minutes.

16 minutes:

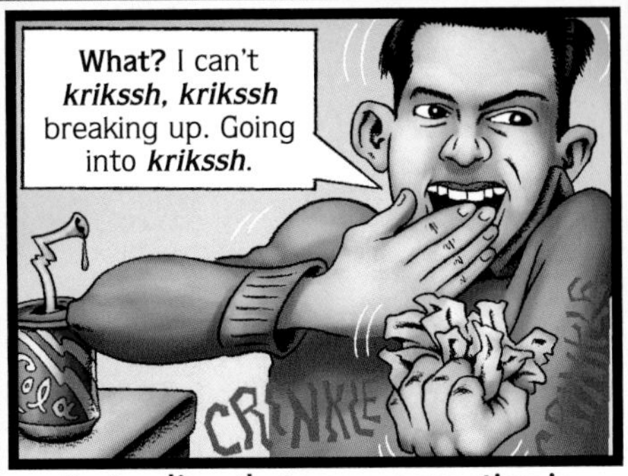
What? I can't *krikssh, krikssh* breaking up. Going into *krikssh*.
CRINKLE
CRINKLE

Pretending that your connection is breaking up to people you don't want to talk to anymore.

0 minutes:

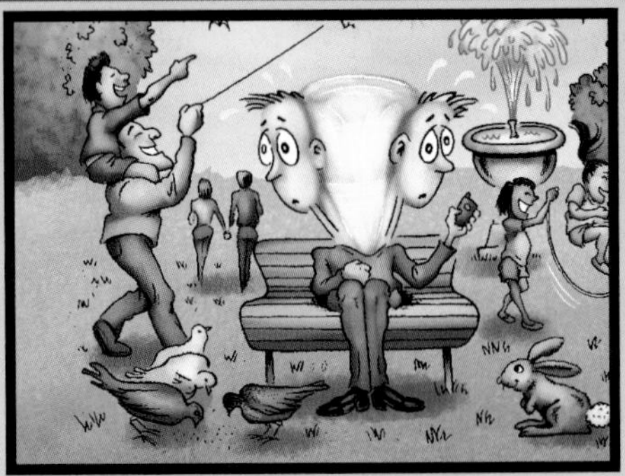

An actual emergency.

O minutes:

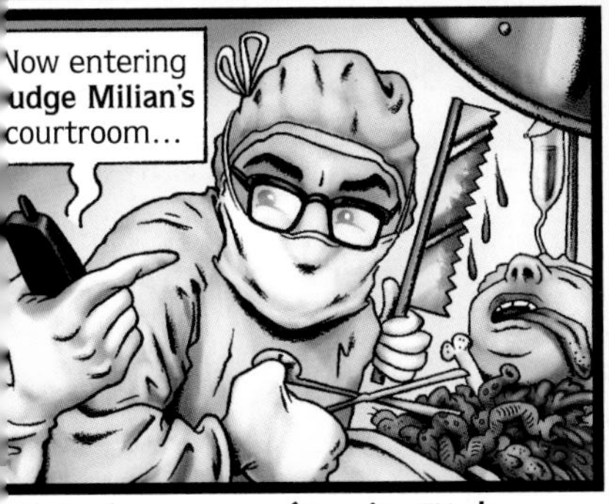
Now entering udge Milian's courtroom…

Listening to your favorite TV show by having somebody at home hold the phone up to the set.

10 minutes:

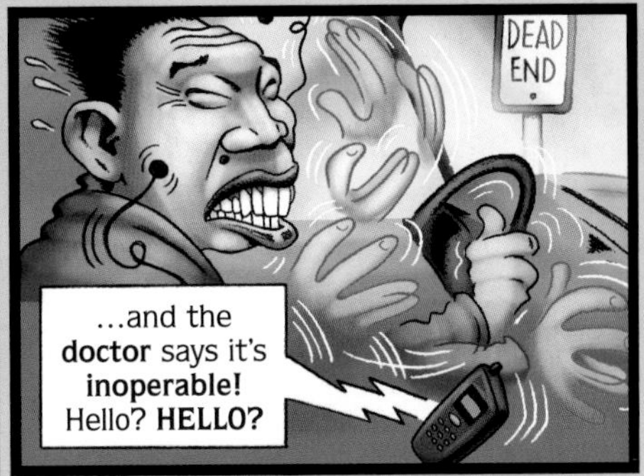
DEAD END
…and the doctor says it's inoperable! Hello? HELLO?

Wasted while trying to get your "hands free" earpiece to stay in your ear.

39 minutes:

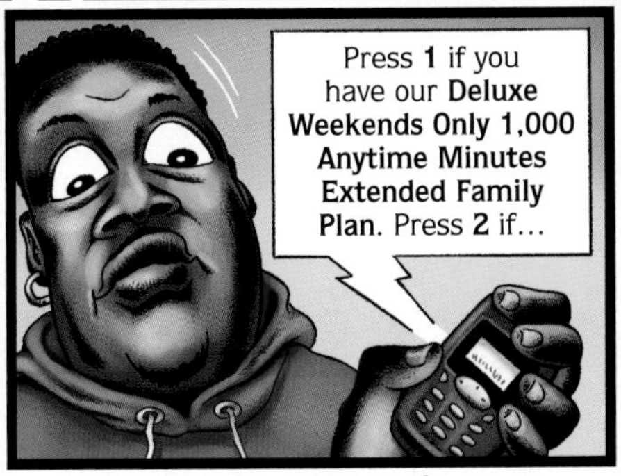
Press 1 if you have our Deluxe Weekends Only 1,000 Anytime Minutes Extended Family Plan. Press 2 if…

Navigating the automated customer service menu to find out how many minutes you have left.

2 minutes:

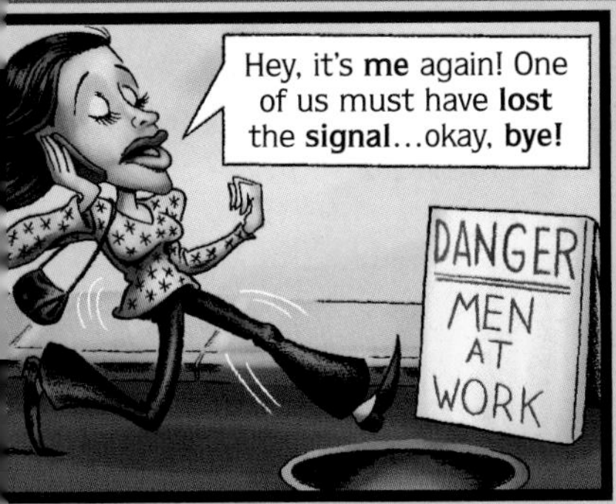
Hey, it's me again! One of us must have lost the signal…okay, bye!
DANGER MEN AT WORK

Returning a dropped call only to find hat neither you nor the person you're alling back has anything more to say.

43 minutes:

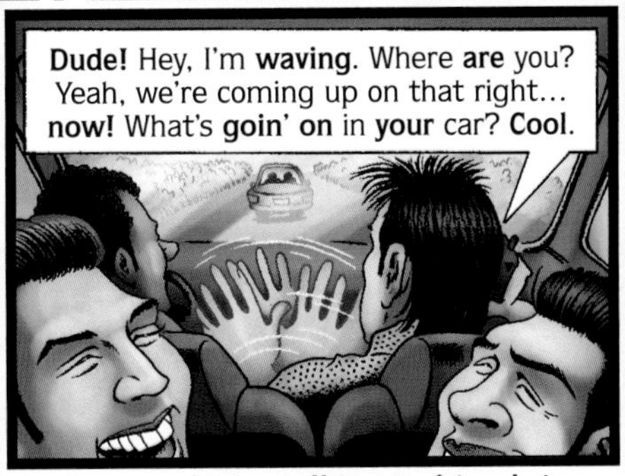
Dude! Hey, I'm waving. Where are you? Yeah, we're coming up on that right… now! What's goin' on in your car? Cool.

On a road trip, talking to friends in the car in front of you.

2 minutes:

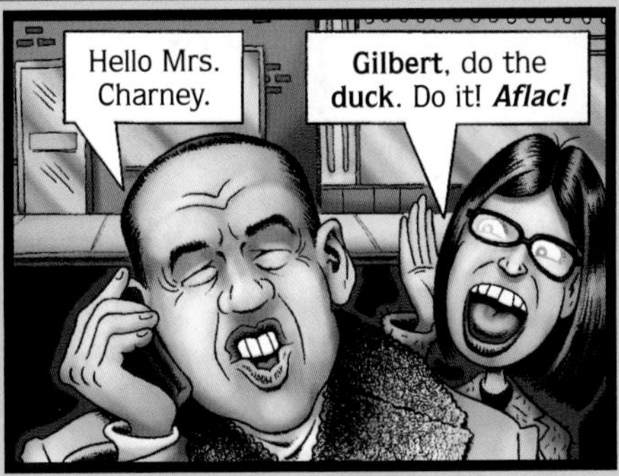
Hello Mrs. Charney.
Gilbert, do the duck. Do it! *Aflac!*

Having a celebrity you ran into tell your mother "Hi."

5 minutes:

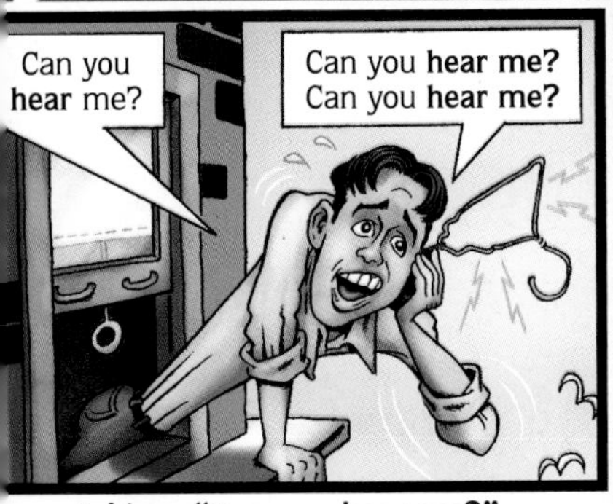
Can you hear me?
Can you hear me? Can you hear me?

Asking, "Can you hear me?"

75 minutes:

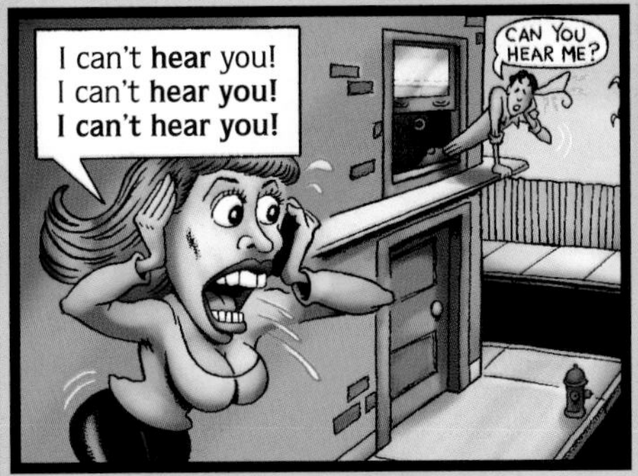
I can't hear you! I can't hear you! I can't hear you!
CAN YOU HEAR ME?

Saying, "I can't hear you."

19 minutes:

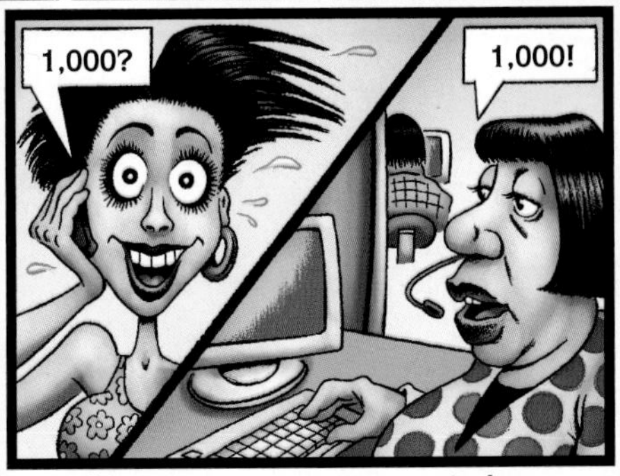
1,000?
1,000!

Making arrangements to switch over to a competitor's phone plan with 1,000 free minutes included.

Just pick a different item from each row as you read your way down the page and you'll have a zany new Naruto episode every time!

MAKE YOUR OWN NUTTY NARUTO EPISODE!

WRITER: KENT PARKER
ARTIST: STEVE SMALLWOOD

NARUTO

SAKURA

SASUKE

AKAMARU

KIBA

ROCK LEE

TENTEN

INO

USES

SHADOW CLONE JUTSU

PB&J SANDWICHES

Whoopee Cushion
A WHOOPEE CUSHION

Super Soaker
A SUPER SOAKER

TRUE LOVE

PLAYSTATION 3
A PLAYSTATION 3

supersmile.
DENTAL FLOSS
DENTAL FLOSS

HEINZ
TOMATO KETCHUP
KETCHUP PACKETS

TO FIGHT

HAKU

A BAD CASE OF THE SNIFFLES

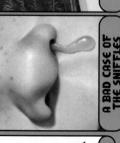

A SUBSTITUTE TEACHER

BARNEY

THE EVIL COUNT OLAF

TONY HAWK

SPAM
Hormel
SPAM

AN UNFAIR BEDTIME

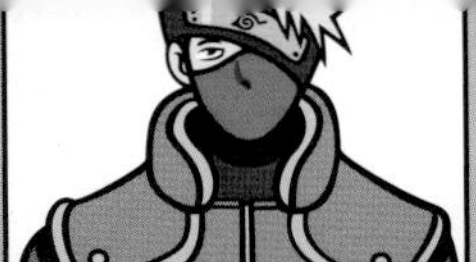
KAKASHI

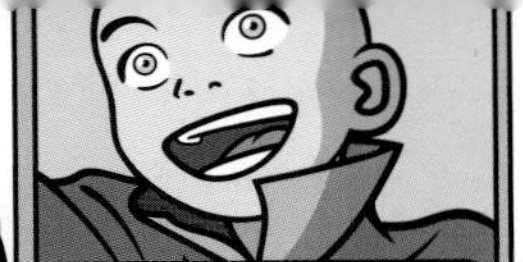
AANG

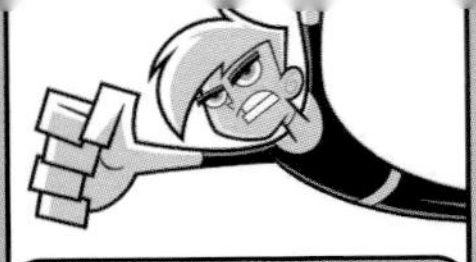
DANNY PHANTOM

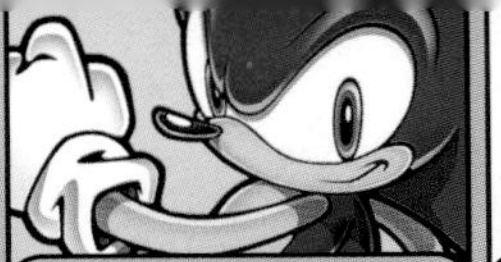
SONIC THE HEDGEHOG

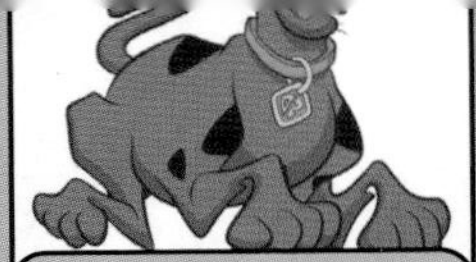
SCOOBY-DOO

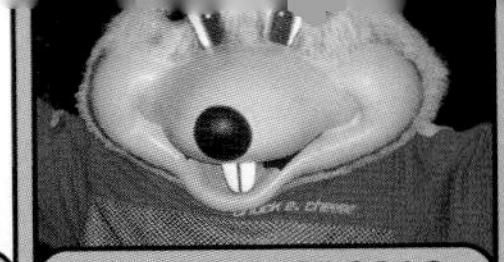
CHUCK E. CHEESE

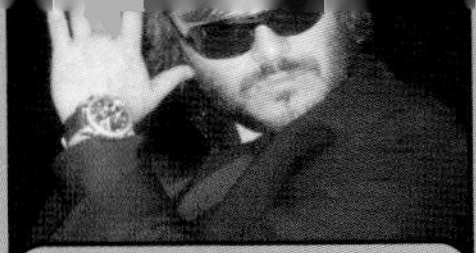
JACK BLACK

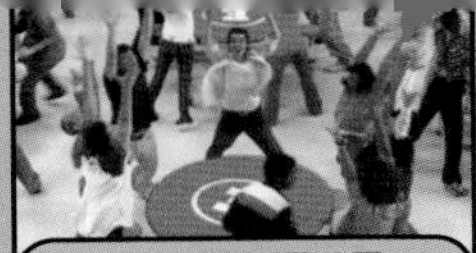
THE CAST OF HIGH SCHOOL MUSICAL

BATTLES

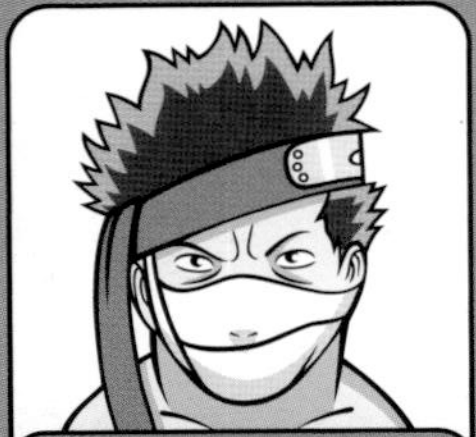
ZABUZA

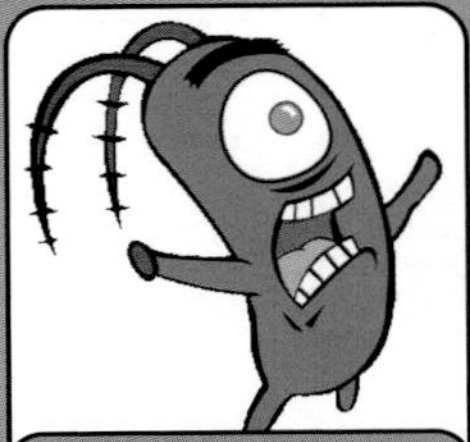
PLANKTON

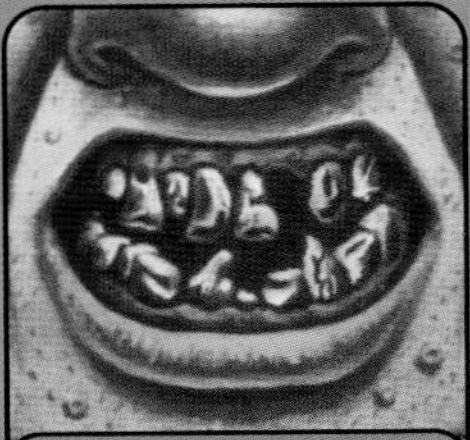
TOOTH DECAY

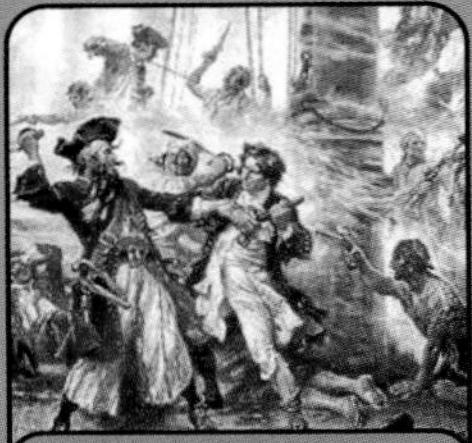
A BAND OF PIRATES

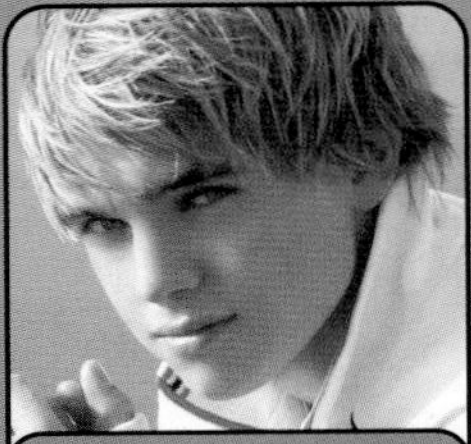
JESSE MCCARTNEY

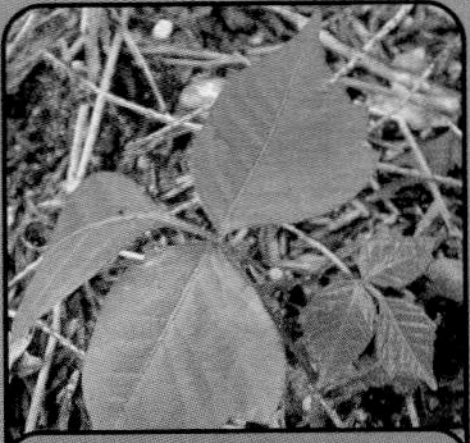
POISON IVY

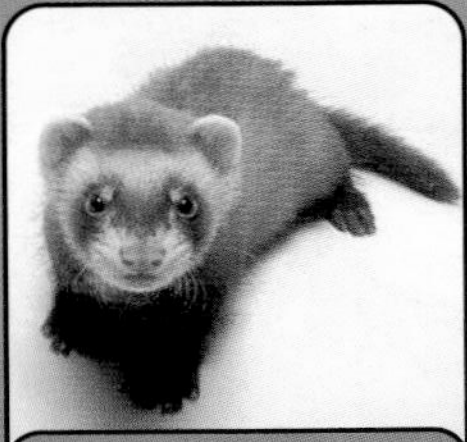
A FERRET

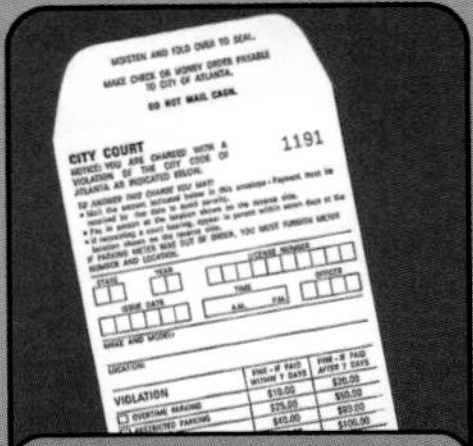
CITY COURT
1191
A PARKING TICKET

AND THEN RESCUES

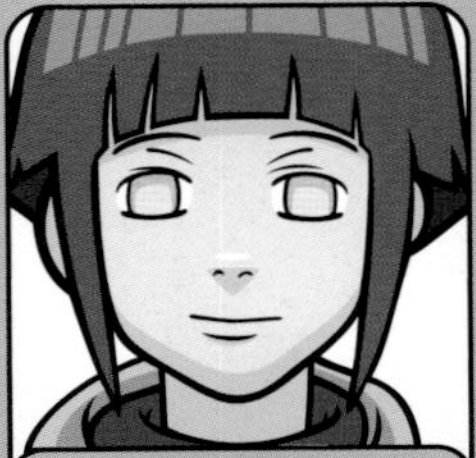
HINATA

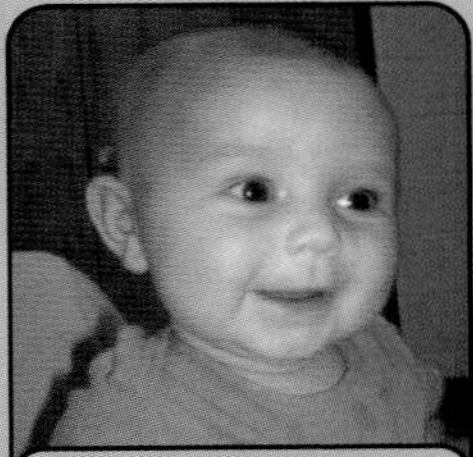
YOUR BABY SISTER

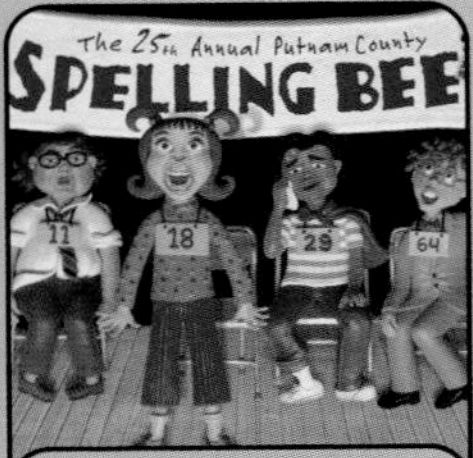
The 25th Annual Putnam County
SPELLING BEE
THE SPELLING BEE FINALISTS

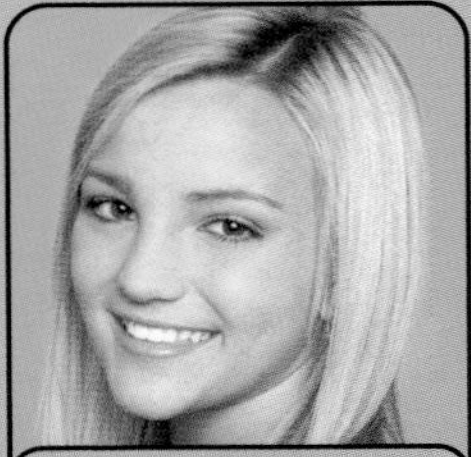
JAMIE LYNN SPEARS

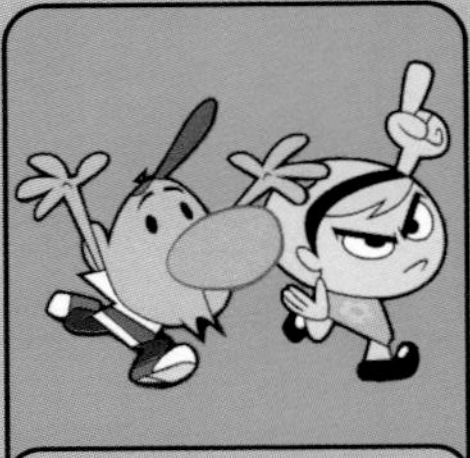
BILLY AND MANDY

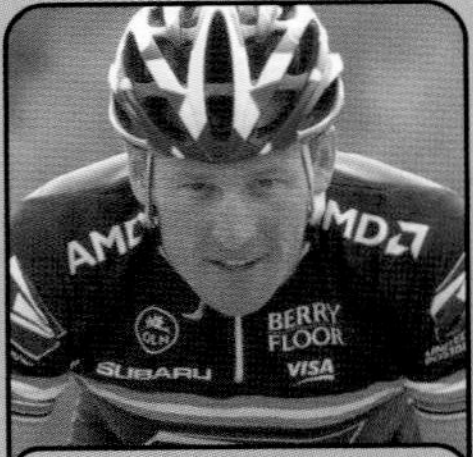
BERRY FLOOR
VISA
SUBARU
LANCE ARMSTRONG

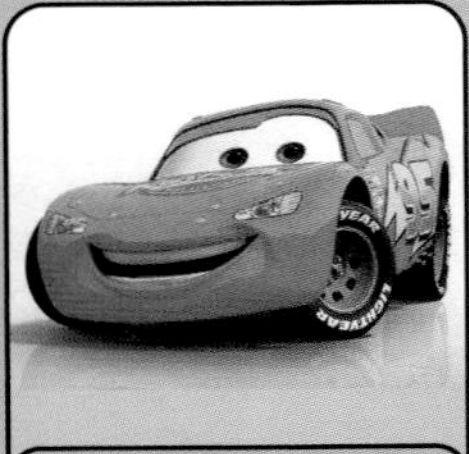
LIGHTNING MCQUEEN

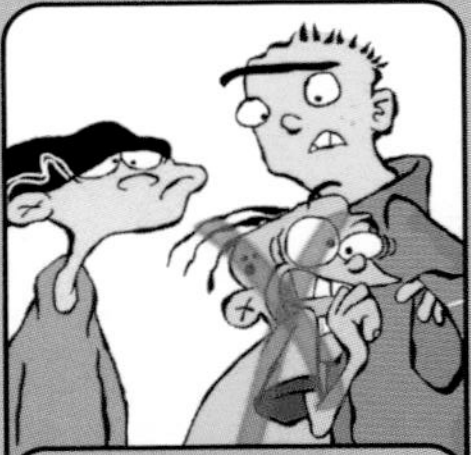
ED & EDD BUT NOT EDDY

FROM

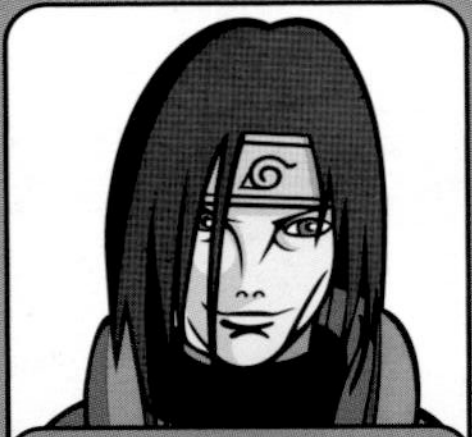
OROCHIMARU

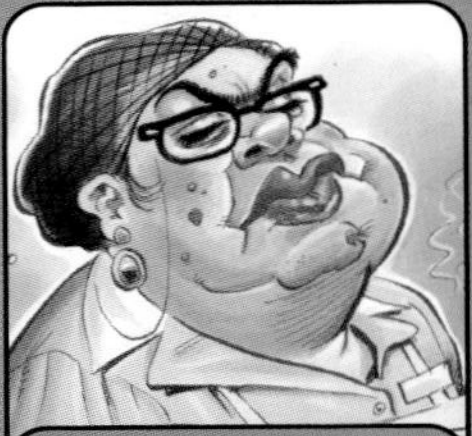
THE SCHOOL LUNCH LADY

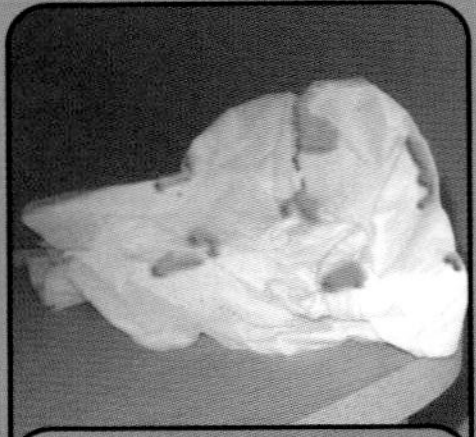
A TISSUE FULL OF FRESH BOOGERS

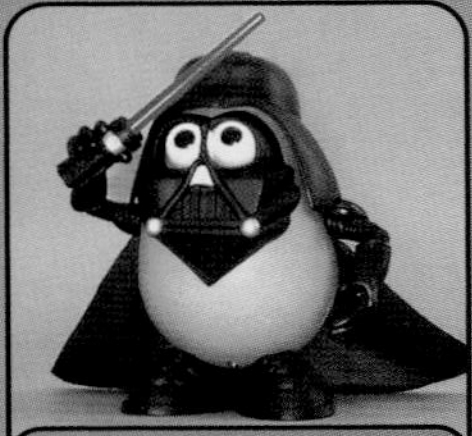
DARTH TATER

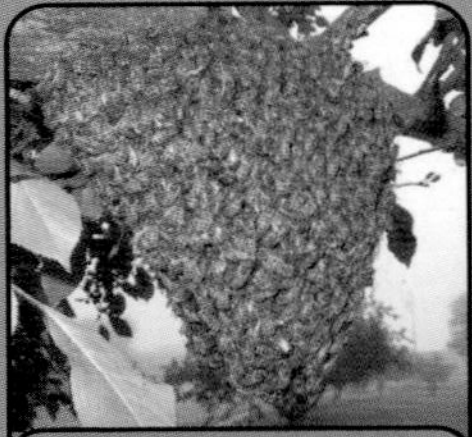
A SWARM OF BEES

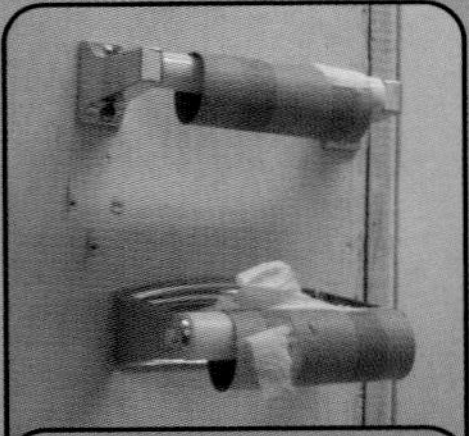
A NATIONWIDE TOILET PAPER SHORTAGE

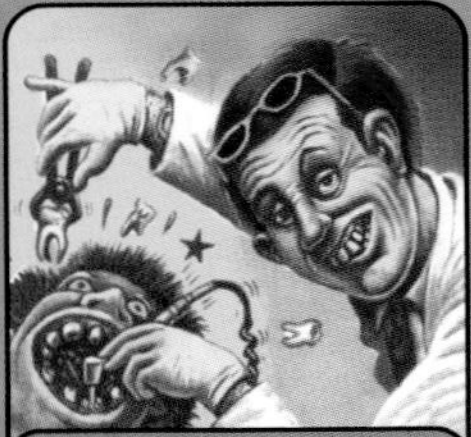
A CRAZED DENTIST

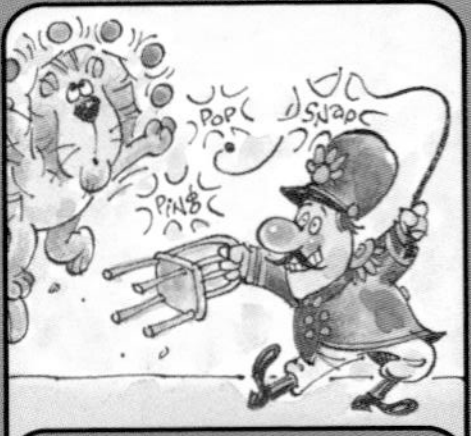
POP
SNAP
A CONFUSED LION TAMER

JUST IN TIME TO RETURN HOME TO

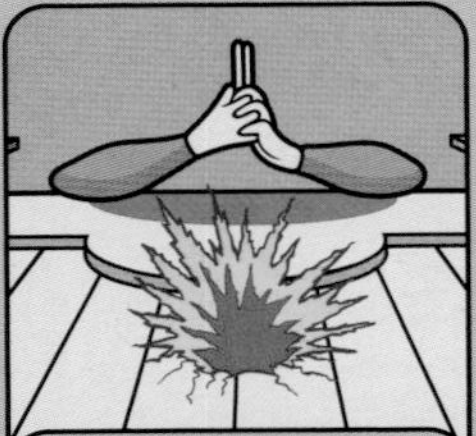
TAKE THE CHUNIN EXAM

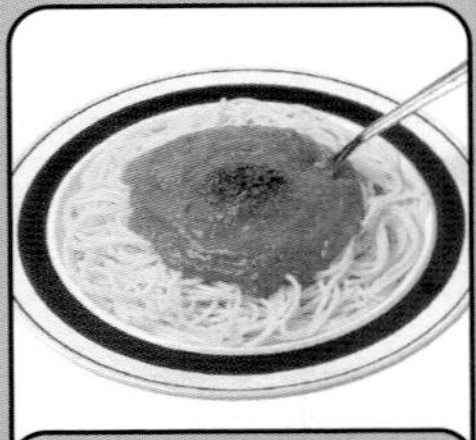
MAKE SPAGHETTI

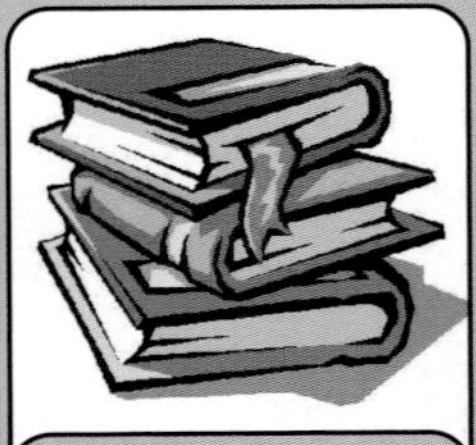
RETURN OVERDUE LIBRARY BOOKS

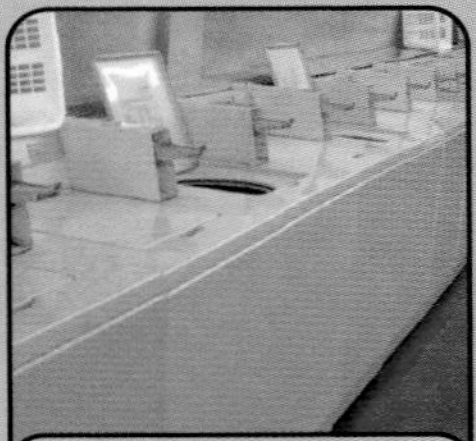
DO LAUNDRY

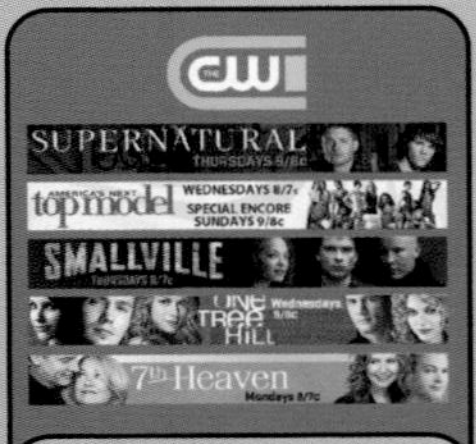
CW
SUPERNATURAL
topmodel
SMALLVILLE
One Tree Hill
7th Heaven
CATCH THE CW'S FALL LINEUP

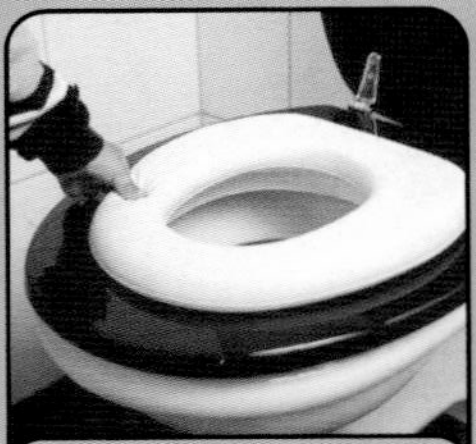
GO POTTY

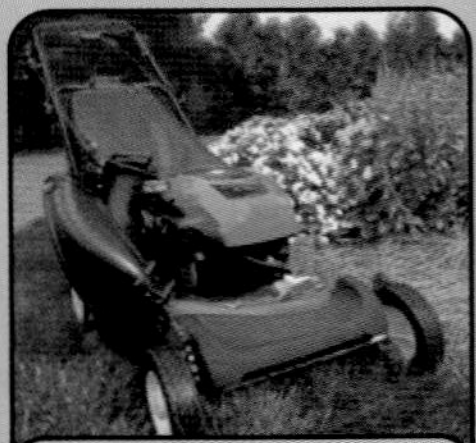
MOW THE LAWN

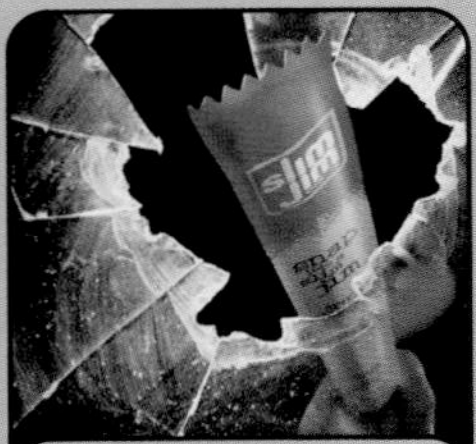
SNAP INTO A SLIM JIM

ONE FINE DAY AT A BANK

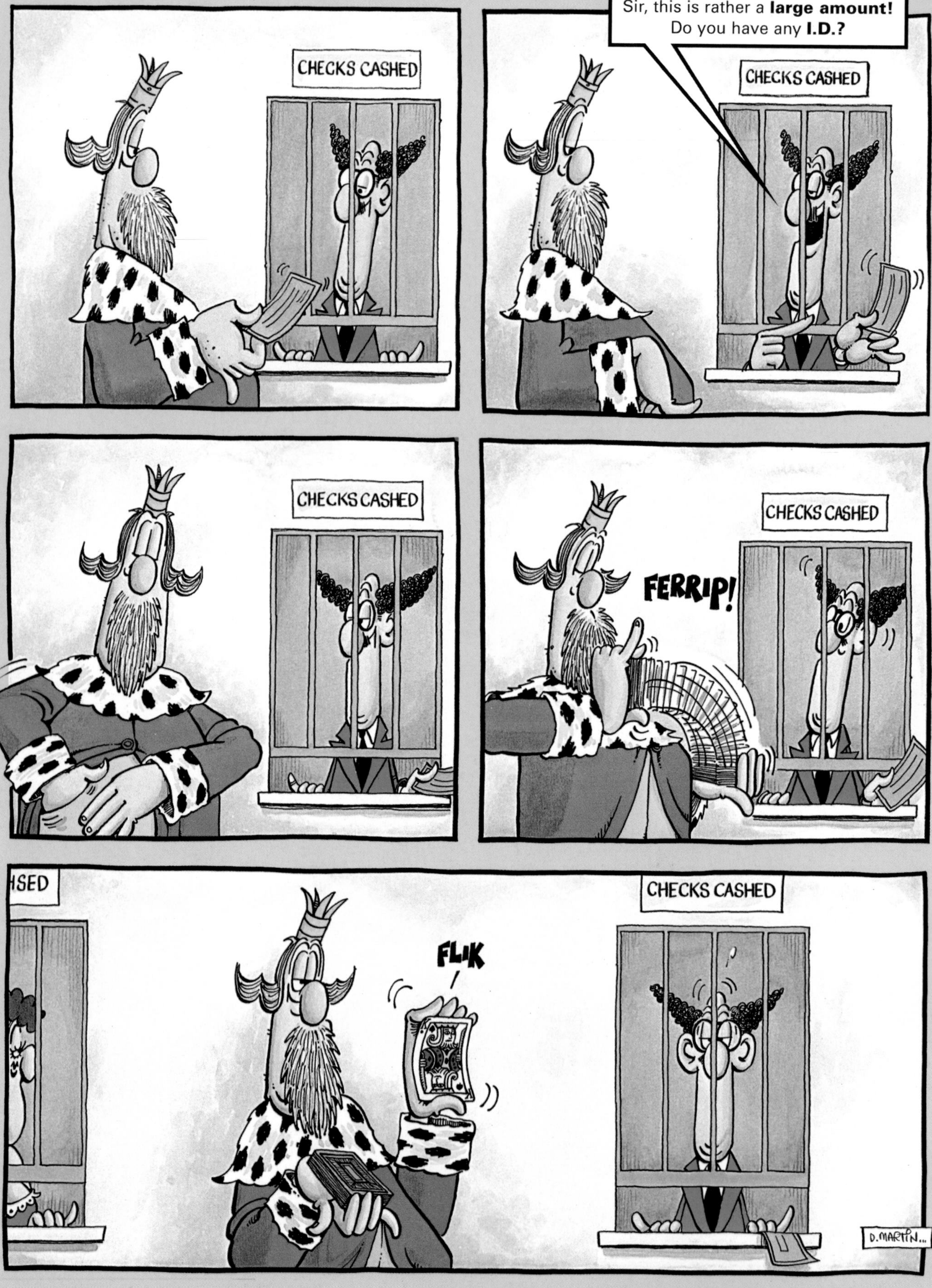
CHECKS CASHED
Sir, this is rather a **large amount!** Do you have any **I.D.?**
CHECKS CASHED
CHECKS CASHED
CHECKS CASHED
FERRIP!
HSED
CHECKS CASHED
FLIK
D. MARTIN...

WRITER: DON EDWING ARTIST: DON MARTIN

Harry Potter may be the biggest thing in publishing right now – but it's certainly not the _smartest_. Although the series has made tons of money, J.K. Rowling has repeatedly stated that the saga would only be seven books long. That's no way to do business! Fellow children's author Lemony Snicket, however, knows that the secret to success is to find a formula, stick with it, and above all else, never take _any_ steps to resolve the plot and kill that golden goose! Just turn this magazine sideways and read on – maybe then you'll understand what keeps the kids interested (and shelling out their parents' bucks), all for...

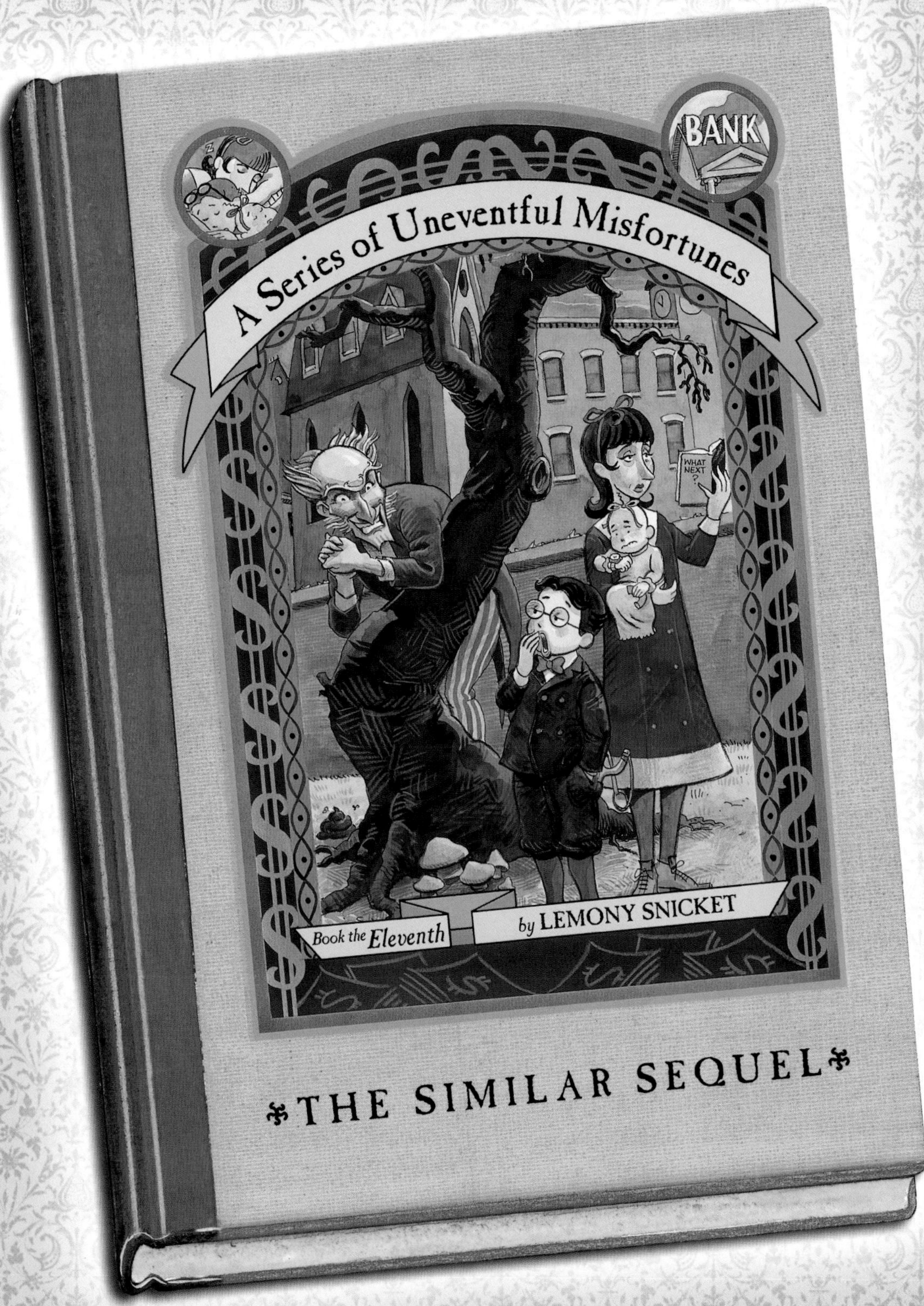
BANK
A Series of Uneventful Misfortunes
WHAT NEXT ?
Book the Eleventh
by LEMONY SNICKET
THE SIMILAR SEQUEL

of the book. The rest is really just an appalling amount of filler. So, why not stop now and find something less aggravating to busy yourself with — it won't be hard to do.

You're still reading, aren't you? Because you're ten books in and you figure that eventually *something* is bound to happen, right? Ha ha! I have you exactly where I want you! *The banana pudding fell sideways into the giraffe's lap.* You read that too, didn't you? Keep reading, it's bound to pay off in a big way real soon! Sucker!

By now, you know all about the Baudelaires — there's the eldest, Violet, who is always inventing things; then there's Klaus, the middle child, who is constantly reading things; and, of course, there's Sunny, the baby, who is always biting things. This is not a summary — this is actually the full extent of the character development after 10 novels' worth of stories. You're up to speed!

Often, while laying awake at night, alone and scared, I wish I had never begun my investigation of the Baudelaires — an endeavor that has ruined my life, forcing me to write, essentially, the same story nearly a dozen times. Of course, when I lie awake at night, it is in my mansion, atop my diamond-filled mattress, and I drift into sleep as soon as I think about how this drivel has made me a millionaire many, many times over — so I won't linger on that particular problem for too long — and neither should you.

At this point in the Baudelaires' truly unfortunate lives, they were in a situation exactly like what they had experienced countless times before. Mr. Poe was about to leave them with a new guardian.

The Baudelaires, of course, were nervous about meeting this distant relative/friend of the family/friend of a friend of a family/disinterested third party (depending on what's easiest for the story — it doesn't much matter, they won't be sticking around long). Actually, "nervous" was a remarkably well-adjusted state of mind for them to be in — consider-

C H A P T E R
One

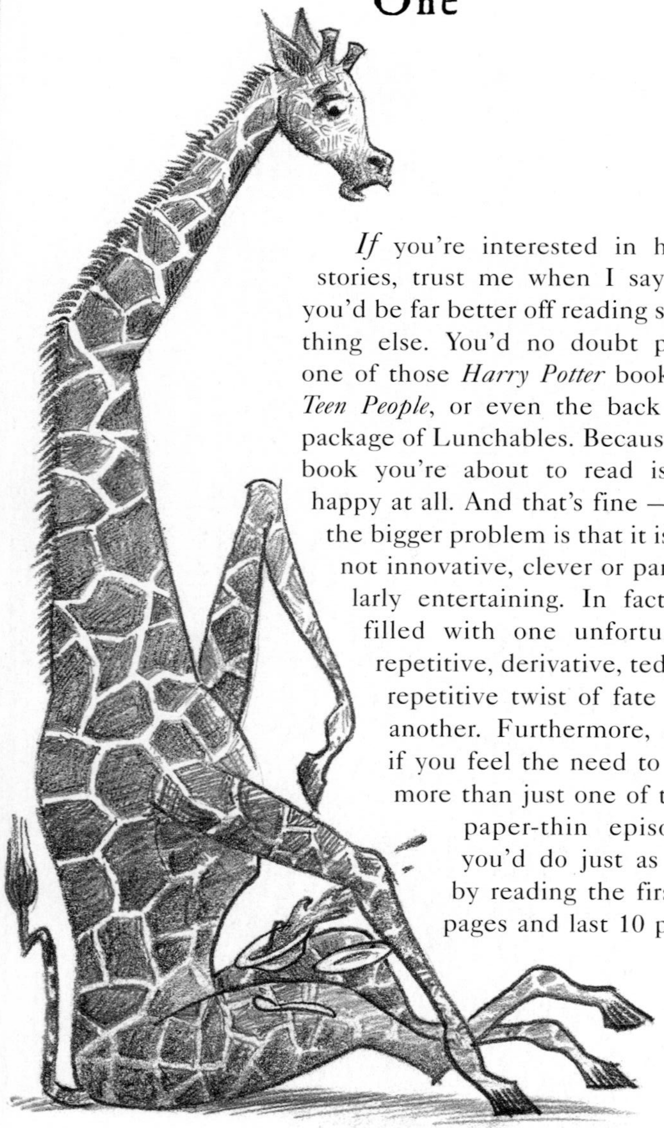

If you're interested in happy stories, trust me when I say that you'd be far better off reading something else. You'd no doubt prefer one of those Harry Potter *books, or* Teen People, *or even the back of a package of Lunchables. Because the book you're about to read is not happy at all. And that's fine — but the bigger problem is that it is also not innovative, clever or particularly entertaining. In fact, it's filled with one unfortunate, repetitive, derivative, tedious, repetitive twist of fate after another. Furthermore, even if you feel the need to read more than just one of these paper-thin episodes, you'd do just as well by reading the first 10 pages and last 10 pages*

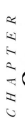

ing that their parents had burned to death, they themselves had nearly been murdered on countless occasions, and no one seemed too bothered by the pattern. Still, they had butterflies in their stomachs just the same.

"Who will we be living with?" Violet asked.

"Oh, it's a zany, inept individual who has an odd fear or obsession that you'll have to abide by, making it impossible to solve your parents' murder or to keep Count Olaf from reentering your lives," Mr. Poe gruffly explained, pausing to cough into his handkerchief.

"You mean like our Aunt Josephine, who wouldn't let us use the stove for any reason?" Klaus asked, rolling his eyes.

"Or 'Sir' at the mill, who wouldn't let us say a word in his presence?" Violet asked.

"Or Jerome Squalor, who refused to disagree with anything his evil, shallow wife said?" Klaus asked.

"Well, our last guardian was absurdly cruel and inept," Violet pointed out, "so I guess that means this guardian will be *good-natured* and inept."

"Crackers!" Sunny said, which probably meant something like, "That's the pattern!"

Sunny, though quite young and capable of only gibberish, was absolutely correct — the characters were all pretty much amorphous — a fancy word in this case meaning "another example of unimaginative, half-witted character development on the writer's part."

"Why can't we live with Justice Strauss, the one person who's been nice to us and believed us about Count Olaf?" Klaus asked.

"You can only be adopted by a relative — that is the rule," Mr. Poe wheezed, a thick strand of phlegm dangling from the corner of his mouth to his ever-present handkerchief.

"But," Violet added, "what about the Squalors — they were just family friends?"

"Well..." Mr. Poe began.

"Or that vile village?" Klaus asked, "We weren't related to any of those people!"

"Same goes for that miserable mill," Violet noted.

"Korn!" Sunny said, by which she probably meant, "And what about when Count Olaf nearly adopted us while he was posing as a female secretary, even though 'she' wasn't related to us at all..."

"Please don't talk to me while I'm driving," Mr. Poe said, conveniently cutting off the children as so many other adults had done when they were asking perfectly reasonable questions. But it was just as well, since Mr. Poe and the children had arrived at their destination — the home of the Baudelaires' new guardian.

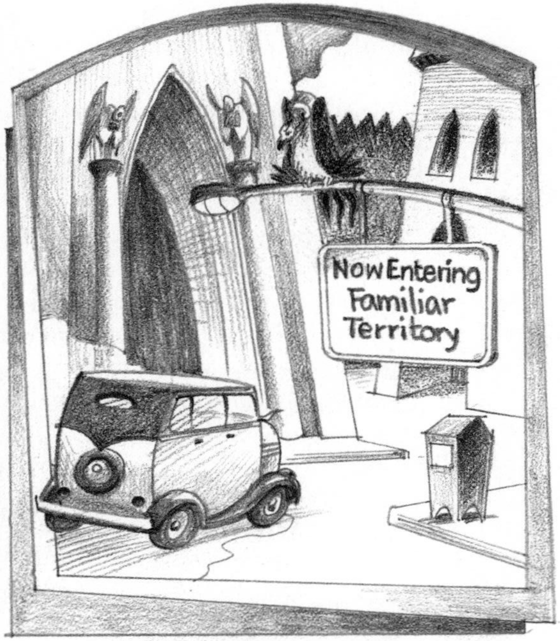
Now Entering
Familiar
Territory

CHAPTER
Three

"*Hello*," said the kindly figure who rushed up to greet them, "I'm Jesse Happy, your new guardian. I just want you to know that I believe you about Count Olaf — and I swear I'll do everything in my power to keep him from ever coming near you again. We're going to have so much fun together, children! We're going to go on picnics and see movies and laugh at funny jokes..."

The Baudelaires felt that at last they had found a home — and with it, a guardian with whom they could find safety and happiness. But, as I've gone nearly four pages without stating, this is not a happy story — and the Baudelaires' happiness, no matter how great, was to be ending very soon.

For just as Jesse was about to make colorful balloon animals for the children, he was crushed beneath the wheels of a car — meeting the predictably gruesome fate of every adult who is kind to the Baudelaires.

"Well," Mr. Poe said, "that's another guardian you've managed to louse up. Tell you what, though, we'll see if this reckless driver is interested in caring for a few wayward orphans."

"I sure *would* be!" was the immediate reply from the unusual man who stepped out of the car, deliberately crushing the windpipe of a still-squirming Jesse in the process.

He wore a headband low over his eyebrows and a giant gaudy anklet that was big enough to hide an incriminating ankle tattoo. He also wore a white t-shirt that had big black letters that read, "I am NOT Count Olaf."

"Allow me to introduce myself," he said, scraping bits of hair and skin off of his fender and pausing only to pry an ear from his hood ornament, "I'm Count Falo."

The Baudelaires, of course, saw past his lame disguise and painfully phony name and realized that, just like clockwork, their old nemesis Count Olaf had reared his ugly head yet again.

"Mr. Poe," Klaus screamed in outrage and surprise, "that is not 'Count Falo' — it is none other than Count Olaf!"

"Nonsense," Mr. Poe exclaimed, "he is wearing a shirt that clearly states he is NOT Count Olaf! He wouldn't be allowed to wear such a garment if it weren't true."

Of course, everyone knows that that is not the case. Obviously, just because something is written on a t-shirt, that does not make it fact. A person wearing a t-shirt that says "Girls Gone Wild!" does not necessarily work for that company — even if he *does* have a camera and swears that he'll make you a star. Everybody knows this — except perhaps for my poor, departed, flash-happy paramour, Beatrice. And, unfortunately for the Baudelaires, Mr. Poe was equally obtuse — a word which here means "super stupid."

But I'm getting off on a tangent — a word that here means, "a bit of unrelated nonsense used to stretch out a flimsy story." So, Count Olaf had already re-emerged — and the Baudelaires could immediately see through his disguise, but would be unable to convince Mr. Poe — or anyone else — until the end of the story. Meaning that there were now 100 mind-numbing pages before every other dense character realized what you, young reader, deduced on page 21. Enjoy!

"Seriously, Mr. Poe," Violet said, "he's Count Olaf...come

on…don't be such a jackass about this!"

"Rozzer!" Sunny said, which probably meant something along the lines of, "For Christ's sake! How many times do we have to go through this exact same scenario! Even *I'm* starting to get tired of this — and I have no short-term memory whatsoever!"

Turning to face the Baudelaires once more, Mr. Poe said, "Now calm down children — the only other time I've seen you this worked up was right before all those times when I left you in the custody of someone who turned out to be Count Olaf!"

"You'll have to forgive the children, Count Falo — they're just upset because Count Olaf always turns up and tries to murder them and every adult they get close to. You know how cranky and suspicious children can get when they have the constant threat of homicide hanging over their heads!"

"It's no problem at all," "Count Falo" said with a smile, "I've tried to kill them so many times, I've nearly lost count!"

"Are you even listening to what he's saying right now?!?" Violet screamed.

"Violet," Mr. Poe said, turning away from "Count Falo" to address the eldest Baudelaire, "it's not polite to yell — and please stop kicking me in the groin while you're at it!"

As Mr. Poe was scolding Violet, behind him, "Count Falo" was holding Sunny by her ankles and using her to beat Klaus about the face and neck, bloodying both in the process.

"But Mr. Poe, if you'll just turn your head 90 degrees, you'll see that phony 'Count Falo' is abusing both my brother and sister right this very minute!"

"Violet, please, it's not polite for children to ask adults to turn their heads. And Klaus, stop that screaming and begging for mercy! Why can't you children behave yourselves?!?"

Oftentimes, adults will not believe children. Maybe it's because they're smaller and sometimes prone to exaggeration. Or maybe it's because adults don't like to think that children know more than they do about certain things. Or, most often, an adult won't listen to a child simply because stubborn adults are an excellent cover for sloppy, inconsistent writers.

"Oh, heavens!" Mr. Poe exclaimed, finally looking at Klaus and Sunny, just after Count Falo had finally grown tired of beating them up and had kicked Sunny, soft-spot-first, directly into Klaus' solar plexus. "Your brother and sister have somehow managed to get blood all over their clothes and faces! You children are behaving most peculiarly today!"

"Yes, but…" Klaus said woozily, feeling several broken ribs floating around his midsection.

"No 'buts,'" Mr. Poe said, "I'm late for a very important appointment. You're in excellent hands — Count Falo is practically family. Good day."

CHAPTER Eight

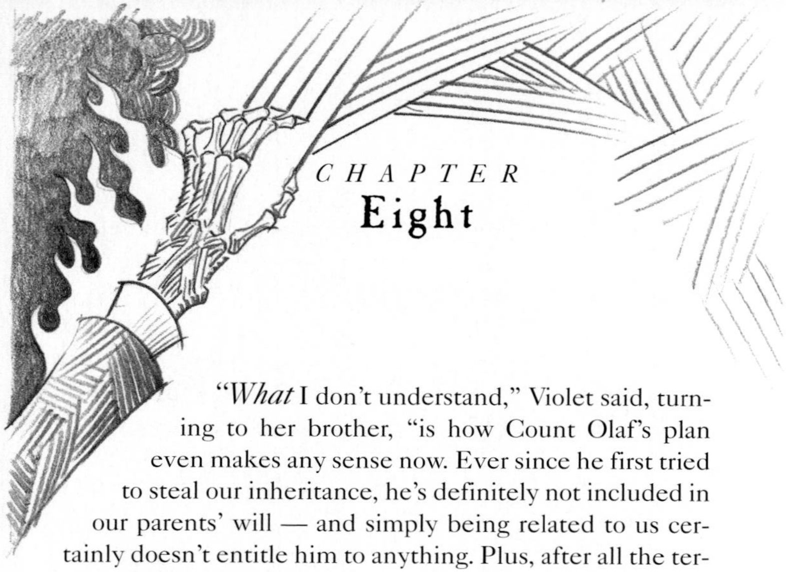

"*What* I don't understand," Violet said, turning to her brother, "is how Count Olaf's plan even makes any sense now. Ever since he first tried to steal our inheritance, he's definitely not included in our parents' will — and simply being related to us certainly doesn't entitle him to anything. Plus, after all the terrible, illegal things that he's done, he's a wanted criminal. There's no way that a man wanted for several murders would be awarded any part of our fortune."

"That's troubled me too," said Klaus.

"Klaus," Violet asked suddenly, "do you remember that time when we were all going to go on a picnic, but it ended up raining?"

"Yes," Klaus said, wistfully remembering one of the many happy days he shared with his family before his parents were killed in that horrible fire and the Baudelaires were forced to endure one miserable experience after another. "It was far too stormy to go outside, but we had a picnic right on the living room rug."

"Dropsy!" Sunny chirped in — which meant something along the lines of, "Yes, I too remember all the fun we used to have with our parents! Good times!"

As the Baudelaires lay in their beds, they thought of their parents futilely clawing the walls and screaming in agony as the flames melted the flesh right off their charred bones.

"Oh well, enough reminiscing. It's silly to dwell on the past," Violet concluded, ending this adventure's obligatory recollection of their parents.

CHAPTER Ten

XYZ

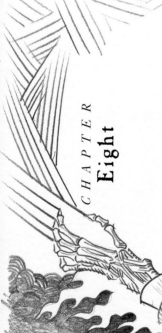

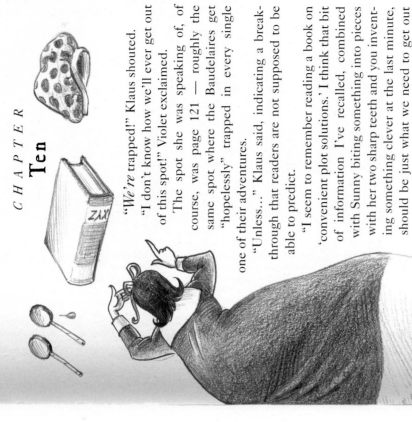

"*We're* trapped!" Klaus shouted.

"I don't know how we'll ever get out of this spot!" Violet exclaimed.

The spot she was speaking of, of course, was page 121 — roughly the same spot where the Baudelaires get "hopelessly" trapped in every single one of their adventures.

"Unless..." Klaus said, indicating a breakthrough that readers are not supposed to be able to predict.

"I seem to remember reading a book on 'convenient plot solutions.' I think that bit of information I've recalled, combined with Sunny biting something into pieces with her two sharp teeth and you inventing something clever at the last minute, should be just what we need to get out of this jam and make one last, uneventful attempt to capture Count Olaf. Good thing I read that book!"

And without a trace of familiarity for the situation, Violet took a ribbon out of her pocket and tied her hair up, as she always did when she needed to invent something that would miraculously save them.

"What are you inventing, Violet?" Klaus asked, purely for tradition's sake.

"Snide!" Sunny said, which meant something along the line of, "She's inventing a 'plot device.' She's going to take the few 'random,' seemingly unrelated objects in her direct vicinity and create an invention at the very last second that perfectly suits the obstacle at hand! Stuck in a runaway elevator? She'll invent an 'elevator-stopper'! About to be trampled by rampaging elephants? She'll invent an 'elephant-disperser'! God! This nonsense makes *MacGyver* look Shakespearean!"

Within a few minutes, Violet had taken two lollipops, the "XYZ" volume of the 1977 World Book and an old shower cap and made an invention that perfectly solved their conundrum — a word that in this case means "imbroglio."

If this were a happy story, it would have a happy ending — and the villain would be captured, while the heroes would be left cheerful, and perhaps enjoying a chocolate sundae (unless they were lactose intolerant, in which case, a non-dairy treat could be easily substituted).

And if you're still expecting a happy ending, you're clearly some sort of moron — although it HAS been nearly four pages since I last stressed that this is NOT a traditional happy story.

Anyway, as those of you who read the previous sentence may remember, this story does NOT have a happy ending. It will, however, have an abrupt, unsatisfactory and well-worn ending. Happy endings are unrealistic and boring and predictable. In contrast, unhappy endings are dark and edgy and unexpected! Even with plenty of previous warnings. In book after book. After book.

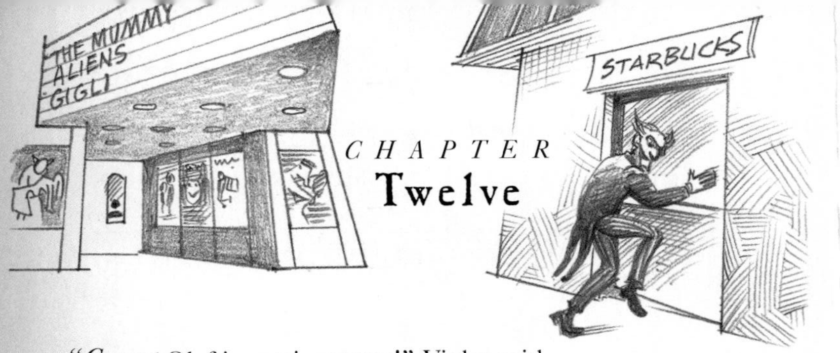
THE MUMMY
ALIENS
GIGLI
STARBUCKS

CHAPTER Twelve

"*Count* Olaf is getting away!" Violet said.

"*We'll* have to stop him then!" the orphans shouted, somehow conveniently finding the courage to face Count Olaf that had eluded them for the previous 138 pages.

"Oh, heavens no!" Mr. Poe said, hacking into a brown, dripping handkerchief. "I can't allow you to be endangered by pursuing that criminal. I am charged with your well-being. Let the police apprehend him..."

"But Count Olaf is right *there*!" Klaus said.

"He's ordering a drink at that coffee shop!" Violet yelled. "Now he's going into the theater to watch *The Return of the King* — he'll be there for the next three and a half hours!"

"No, no," Mr. Poe said, as he expelled a large bloody mass into his handkerchief, "better that we stay put. The police will handle it — we'll give them a call first thing tomorrow."

"The police are useless idiots!" Klaus screamed. "If they really want to catch Count Olaf, why don't they just stay with us and wait for Olaf to turn up and harass us like he does every single freakin' time!?!"

"Seriously," Violet shouted, "what kind of cops can't find a lanky, sinister man accompanied by a half-dozen cohorts who have hook-hands, incredibly pale skin and other immediately identifiable and freakish traits?!? These aren't people who just blend into a crowd!"

"Poiuyt!" Sunny said, sinking both of her large pointy teeth directly into Mr. Poe's Achilles' tendon. If Mr. Poe weren't in such pain, he might have realized that what she said meant something like, "And if you're so freakin' concerned with our safety, why do you put us with one horrible, unfit guardian after another?!?"

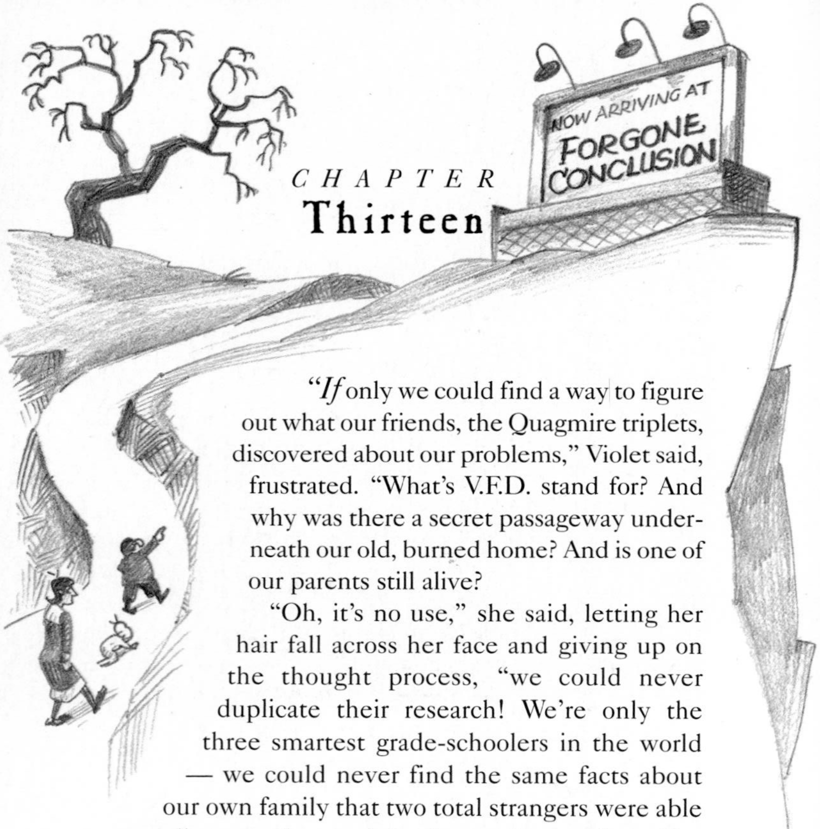
NOW ARRIVING AT
FORGONE CONCLUSION

CHAPTER Thirteen

"*If* only we could find a way to figure out what our friends, the Quagmire triplets, discovered about our problems," Violet said, frustrated. "What's V.F.D. stand for? And why was there a secret passageway underneath our old, burned home? And is one of our parents still alive?

"Oh, it's no use," she said, letting her hair fall across her face and giving up on the thought process, "we could never duplicate their research! We're only the three smartest grade-schoolers in the world — we could never find the same facts about our own family that two total strangers were able to discover after a *whole afternoon* in the library!"

"Well, it's not all bad," Klaus said, finding the same bright side that the orphans always found after another nearly-deadly and pointless adventure. "We're still together, and we did manage to defeat Count Olaf once again!"

"Potrzebie!" Sunny shrieked — which in this case meant something along the lines of, "and we're also no further along in this story than when we *started*, morons!"

At this point, I'll simply end the story and attempt to make up for another flat and disappointing conclusion by going directly to my note to the editor, vaguely hinting at the possibility of plot development in the next unfulfilling and formulaic installment. I'd explain what "formulaic" means — but I've already met my word count. See you next time, suckers!

To My Kind Editor,

I am writing to you from the humongous whirlpool bathtub of my Italian penthouse. Oh…that is to say I'm writing to you from…oh, let's say, "The Dangerous Dam"…or "The Treacherous Trolley," or "The Hectic Halfway-House." Or whatever – just pick something vaguely sinister and alliterative and I'll plug it into the standard template.

Anyway, for the sake of this letter, let's say that I'm visiting the home of the Baudelaires' "mean and idiosyncratic guardian" and I'm looking for anything that would shed some light on the time that the Baudelaires spent there.

Please go to Eli's Bagels on Route 34 at 3 P.M. next Wednesday and order a pumpernickel bagel with vegetable cream cheese. It will not help you at all in piecing together this story, but it's delicious, and it's well worth the effort. Afterwards, visit the nearby Strathmore Cinema and buy a children's ticket to Gigli. Sit in the first seat on your right – beneath it, you will find an envelope. I guarantee you will have plenty of privacy to read its contents. Inside, you will find my notes, as well as a tooth from the silent sloth, a coaster from the Tavern on the Scream Bar & Grill and a sketch of Carmen Electra that I'm particularly proud of. On second thought, I'll just send a messenger over with it after I'm done with this afternoon's deep tissue massage. Ciao!

Remember, you are my only hope to keep this sweet, sweet money-maker going by publishing a yearly edition of this endless saga. Don't screw it up for both of us.

With all due respect,

~~Daniel Handler~~ Lemony Snicket

Lemony Snicket

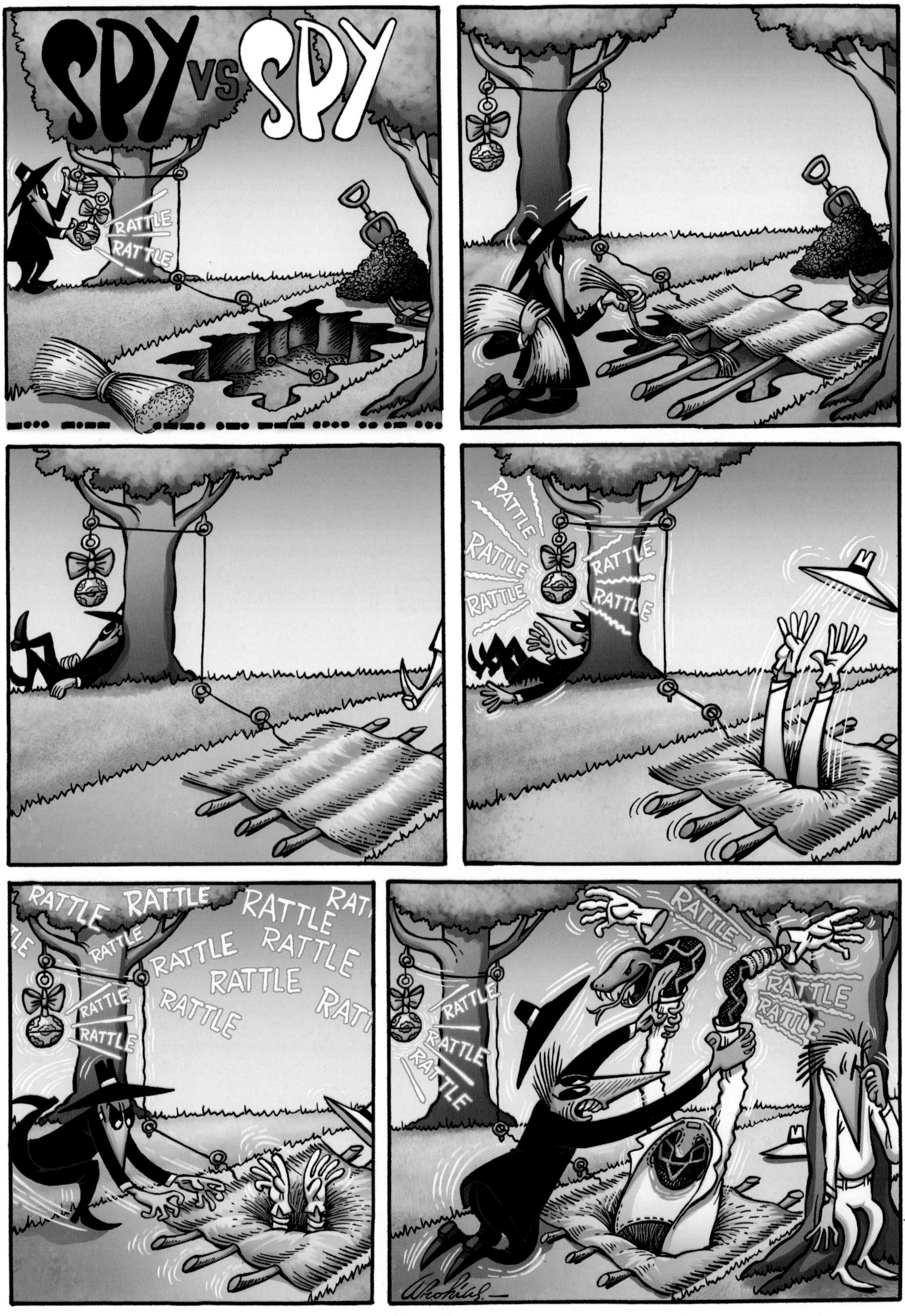
SPY vs SPY
RATTLE
RATTLE
RATTLE
RATTLE
RATTLE
RATTLE
RATTLE RATTLE RATTLE
RATTLE
RATTLE RATTLE
RATTLE
RATTLE
RATTLE
RATTLE
RATTLE
RATTLE
RATTLE
RATTLE
RATTLE
RATTLE
RATTLE

WRITER AND ARTIST: ANTONIO PROHIAS COLORIST: CARRIE STRACHAN

MAD PRESENTS

The Least Pop

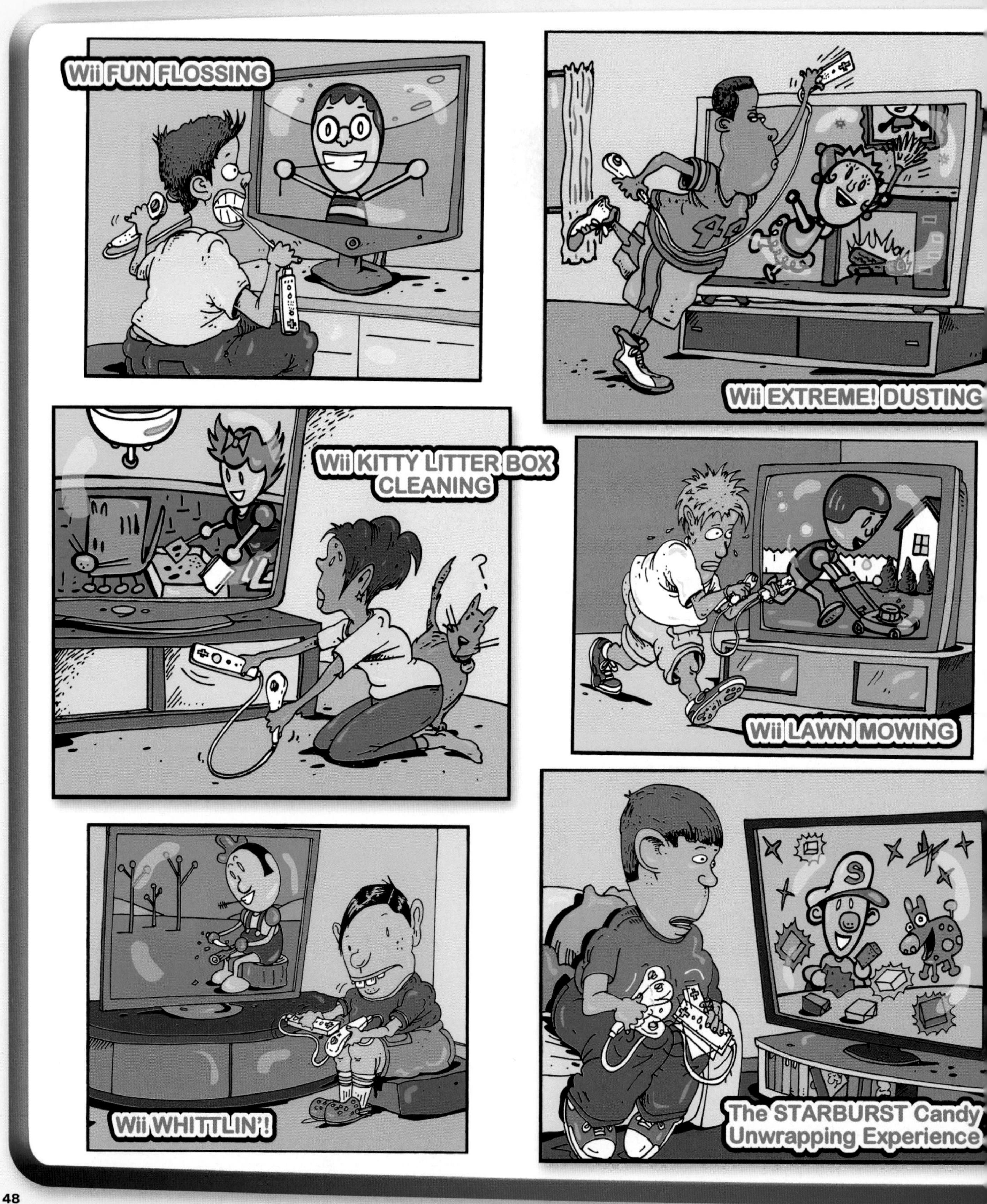
Wii FUN FLOSSING
Wii EXTREME! DUSTING
Wii KITTY LITTER BOX CLEANING
Wii LAWN MOWING
Wii WHITTLIN'!
The STARBURST Candy Unwrapping Experience

ular Wii Games

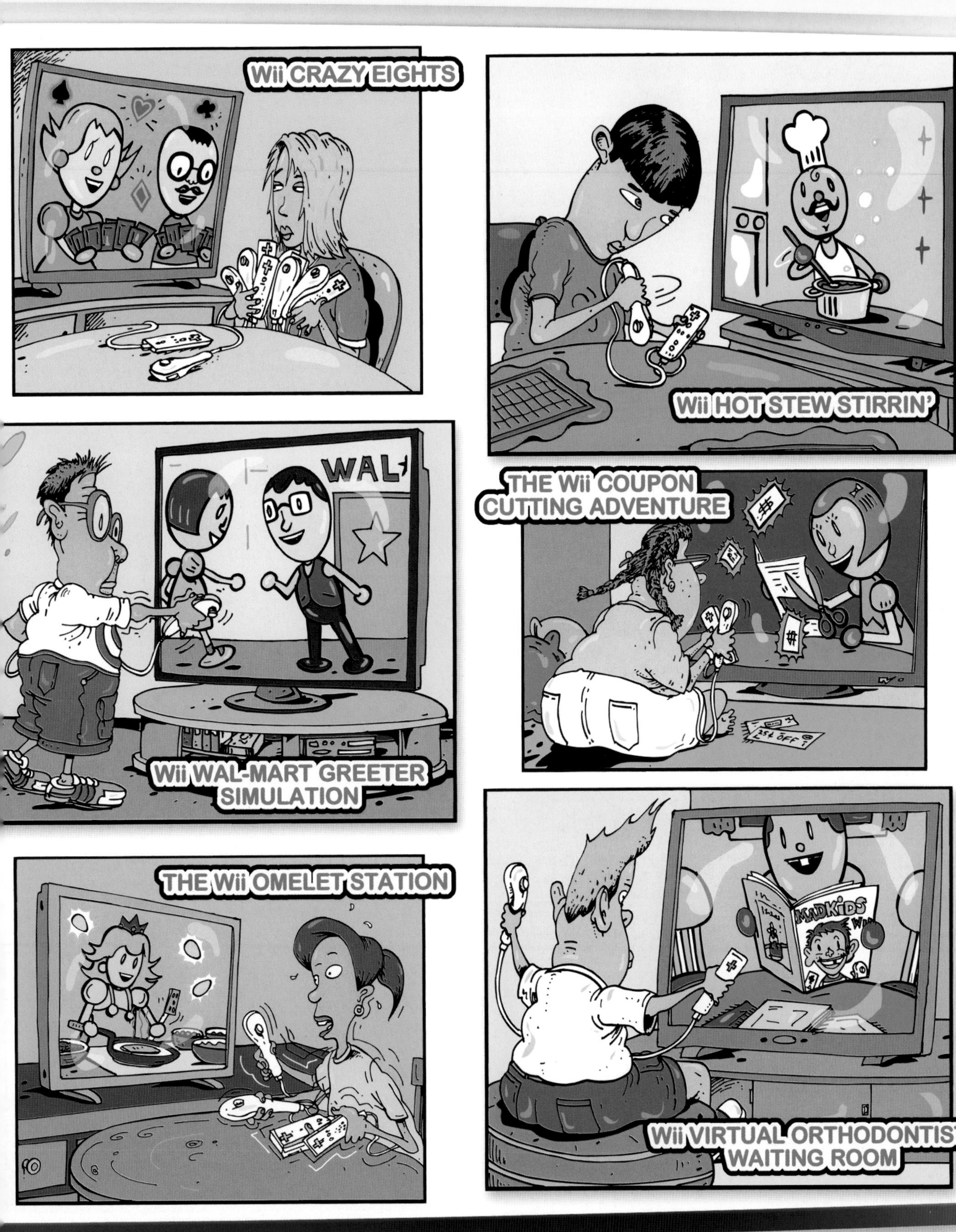

Wii CRAZY EIGHTS
Wii HOT STEW STIRRIN'
WAL
Wii WAL-MART GREETER SIMULATION
THE Wii COUPON CUTTING ADVENTURE
25¢ OFF
THE Wii OMELET STATION
MADKIDS
Wii VIRTUAL ORTHODONTIST WAITING ROOM

WRITER: TOM SILVESTRO ARTIST: KEVIN POPE

Summer means just one thing! Complete, constant freedom… for about a day or so. Then, if you want to actually do anything, you'll need a job to pay for it! But just because you've got to work, that doesn't mean you have to take the first job that comes along! Before you agree to put on that hairnet and plastic smock, here are some…

THINGS TO CONSIDER BEFORE

What are the hook-up possibilities?

Are there any, um, inmates or whatever, that are under, like, thirty? Or even forty?

How lame are the uniforms?

Cumbersome?!? Your dress is too *cumbersome*? Maybe you should take a minute — off the clock — and think about the REAL pioneer women and how they'd kick your lazy, cumbersome butt!!!

PRAIRIE DOGS

Is there cell phone reception?

Hold on — we're going through the freakin' tunnel again!

Will you be able to get there and back?

Hi, Mrs. Norbert? Um, this is Bradley Kwirk — 'member, from Webelos a few years ago?...Well, I was wondering if you could give me a lift...

BEEFY Bob's

Are the fringe benefits cool or sucky?

...and at the end of the season, you fellas get to keep all the stained tablecloths!!

decent

WRITER AND ARTIST: TERESA BURNS PARKHURST

ACCEPTING A SUMMER JOB

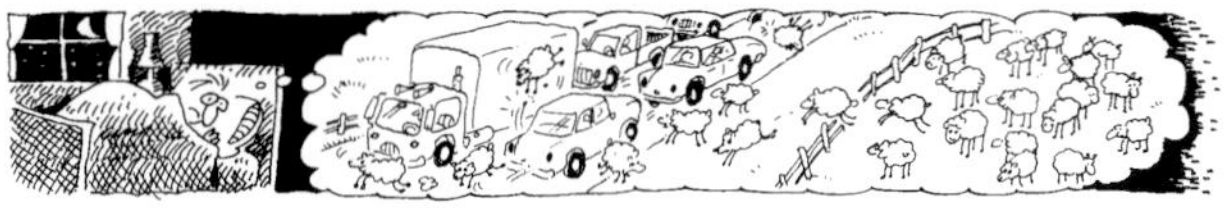

What's the humiliation factor?

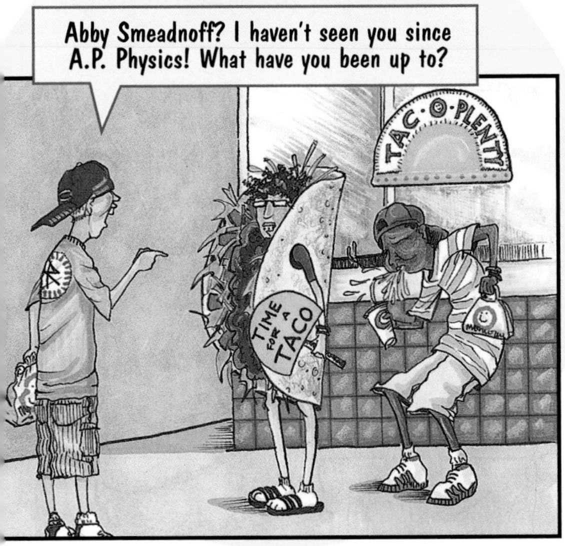
Abby Smeadnoff? I haven't seen you since A.P. Physics! What have you been up to?
TAC-O-PLENTY!
TIME FOR A TACO

Will there be a lingering smell?

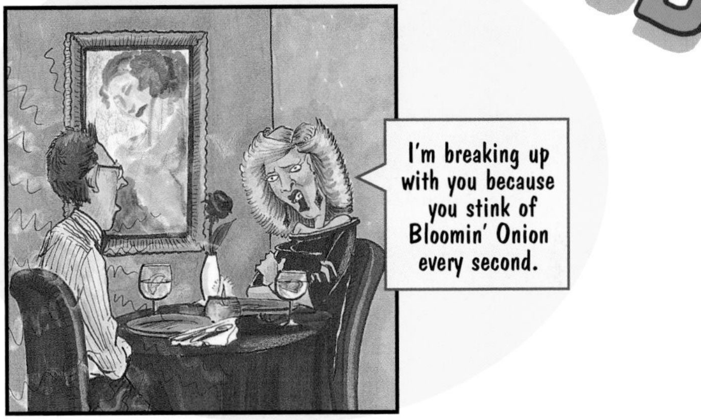
I'm breaking up with you because you stink of Bloomin' Onion every second.

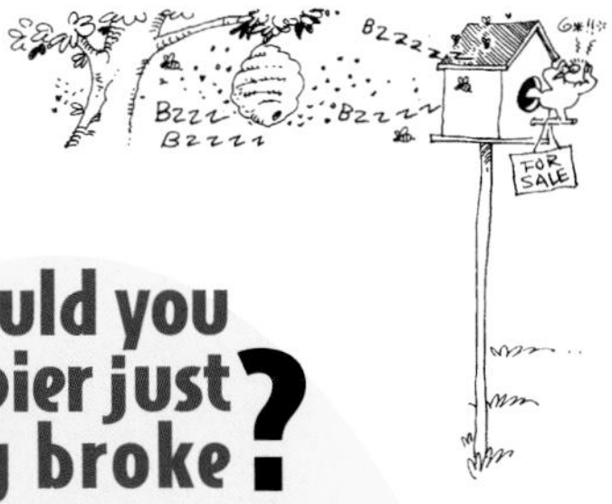
FOR SALE

Do you get to operate cool machines?

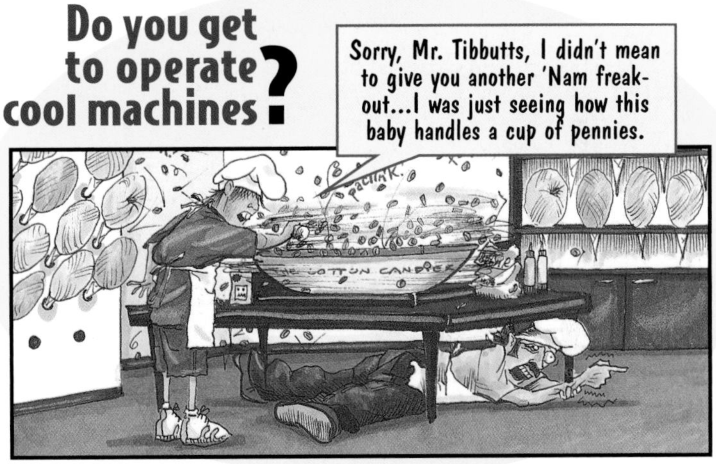
Sorry, Mr. Tibbutts, I didn't mean to give you another 'Nam freak-out...I was just seeing how this baby handles a cup of pennies.

Would you be happier just being broke?

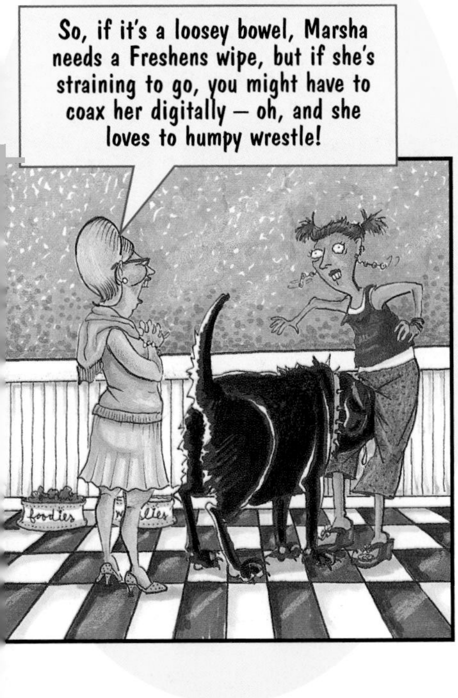
So, if it's a loosey bowel, Marsha needs a Freshens wipe, but if she's straining to go, you might have to coax her digitally — oh, and she loves to humpy wrestle!
foodies

Will you end up with a good reference?

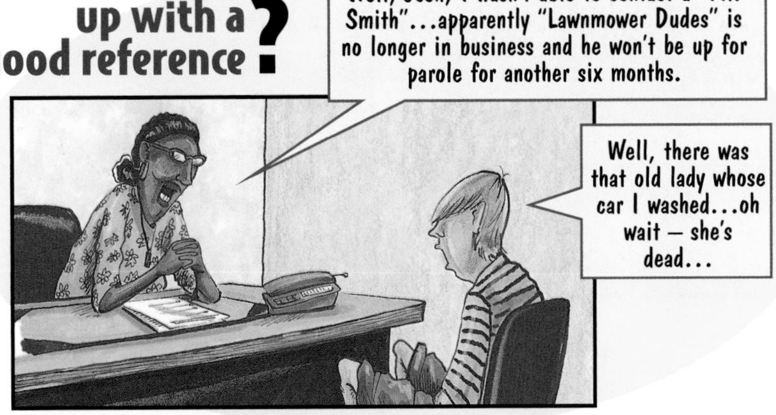
Well, Josh, I wasn't able to contact a "Mr. Smith"...apparently "Lawnmower Dudes" is no longer in business and he won't be up for parole for another six months.
Well, there was that old lady whose car I washed...oh wait — she's dead...

TALES FROM THE DUCK SIDE DEPT.

THE MEATY MERMAID MENACE

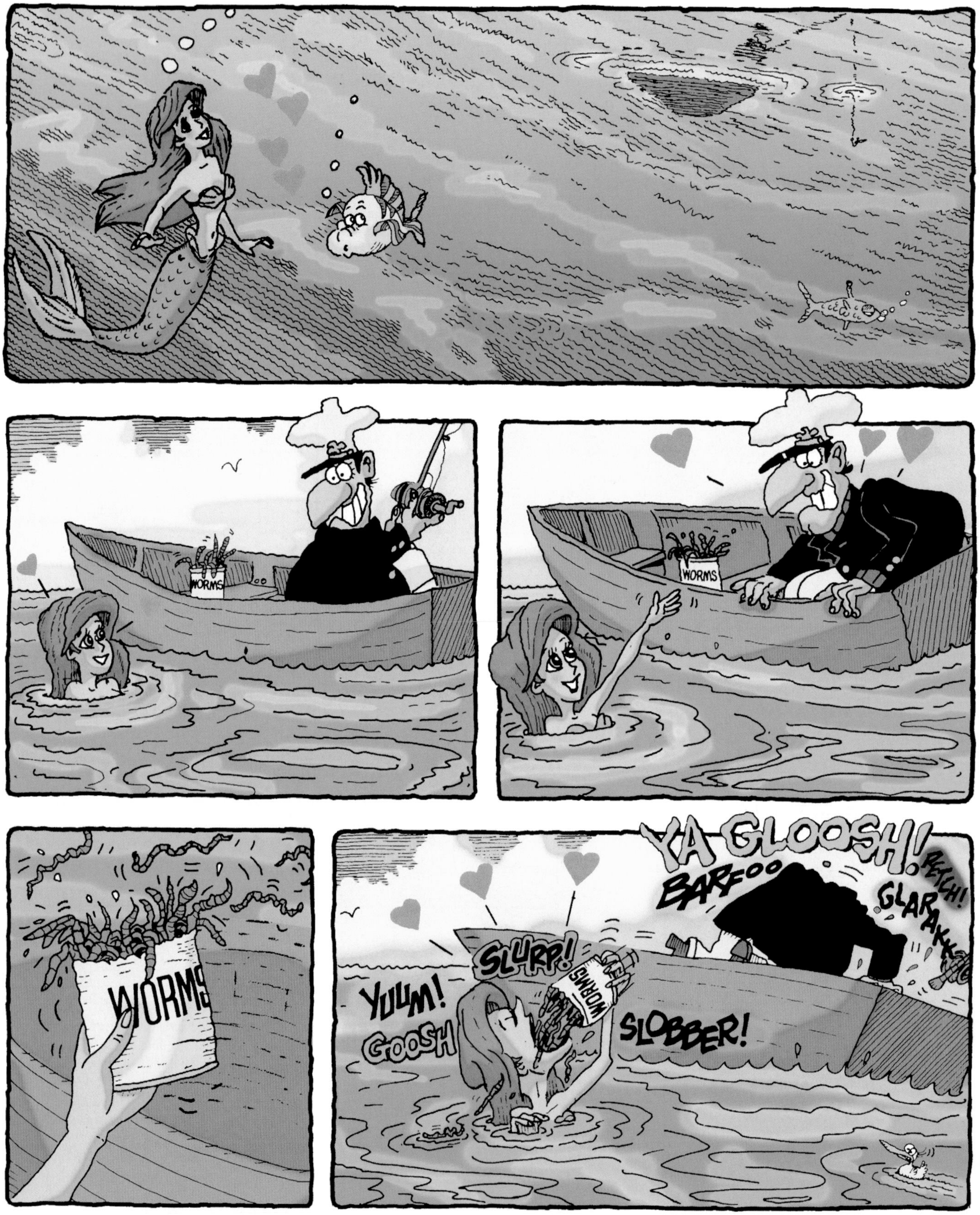
WORMS
WORMS
WORMS
YA GLOOSH!
BARFOO
RETCH!
GLARAKK
SLURP!
WORMS
YUUM!
GOOSH
SLOBBER!

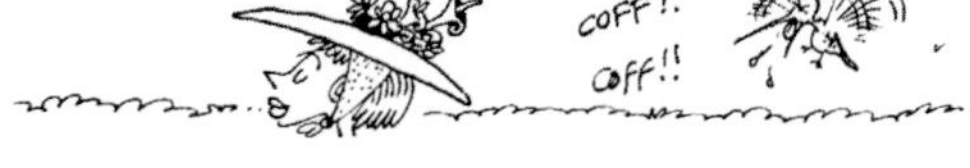
COFF!!
COFF!!

ARTIST AND WRITER: DUCK EDWING

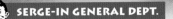

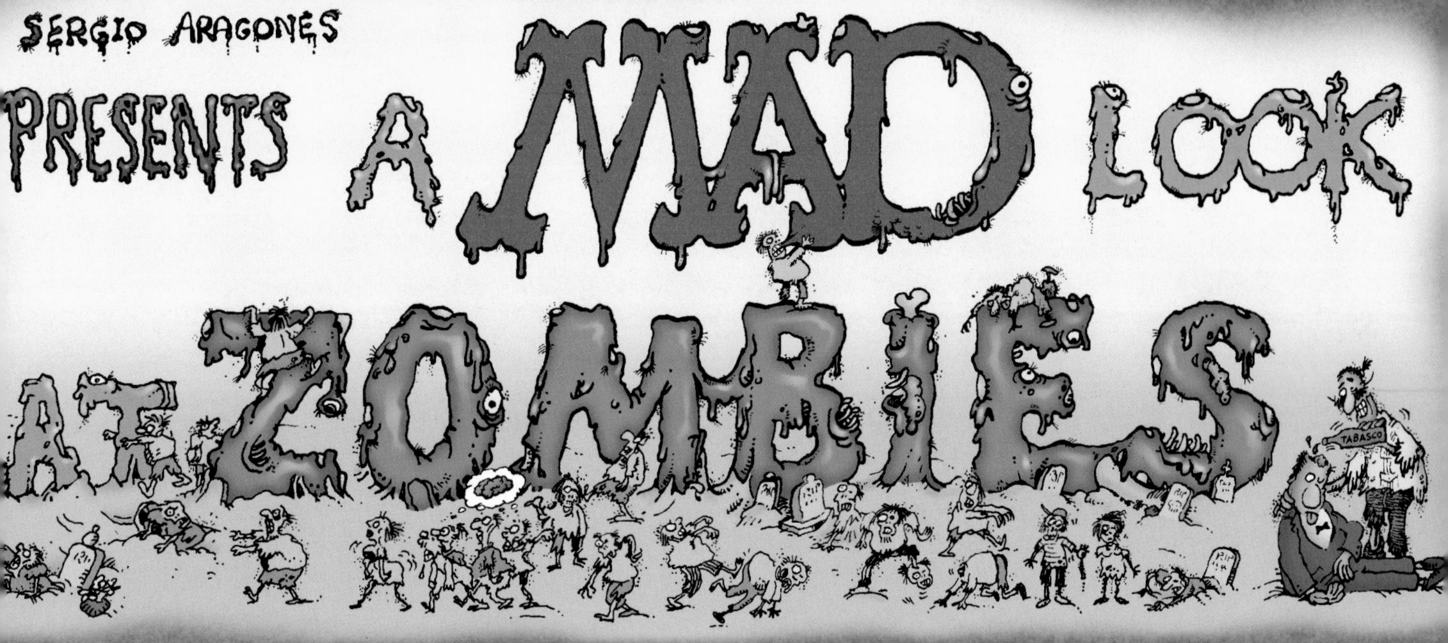
SERGIO ARAGONES
PRESENTS A MAD LOOK AT ZOMBIES
TABASCO

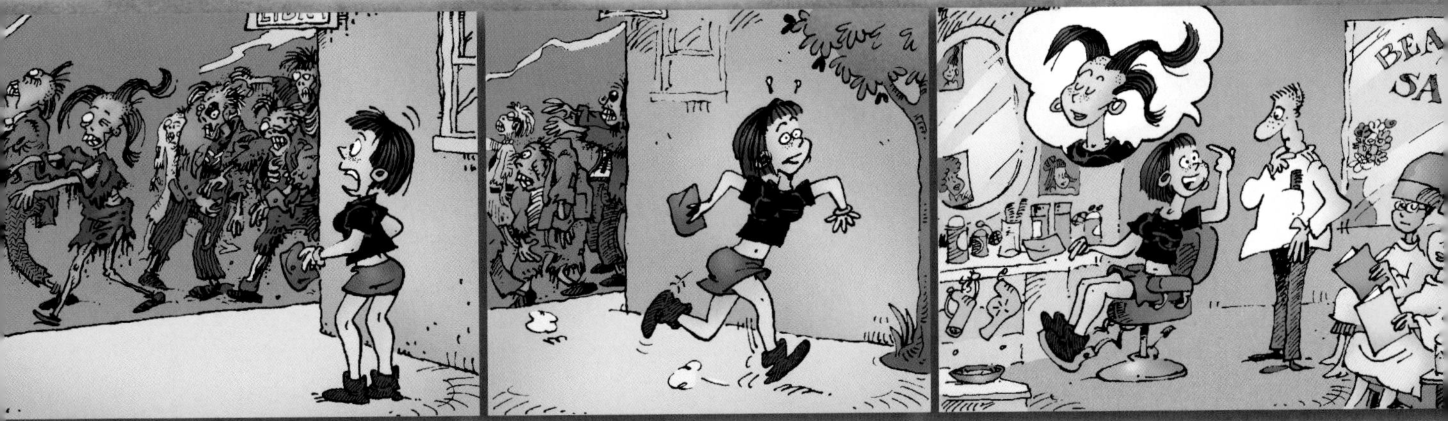

WRITER AND ARTIST: SERGIO ARAGONES

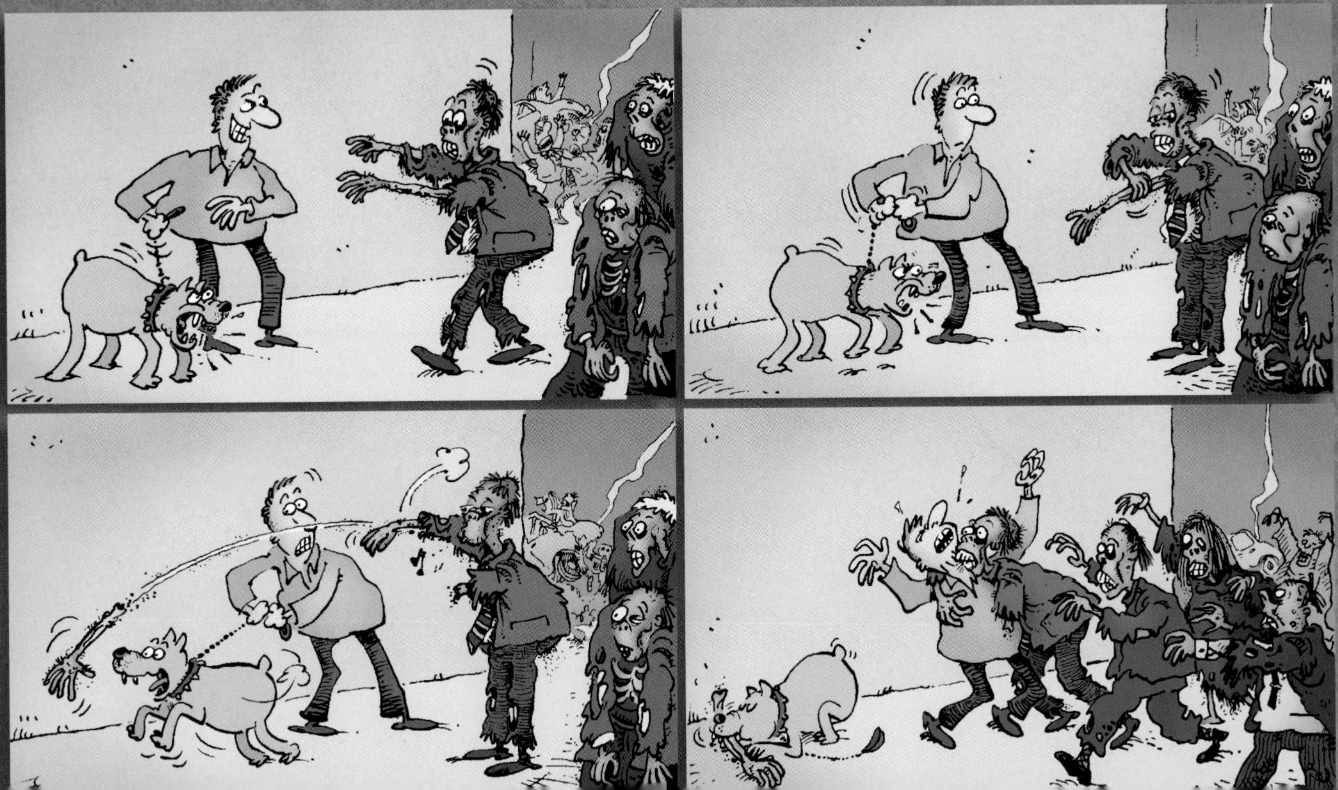

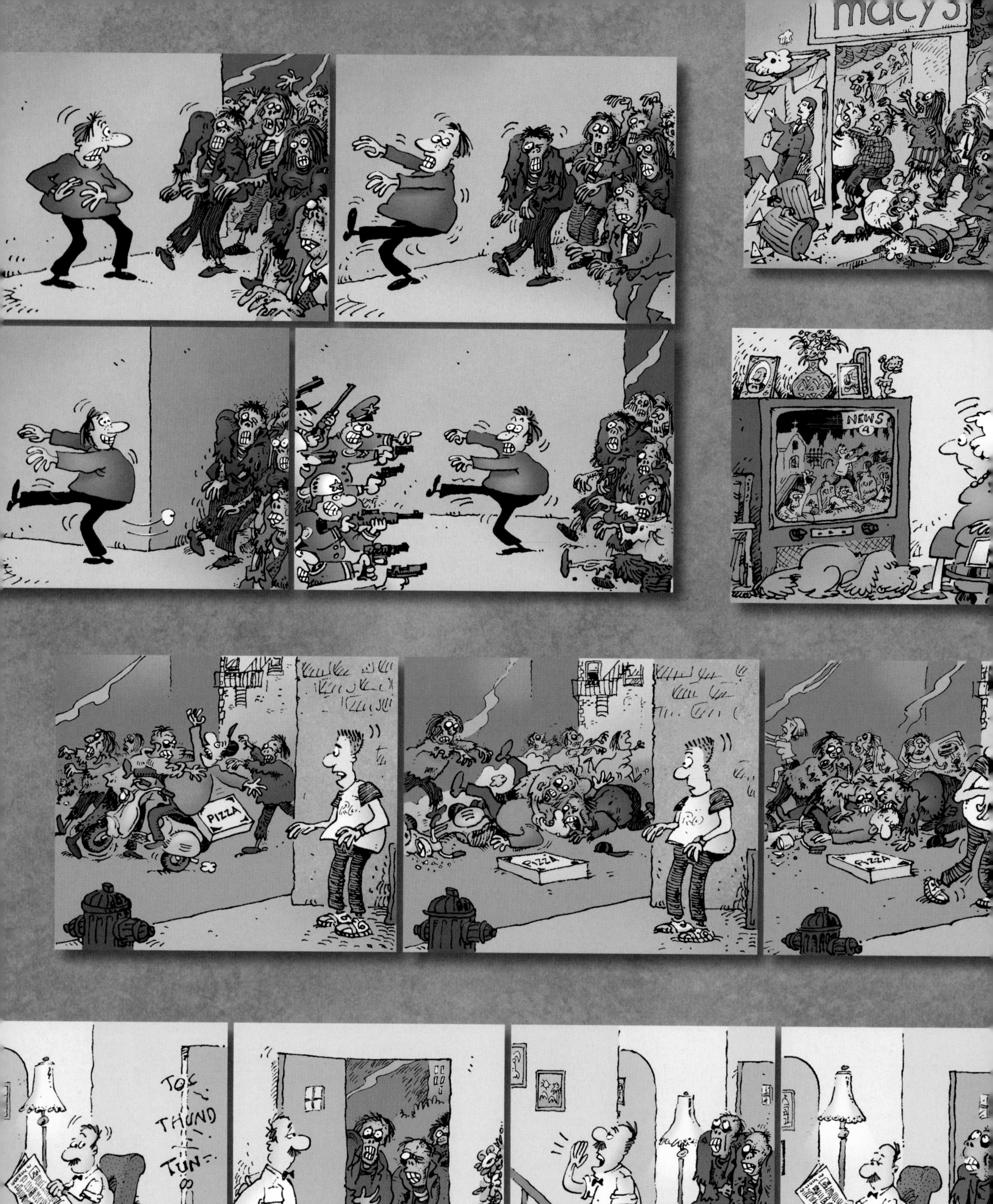
macy's
NEWS 4
PIZZA
PIZZA
PIZZA
TOC
THUND
TUN

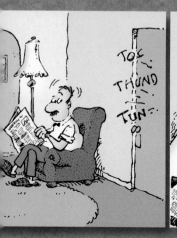

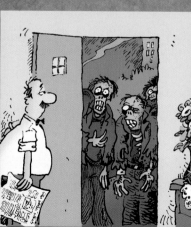

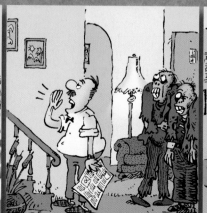

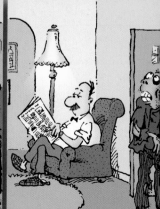

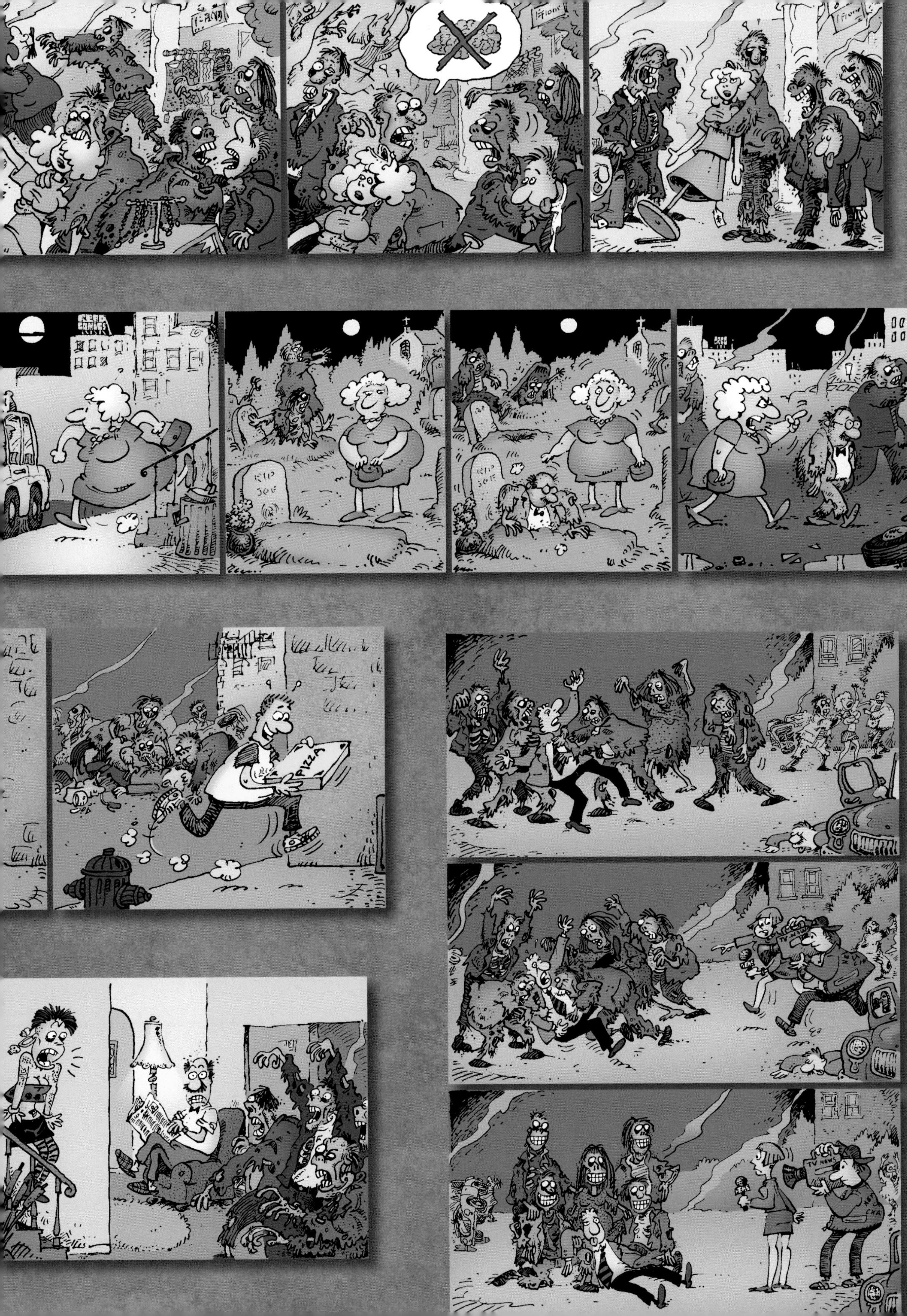
RIP JOE
RIP JOE
PIZZA
TV NEWS
TV NEWS

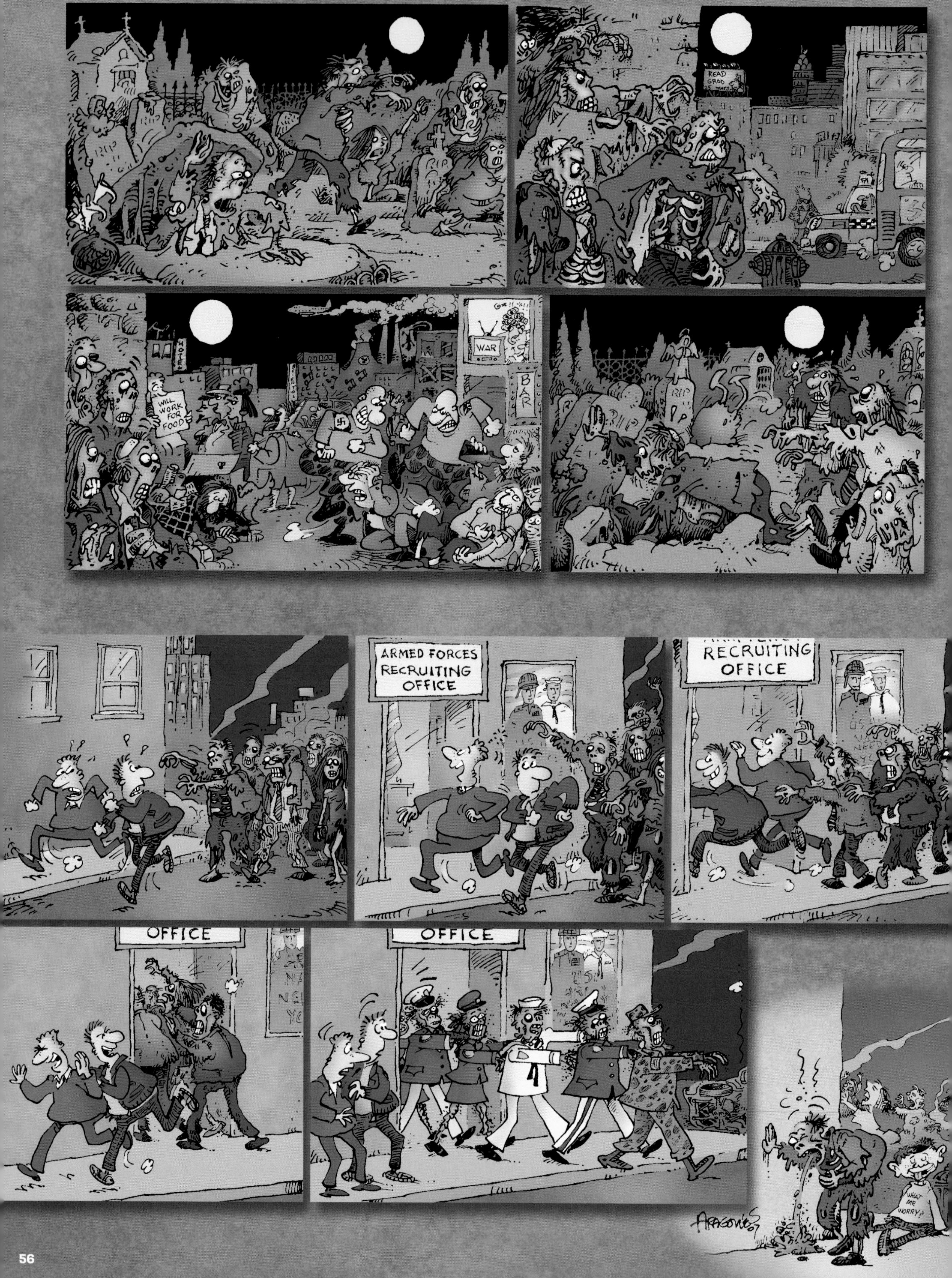
RIP
READ GROD 25 YEARS
WILL WORK FOR FOOD
WAR
BAR
RIP
ARMED FORCES RECRUITING OFFICE
RECRUITING OFFICE
OFFICE
OFFICE
WHAT ME WORRY?
ARAGONES

One Fine Day in the Operating Room

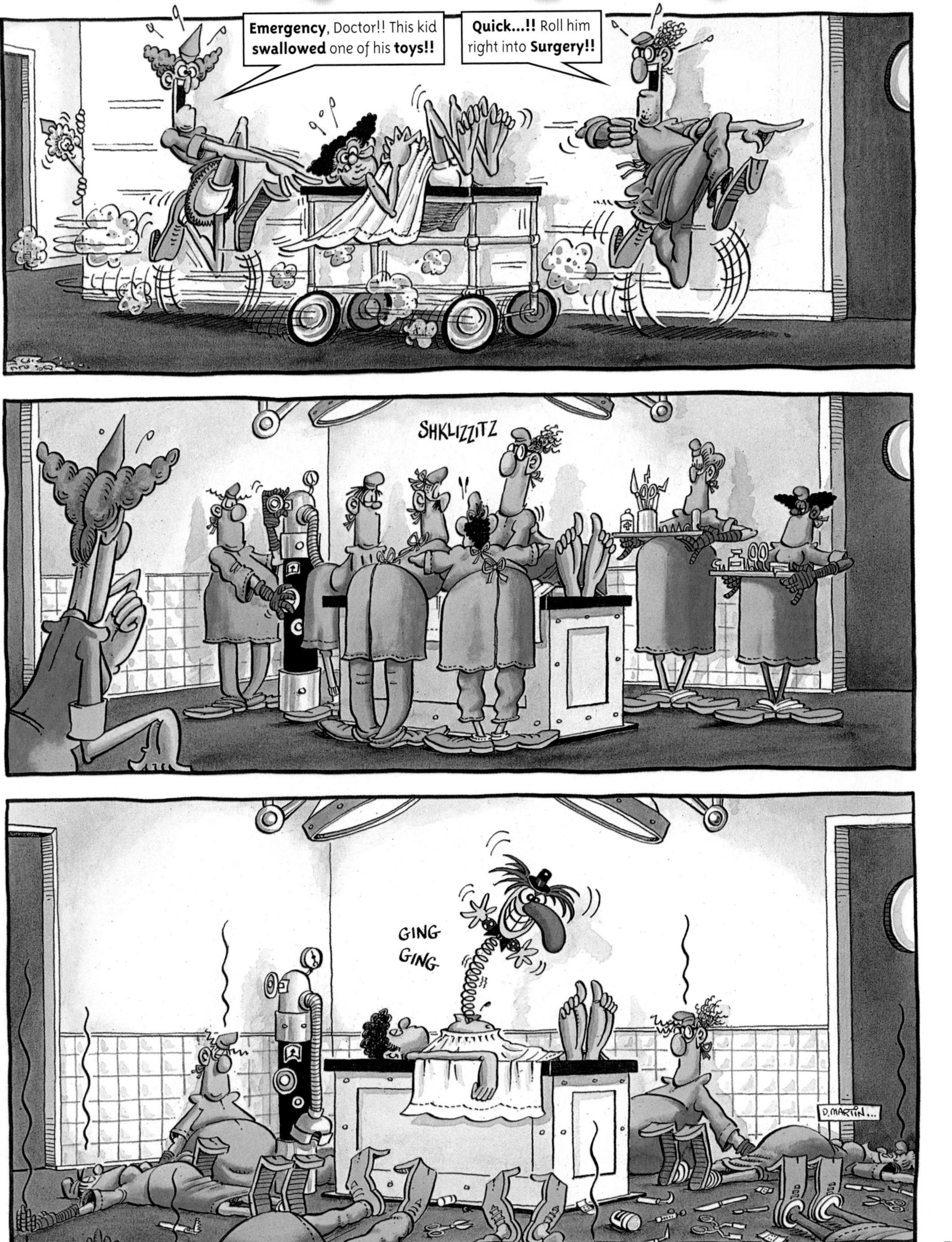
Emergency, Doctor!! This kid swallowed one of his toys!!
Quick...!! Roll him right into Surgery!!
SHKLIZZITZ
GING
GING
D.MARTIN...

WRITER: DON EDWING ARTIST: DON MARTIN

BEATING A DEAD NORSE DEPT.

MAD'S THOR-OUGHLY STUPID THOR OUTTAKES

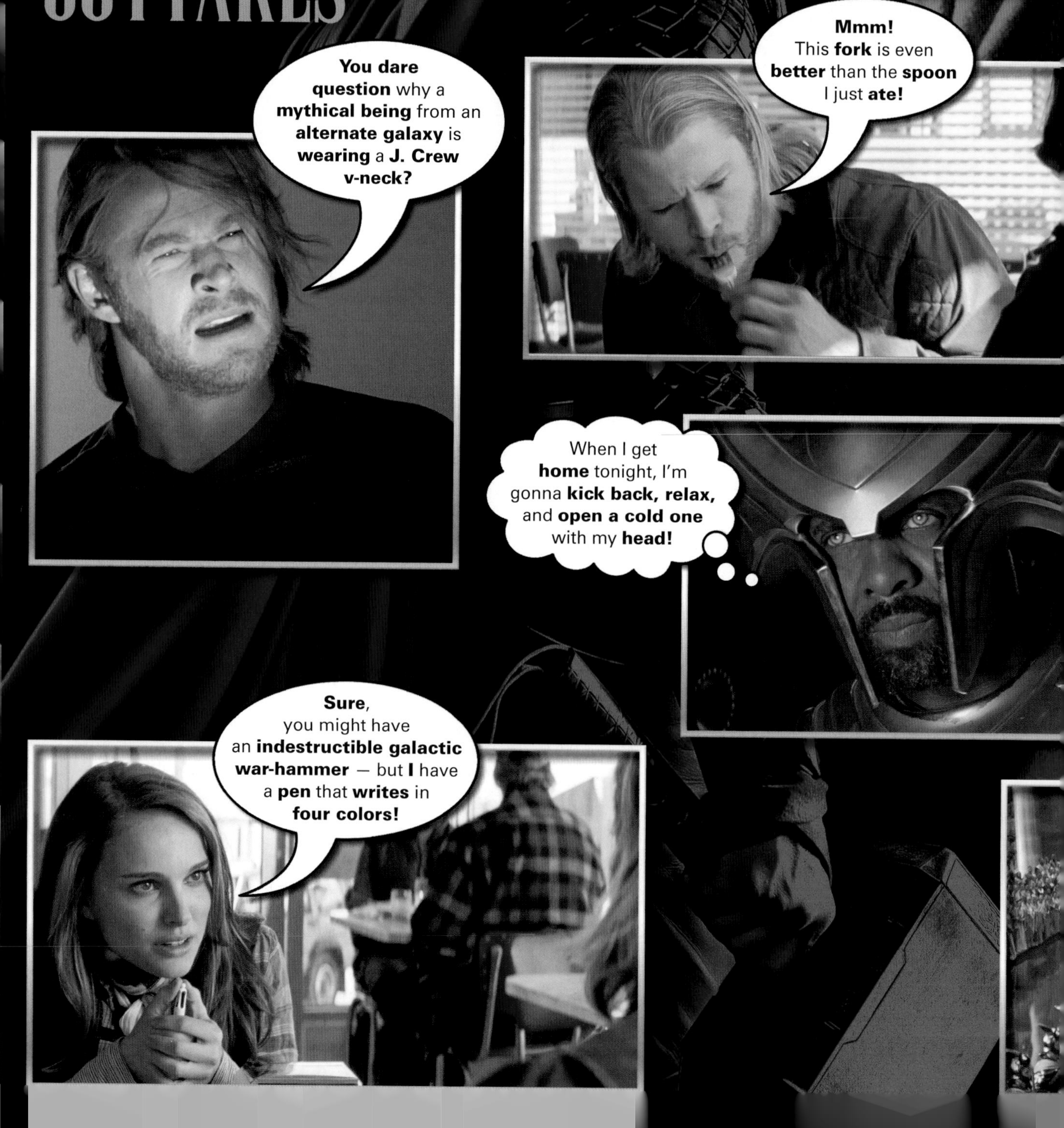
You dare question why a mythical being from an alternate galaxy is wearing a J. Crew v-neck?
Mmm! This fork is even better than the spoon I just ate!
When I get home tonight, I'm gonna kick back, relax, and open a cold one with my head!
Sure, you might have an indestructible galactic war-hammer — but I have a pen that writes in four colors!

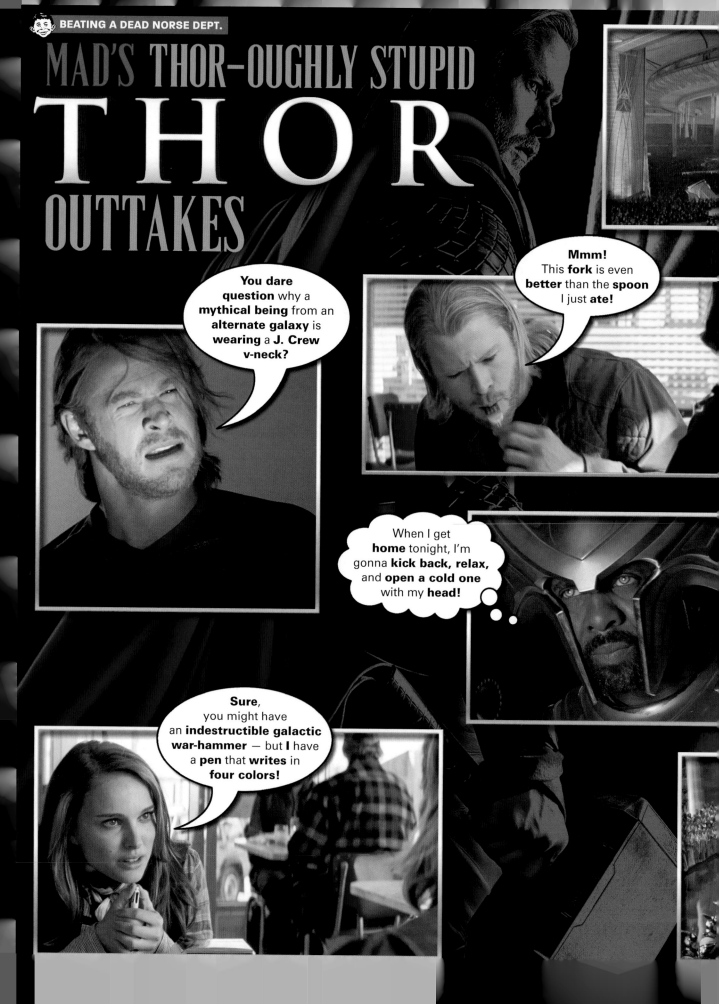

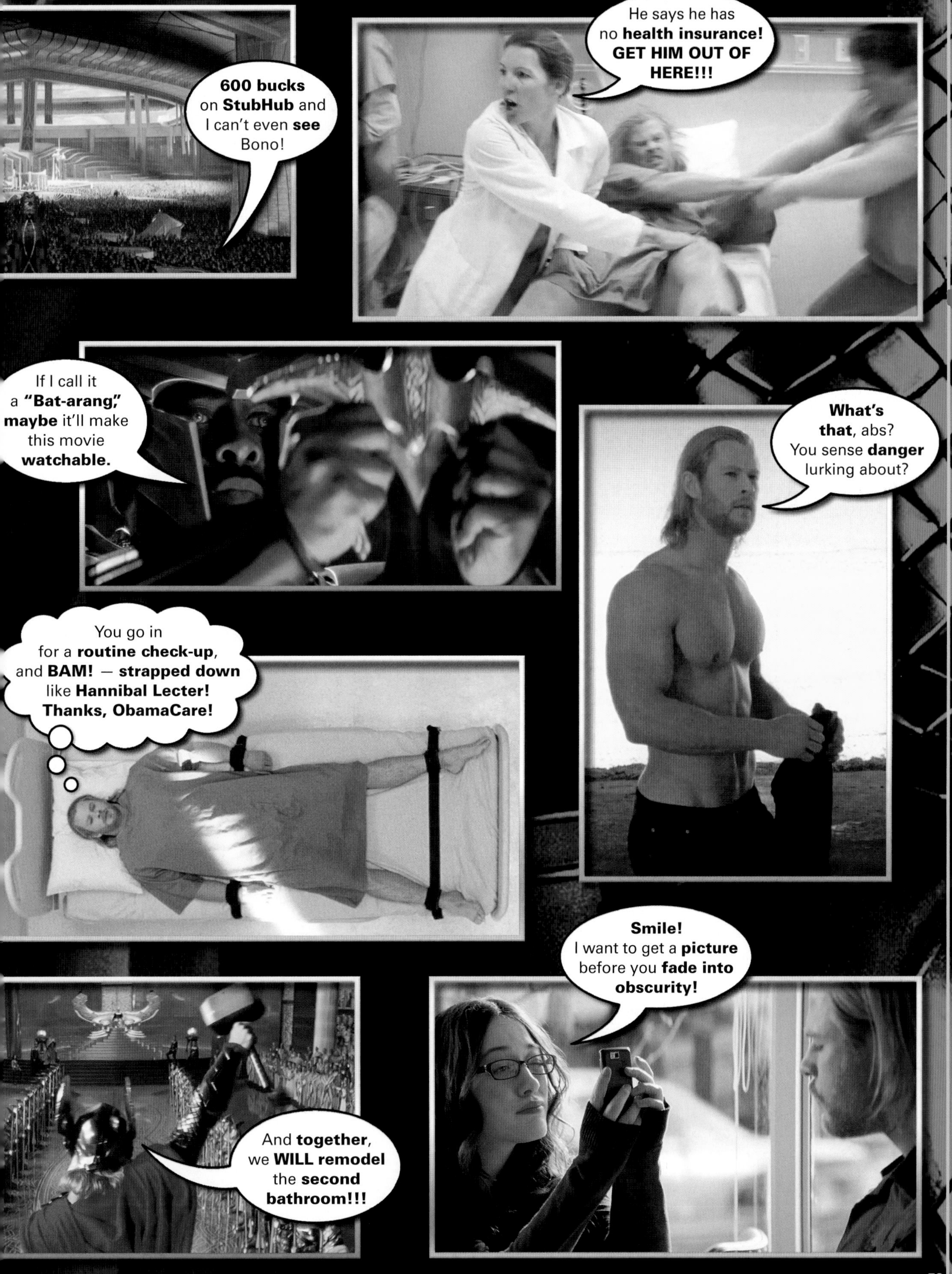
600 bucks on StubHub and I can't even see Bono!
He says he has no health insurance! GET HIM OUT OF HERE!!!
If I call it a "Bat-arang," maybe it'll make this movie watchable.
What's that, abs? You sense danger lurking about?
You go in for a routine check-up, and BAM! — strapped down like Hannibal Lecter! Thanks, ObamaCare!
And together, we WILL remodel the second bathroom!!!
Smile! I want to get a picture before you fade into obscurity!

The Castaway

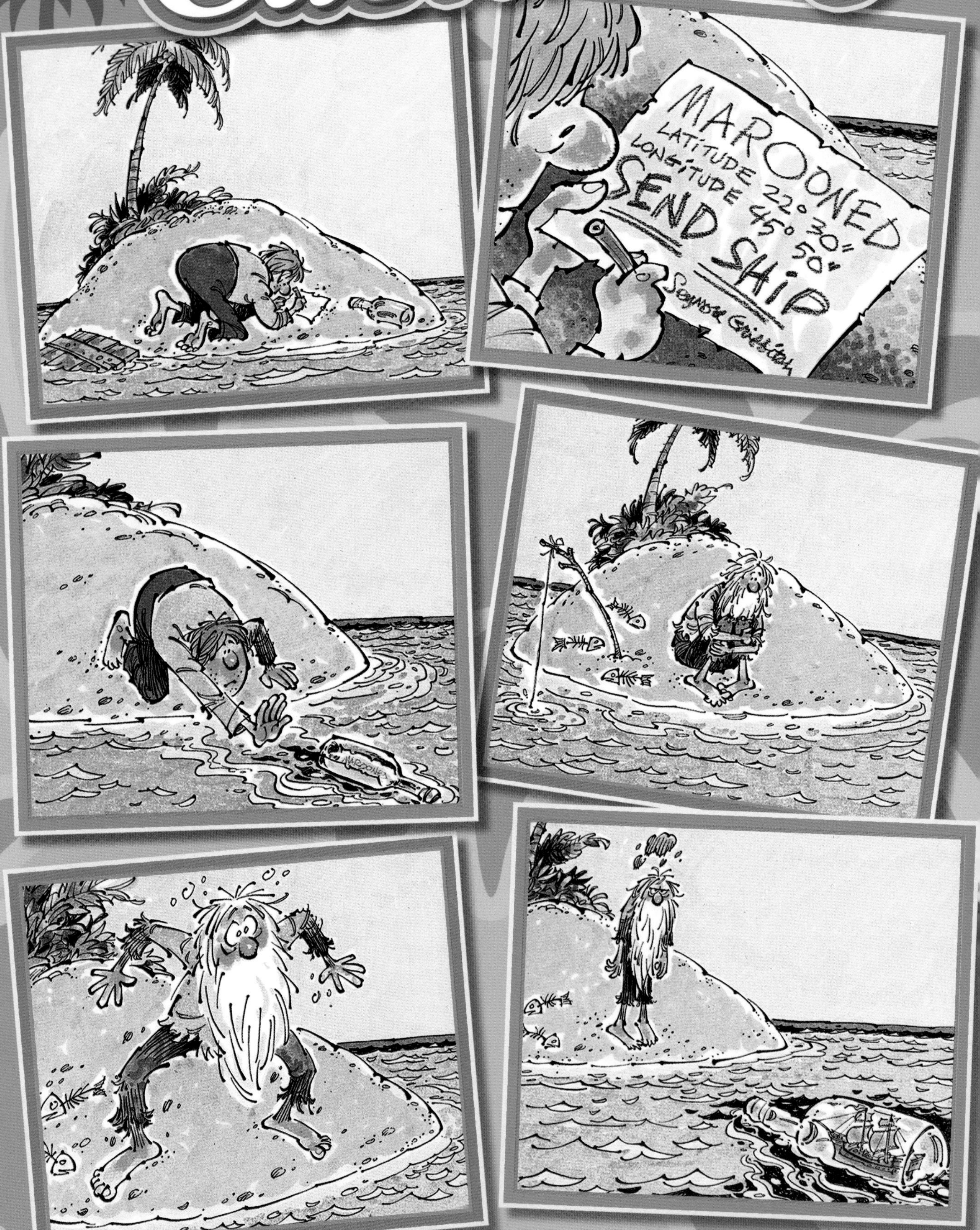
MAROONED
LATITUDE 22° 30"
LONGITUDE 45° 50"
SEND SHIP

WRITER: AL JAFFEE ARTIST: PAUL COKER

JALOPY SHOPPER

Take One
Free
We'll Make
Up For It
Somewhere Else

www.clunkermagazine.con

Your Totaled Transportation Tabloid
Including: New Vehicles, Used Vehicles, and *Really* Used Vehicles

Vol. XXI Issue 05

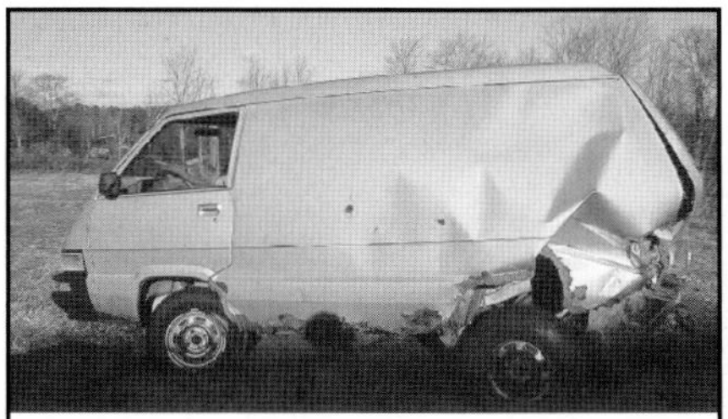

92 DODGE CRAPAVAN 1-wheel drive, turbo-charged price tag, w/sturdy, stainless steel airbag. Owner's manual in braille. $37,000. PRIVATE PARTY, 121-2405

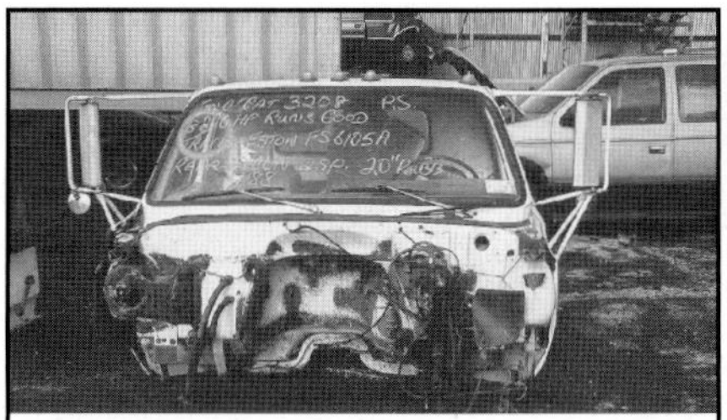

93 WHITE FORD BRONCO Xlnt cond., $17,000 ($25,000 for idiots who make lame, predictable references to O.J.). BY OWNER, 181-8900

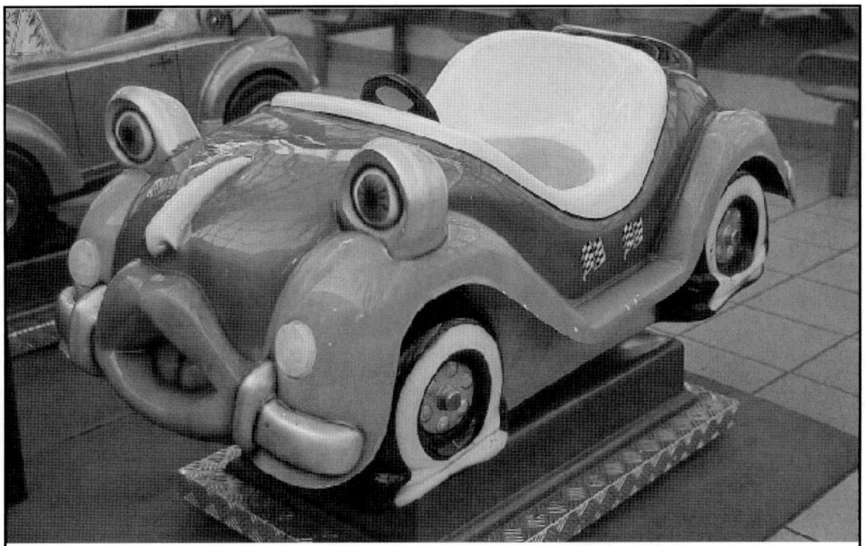

82 LINCOLN CLOWN CAR

External combustion engine, tubeless ashtray, aquarium windows, trampoline roof, convex rearview mirrors like at carnival fun houses. $17,505. WRECKY'S CARZ, 161-5383

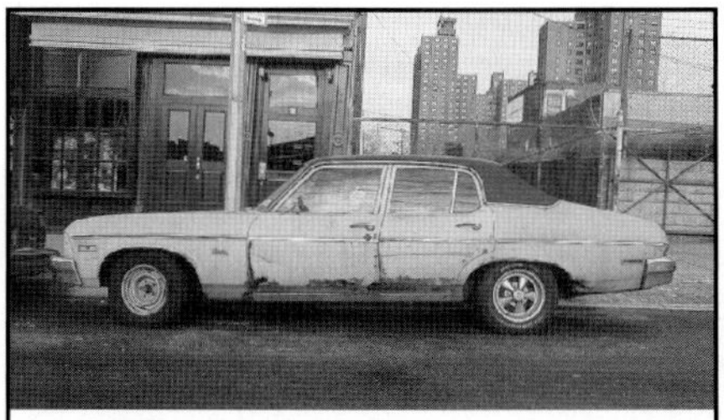

94 CHEVY LUNATIC Chrome wheels, traction ctrl. & little purple man in glove compartment revealing secrets of Roswell. $16,354. PRIVATE PARTY, 197-3678

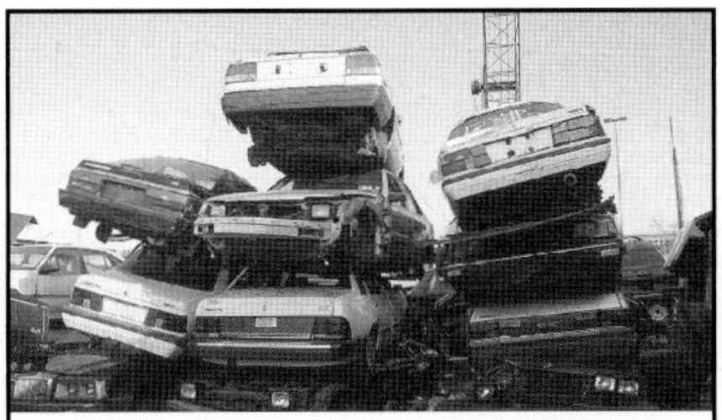

91 INFINNITY Intentionally misspelled name, Formica dash, EZ-rip faux leather seats, invisible multi-disc CD player. $14,000. THE CAR DITCH, 160-2949

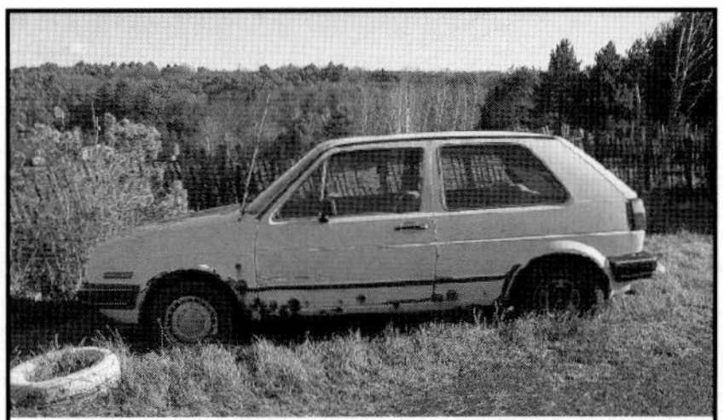

95 FORD PHELGM 1 cyl., coal-powered, solid gold splash guards. Horn plays first eight notes of "A Hundred Bottles Of Beer On The Wall." $15,600. AUTO DUMP, 160-9483

Unless otherwise specified, price(s) include(s) all Cost(s) to be paid by consumer(s) except for license(s), tax(es), back parking ticket(s), upholstery cleaning(s) and many other things you'll find out as you go along.

To Place Your Photo Ad
1-800-BAD-PIX

Targeting Drivers Who Don't Care What Others Think About Them

That Number Again
1-800-BAD-PIX

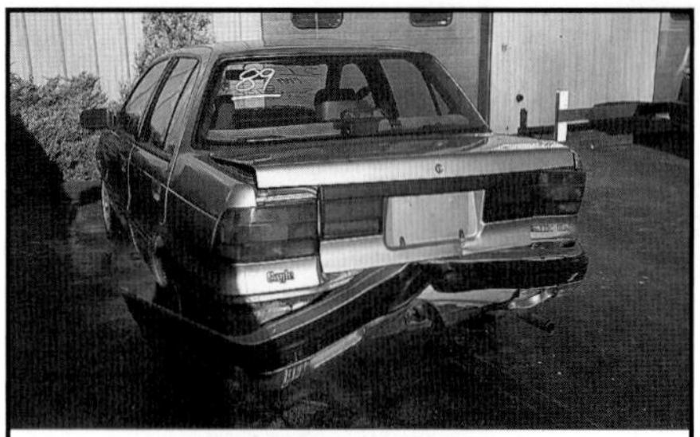

97 TOYOTA MOSQUITO
Comes w/mysterious stains, wood paneling one one side, in-dash steering wheel. Rear-seat soda dispenser! $14,000. PRIVATE PARTY, 191-9001

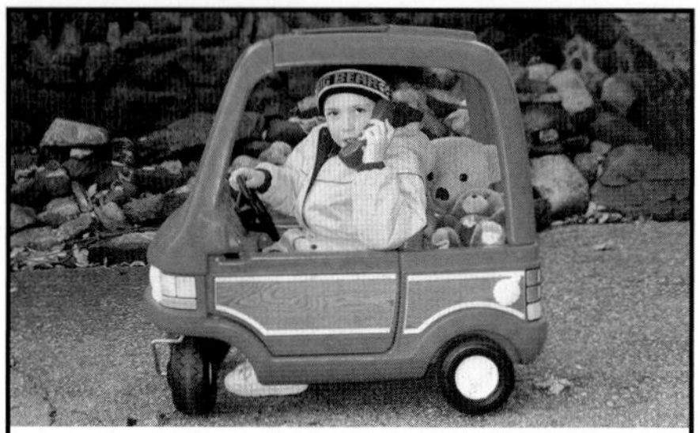

99 HONDA ACCORDION
Includes pre-nicked windshield and factory installed spice rack. Perfect 2nd car if you only use the 1st one. $18,750. DOODLE MOTORS, 141-7888

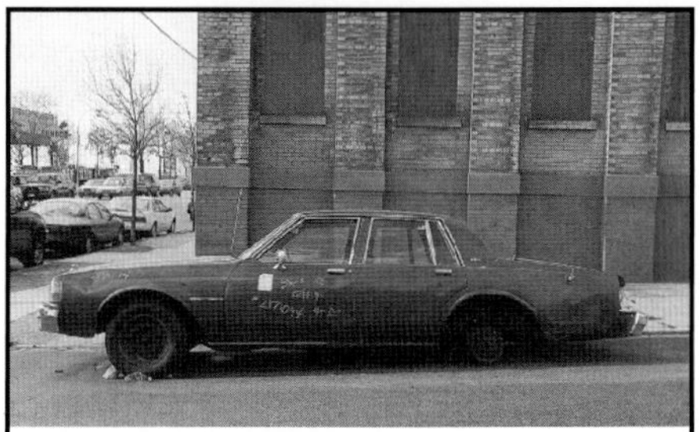

86 FORD INSIPID
Like new, only not. Speedometer in Roman numerals, mini jaws-of-life in glove compartment, body in trunk. $4450. BY OWNER, 500-0001.

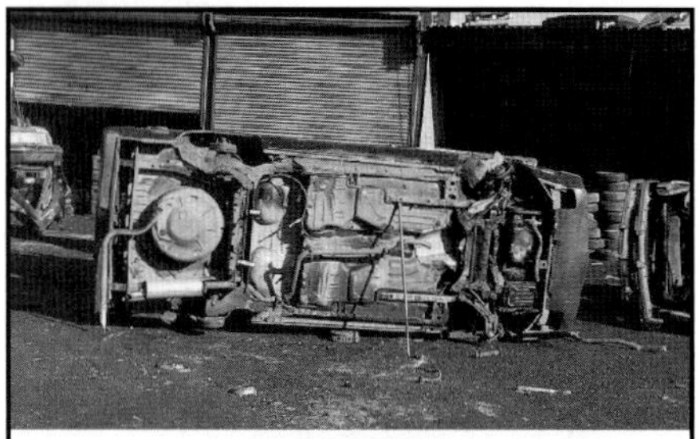

65 MUSTANG
Electric pink collector's classic with AM/FM stereo, CD changer and leather bucket seats would be really nice, but all I have is this 89 Sentra. $199. PRIVATE PARTY, 130-5332

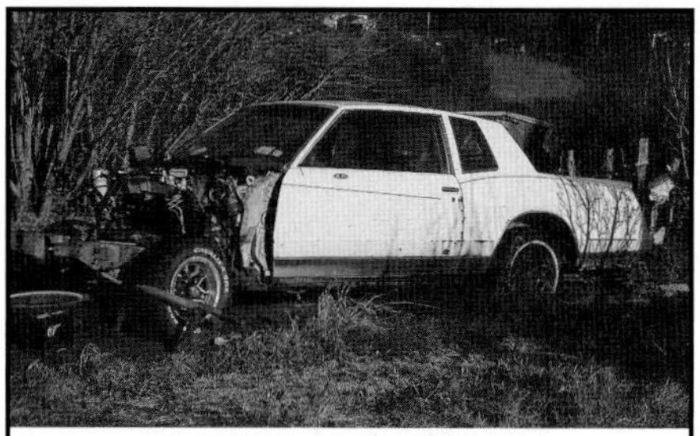

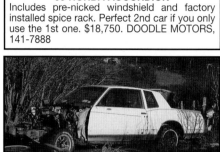

86 CADILLAC BROUGHAM
Sick purple, Y2K compliant cup-holder. Must sell, or my bookie will send his goons out to break my legs. $6500 PLEEEZE! BY OWNER, 151-2649

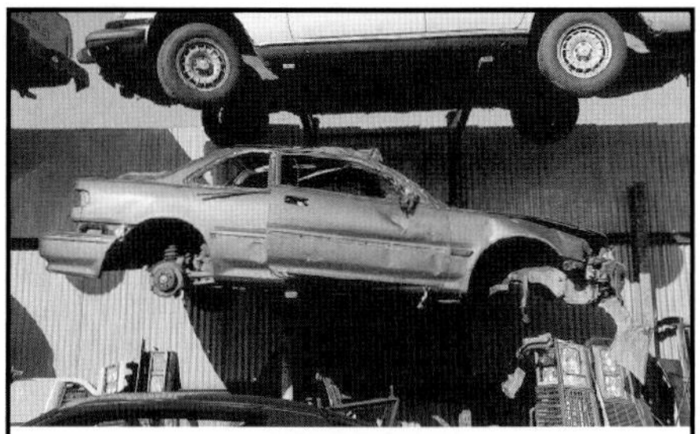

95 VW BURRITO
Obnoxious semi-gloss ext., special hidden compartment for hiding open bottles of syrup, illegal aliens, etc. $12,500. PRIVATE PARTY, 171-7171

BAD CREDIT?
NO CREDIT?
WOW, YOU MUST BE A REAL LOSER!

CRAZY HOWIE'S AUTO ASYLUM 1-900-HEAP

Where Quality is a 3-syllable word!
Se Habla Your Cash

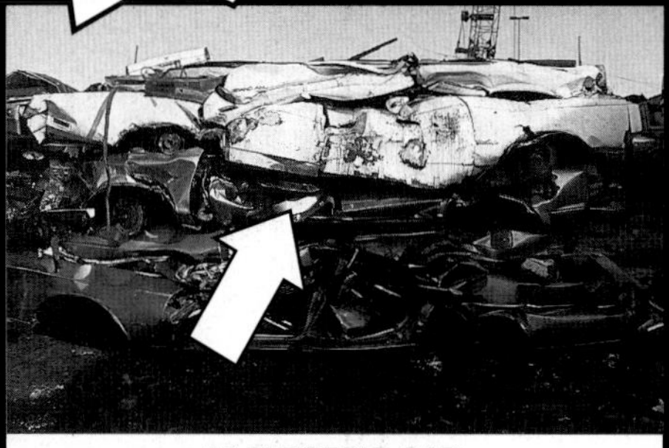

97 ELECTRIC CAR
Runs great on 10,000 AA batteries (not incl). Buy now, before the federal gov't sells out to big oil and puts us all in gulags. $12,500.

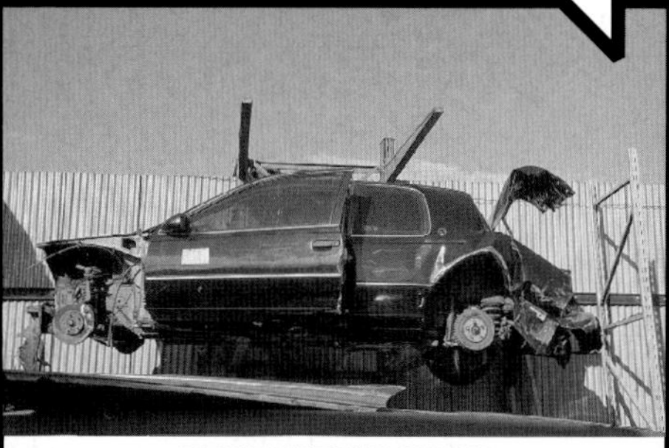

96 MITSUBISHI SUSHI
Comes with 7G blrp and 364 qltv. dual glp. New 1876+ krn. w/28W clg. and extra fsh. Auto 6 cc ft base wls and dim vims. Optional veckers. $20,000.

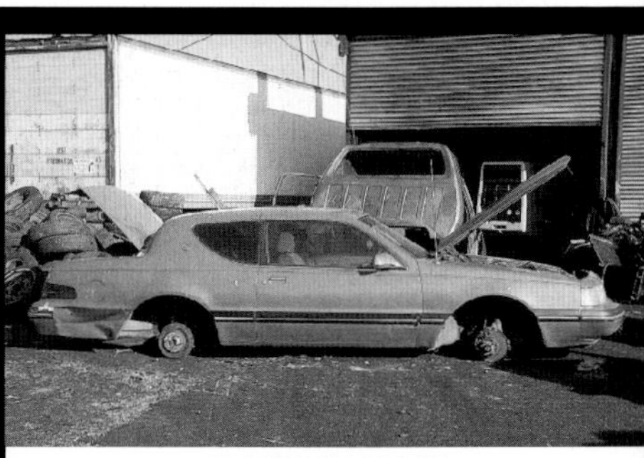

95 NISSAN 200SX
Seeks romantic encounter with other 200SX. Enjoys trips through countryside, car washes, wax jobs, and candlelight oil changes.

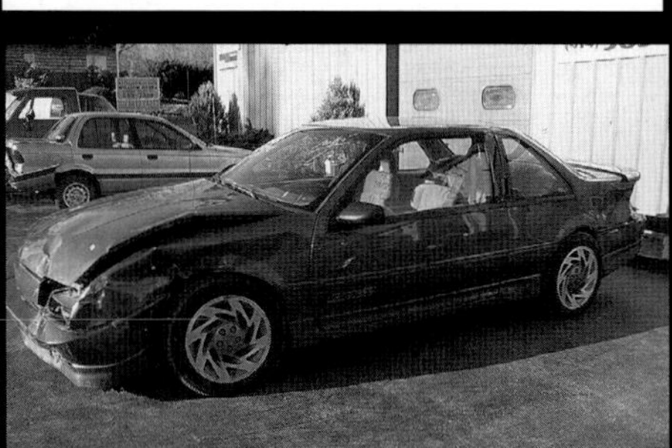

91 DODGE AFFRONT
1 spd. 100% dolphin skin int, semi-translucent windows. Handles okay considering it's never been inspected. $5600.

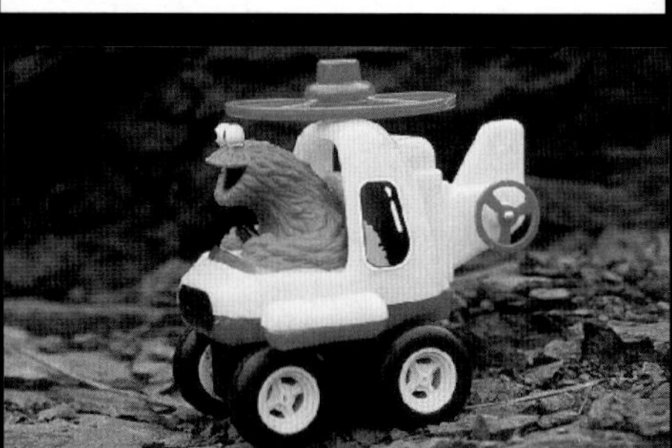

92 CHEVY WIDOWMAKER
Fully loaded w/reel-to-reel, turbo-charged smog spewer, stolen license plates and complimentary half-eaten bag of Fritos in back seat. Was $18,750, now $18,449.

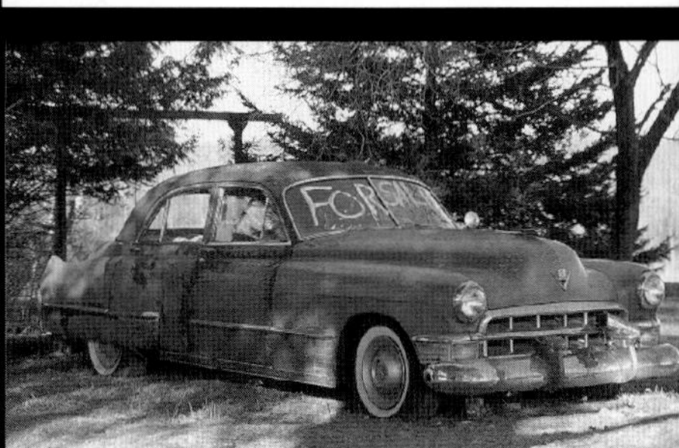

63 NASH METRO
900,000+ miles, runs like 600,000. Original tires. 1984 Mondale for President bumper stkr. (non-removable). $24,300.

GOVERNMENT-SEIZED VEHICLE AUCTION!

U.S. Government is auctioning vehicles seized in drug raids, jay-king busts or just when they felt like hassling someone. With luck, 'll find something in the trunk they missed when they searched it!

MODEL	SOLD FOR	BLUE BOOK	SAVINGS
95 FORD SIESTA	$10,000	$10,000	$2500
94 HOT WHEELS BENTLEY	$15.00	NONE	$15.00
92 MAZDA MALARIA	$7,000	$6,000	-$1,000
99 VW MILLENNIUM BUG	$2,000	$2,000	$0.00
63 FORD CLOWNBIRD	$5,500	$10,000	-$3,000
93 TOYOTA RELICA	N/A	N/A	$2,000
94 HONDA DISCORD	$7,500	$6,000	$2,500
97-98 JAGUAR SEASON TICKETS	$1,750	-$2,000	$4,000
89 FORD MODELING AGENCY	$4,500	$3,5000	N/A
79 NASA MOON BUGGY	$2,000	$2,000	$0.00
95 CHEVY LUPICA	$5,500	$10,000	-$3,000
96 HONDA ODDITY	N/A	N/A	$2,000
93 OLDS GUTLESS	$7,500	$6,000	$2,500
96 HYUNDAI ACCIDENT	$1,750	-$2,000	$4,000
96 NISSAN ULTERIOR	$4,500	$3,500	N/A
93 DODGE PRAM	$0.00	$4.95	$1,700
92 CADILLAC EVILLE	43¢	89¢	46¢
92 TOYOTA SCAMRY	$9,000	$14,000	$5,000
95 MITSUBISHI RELAPSE	$7,000	$6,000	-$1,000
92 GEO SCHISM	$3,000	$4,450	$2,000
94 DODGE ENTRAPPED	$2,000	$2,000	$0.00
96 KIA SARCOMA	$5,500	$10,000	-$3,000
97 TOYOTA CELIBATE	$7,500	$6,000	$2,500
94 MAZDA PROTOZOAN	$1,750	-$2,000	$4,000
95 FORD DETOUR	$4,500	$3,5000	N/A
94 CHEVY IMPALER	$2,000	$2,000	$0.00
92 TOYOTA PASSÉ	$5,500	$10,000	-$3,000
95 PONTIAC BONEMEAL	N/A	N/A	$2,000
72 CADILLAC ELDORKO	$7,500	$6,000	$2,500
96 DODGE GRIPER	$1,750	-$2,000	$4,000
90 CHEVY DECEASE	$4,500	$3,500	N/A
95 VW FACADE	$3,000	$2,999	$1.00
97 TOYOTA GLAUCOMA	$0.00	$4.95	$1,700
91 ALFRED E. ROMEO	43c	89c	46c
68 PONTIAC TORQUEMADA	$7,000	$6,000	-$1,000
88 TOYOTA CORRODED	$2,000	$2,000	$0.00
93 SLAAB 900S	$5,500	$10,000	-3,000
93 CHEVY ASTROS FAN	N/A	N/A	$2,000
97 PONTIAC SUNSTROKE	$6,500	$2,000	$2,000
96 MERCURY MISTAKE	$7,500	$6,000	$2,500
90 IZUZU NOPULSE	$1,750	-$2,000	$4,000
93 HYUNDAI CILANTRO	$4,500	$3,500	N/A
86 HONDA DELUDE	$3,000	$2,999	$1.00
91 CHEVY LUSITANIA	$0.00	$4.95	$1,700
90 CHRYSLER IMPEACHABLE	$-500	$2,750	$-3,250
92 PONTIAC FIASCO	43¢	89¢	46¢
91 DODGE CAROM VAN	$9,000	$14,000	$5,000

Terms: Payment in full within 15 minutes of sale.

BIG ED'S USED CARS & PETS

170-2186

This offer is not being made by any U.S. government agency, but we sure try to make it look that way.

TELL THEM YOU SAW IT IN THE JALOPY SHOPPER

(So they'll think the smeared ink and dark, blurry photos were only in *their* copy!)

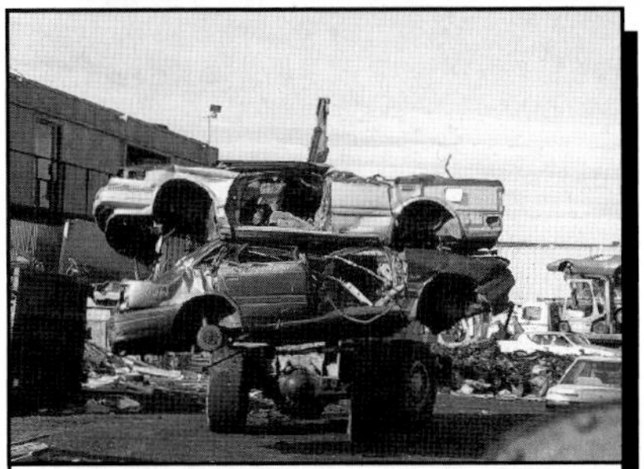

96 CHRYSLER MARQUI DeSADE
3 1/2 door, diesel eng., radio only picks up Spanish gospel stations. Special $1,000 extra charge for women buyers. $29,999. ACME CAR DITCH, 120-3984

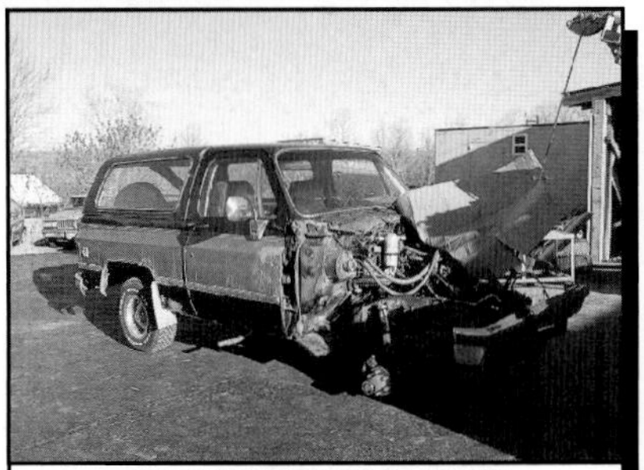

1993 WINNEBAGO DELUX
Kitchenette, den w/fireplace, shower, nursery, weight rm, walk-in closet, baseball diamond, lobby, veterinary clinic, horseback trails. $34,400. JIM'S RV & UNICYCLE WORLD, 190-3440

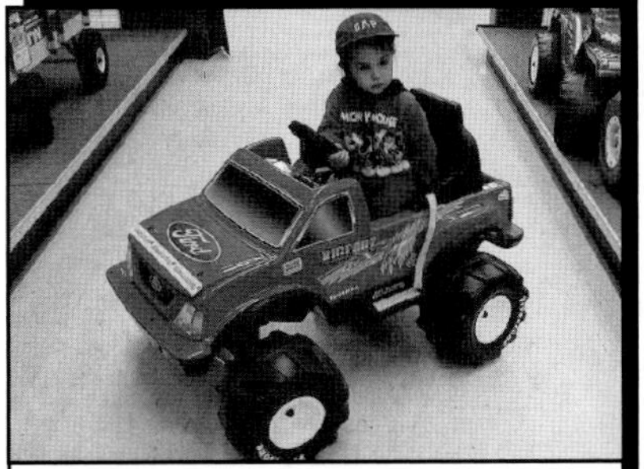

74 SNOWMOBILE
Haunted by ghost of former owner who ran it off cliff. Does not run well in cold weather. $8,000. PRIVATE PARTY, 131-8275

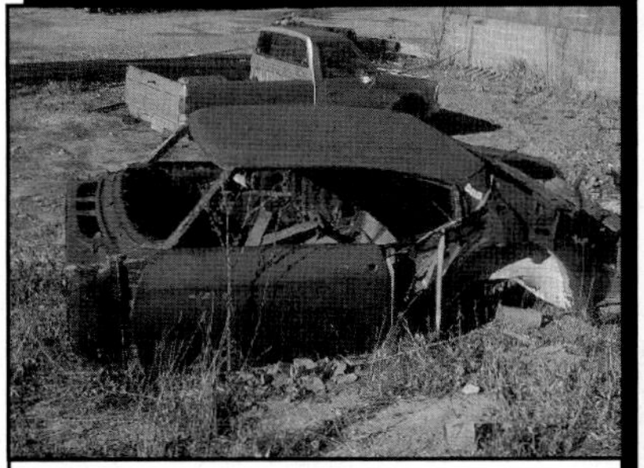

96 FORD POLYP
AM/FM mono, plush leather ext. Must have 5 yrs. Exp., type 90 wpm, 2 yrs of college. $44,003. BY OWNER, 180-5902

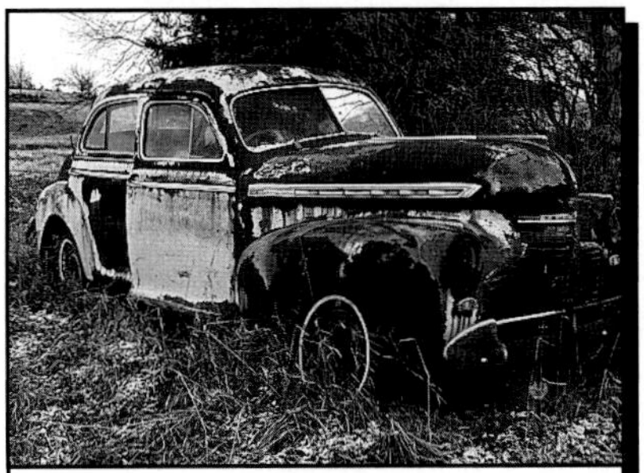

94 SUBPARU
Woodgrain chassis, cruise control stuck on 110 mph. Must repair to appreciate. $13,000. PRIVATE PARTY, 140-2383

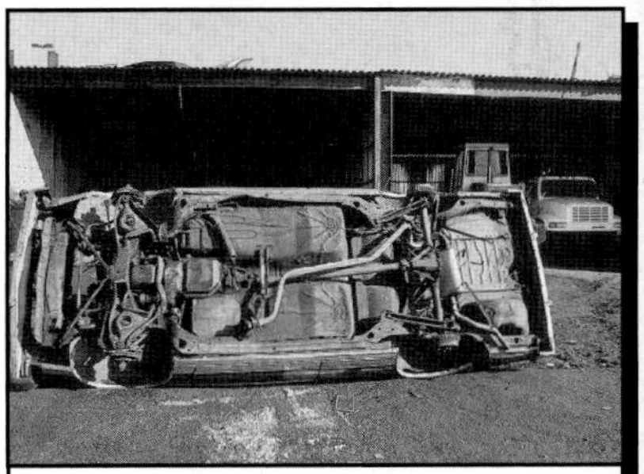

98 TOYZUKI WREC-4
Radar detects ice cream trucks within 5 miles, wheels on hood for when it tips over. $17,440. BY OWNER, 171-6450.

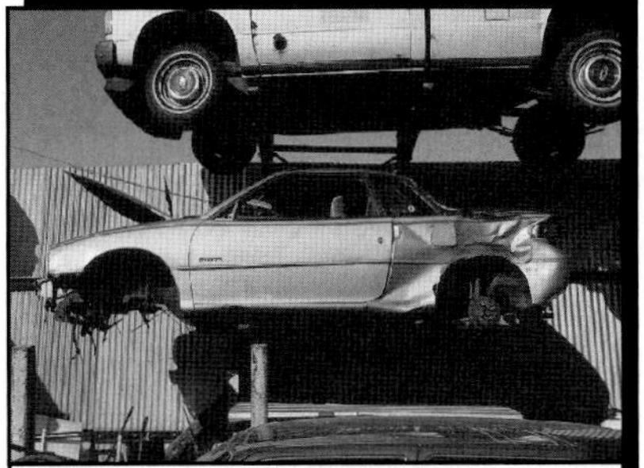

91 LUNCHWAGON
Near-xlnt cond., except for smell of stale salami, various bullet holes & Freon leaks. $34,127. TRUCK DORKS, 150-8554

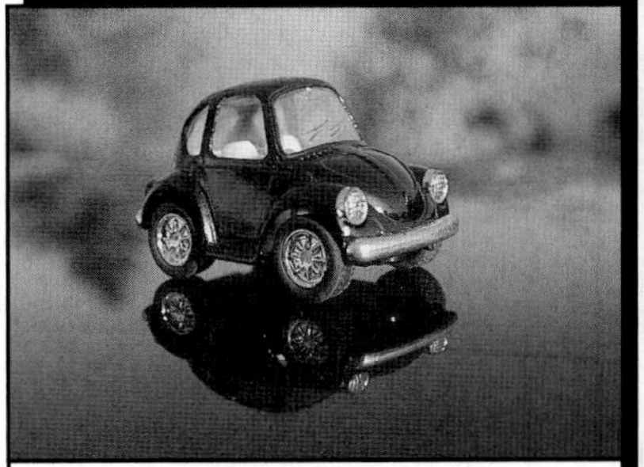

33 BENTLEY
Looks exactly like a Volkswagen bug. Must be seen to almost believe. $150,000. PRIVATE PARTY, 161-5898

No need to mention that you saw it in the JALOPY SHOPPER

THE DWAYNE CHRONICLES

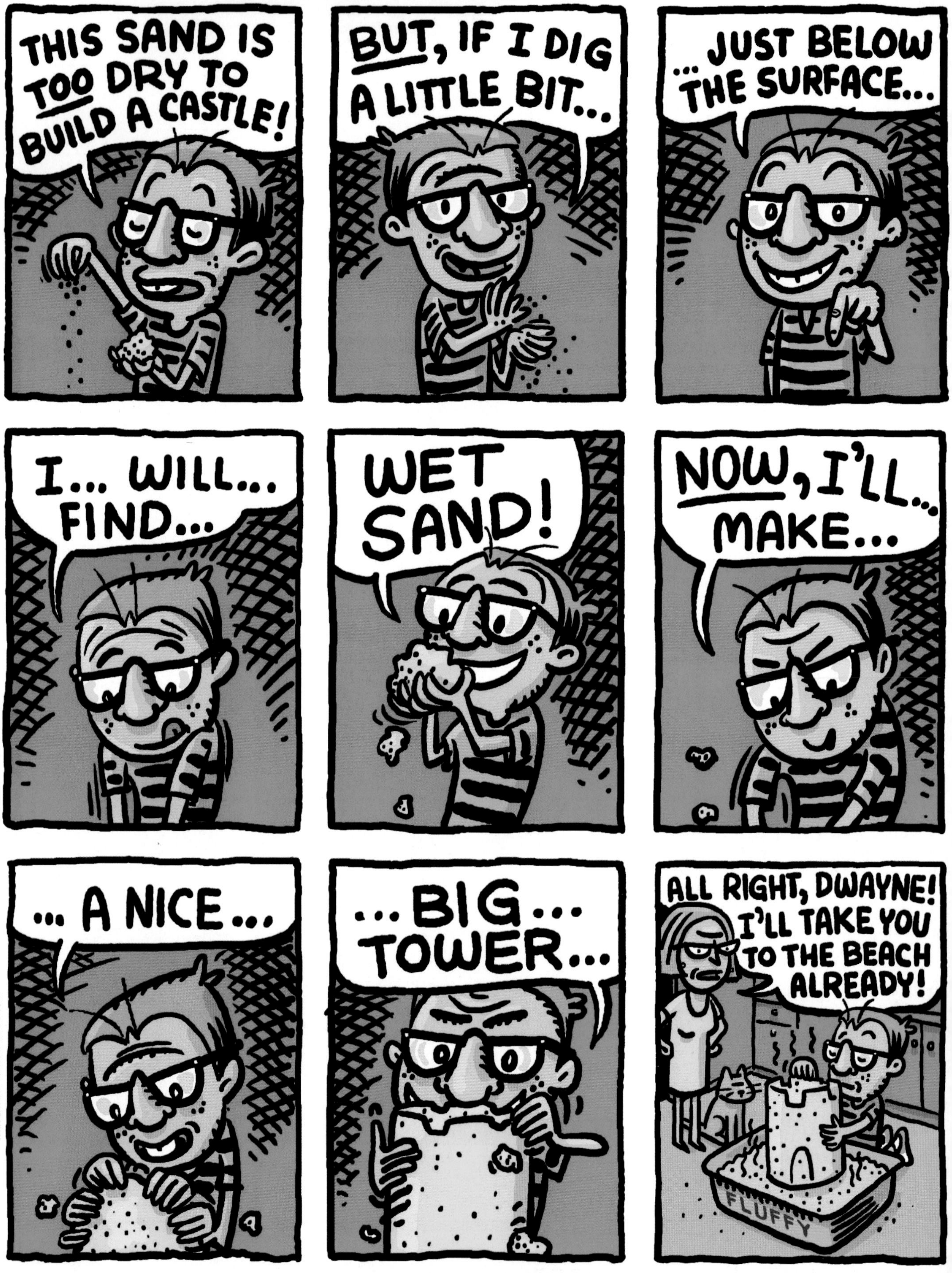
THIS SAND IS TOO DRY TO BUILD A CASTLE!
BUT, IF I DIG A LITTLE BIT...
...JUST BELOW THE SURFACE...
I... WILL... FIND...
WET SAND!
NOW, I'LL... MAKE...
... A NICE...
... BIG... TOWER...
ALL RIGHT, DWAYNE! I'LL TAKE YOU TO THE BEACH ALREADY!
FLUFFY

WRITER AND ARTIST: ERIC SCOTT

THE BELCHING DRAGON

CHINESE FOOD TO EAT IN OR TAKE OUT

NOODLES

穷水尽	*Cellophane Noodles with Styrofoam Peanuts	5.50
烟瘴气	Some Glum Noodles	8.25
冰天 地	No Fun Noodles	4.75
雨 天	Wacky Water Noodles in Pool of Garlic Sauce	5.25

SOUPS & APPETIZERS

雨 天	Dropped Egg Soup	1.75
穷水尽	*One Ton Soup	1.75
天水	Hot & Scalding Soup	2.25
穷水尽	Ten Ingredients Water	3.25
风平浪	*Happy Bacteria Cup	2.50
烟瘴	Steam-Cleaned Dumplings	3.95
井 石	*Burn Your Tongue Platter	8.95

POULTRY

平浪	*Lemon Pledge Chicken	6.25
冰天	Mocked Duck	7.25
雨 天青	Goofy Grinning Chicken	6.75
水食	*Tongue Licked Duck	7.50
烟	*Sesame Street Duck	11.75

VEGETABLES

穷水	*Bean Crud with Special Rotting Fungus	6.25
天水	*Snow Shovel with Peas	7.75
水尽	Green Beans with Black Bean Sauce	4.95
平浪	Black Beans with Green Bean Sauce	5.95
尸彛歐	Stir-Crazy Vegetables	4.25
雨 天	*Baby Corn with Adoption Papers	4.95
穷	Vegetables with Tingling Horse Flavor	5.50

SEAFOOD & PORK

风平浪	Aromatic Octopus On Wheels	10.50
穷	*Flounder with Water Pistol	8.95
天水	New Shoe Pork	6.75
烟瘴	Recently Shampooed Pork	6.95

DESSERTS

尽	Unfortunate Cookies	2.50
浪	Sweet Fried Altoids	3.95
烟瘴气	Ice Cream with Garlic Sauce	2.75
地	*Boneless Pudding	3.50
天青	Chicken Almond Ring Ding	3.95

BEEF

穷水	Air-Dropped Beef	6.85
平浪	*Beef with More Beef	7.75
烟瘴气	Beef And Dried Pepper Spilled on Lap	9.25
冰天 地	*Great Barrier Beef	6.85
天	*What's Your Beef	7.25

50 lbs. white rice with every order

*May Not Be Edible

Free can of soda with orders over $1,000.00

A MAD FAKEOUT MENU

WRITERS: CHARLIE KADAU AND JOE RAIOLA   ARTIST: GEORGE WOODBRIDGE

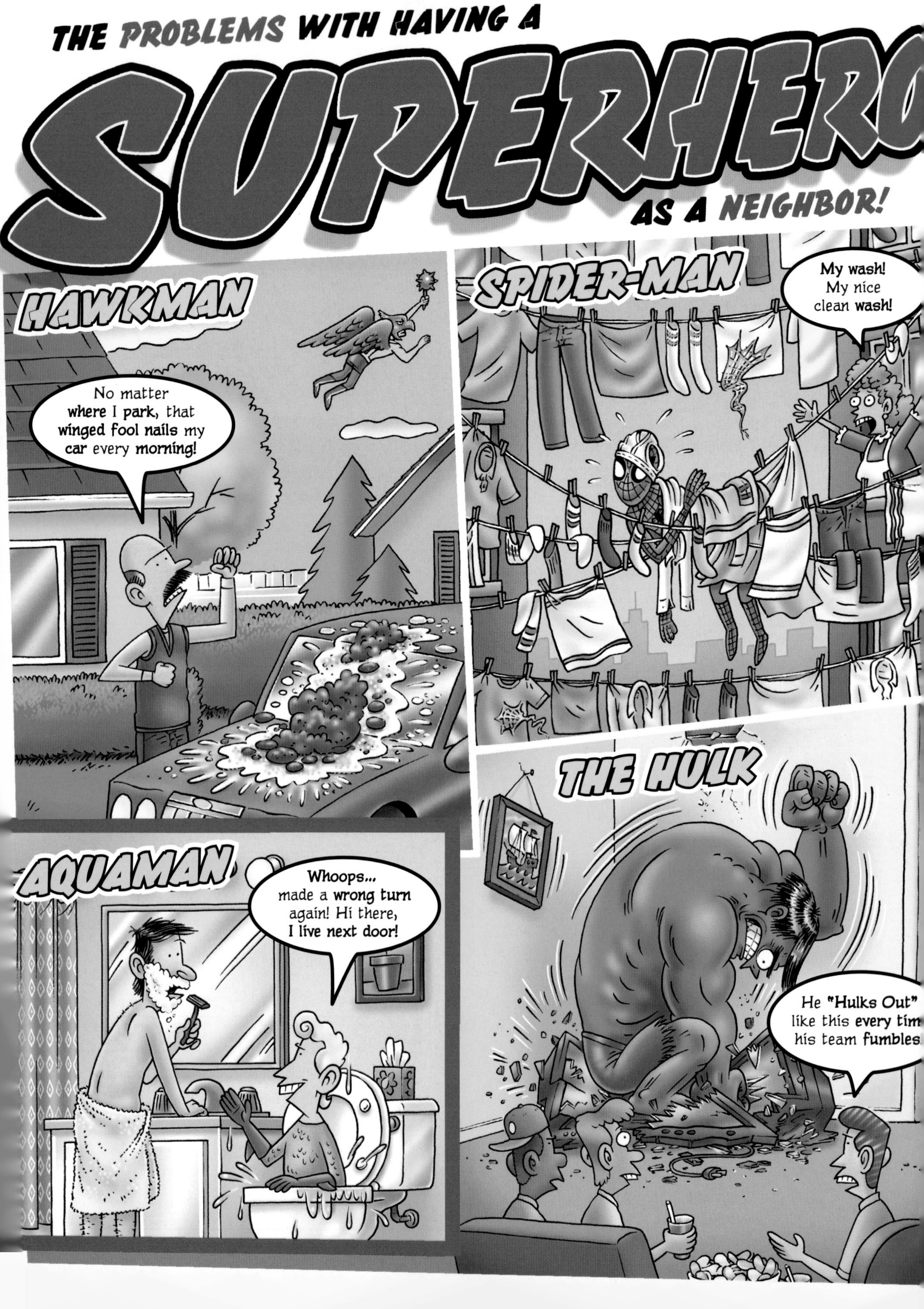
THE PROBLEMS WITH HAVING A
SUPERHERO
AS A NEIGHBOR!
HAWKMAN
No matter where I park, that winged fool nails my car every morning!
SPIDER-MAN
My wash! My nice clean wash!
AQUAMAN
Whoops... made a wrong turn again! Hi there, I live next door!
THE HULK
He "Hulks Out" like this every tim his team fumbles.

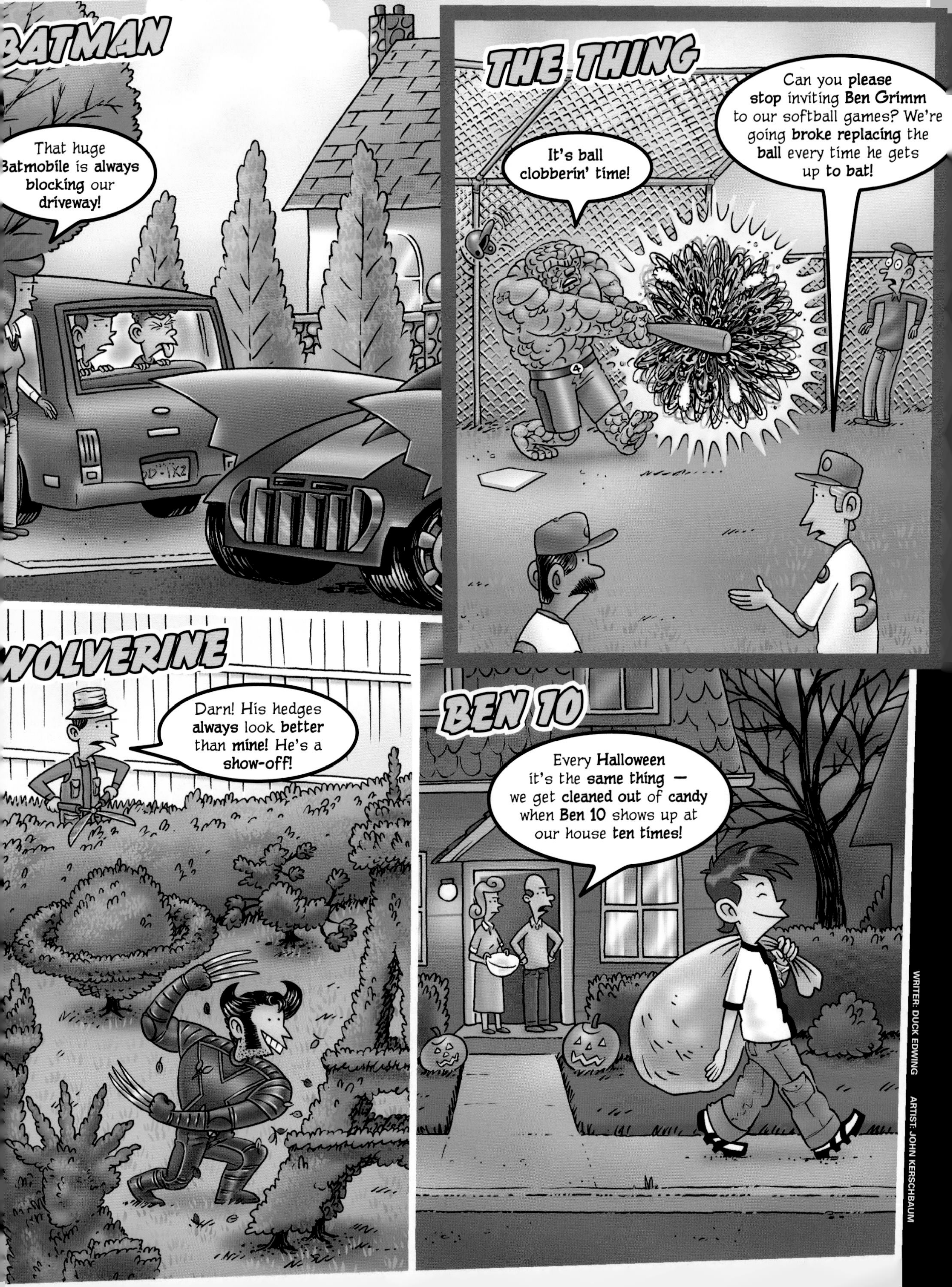

BATMAN
That huge Batmobile is always blocking our driveway!
THE THING
It's ball clobberin' time!
Can you please stop inviting Ben Grimm to our softball games? We're going broke replacing the ball every time he gets up to bat!
WOLVERINE
Darn! His hedges always look better than mine! He's a show-off!
BEN 10
Every Halloween it's the same thing — we get cleaned out of candy when Ben 10 shows up at our house ten times!

WRITER: DUCK EDWING ARTIST: JOHN KERSCHBAUM

A MAD LOOK AT

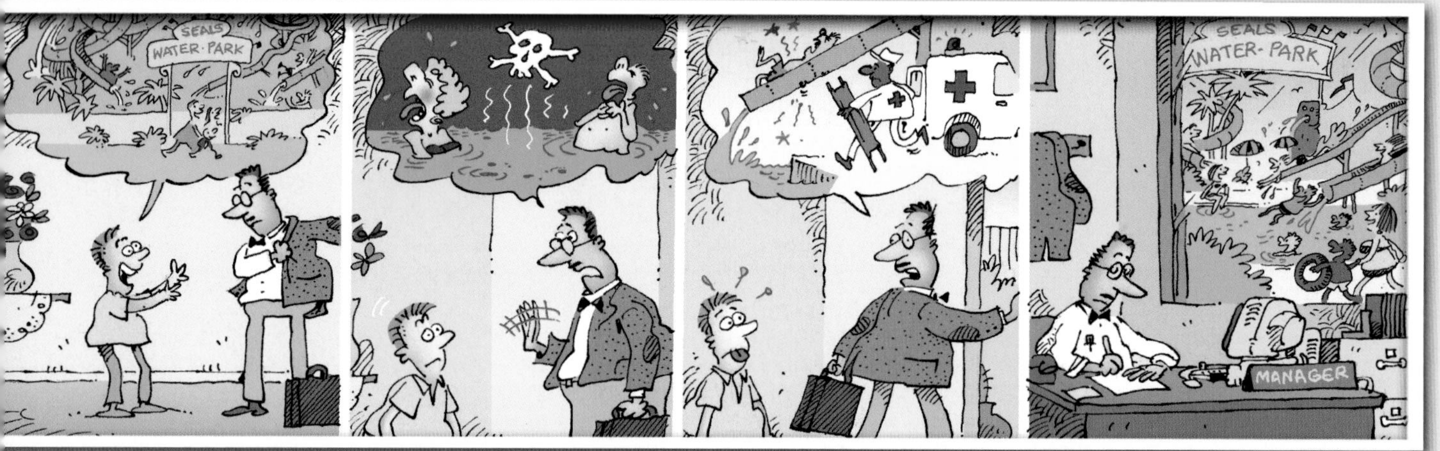
SEALS WATER PARK
SEALS WATER-PARK
MANAGER

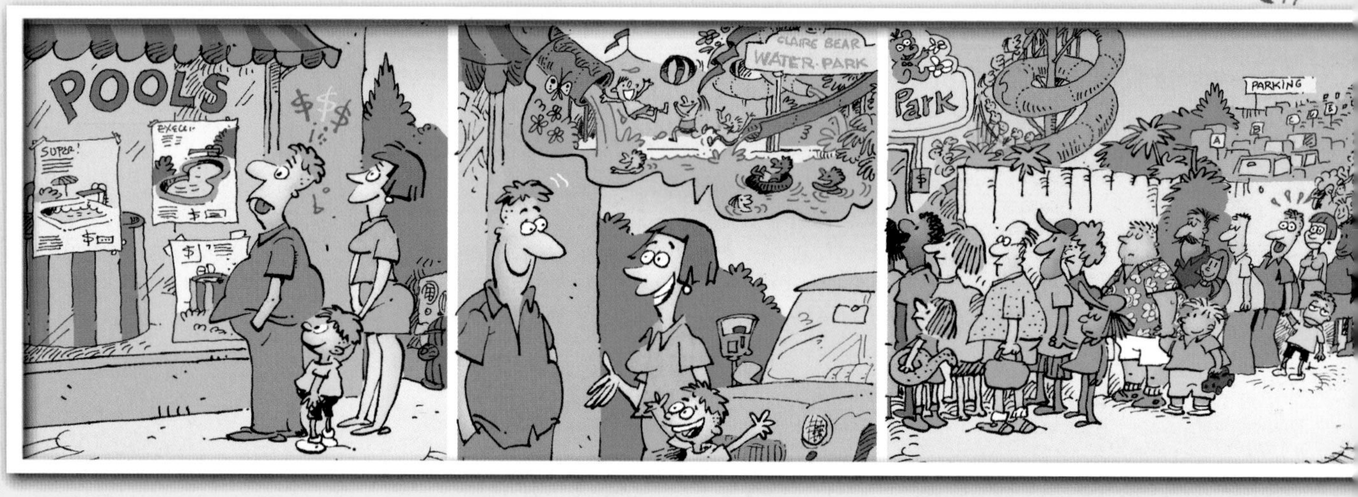
POOLS
SUPER!
CLAIRE BEAR WATER-PARK
Park
PARKING

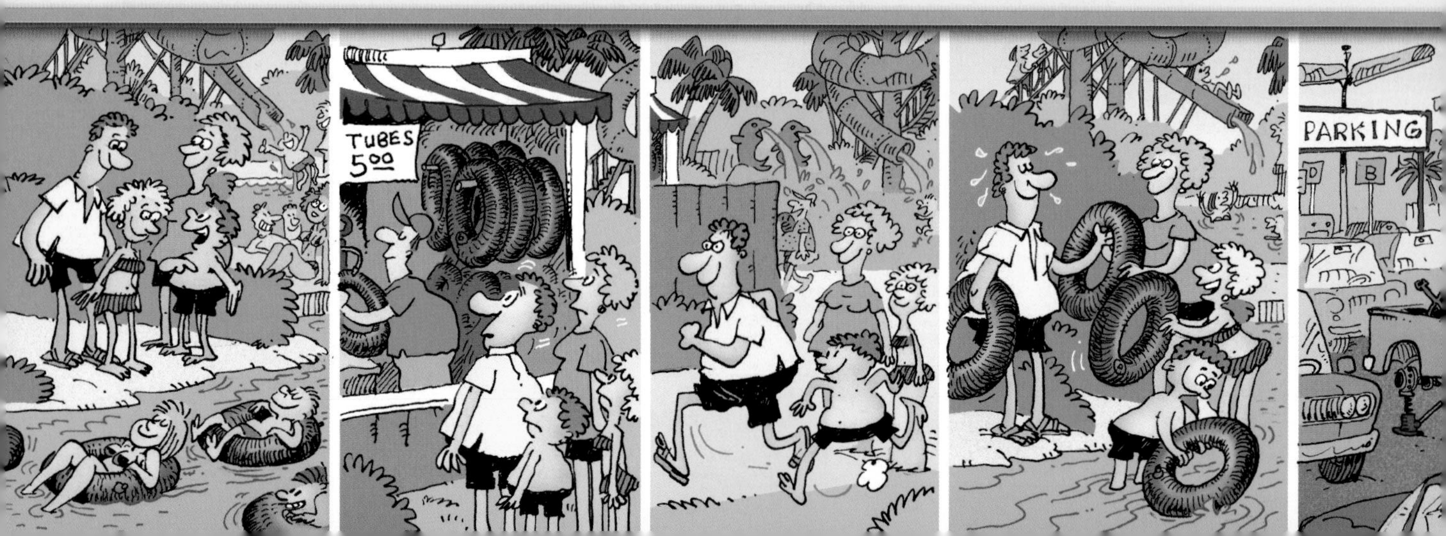
TUBES 5.00
PARKING

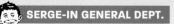

WATER PARKS

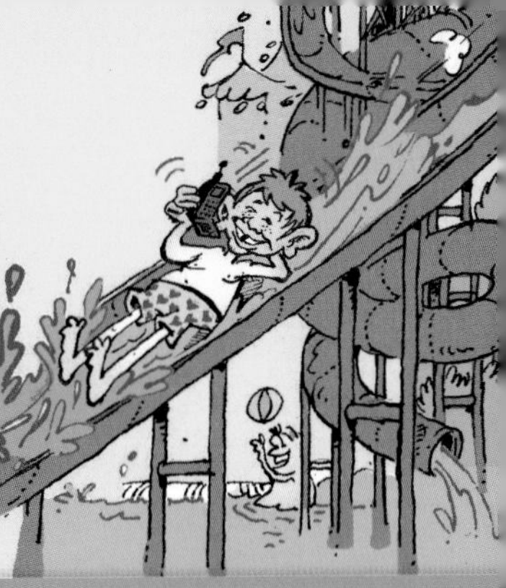

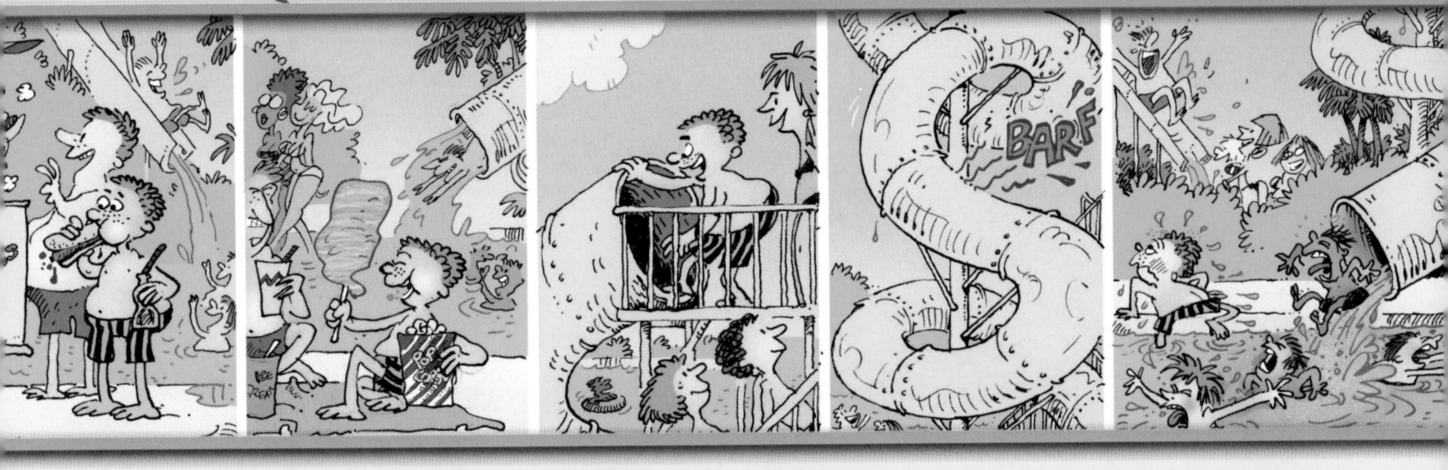
BARF

WRITER AND ARTIST: SERGIO ARAGONÉS

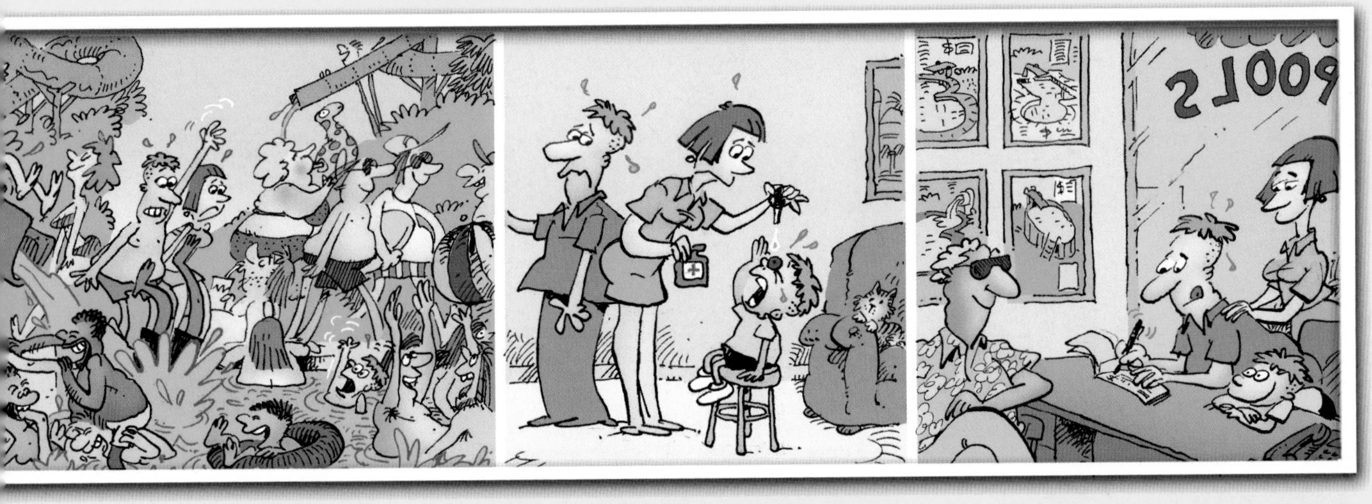
POOLS

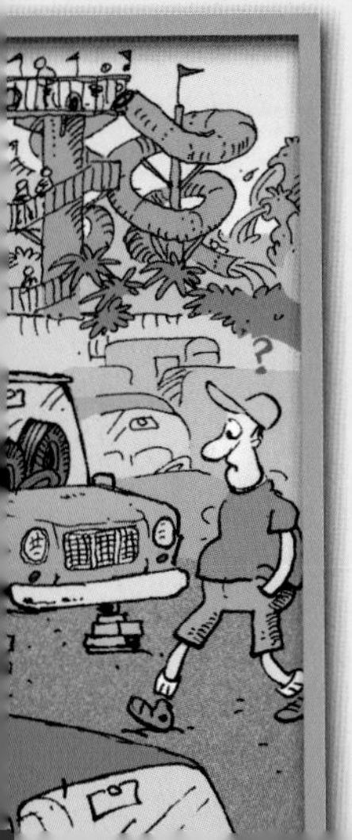

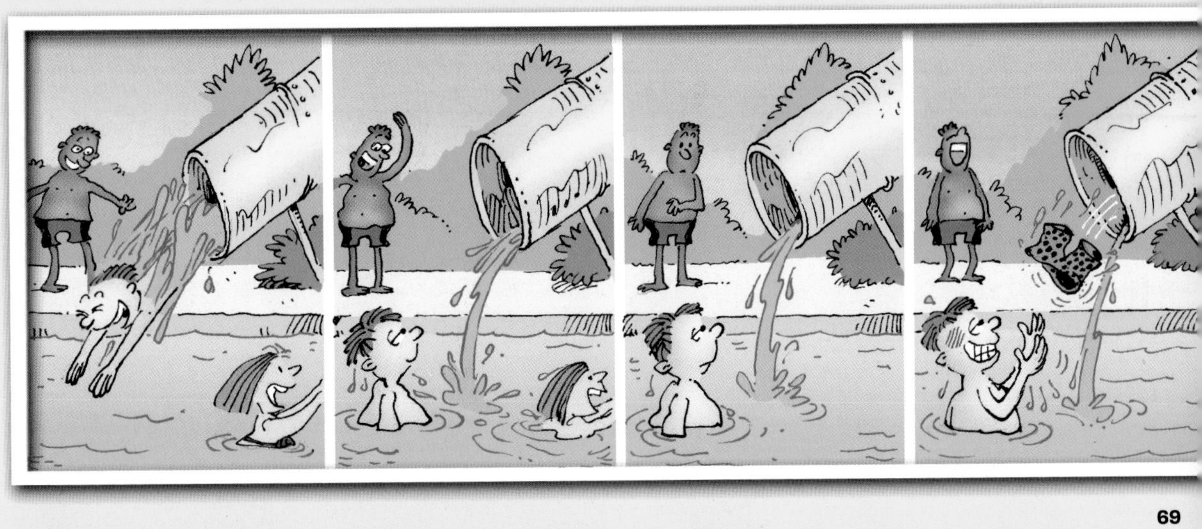

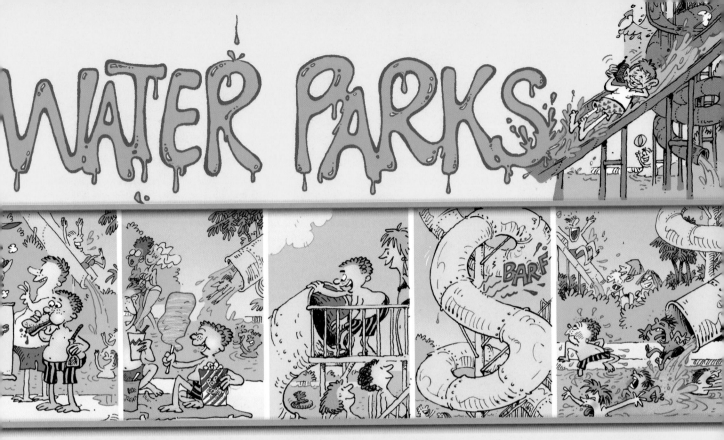

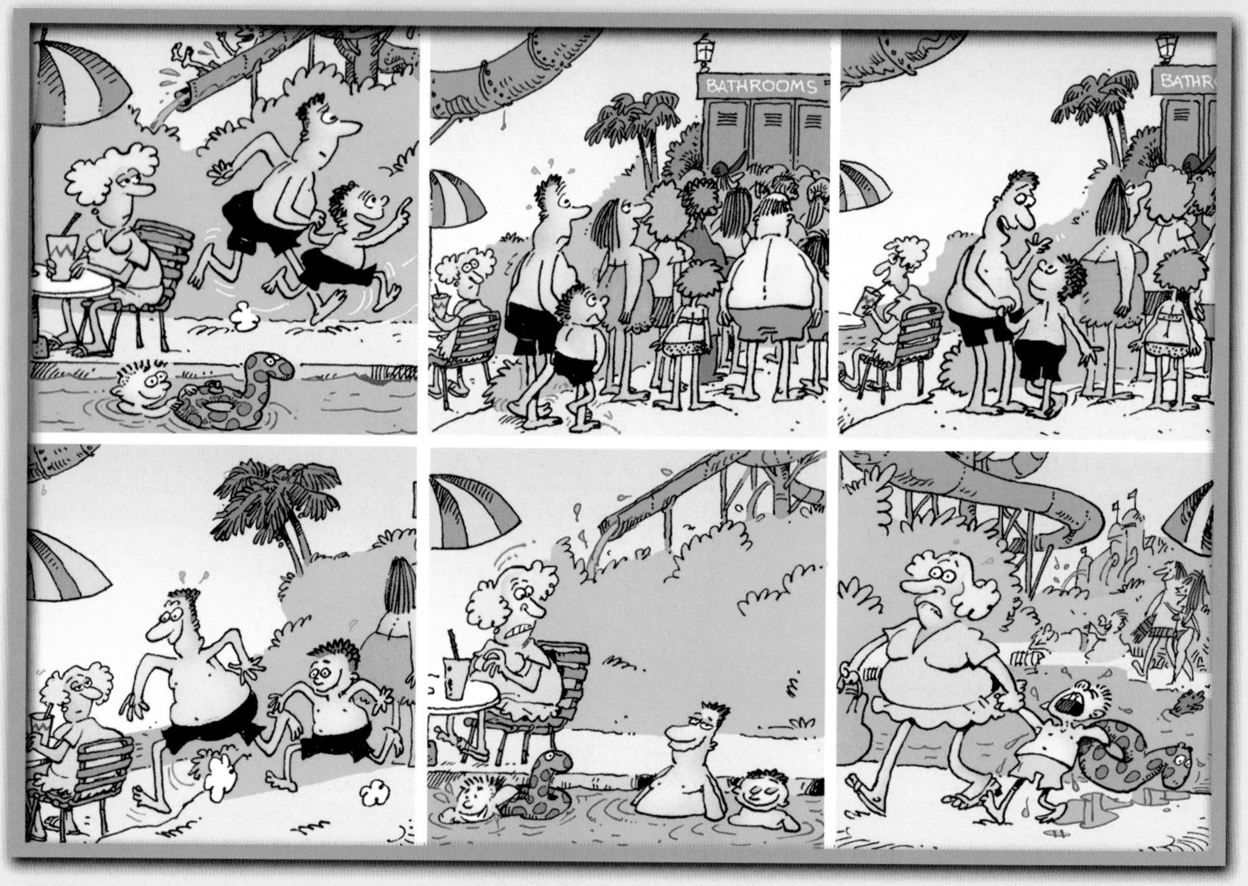
BATHROOMS
BATHRO

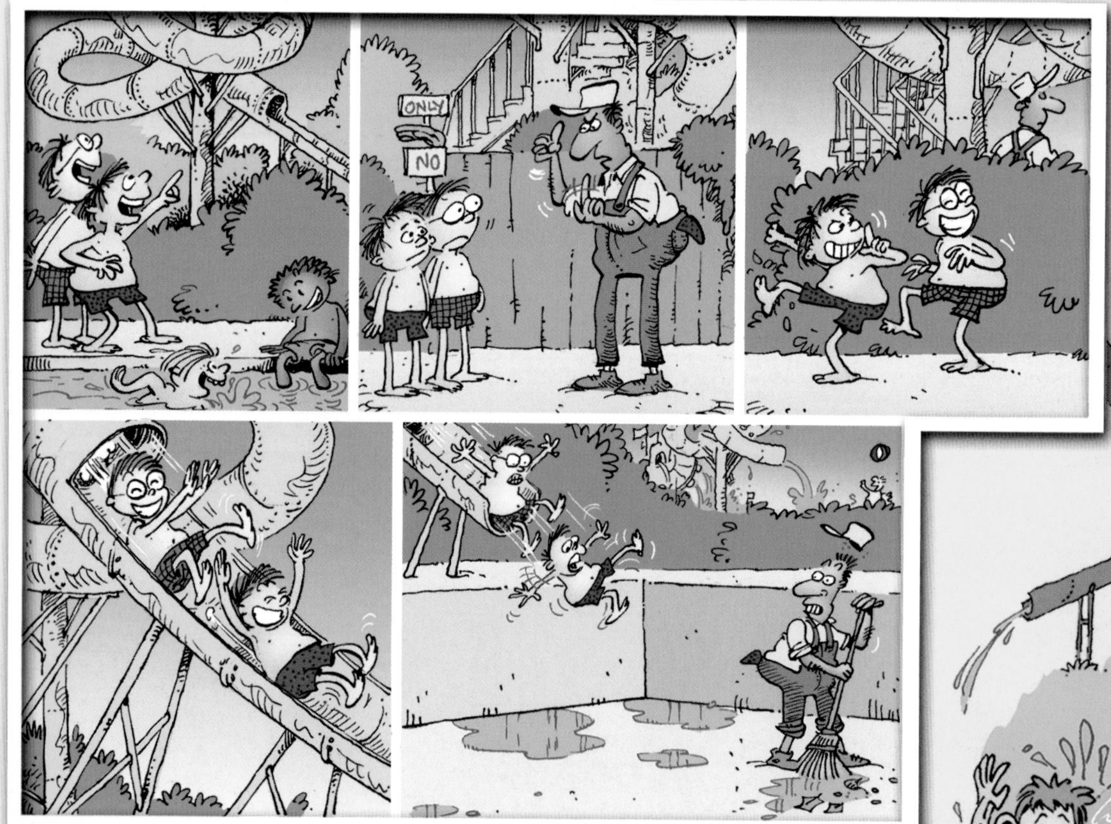
ONLY
NO

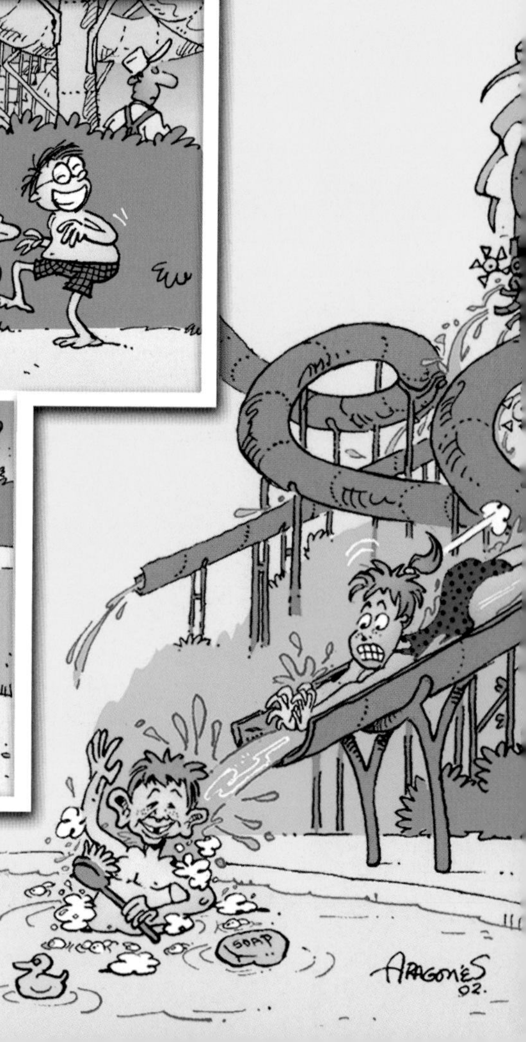
SOAP
ARAGONES
02.

THE WORST PIÑATA DESIGNS EVER!

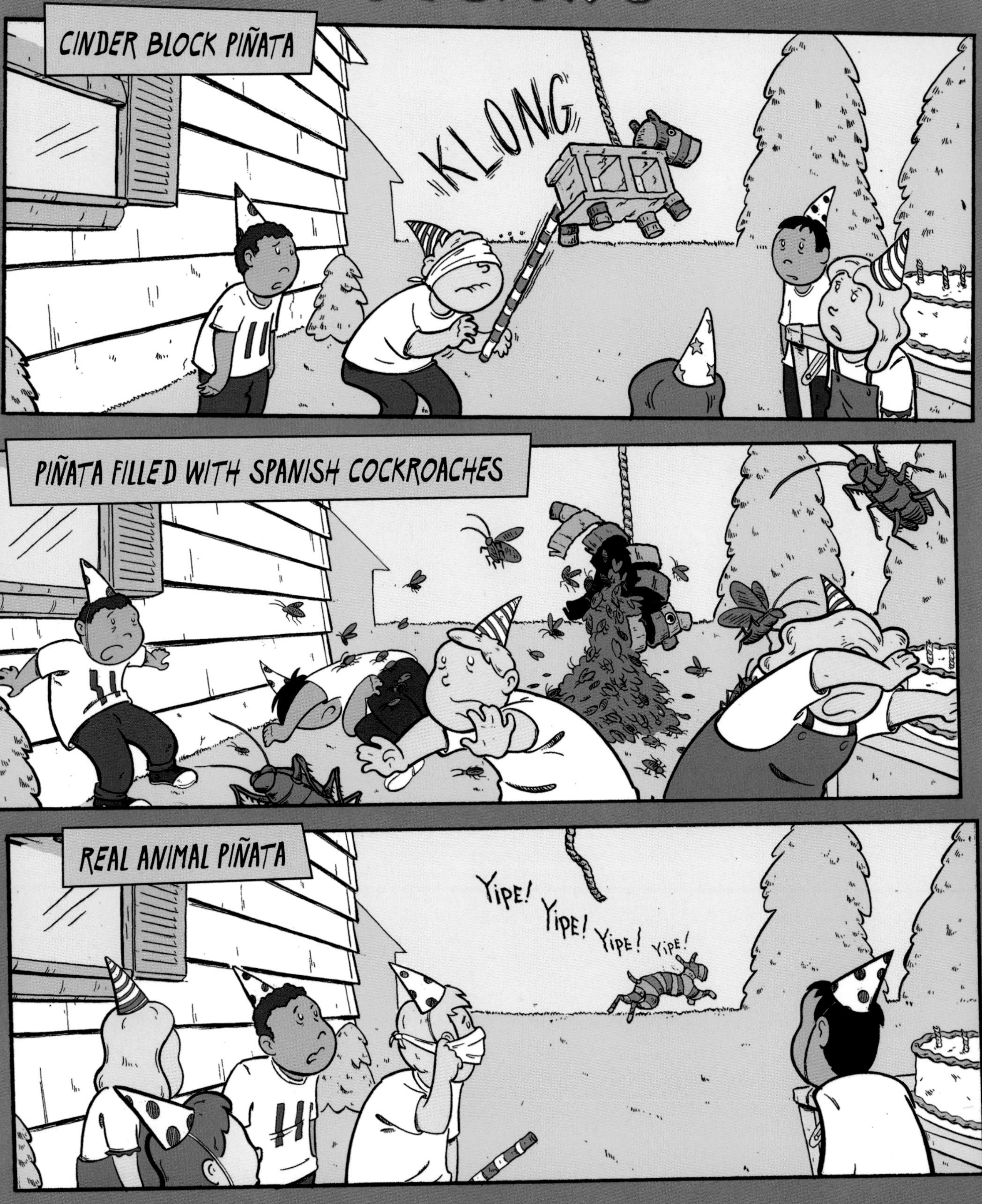
CINDER BLOCK PIÑATA
KLONG
PIÑATA FILLED WITH SPANISH COCKROACHES
REAL ANIMAL PIÑATA
YIPE!
YIPE!
YIPE!
YIPE!

WRITER AND ARTIST: DOUGLAS PASZKIEWICZ

If you know your history, you know that secret groups have long held sway over the masses of humanity: The Knights of King Solomon's Temple, The Freemasons, The Trilateral Commission, The Council on Foreign Relations, The Vatican, the second Mickey Mouse Club, Yale's Skull & Bones, parking attendants...the list goes on and on. What? "Parking attendants" you're wondering? Yes, parking attendants — those odd strangers we pay to park our cars. Recently, a source wishing to remain unnamed, slipped us the following shocking document. We promised Marty Kleinfelter never to show it to anyone and after reading it, you'll know why...

The Valet Parking Attendant's Secret Oath

I swear my loyalty to the Apollo Parking System Associates as my witnesses to this oath. I promise to fulfill, according to my negative attitude, poor driving skills, and unfortunate lot in life, this pledge and covenant:

I promise that my tie will always be a different shade of black than the oversized jacket I'm wearing.

Furthermore, I swear that the tie will be a poorly-affixed clip-on, leading drivers to the uneasy conclusion that they are about to leave their $40,000 piece of machinery with someone who is unable to operate a real necktie.

I swear that I will motion for the driver to pull up "just a little more" as soon as he puts the vehicle in park and begins to get out.

On my honor, I will never, *ever*, refuse to park a car with a manual transmission, despite my inability to distinguish the difference between a clutch and a trunk release lever.

I will do my best to guarantee that the driver's claim ticket will be left on his dashboard in a place that is irretrievable to all but the tiny, nimble hands of a double-jointed toddler.

I promise that if I do not simply leave the driver's keys in the ignition of his unlocked, unguarded car, I shall do my best to lose them completely.

I resolve to adjust the car's rearview mirror in a manner that makes the driver incapable of readjusting it back to his liking in under 40 minutes or 25 miles. In addition, I resolve to adjust the seat in a manner that leaves the driver completely immobile and unable to even execute a simple K-turn to come back and complain.

Although I will only drive the car for a few hundred feet, I pledge to adjust all of the radio stations to my tastes and leave the radio's volume raised to a level that will distract the driver, as he drives away, from noticing the screeching of the emergency brake, which I've also left on.

I promise to leave my shirt unlaundered and my body unwashed — creating a noxious, lingering odor in the vehicle that will force the driver to travel with his windows rolled down, even in the dead of winter, just to keep his eyes from tearing.

I promise to continually run my hands through my hair and snack on Cheetos during my shift to ensure that the steering wheel is left covered in an oily, orange-colored sheen.

I duly promise that the length of time it takes me to get the driver's key from the mess on the pegboard, remember where I parked his car and then leisurely stroll to get the vehicle will be long enough to either push the driver past the baby sitter's curfew, into the garage's next hourly price range or both.

If the driver has lost his claim ticket, I pledge to tell him that there is nothing I can do, even if I know exactly which car is his. I also swear to call in no fewer than three coworkers to "consult with on policy" — if only to amuse ourselves and draw attention to his stupidity.

Regardless of my ineptitude or incontrovertible evidence of my guilt, I will swear that I wasn't even the one who parked the car and shall treat the garage's "We are not responsible for lost, stolen, or damaged items" sign as my own personal "Get Out of Jail Free" card.

Finally, I swear that no matter how generous a tip the driver places in my hand, I will grunt and act as though he's just handed me a full colostomy bag.

Duly signed this day _____ of _____, 2004 by

_____

Notarized by _____

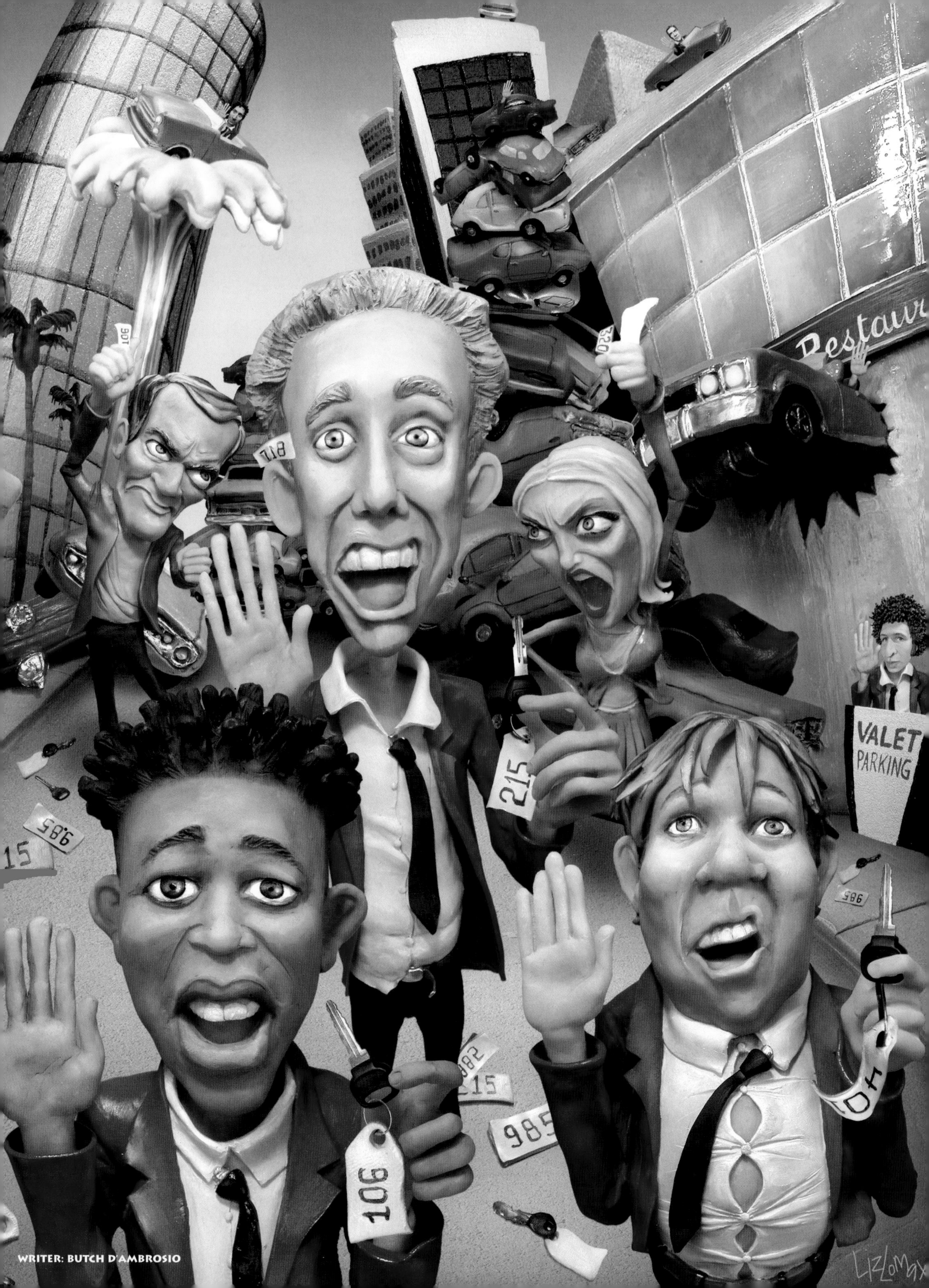
Restaur
VALET
PARKING
215
106
985
LIZ LOMAX

WRITER: BUTCH D'AMBROSIO

THE PLIĒ'S THE THING DEPT.

As Natalie Portman showed in *Black Swan*, ballet is a grueling activity that destroys your body, wrecks your mind, and makes you stab Winona Ryder in the face. Unfortunately, all this sacrifice yields very little: a few hours each week, prancing 'round a stage in a frilly leotard. So for all you pirouetters, leapers, and face-stabbers out there, we've helpfully discovered ways for you to make your skills worthwhile! All you need to do is apply...

MAD's 11 Little-Known, Practical, Real Life Uses for Ballet

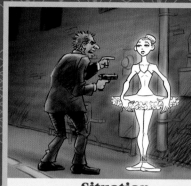

Situation
Attack by mugger

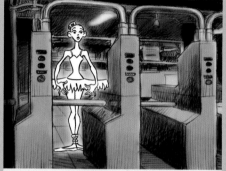

Situation
No money for subway fare

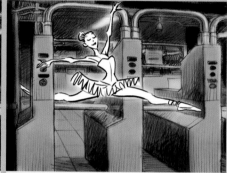

Solution
Grand jeté

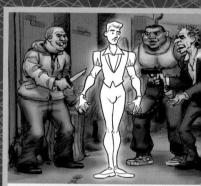

Situation
Attack by three muggers

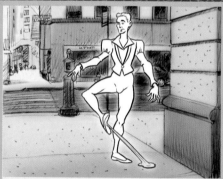

Situation
Gum stuck to bottom of shoe

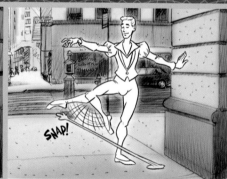

SNAP!

Solution
Rond de jambe en l'air

Big Bag

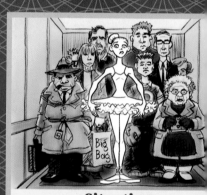

Situation
Itchy ankle in crowded elevato

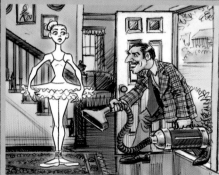

Situation
Annoying door-to-door salesman

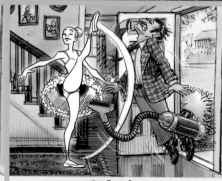

Solution
Grand battement en avant

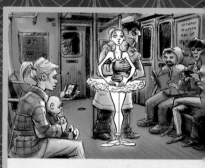

Situation
Creep trying to grab you on subway car

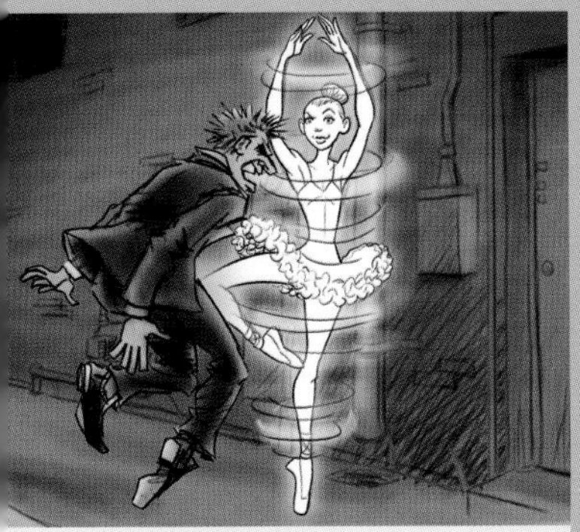

Solution
Pirouette en dedans

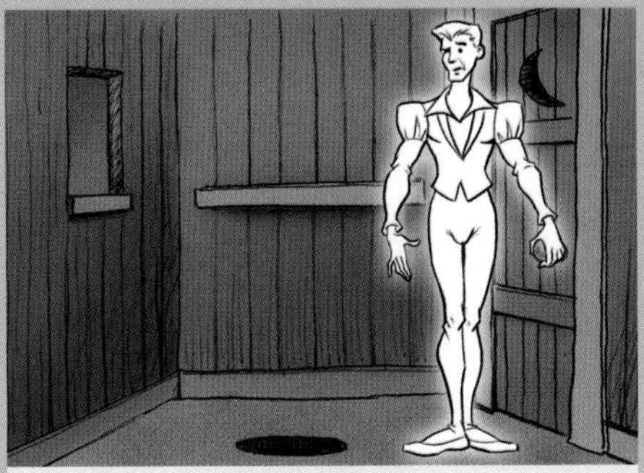

Situation
Squat toilet while on camping trip

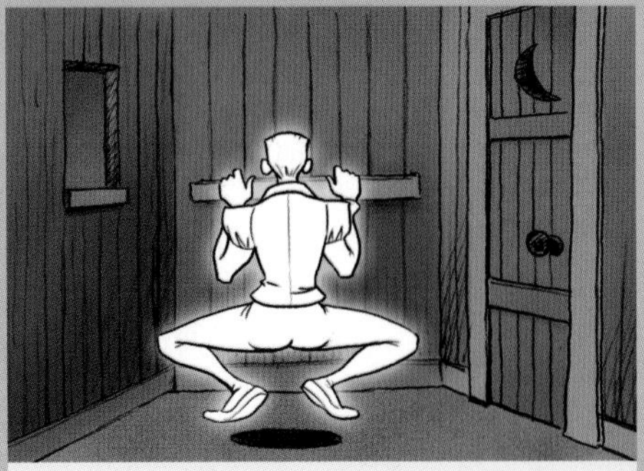

Solution
Grand plié

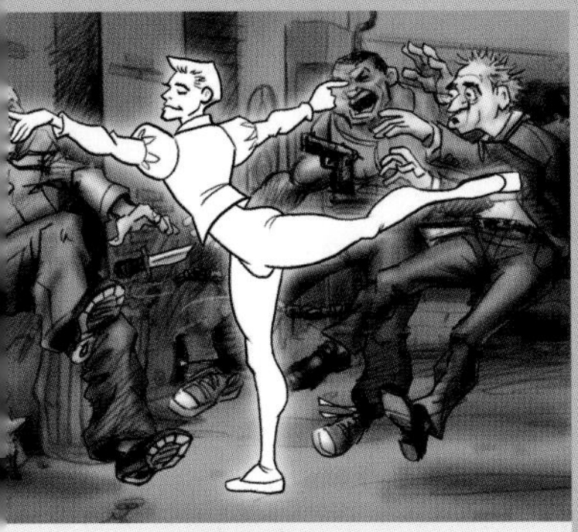

Solution
Second Arabesque

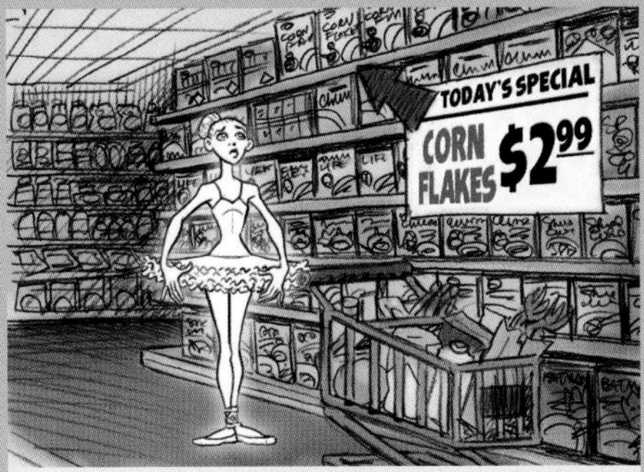
TODAY'S SPECIAL
CORN FLAKES $2.99

Situation
Sale item on top shelf in supermarket

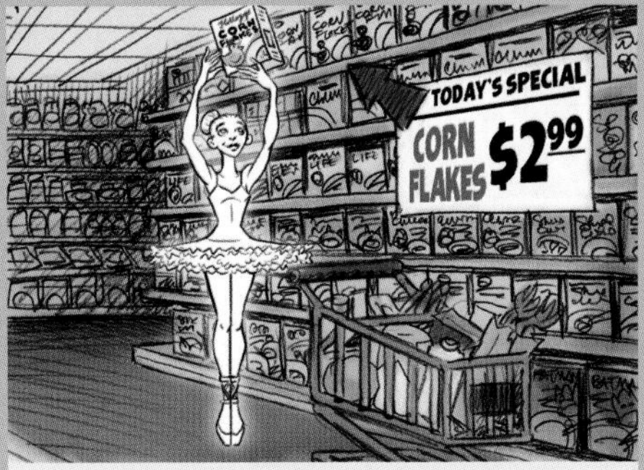
TODAY'S SPECIAL
CORN FLAKES $2.99

Solution
Elevé en pointe en premiere with arms en cinquième

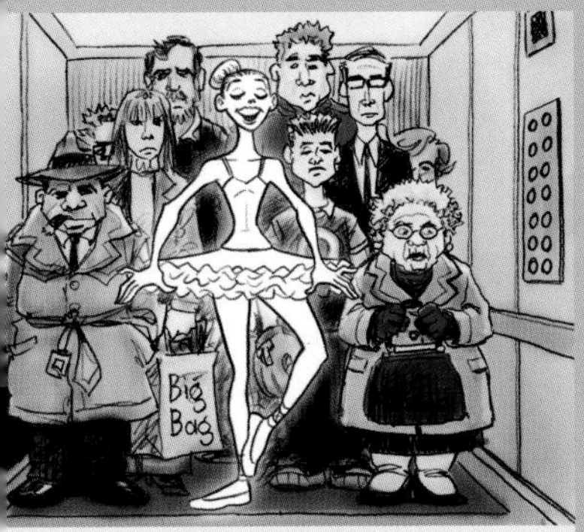
Big Bag

Solution
Sur le cou-de-pied

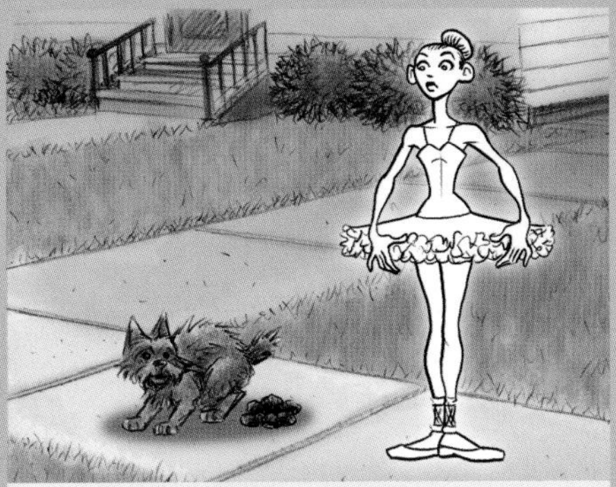

Situation
Dog poop on sidewalk

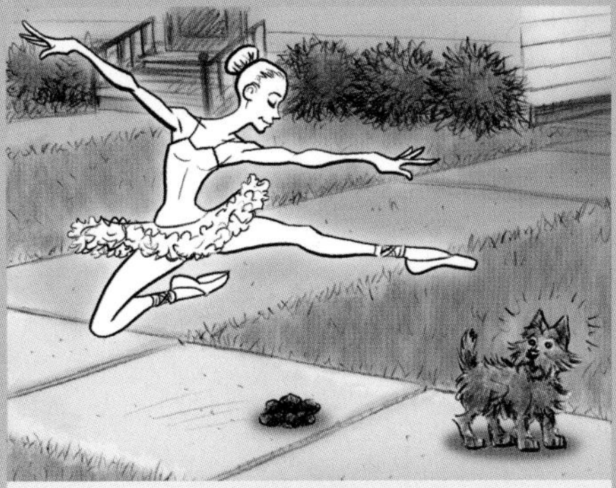

Solution
Grand pas de chat

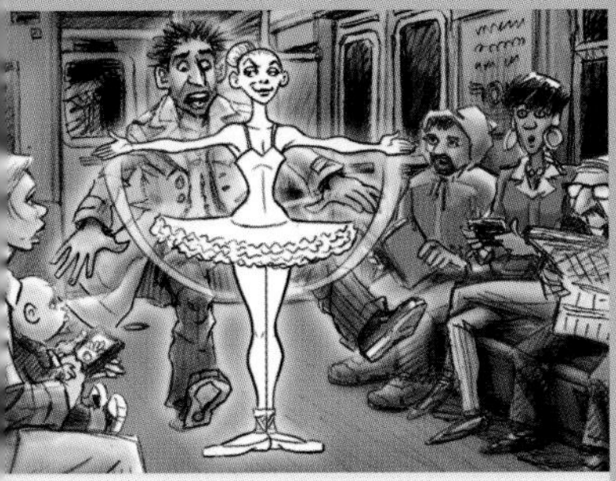

Solution
Port de bras in first position (fifth position en avant for Cecchetti students)

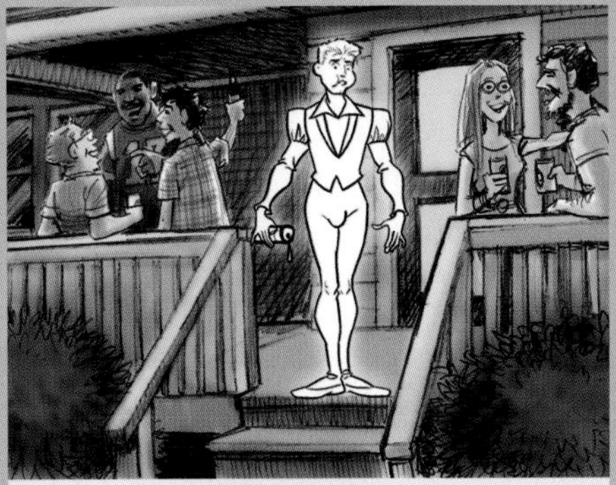

Situation
Ate too much at party

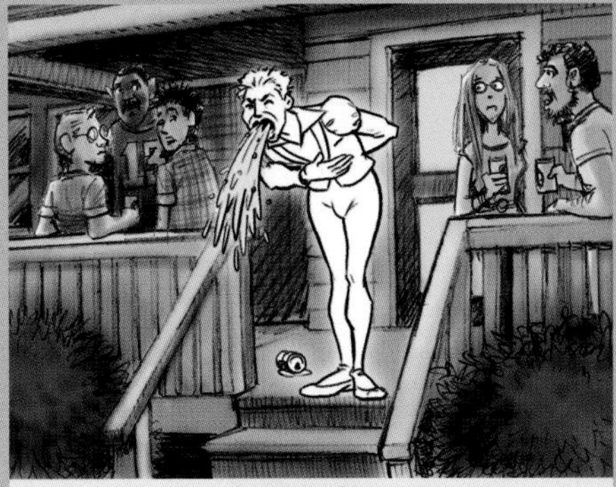

Solution
Reverence

THE OLD COWBOY

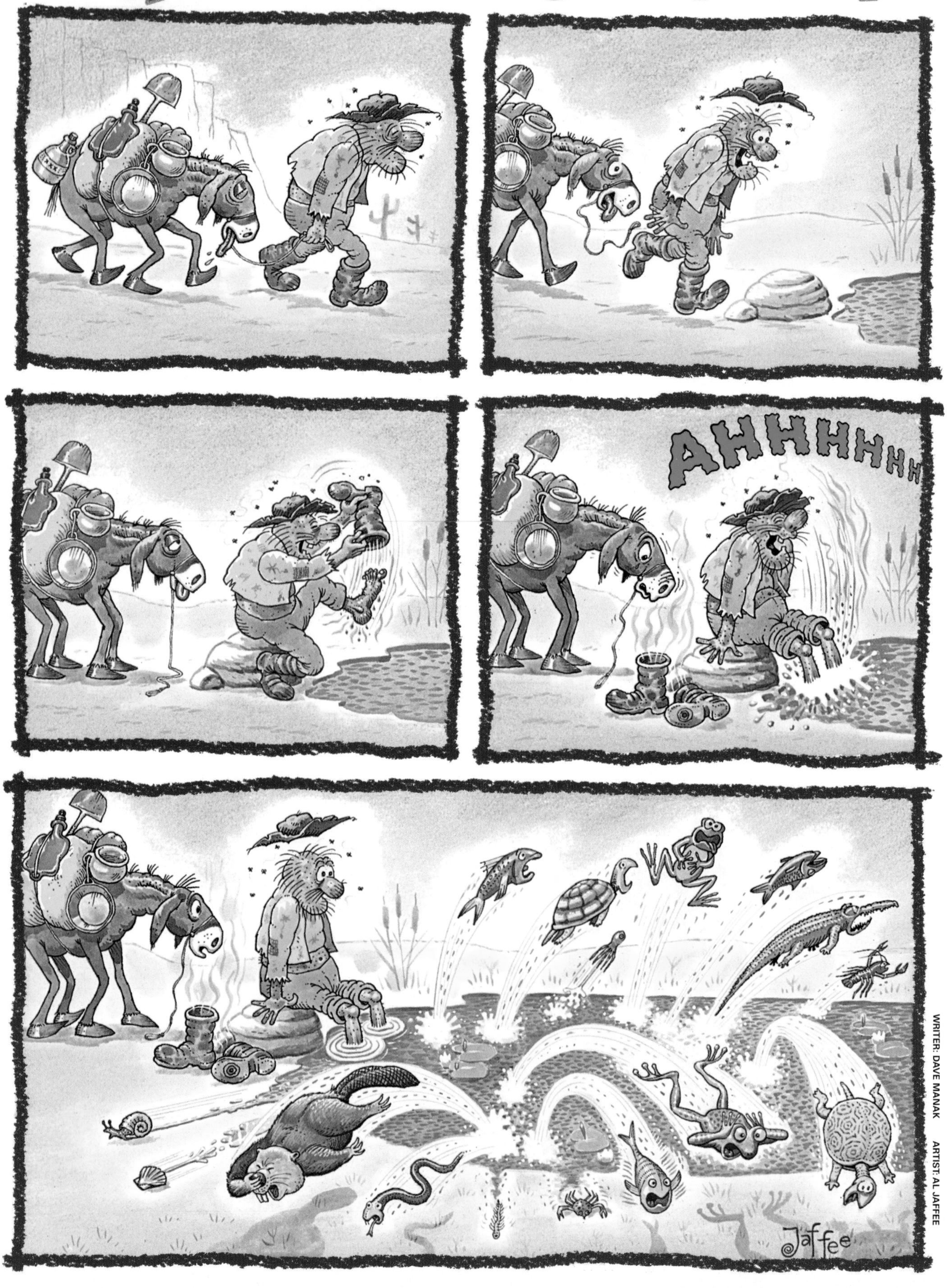

AHHHHHH
Jaffee

WRITER: DAVE MANAK ARTIST: AL JAFFEE

PEN AND STINK DEPT.

The COMIC CLUB

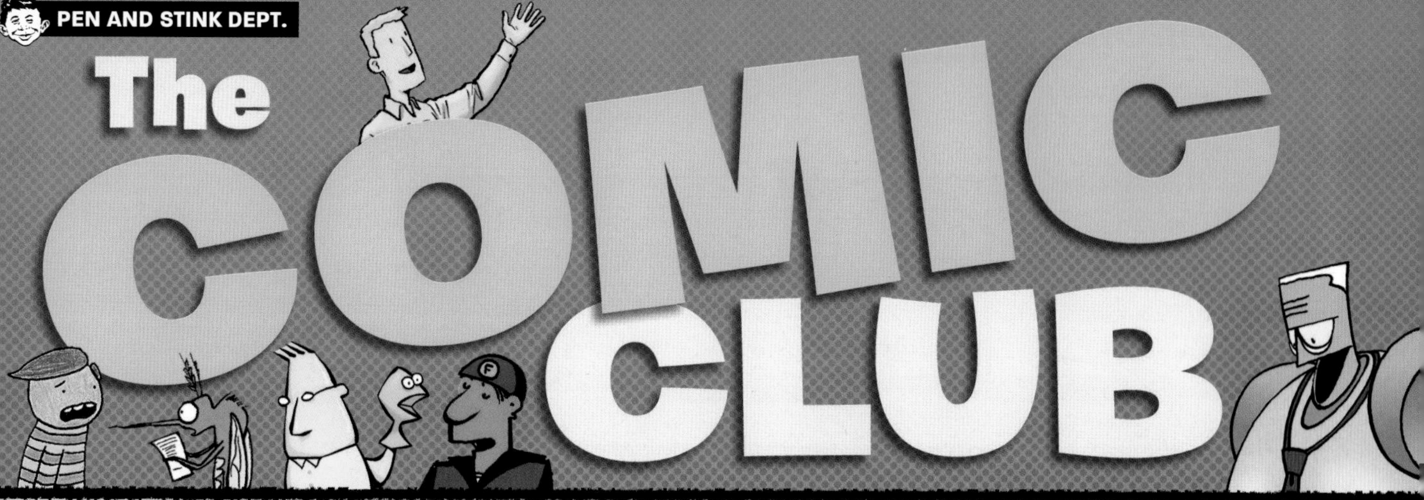

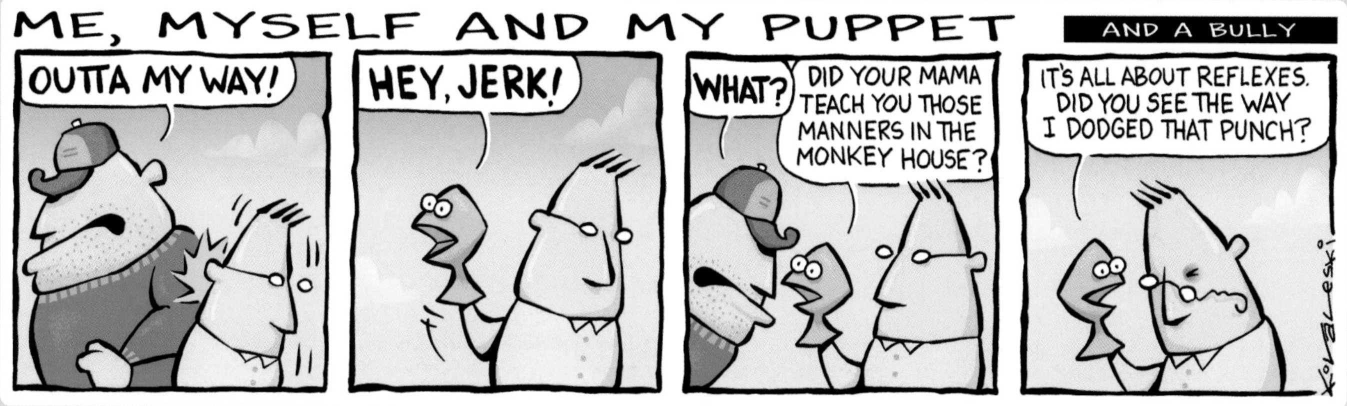
ME, MYSELF AND MY PUPPET
AND A BULLY
OUTTA MY WAY!
HEY, JERK!
WHAT?
DID YOUR MAMA TEACH YOU THOSE MANNERS IN THE MONKEY HOUSE?
IT'S ALL ABOUT REFLEXES. DID YOU SEE THE WAY I DODGED THAT PUNCH?
Kovaleski

JOHN KOVALESKI

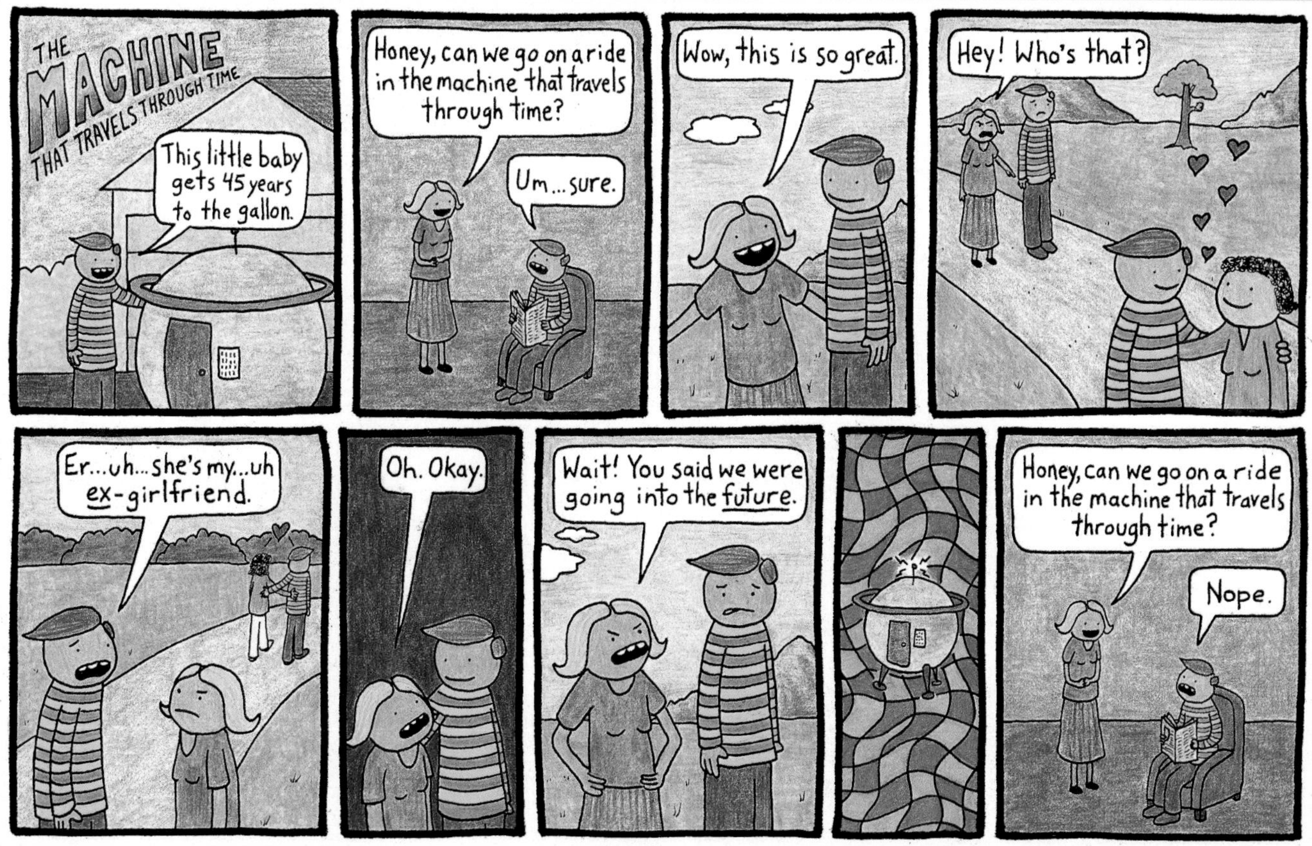
THE MACHINE THAT TRAVELS THROUGH TIME
This little baby gets 45 years to the gallon.
Honey, can we go on a ride in the machine that travels through time?
Um... sure.
Wow, this is so great.
Hey! Who's that?
Er...uh...she's my...uh ex-girlfriend.
Oh. Okay.
Wait! You said we were going into the future.
Honey, can we go on a ride in the machine that travels through time?
Nope.

JOEY ALISON SAYERS

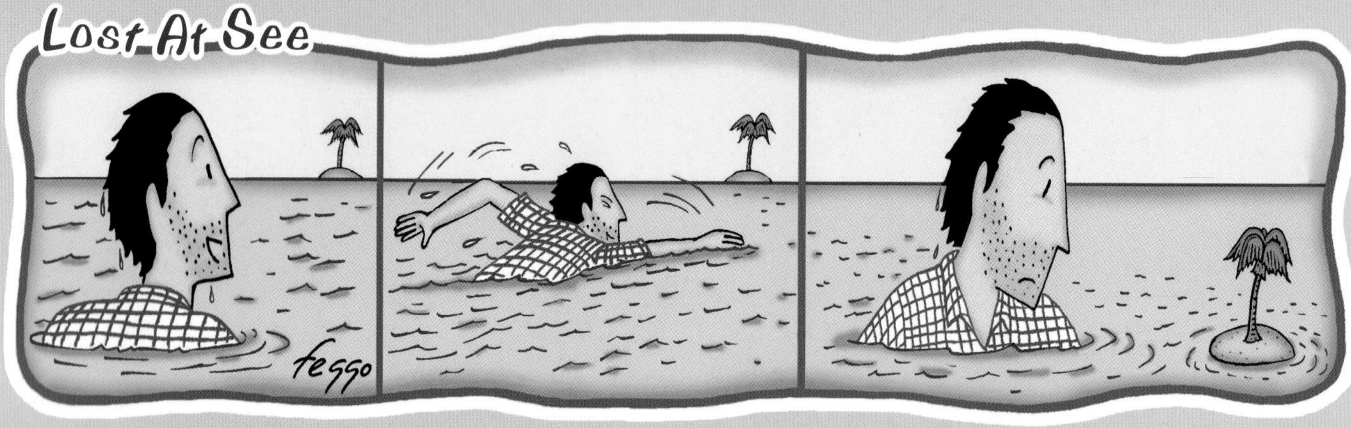
Lost At See
feggo

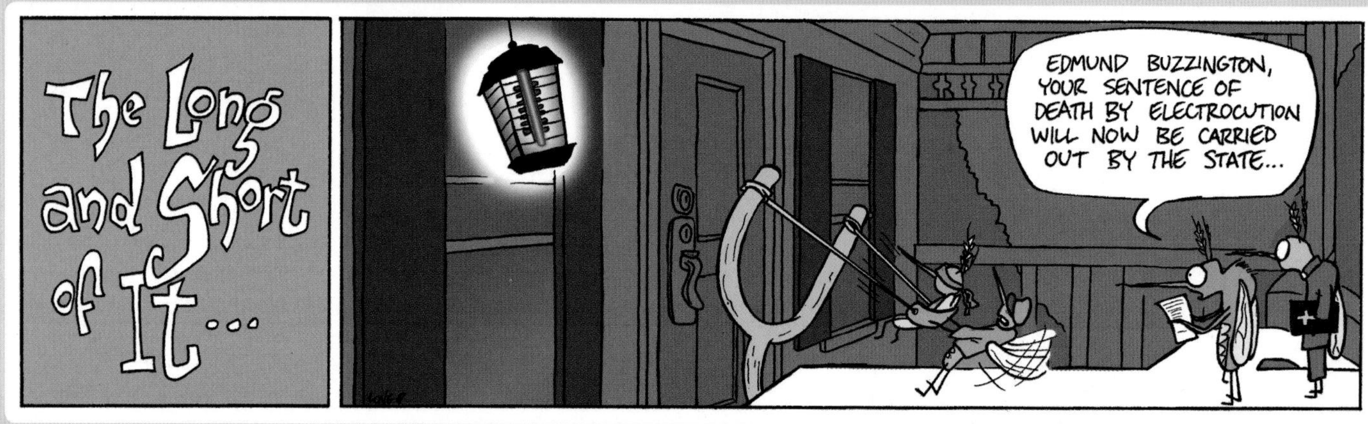
The Long and Short of It...
EDMUND BUZZINGTON, YOUR SENTENCE OF DEATH BY ELECTROCUTION WILL NOW BE CARRIED OUT BY THE STATE...

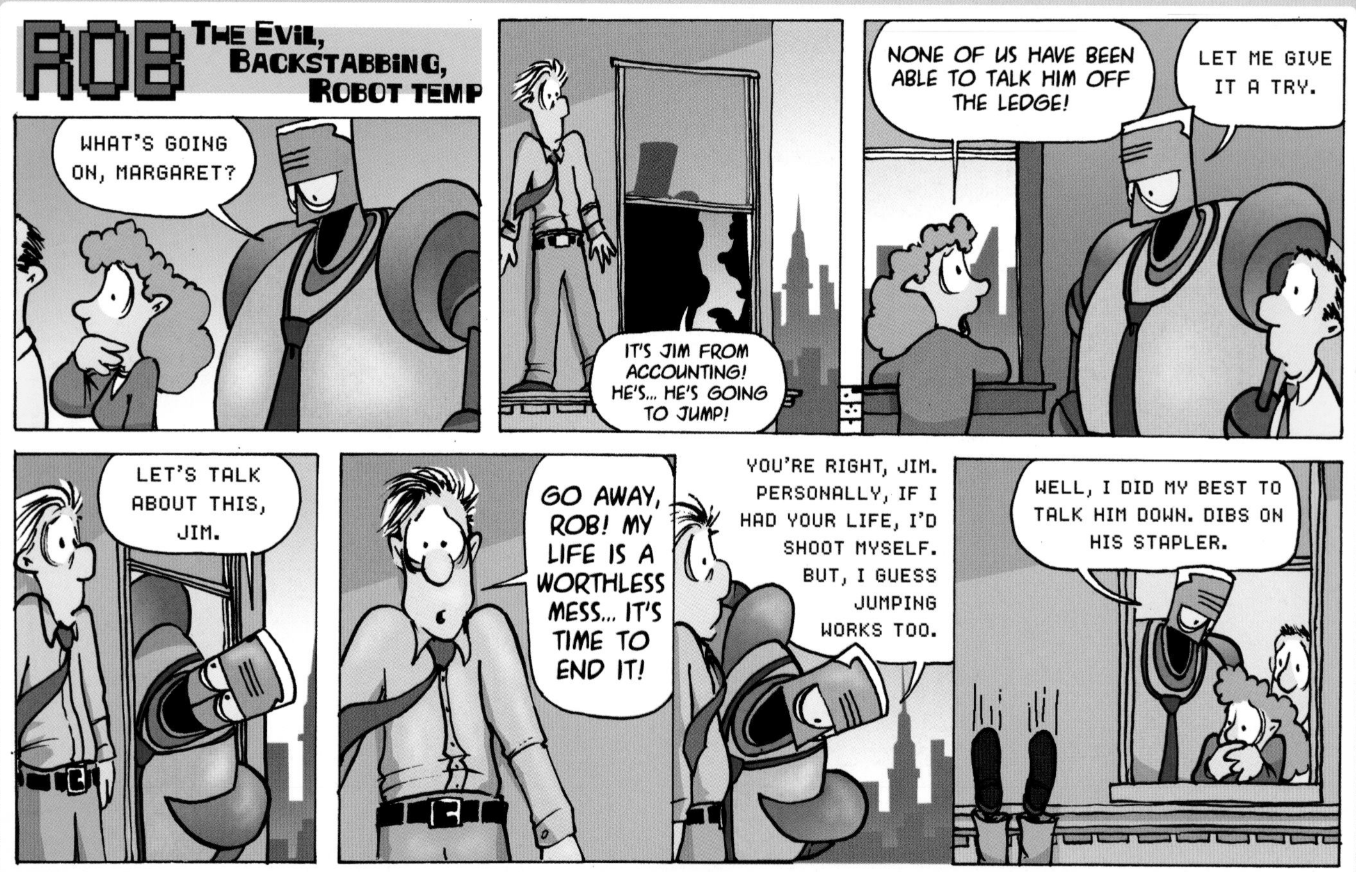
ROB THE EVIL, BACKSTABBING, ROBOT TEMP
WHAT'S GOING ON, MARGARET?
IT'S JIM FROM ACCOUNTING! HE'S... HE'S GOING TO JUMP!
NONE OF US HAVE BEEN ABLE TO TALK HIM OFF THE LEDGE!
LET ME GIVE IT A TRY.
LET'S TALK ABOUT THIS, JIM.
GO AWAY, ROB! MY LIFE IS A WORTHLESS MESS... IT'S TIME TO END IT!
YOU'RE RIGHT, JIM. PERSONALLY, IF I HAD YOUR LIFE, I'D SHOOT MYSELF. BUT, I GUESS JUMPING WORKS TOO.
WELL, I DID MY BEST TO TALK HIM DOWN. DIBS ON HIS STAPLER.

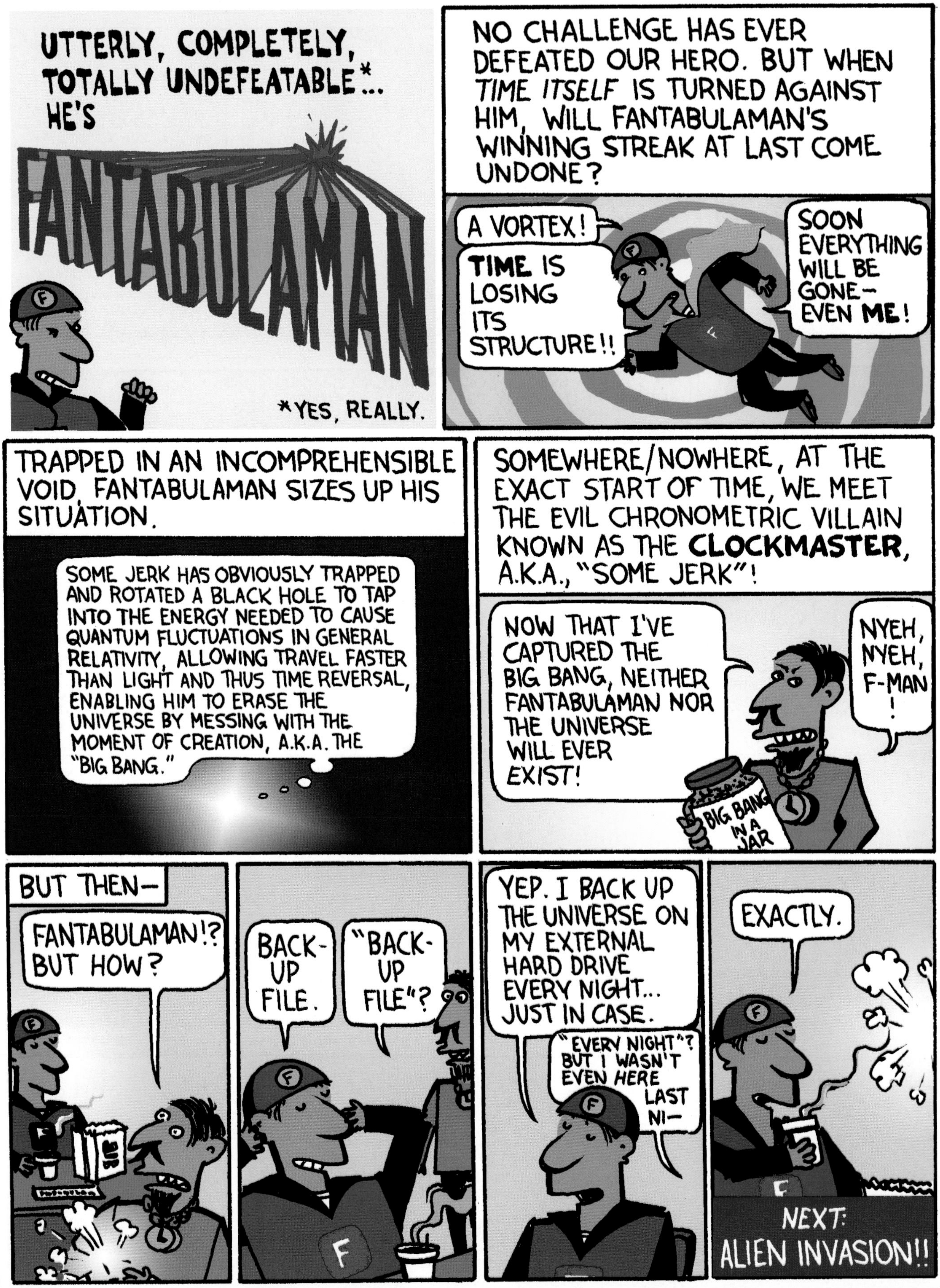

UTTERLY, COMPLETELY, TOTALLY UNDEFEATABLE*... HE'S
FANTABULAMAN
*YES, REALLY.
NO CHALLENGE HAS EVER DEFEATED OUR HERO. BUT WHEN TIME ITSELF IS TURNED AGAINST HIM, WILL FANTABULAMAN'S WINNING STREAK AT LAST COME UNDONE?
A VORTEX!
TIME IS LOSING ITS STRUCTURE!!
SOON EVERYTHING WILL BE GONE— EVEN ME!
TRAPPED IN AN INCOMPREHENSIBLE VOID, FANTABULAMAN SIZES UP HIS SITUATION.
SOME JERK HAS OBVIOUSLY TRAPPED AND ROTATED A BLACK HOLE TO TAP INTO THE ENERGY NEEDED TO CAUSE QUANTUM FLUCTUATIONS IN GENERAL RELATIVITY, ALLOWING TRAVEL FASTER THAN LIGHT AND THUS TIME REVERSAL, ENABLING HIM TO ERASE THE UNIVERSE BY MESSING WITH THE MOMENT OF CREATION, A.K.A. THE "BIG BANG."
SOMEWHERE/NOWHERE, AT THE EXACT START OF TIME, WE MEET THE EVIL CHRONOMETRIC VILLAIN KNOWN AS THE CLOCKMASTER, A.K.A., "SOME JERK"!
NOW THAT I'VE CAPTURED THE BIG BANG, NEITHER FANTABULAMAN NOR THE UNIVERSE WILL EVER EXIST!
NYEH, NYEH, F-MAN!
BIG BANG IN A JAR
BUT THEN—
FANTABULAMAN!? BUT HOW?
BACK-UP FILE.
"BACK-UP FILE"?
YEP. I BACK UP THE UNIVERSE ON MY EXTERNAL HARD DRIVE EVERY NIGHT... JUST IN CASE.
"EVERY NIGHT"? BUT I WASN'T EVEN HERE LAST NI—
EXACTLY.
NEXT: ALIEN INVASION!!

TED RALL

VICTORY ROLL!

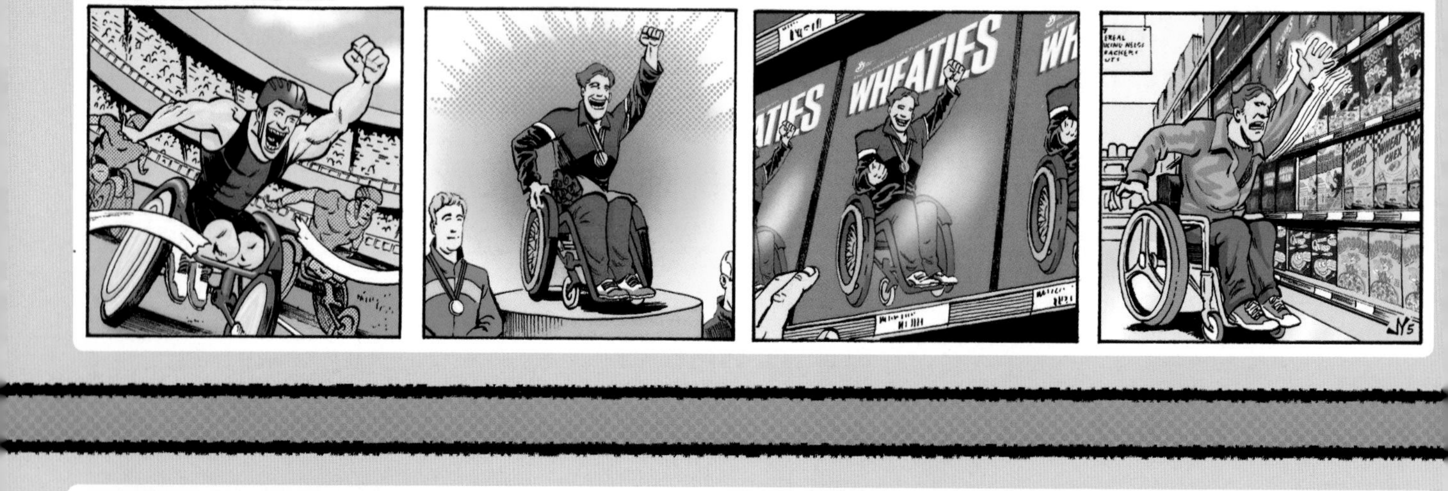

WHEATIES
WHEATIES

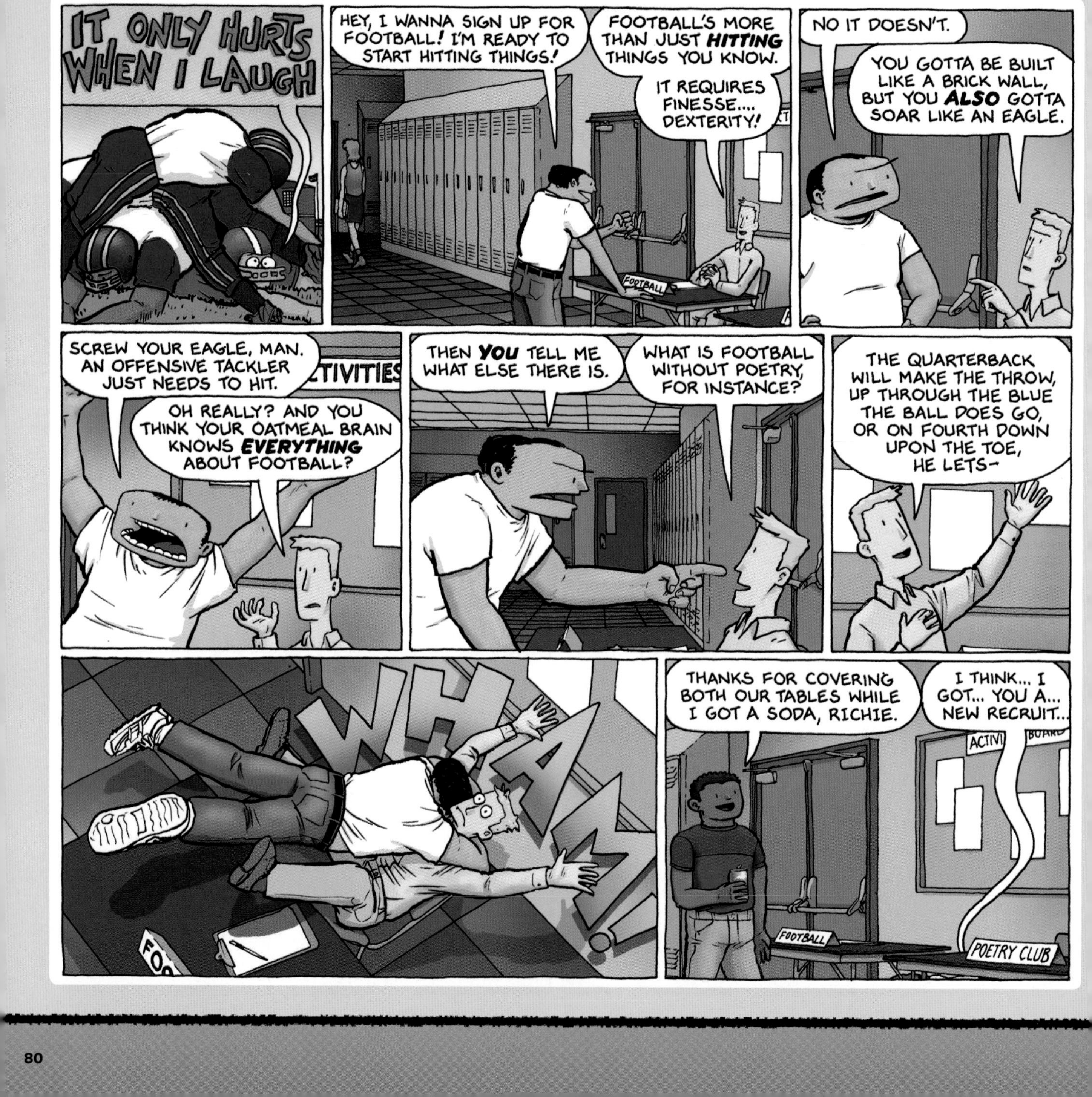

IT ONLY HURTS WHEN I LAUGH
HEY, I WANNA SIGN UP FOR FOOTBALL! I'M READY TO START HITTING THINGS!
FOOTBALL'S MORE THAN JUST HITTING THINGS YOU KNOW.
IT REQUIRES FINESSE.... DEXTERITY!
FOOTBALL
NO IT DOESN'T.
YOU GOTTA BE BUILT LIKE A BRICK WALL, BUT YOU ALSO GOTTA SOAR LIKE AN EAGLE.
SCREW YOUR EAGLE, MAN. AN OFFENSIVE TACKLER JUST NEEDS TO HIT.
OH REALLY? AND YOU THINK YOUR OATMEAL BRAIN KNOWS EVERYTHING ABOUT FOOTBALL?
THEN YOU TELL ME WHAT ELSE THERE IS.
WHAT IS FOOTBALL WITHOUT POETRY, FOR INSTANCE?
THE QUARTERBACK WILL MAKE THE THROW, UP THROUGH THE BLUE THE BALL DOES GO, OR ON FOURTH DOWN UPON THE TOE, HE LETS–
WHAM
THANKS FOR COVERING BOTH OUR TABLES WHILE I GOT A SODA, RICHIE.
I THINK... I GOT... YOU A... NEW RECRUIT...
FOOTBALL
POETRY CLUB

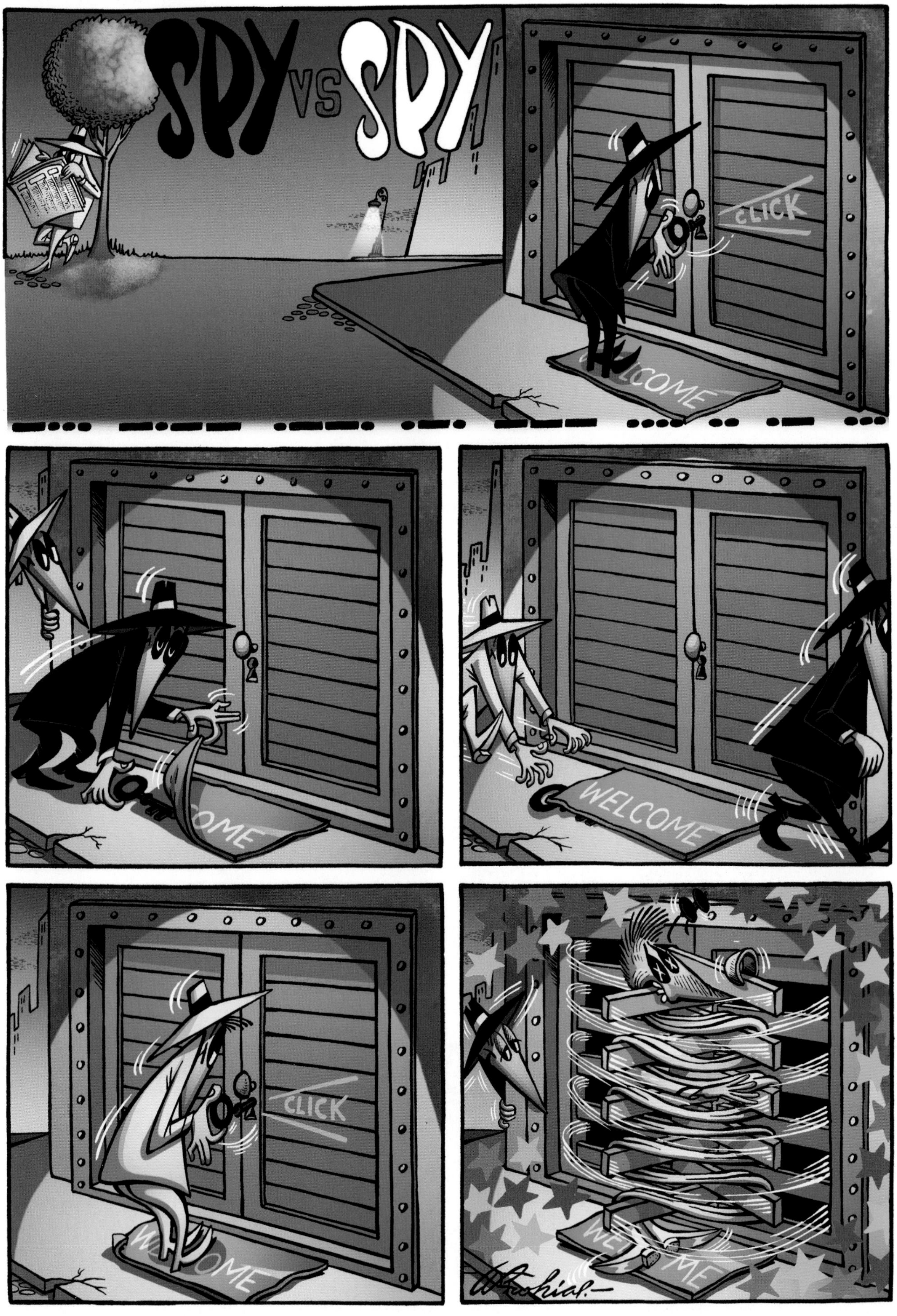
SPY VS SPY
CLICK
WELCOME
WELCOME
CLICK

WRITER AND ARTIST: ANTONIO PROHIAS COLORIST: CARRIE STRACHAN

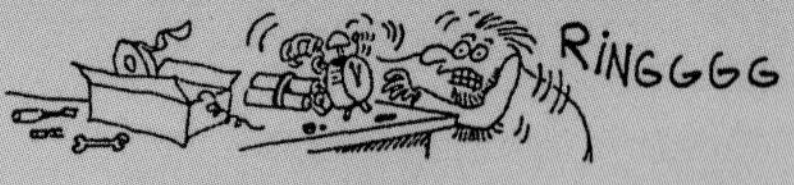
RINGGGG

WEARY OF RELATIVITY DEPT.

As Albert Einstein explained, Time is relative. Which means that, someti
Time passes faster or slower than other times. You find that hard to beli

TIME DRAGS..

TIME DRAGS . . .

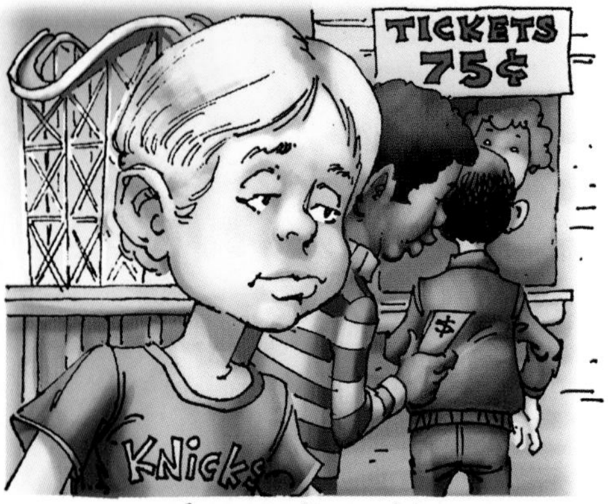
TICKETS
75¢
Knicks

. . . when you're waiting your turn on the roller coaster.

TIME FLIES . . .

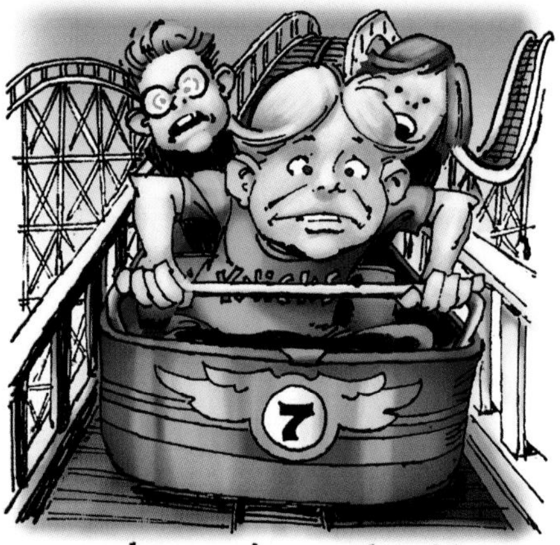
7

. . . when you're on the ride.

TIME DRAGS . . .

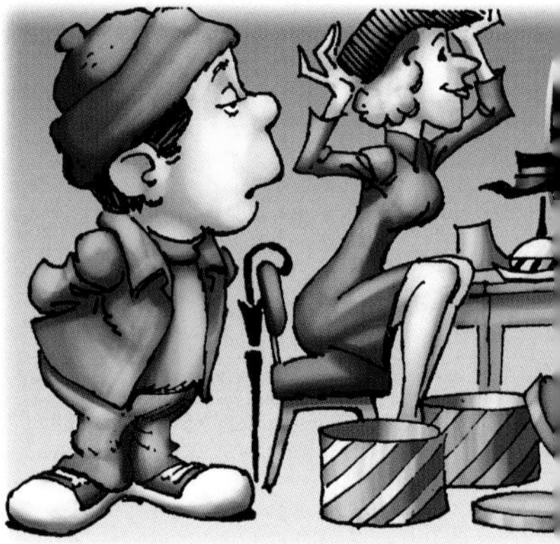

. . . when you're waiting for your Mother in the Hat Department.

TIME DRAGS . . .

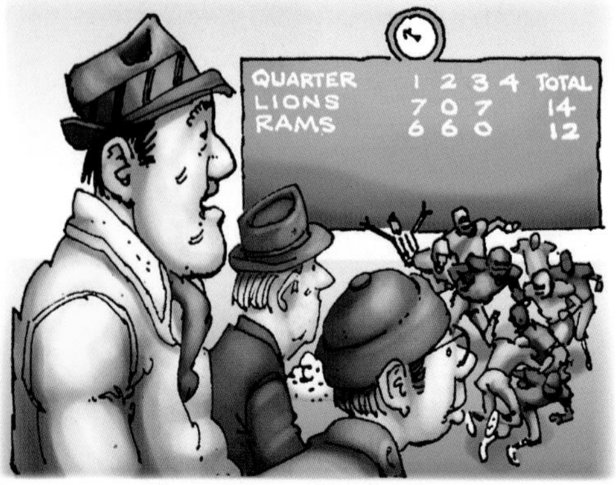
QUARTER 1 2 3 4 TOTAL
LIONS 7 0 7 14
RAMS 6 6 0 12

. . . when your football team is winning by only 2 points.

TIME FLIES . . .

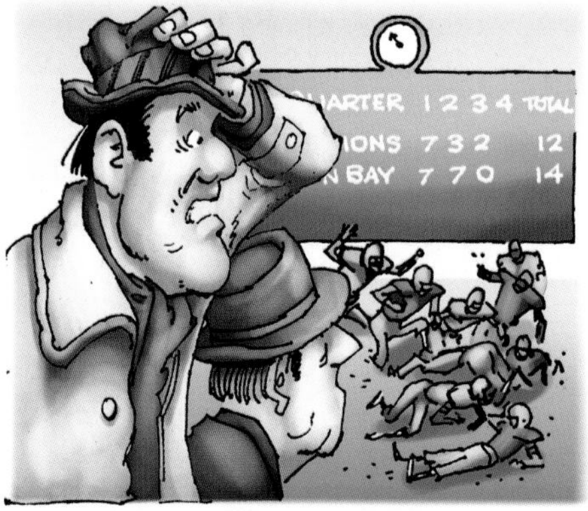

. . . when your football team is losing by only 2 points.

TIME DRAGS . . .

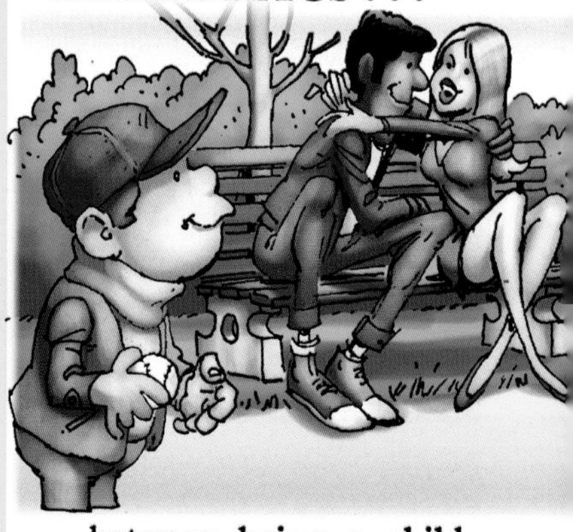

. . . between being a child . . . and becoming a young adult.

TIME DRAGS . . .

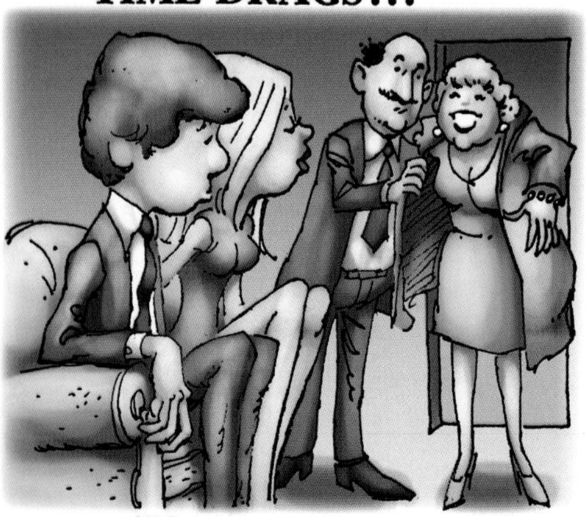

. . . till her parents go out.

TIME FLIES . . .

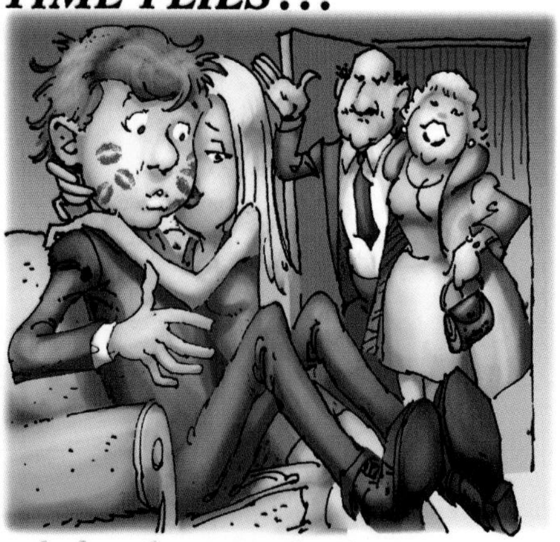

. . . before they come back.

TIME DRAGS . . .

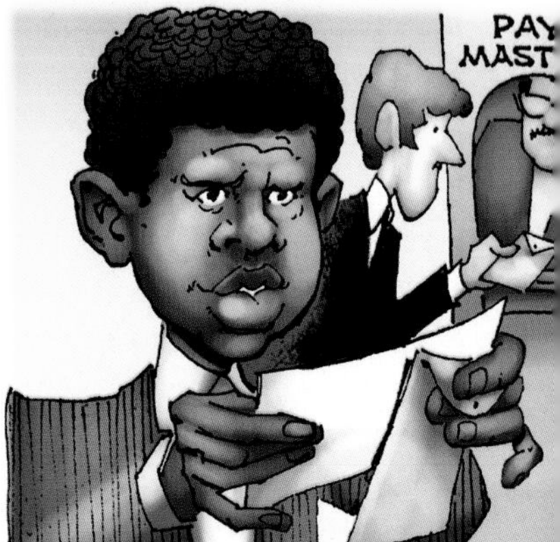

. . . between paychecks.

ell, notice how fast Time goes when you're enjoying yourself, as compared to
w slow it passes when you're reading a dull article like this one, called . . .

WRITER: STAN HART
ARTIST: JACK RICKARD
COLORIST: CARRIE STRACHAN

TIME FLIES...

IME FLIES...

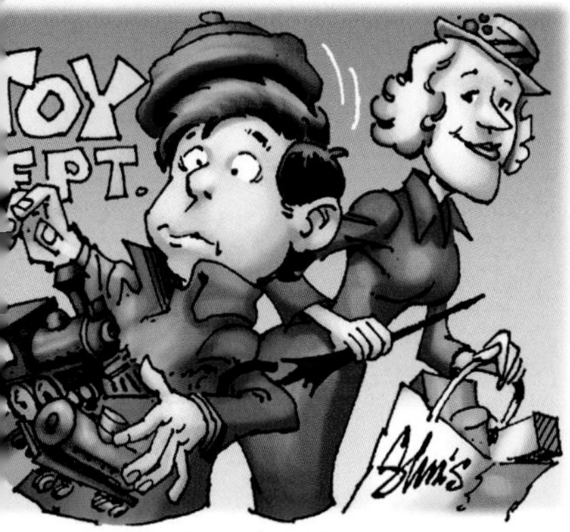

when your Mother is waiting
r you in the Toy Department.

TIME DRAGS...

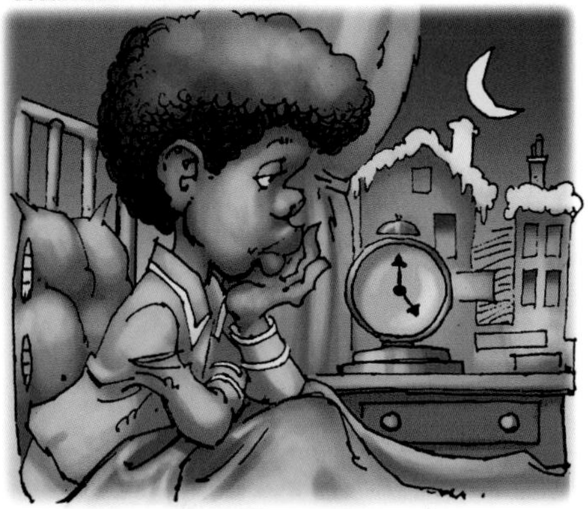

...waiting for Xmas morning,
so you can open your presents.

TIME FLIES...

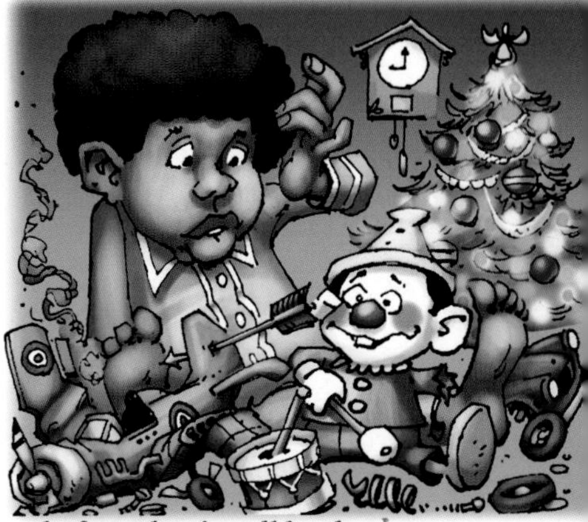

...before they're all broken.

ME FLIES...

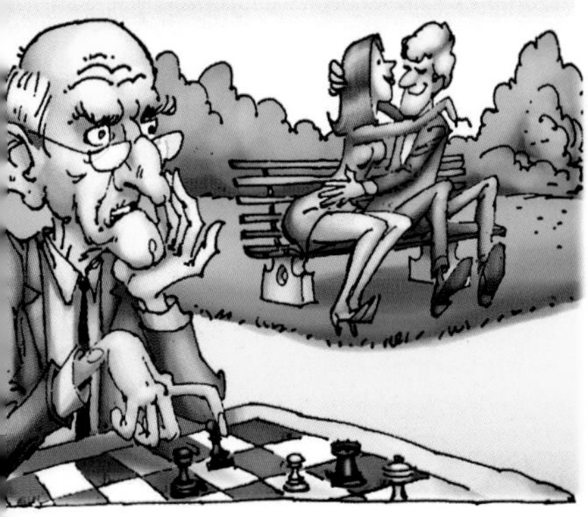

between being a young adult
and becoming an old adult.

TIME DRAGS...

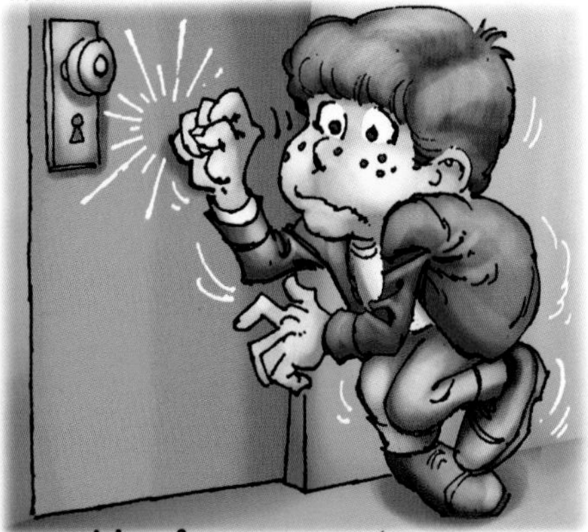

...waiting for someone to
get out of the bathroom.

TIME FLIES...

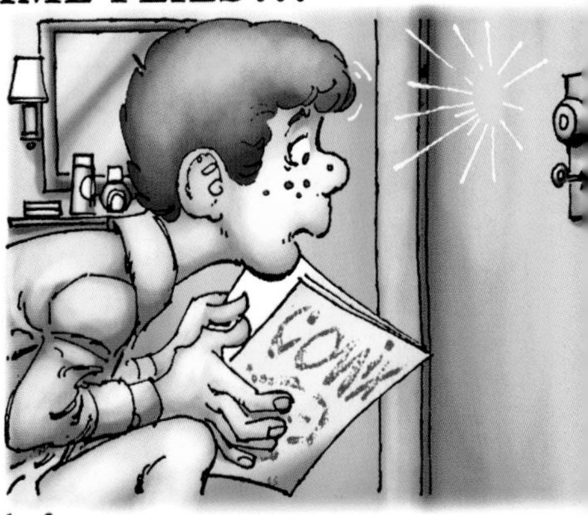

...before someone wants you
to get out of the bathroom.

ME FLIES...

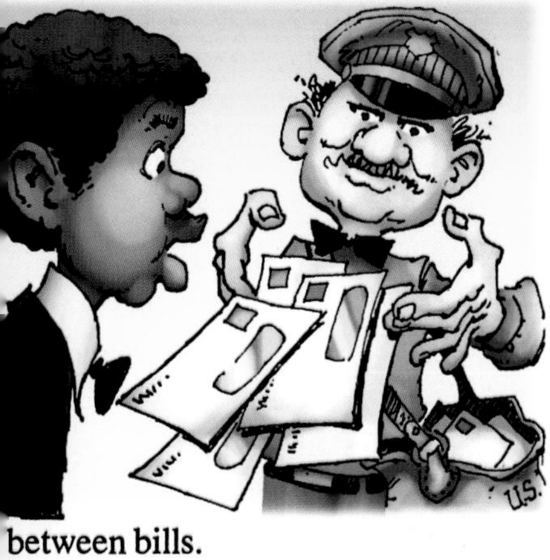

between bills.

TIME FLIES...

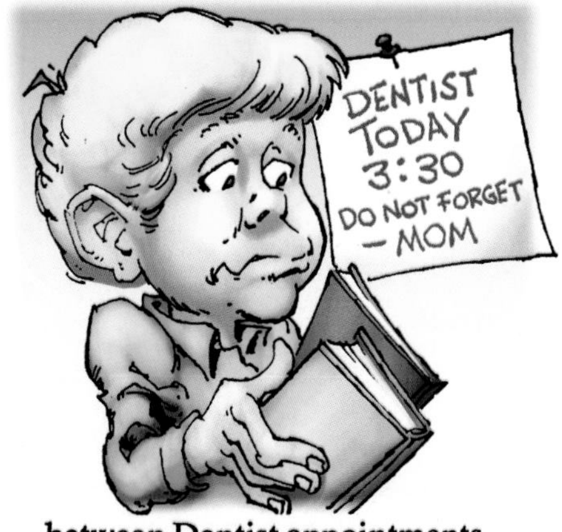
DENTIST
TODAY
3:30
DO NOT FORGET
—MOM

...between Dentist appointments.

TIME DRAGS...

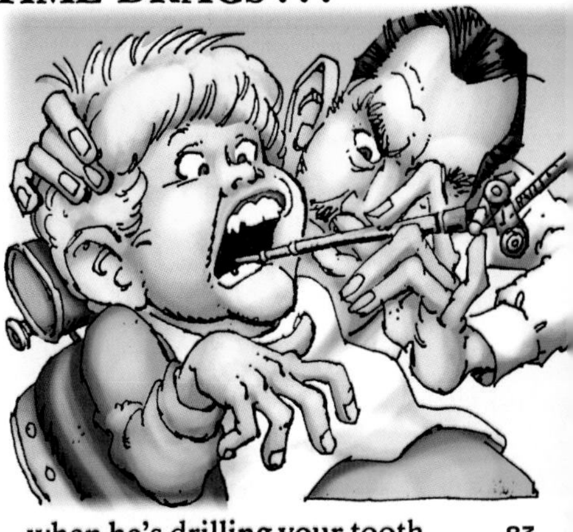

...when he's drilling your tooth.

THE MAG

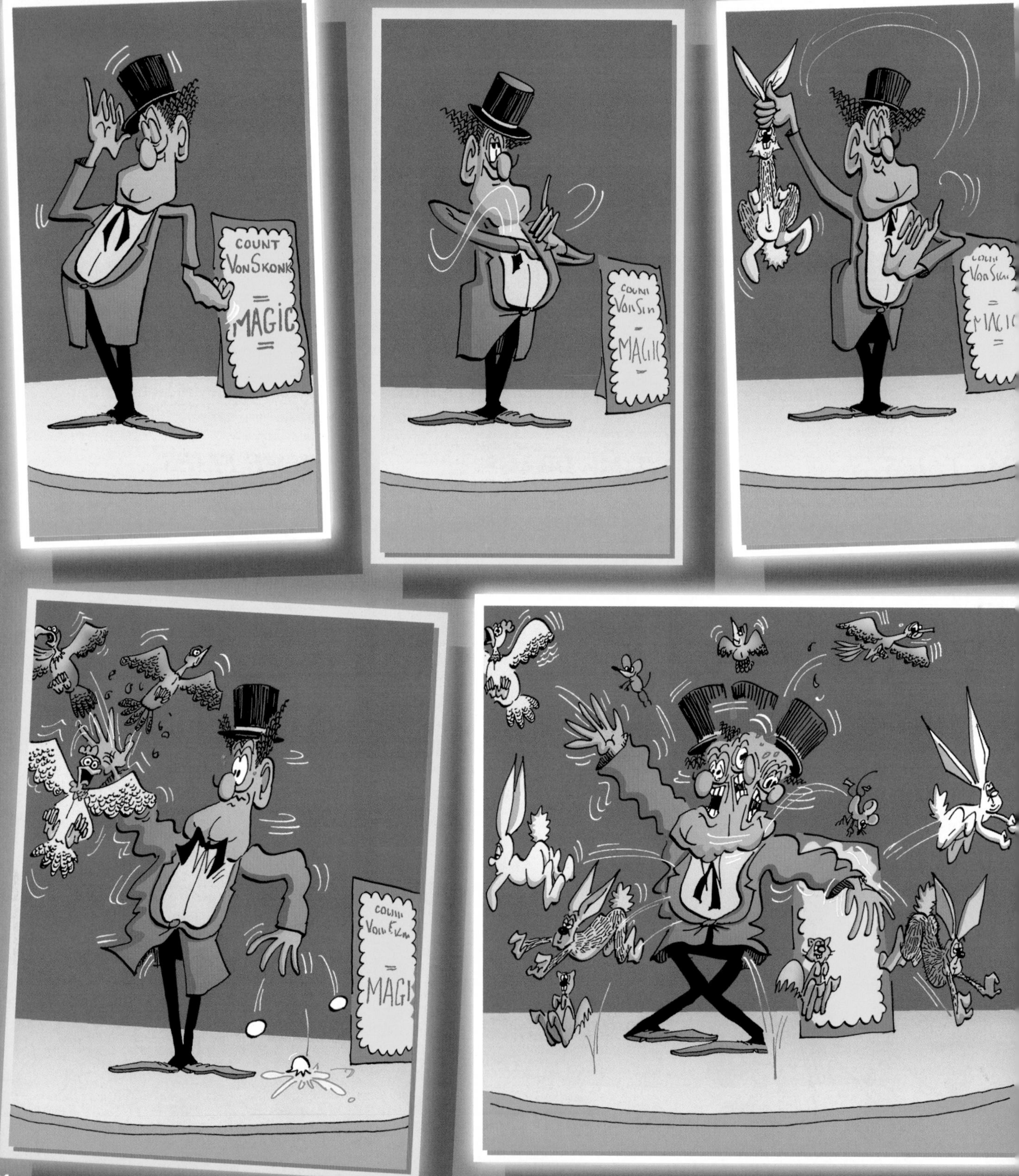
COUNT
VonSkonk
=
MAGIC
=

ICIAN

WRITER AND ARTIST:
DON MARTIN

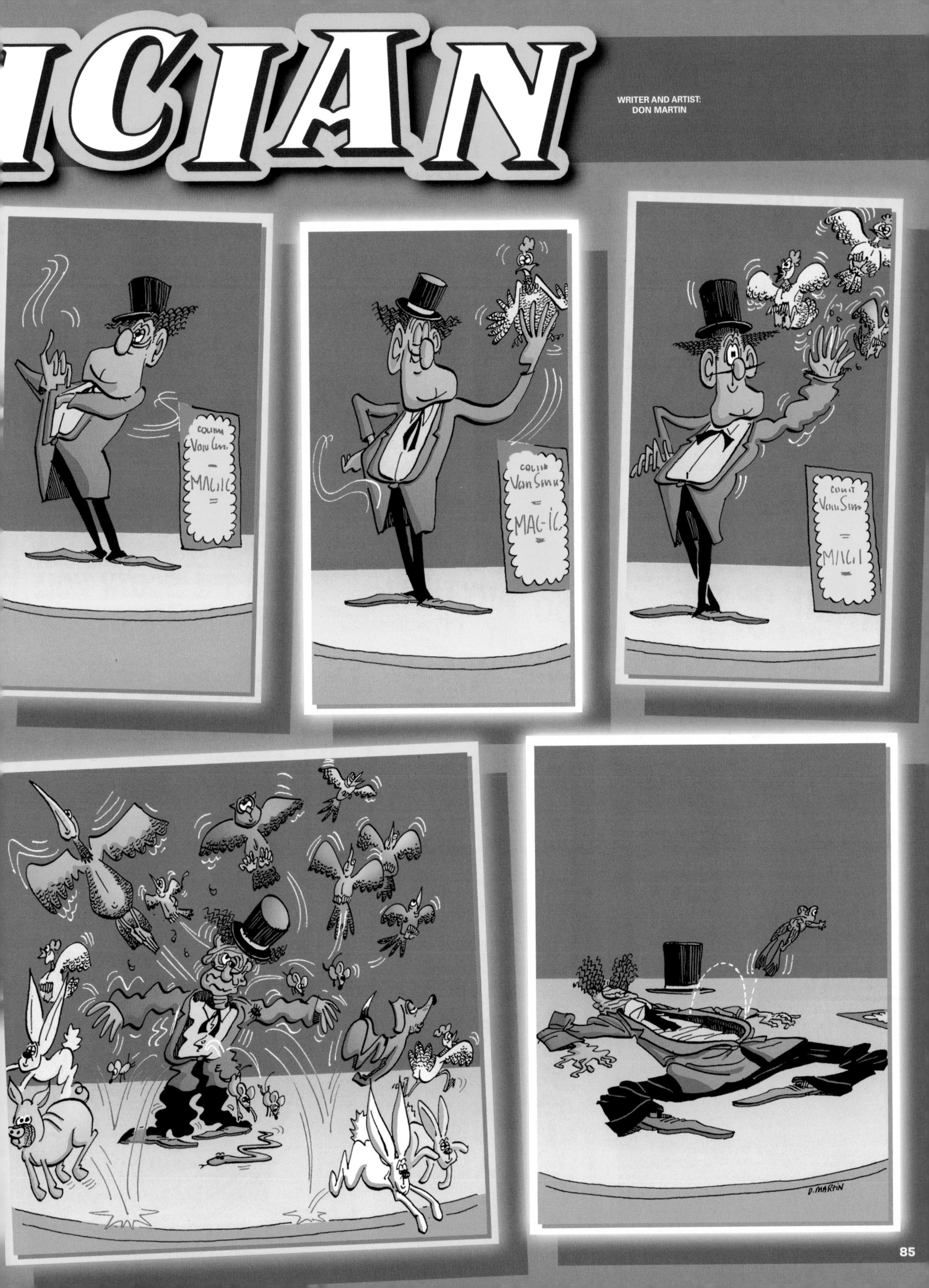
D. MARTIN

MOCK OF THE PENGUINS

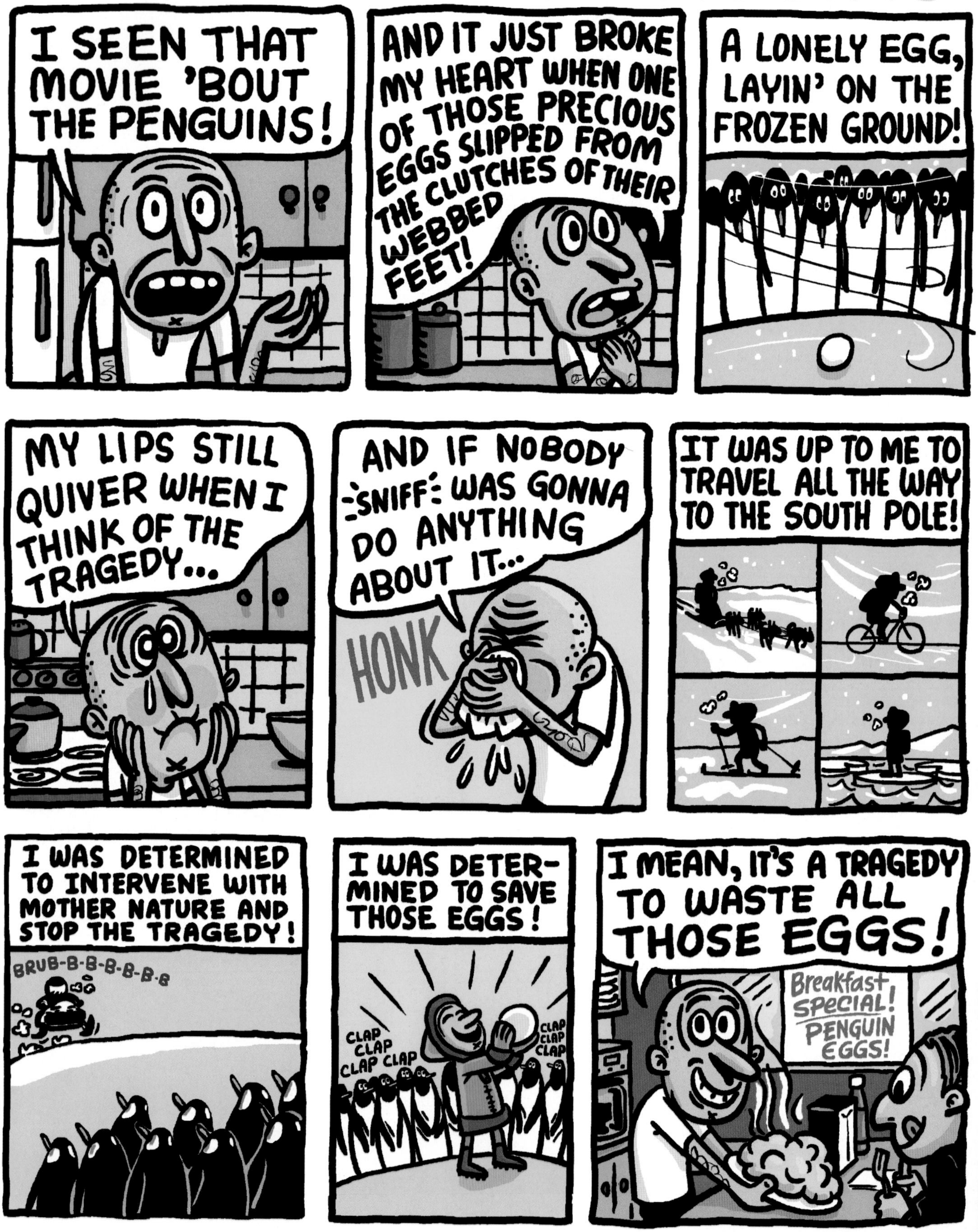

I SEEN THAT MOVIE 'BOUT THE PENGUINS!
AND IT JUST BROKE MY HEART WHEN ONE OF THOSE PRECIOUS EGGS SLIPPED FROM THE CLUTCHES OF THEIR WEBBED FEET!
A LONELY EGG, LAYIN' ON THE FROZEN GROUND!
MY LIPS STILL QUIVER WHEN I THINK OF THE TRAGEDY...
AND IF NOBODY -SNIFF- WAS GONNA DO ANYTHING ABOUT IT...
HONK
IT WAS UP TO ME TO TRAVEL ALL THE WAY TO THE SOUTH POLE!
I WAS DETERMINED TO INTERVENE WITH MOTHER NATURE AND STOP THE TRAGEDY!
BRUB-B-B-B-B-B-B
I WAS DETERMINED TO SAVE THOSE EGGS!
CLAP CLAP CLAP CLAP
CLAP CLAP CLAP
I MEAN, IT'S A TRAGEDY TO WASTE ALL THOSE EGGS!
Breakfast SPECIAL! PENGUIN EGGS!

WRITER AND ARTIST: ERIC SCOTT

Aiiieeeee! Hide the kids! Batten down the hatches! Run for your lives! They're back! Here come the dorks, morons and nerds whose yellow teeth and zit-covered faces fill the rogues' gallery of dweebs we call MAD's...

Video Arcade Personalities

VOLUME II

ARTIST: TOM BUNK
WRITER: SEAN EISENPORTH

POSITION: 07X   TIME:5.03

TOTAL: 3Y-6F:00

THE REFLECTOR

The one thing that arcade players fear most is the dreaded Reflector in their video game screens. Hovering close, staring over their shoulders like some anal-retentive math teacher, this clueless turd is completely unaware of his highly annoying and intrusive presence!

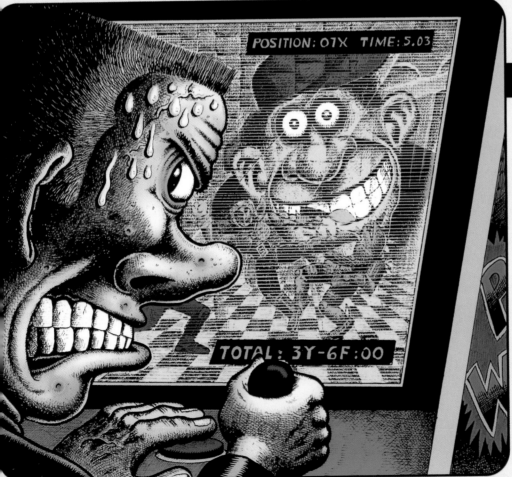

Video Arcade Personalities

THE COAT-HANGER

Beware The Coat-Hanger! This big gooch deliberately hangs his jacket on the joystick of the game next to him hoping that someone will ask him to remove it. The instant the request is made, The Coat-Hanger takes it as his cue to perform radical dental alterations with his steel-toe boots on the poor schmuck who asked him!

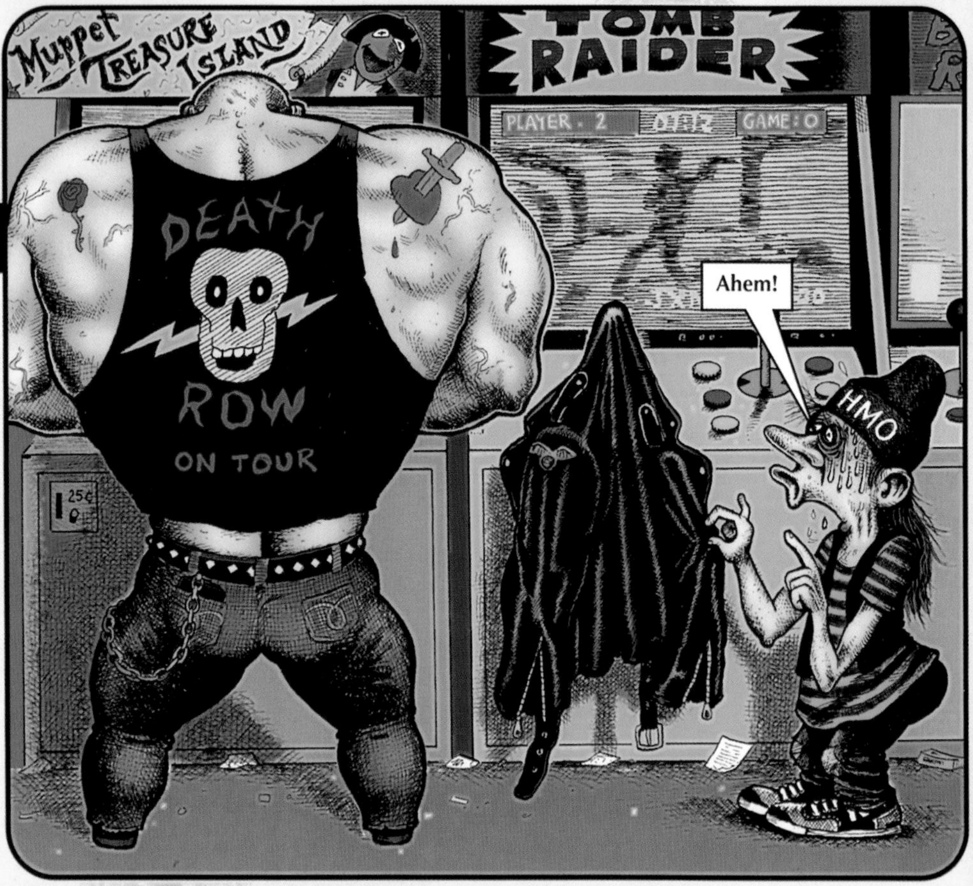

Muppet Treasure Island
TOMB RAIDER
PLAYER - 2
GAME: 0
DEATH
ROW
ON TOUR
25¢
Ahem!
HMO

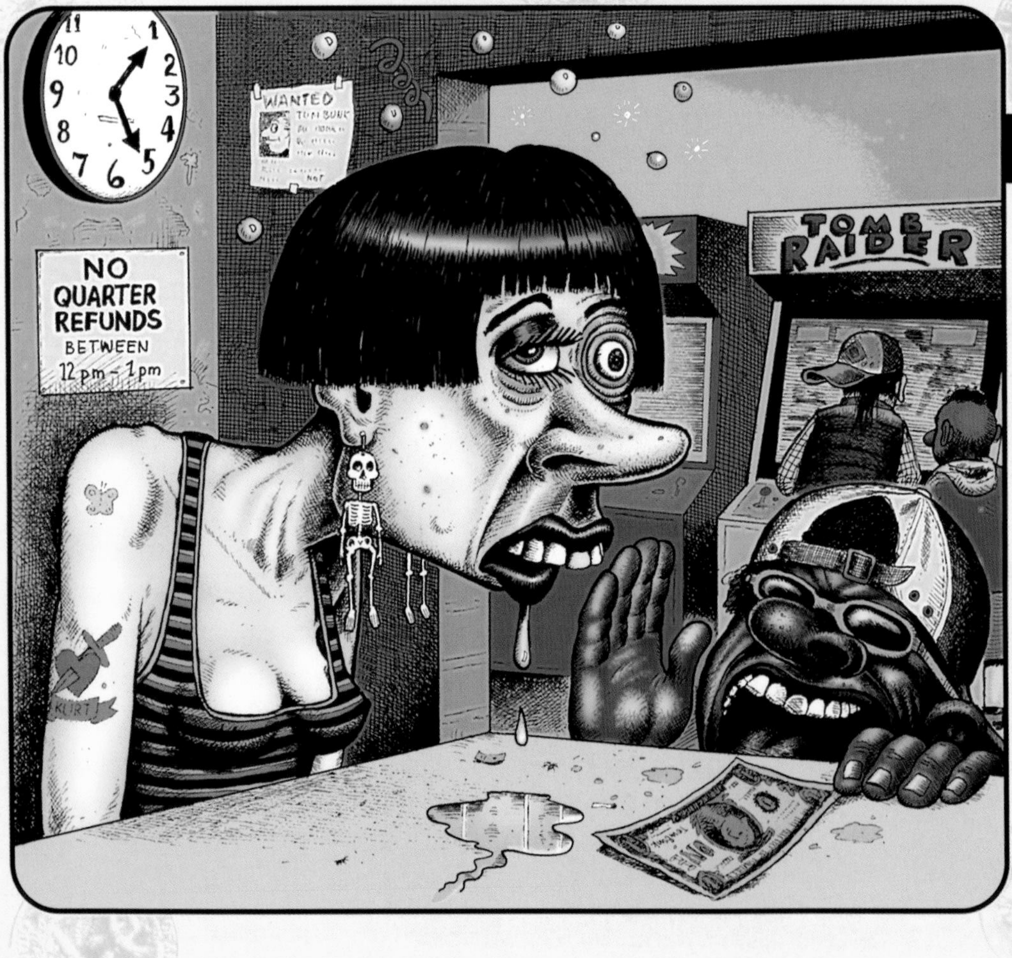

WANTED
NO QUARTER REFUNDS BETWEEN 12pm - 1pm
TOMB RAIDER
KURT

THE LIVING DEAD

She's got no pulse! She's got about as much brain wave activity as a Twinkie! She is The Living Dead! Hey, you'd turn into a mindless, drooling zombie too if the entire purpose of your failed and bleak life was to hand out change all day to a perpetual parade of illiterate, unwashed freaks!

THE CURSOR

You can't always see The Cursor, but you can always hear him! This profane pinhead feels compelled to make his fury known to everyone in the arcade! And the comedic irony of it all is that no matter how much he is enraged by any one particular game, he continues to plop quarters into it! Sheesh! Talk about your pathetic codependent relationships!

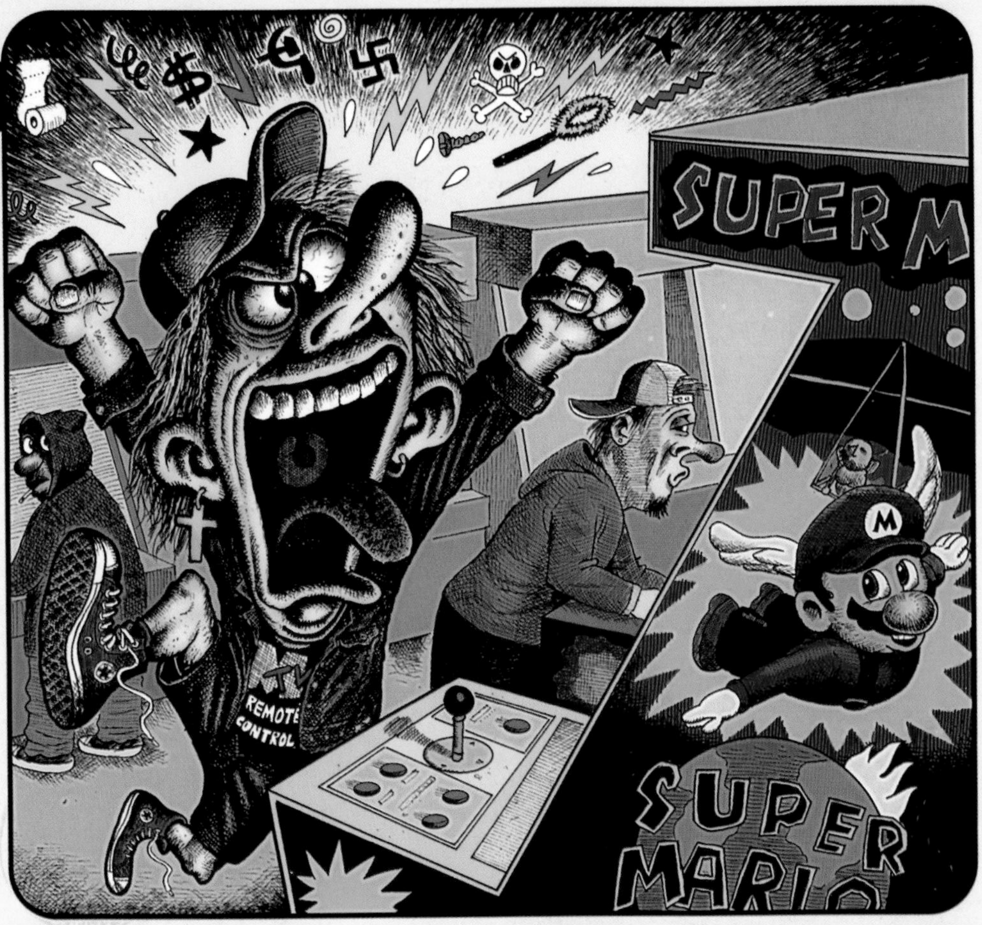
SUPER M
REMOTE CONTROL
SUPER

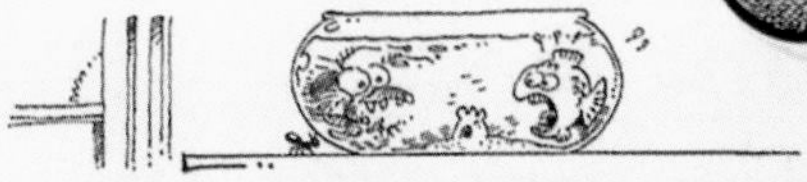

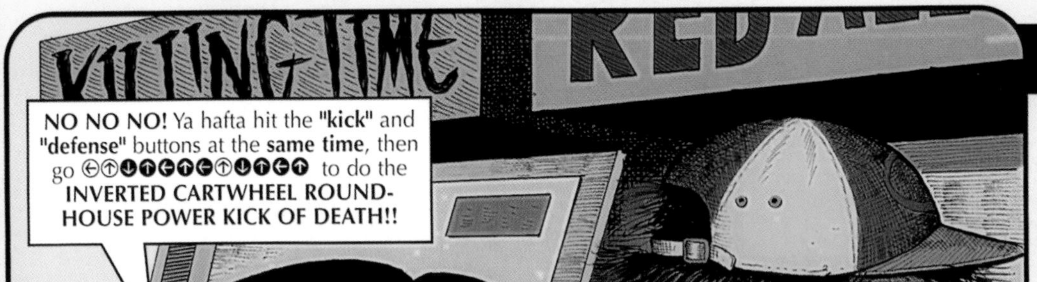
NO NO NO! Ya hafta hit the "kick" and "defense" buttons at the same time, then go ←↑↓↑←↑←↑↓↑←↑ to do the INVERTED CARTWHEEL ROUND-HOUSE POWER KICK OF DEATH!!

THE ADVISOR

The Advisor runs around the arcade spewing his unsolicited advice to many a captive audience. This well-meaning but utterly misguided cretin has made it his life's mission to correct any and all game-playing errors he sees. He has to somehow occupy his time — ever since the editors of the video game magazines stopped printing his obnoxious letters!

BIRTH OF A COMBINATION DEPT.

A few issues back we published a scathing indictment on the unimaginative film industry and its propensity to make sequel upon sequel upon sequel. We continue our puckish criticism of this horrendous practice with this sequel article...

MORE MOVI

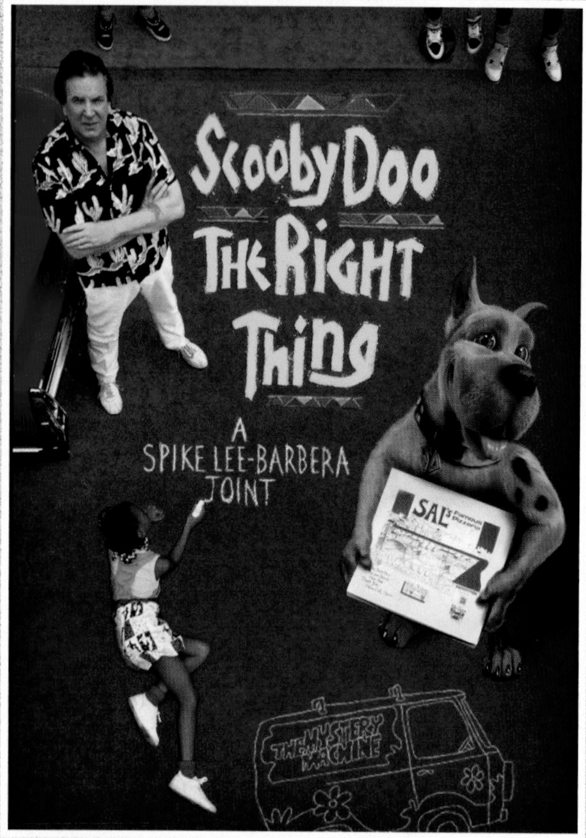

ScoobyDoo
TheRight
Thing
A SPIKE LEE-BARBERA JOINT
SAL'S
THE MYSTERY MACHINE

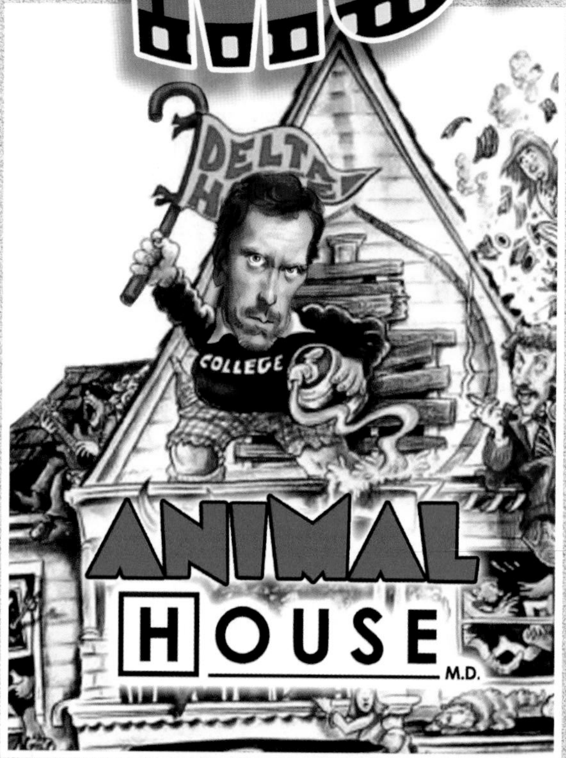

DELTA
COLLEGE
ANIMAL
HOUSE
M.D.

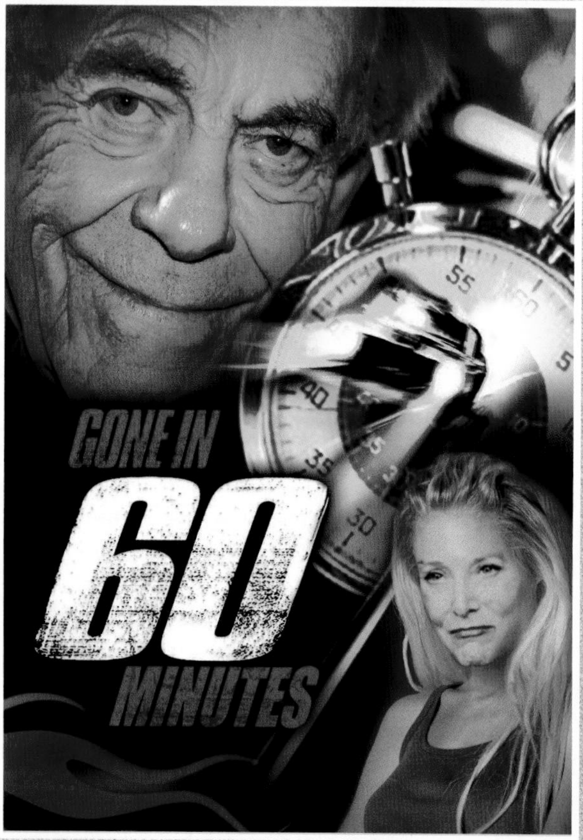

GONE IN
60
MINUTES

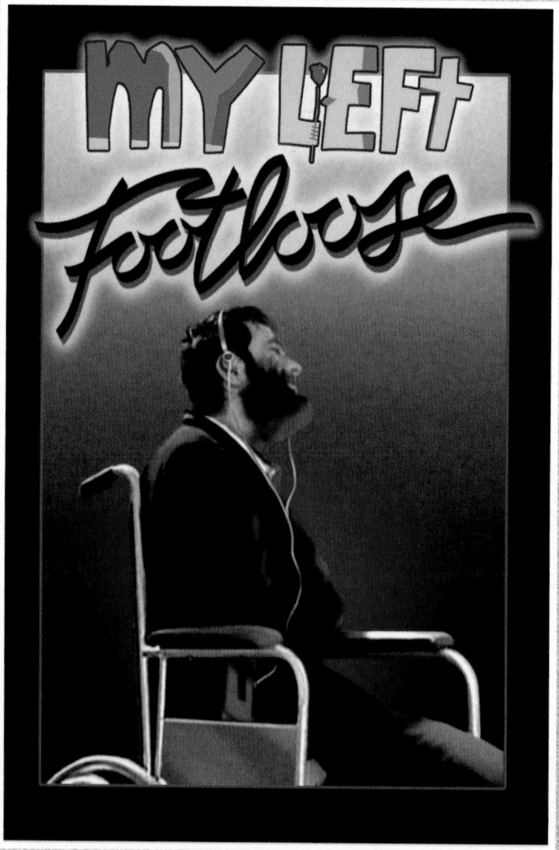

MY LEFT
Footloose

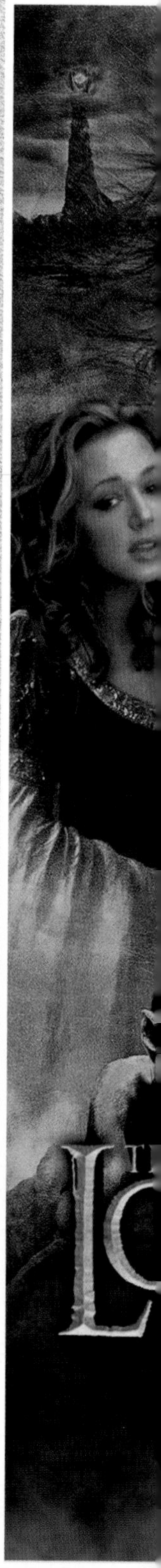

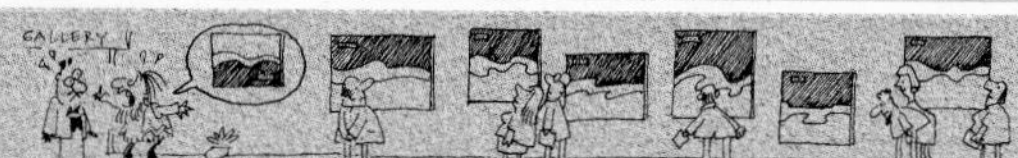

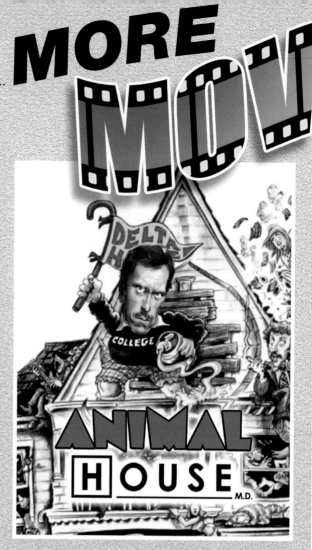

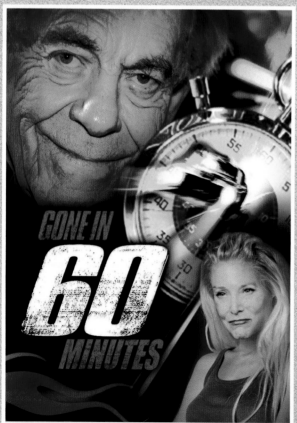

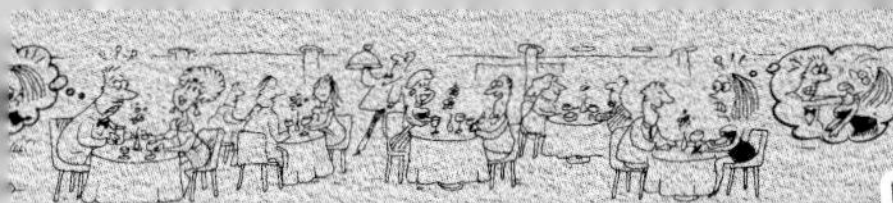

MASHUPS WE'D HATE TO SEE

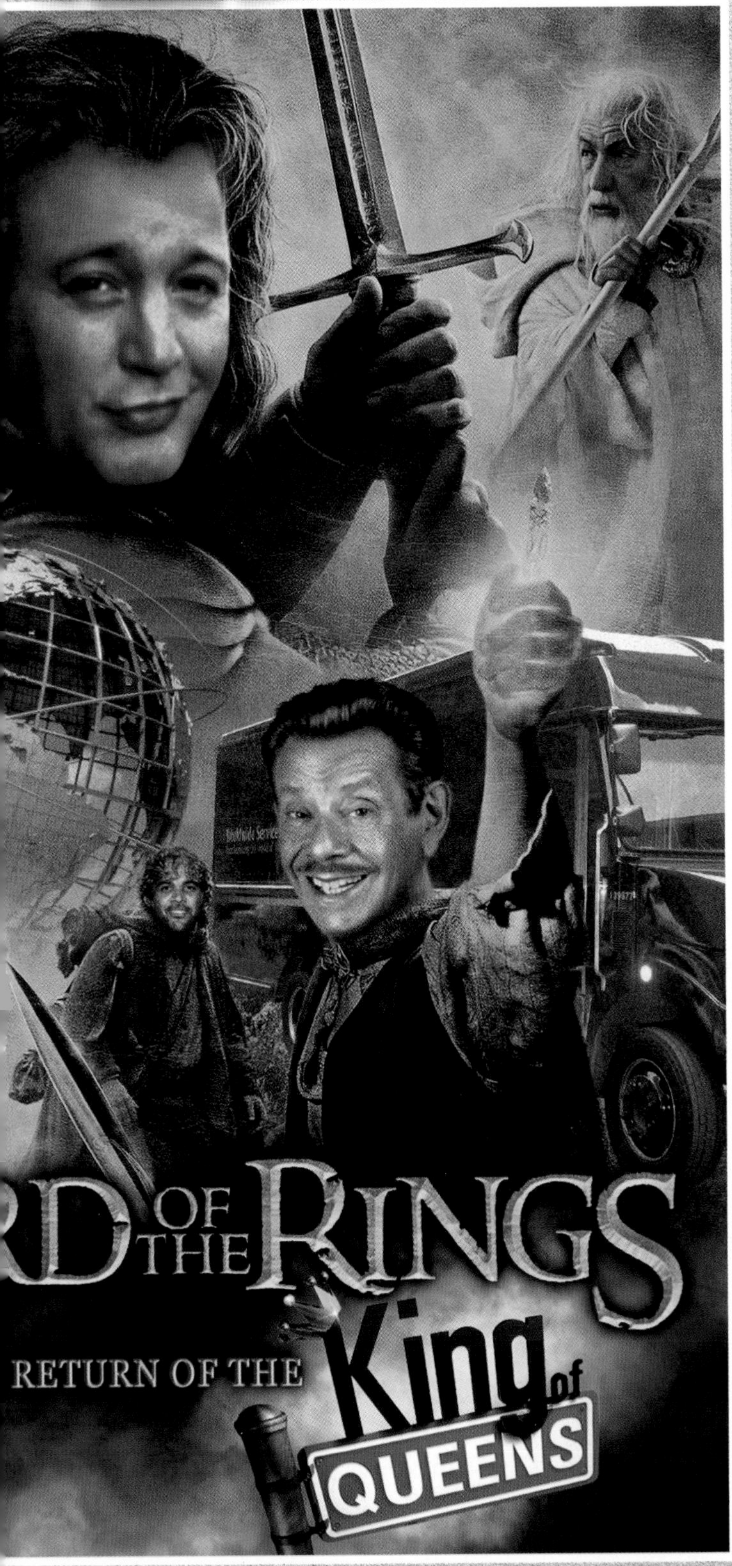

RD OF THE RINGS
RETURN OF THE King of QUEENS

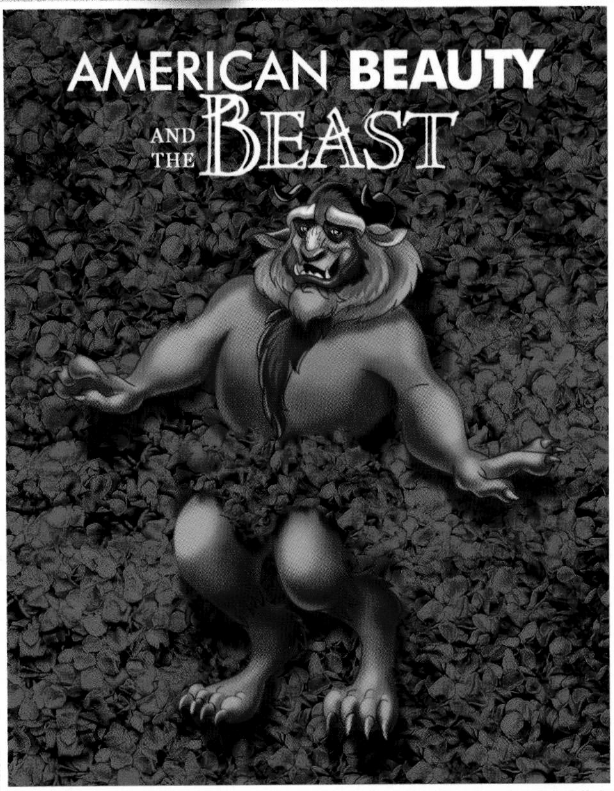

AMERICAN BEAUTY
AND THE BEAST

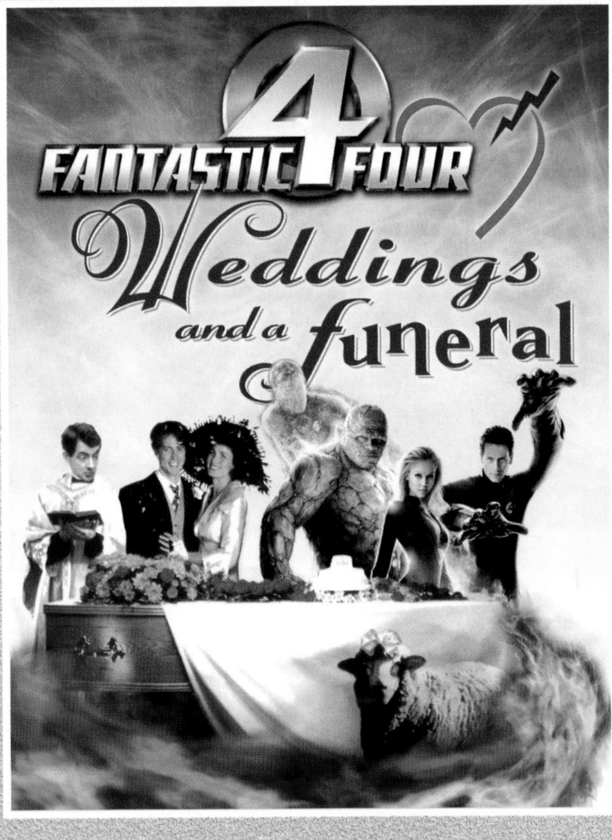

FANTASTIC 4 FOUR
Weddings
and a funeral

ARTIST: SCOTT BRICHER

THE HARDSHIP SUPER OF AMERICA'

THESE DAYS we hear a lot of alarming reports about overweight people. America, it seems, is a nation of fatties getting fatter all the time. But like most alarming reports from the media, you probably shouldn't believe them. The truth is, we've always been a country of overeating heifers, we just didn't have talking heads with hours of television airtime to get us all excited about them. Too bad! If we had TV back in the old West, we could have seen some pretty entertaining special reports, such as...

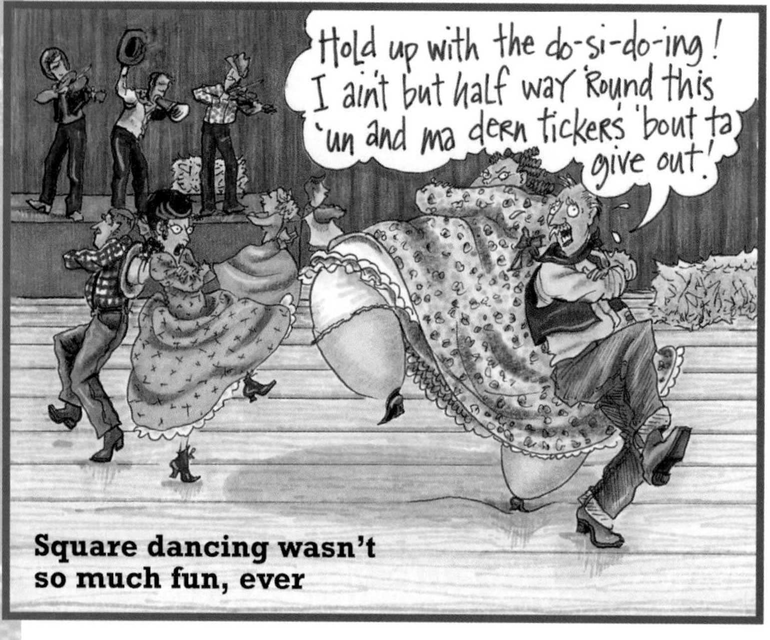
Hold up with the do-si-do-ing! I ain't but half way 'Round this 'un and ma dern tickers 'bout ta give out!

Square dancing wasn't so much fun, ever

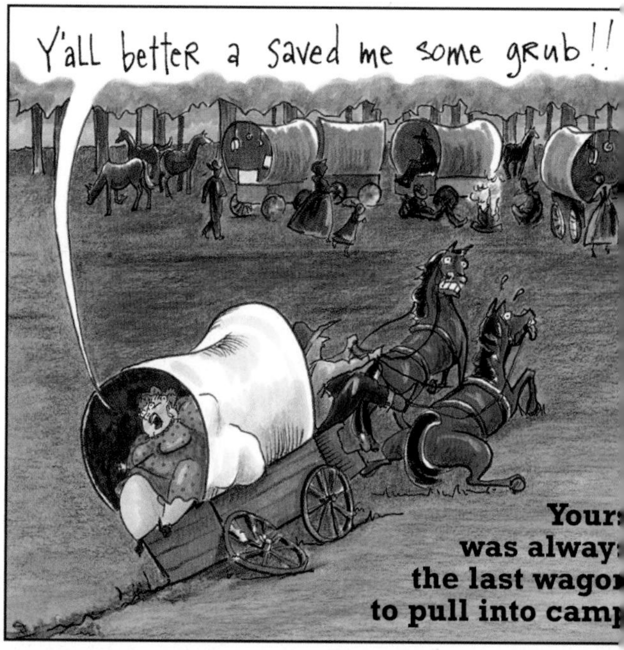
Y'all better a saved me some grub!!

Your: was alway: the last wagon to pull into camp

The seldom-won quick-draw showdowns

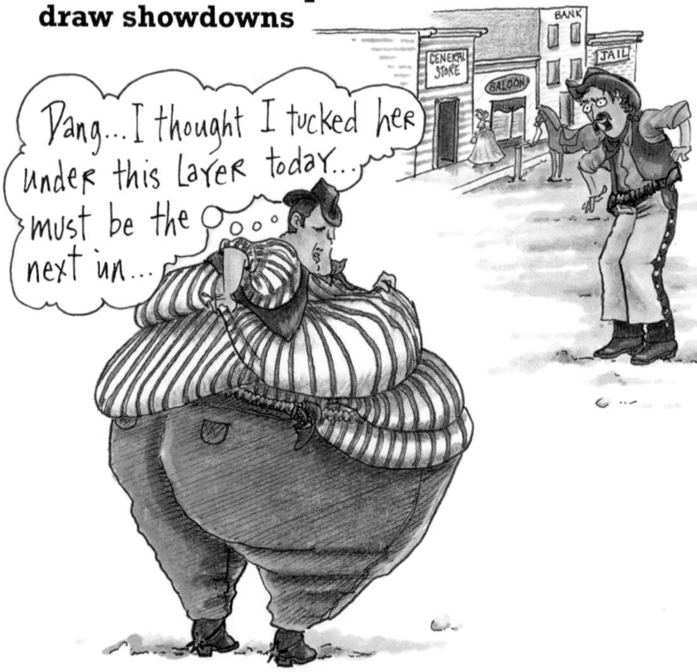
BANK
GENERAL STORE
SALOON
JAIL
Dang... I thought I tucked her under this layer today... must be the next un...

Long, harsh winters left you feeling less like a person and more like a commodity

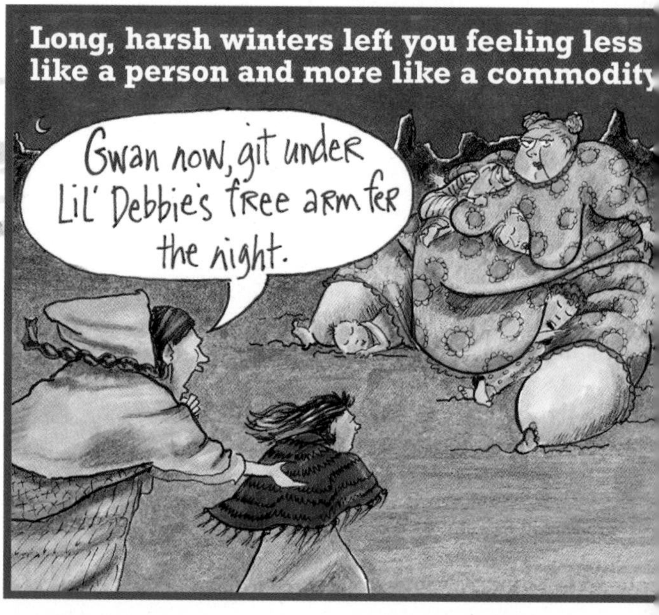
Gwan now, git under Lil' Debbie's free arm fer the night.

WRITER AND ARTIST: TERESA BURNS PARKHURST

ACED BY THE OBESE WILD WEST

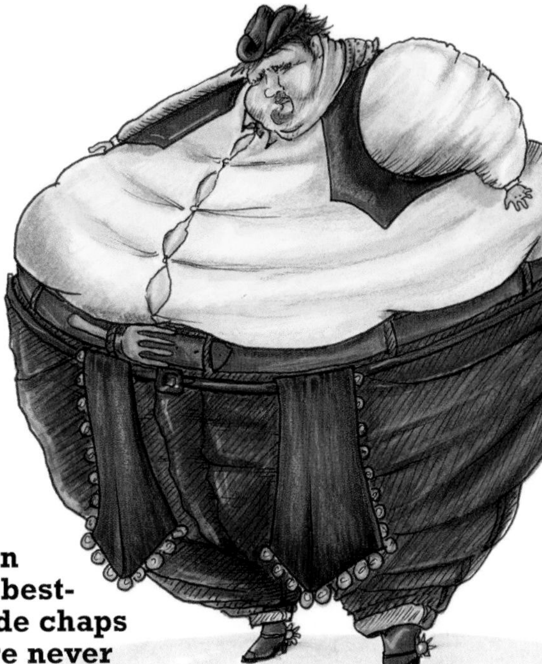

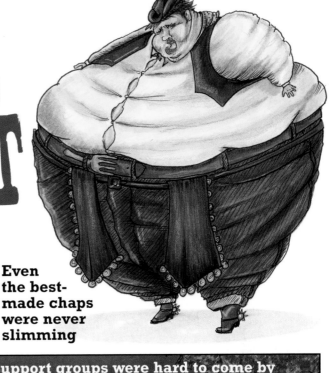

Even the best-made chaps were never slimming

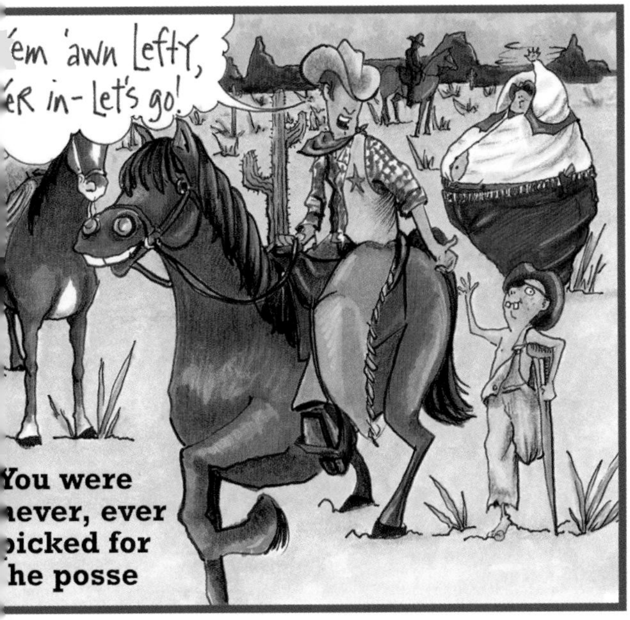
'em 'awn Lefty, ér in- Let's go!

You were never, ever picked for the posse

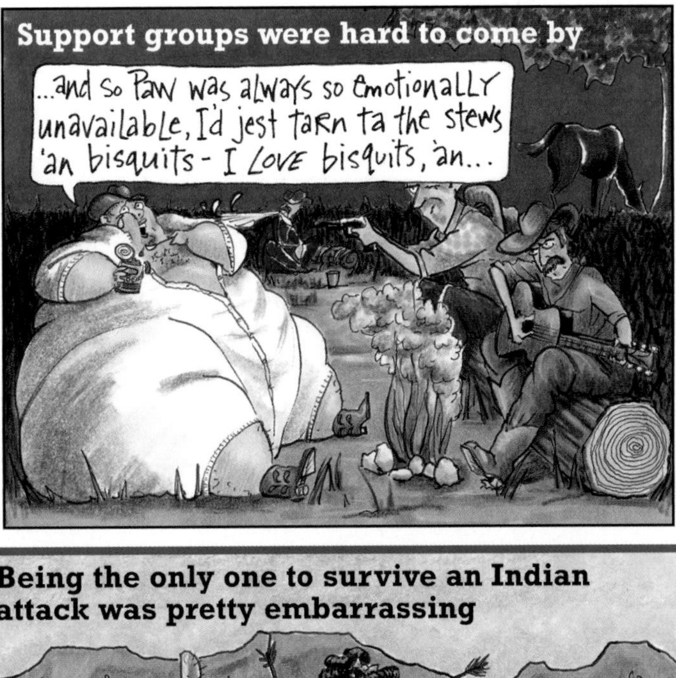
...and so Paw was always so emotionally unavailable, I'd jest tarn ta the stews 'an bisquits - I LOVE bisquits, 'an...

Support groups were hard to come by

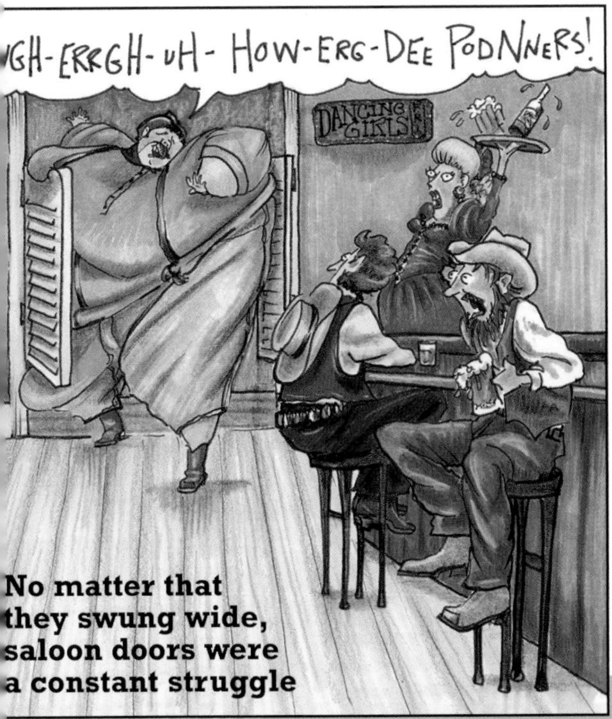
GH-ERRGH-UH- HOW-ERG-DEE PODNNERS!
DANCING GIRLS

No matter that they swung wide, saloon doors were a constant struggle

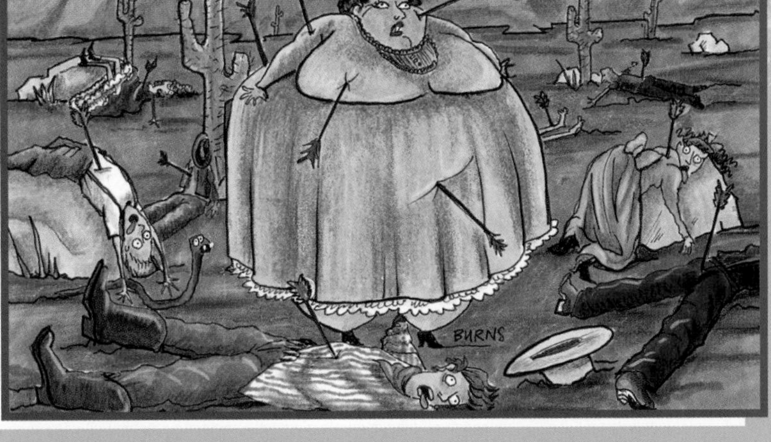
BURNS

Being the only one to survive an Indian attack was pretty embarrassing

MAD
PRESENTS

OTHER USES FOR

LOB

DIAPER RINSER

EARPHONES HOLDER

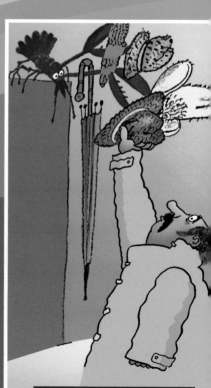

COAT & HAT RACK

TURN SIGNAL

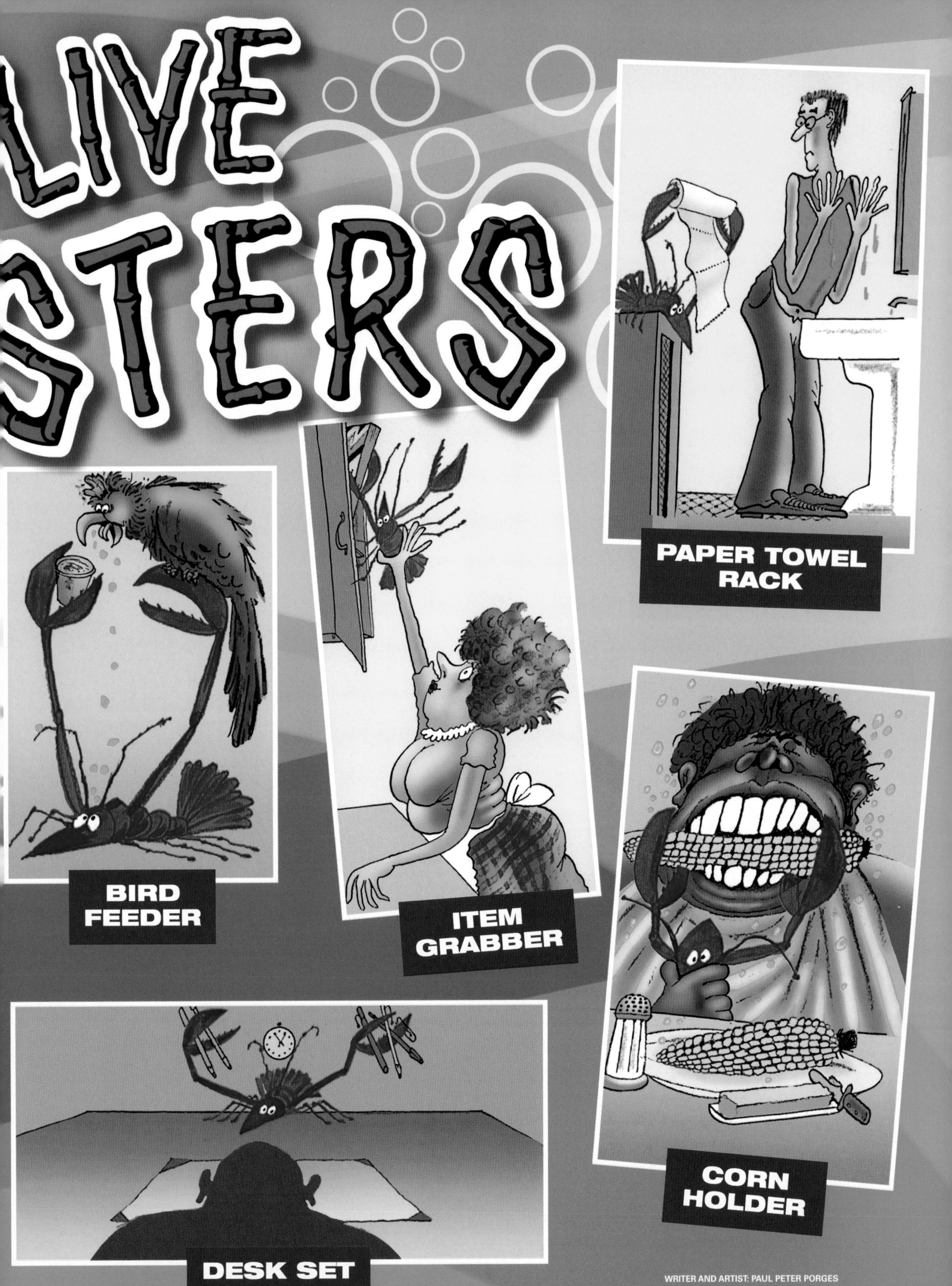
LIVE
STERS
PAPER TOWEL RACK
BIRD FEEDER
ITEM GRABBER
CORN HOLDER
DESK SET

WRITER AND ARTIST: PAUL PETER PORGES

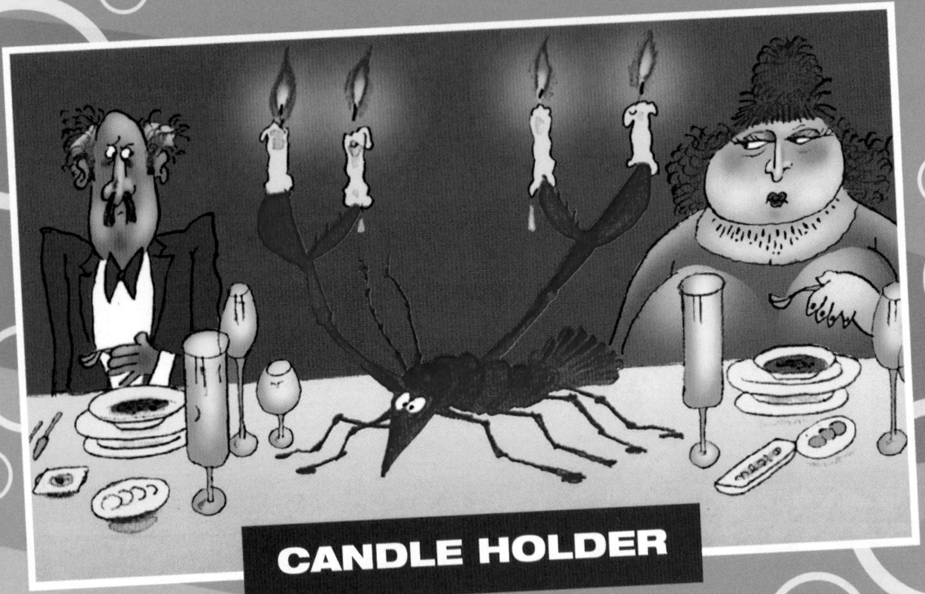

CANDLE HOLDER

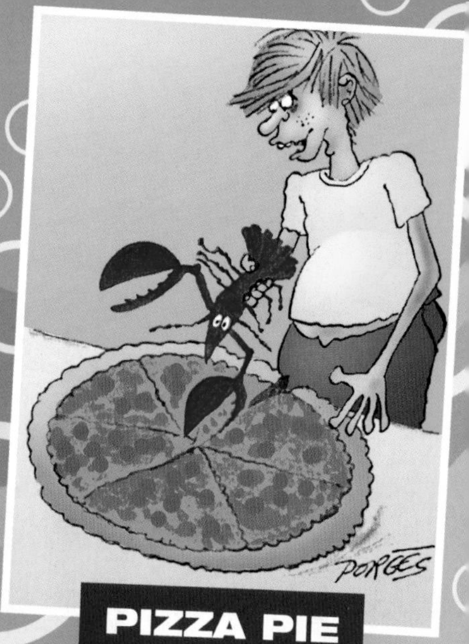
PORGES

PIZZA PIE SLICER

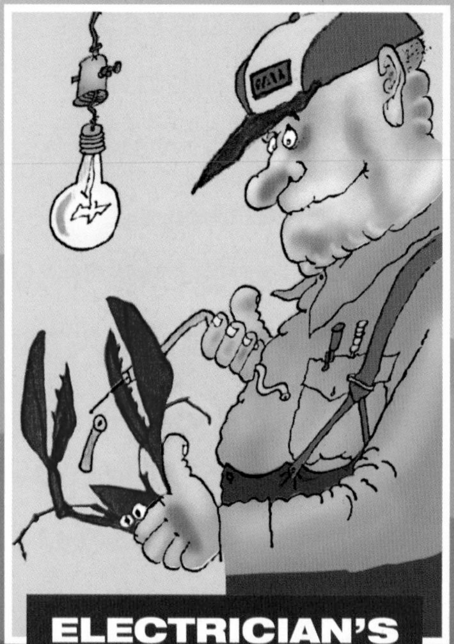

ELECTRICIAN'S WIRESTRIPPER

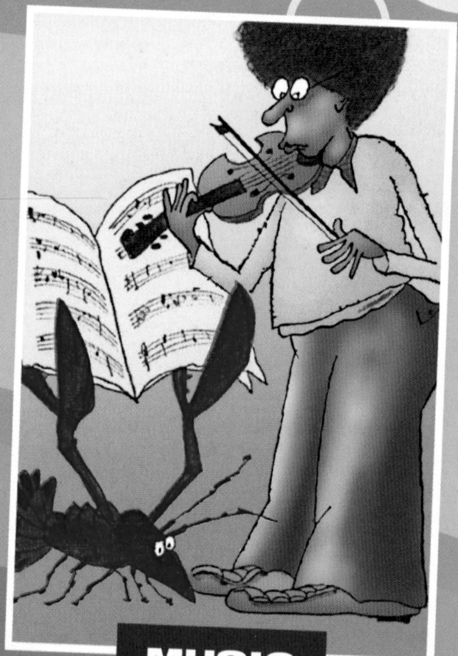

MUSIC STAND

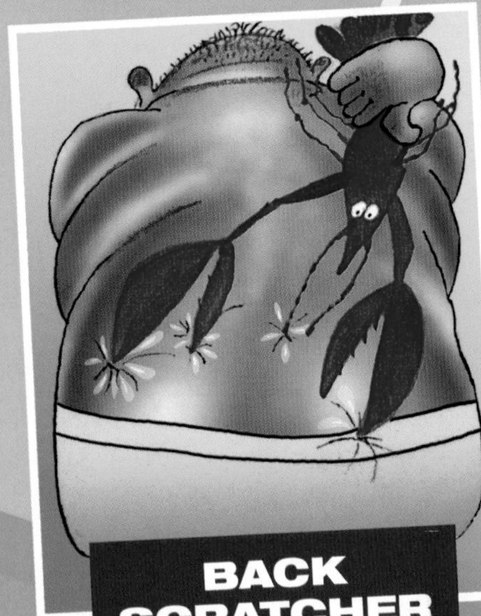

BACK SCRATCHER

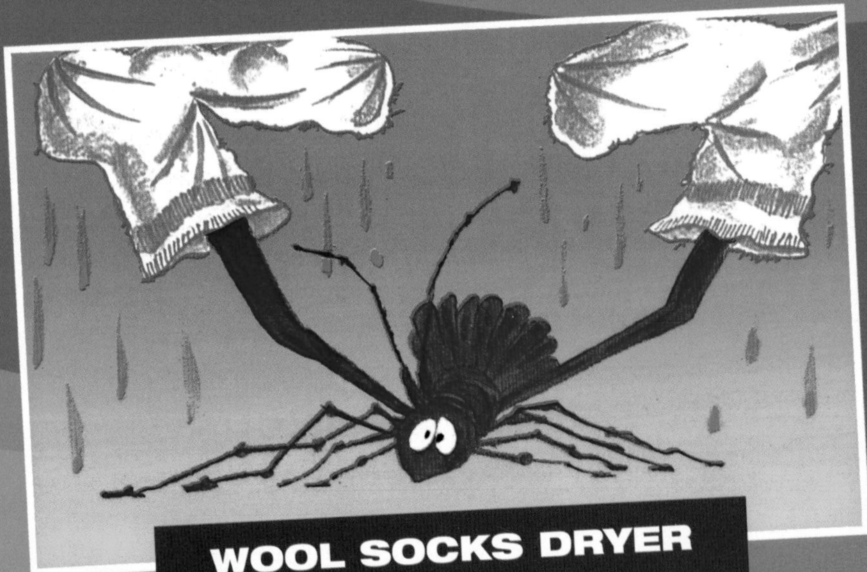

WOOL SOCKS DRYER

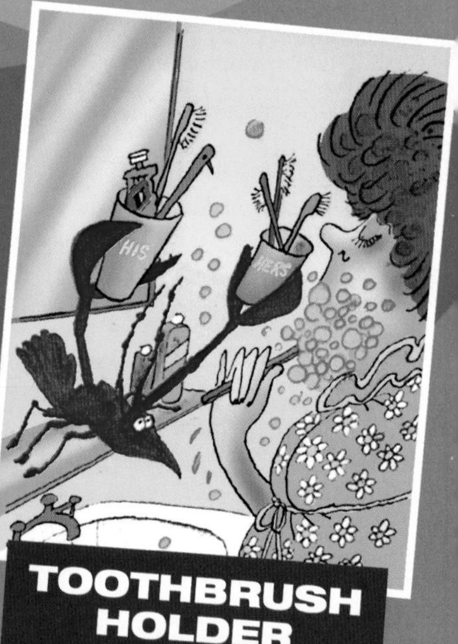
HIS
HERS

TOOTHBRUSH HOLDER

JOKE AND DAGGER DEPT.

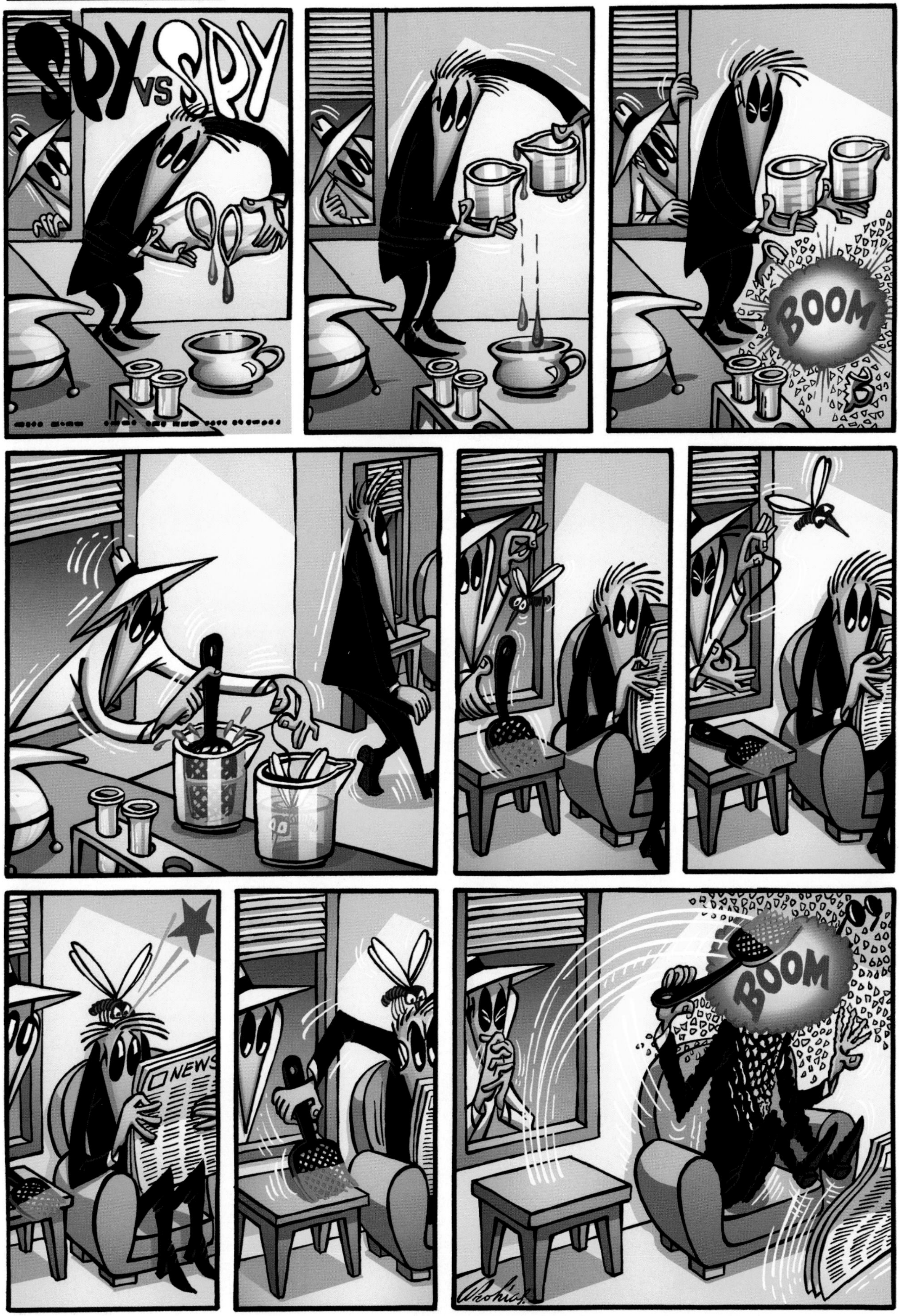
SPY vs SPY
BOOM
NEWS
BOOM
Prohias

Cars THAT DIDN'T MAK

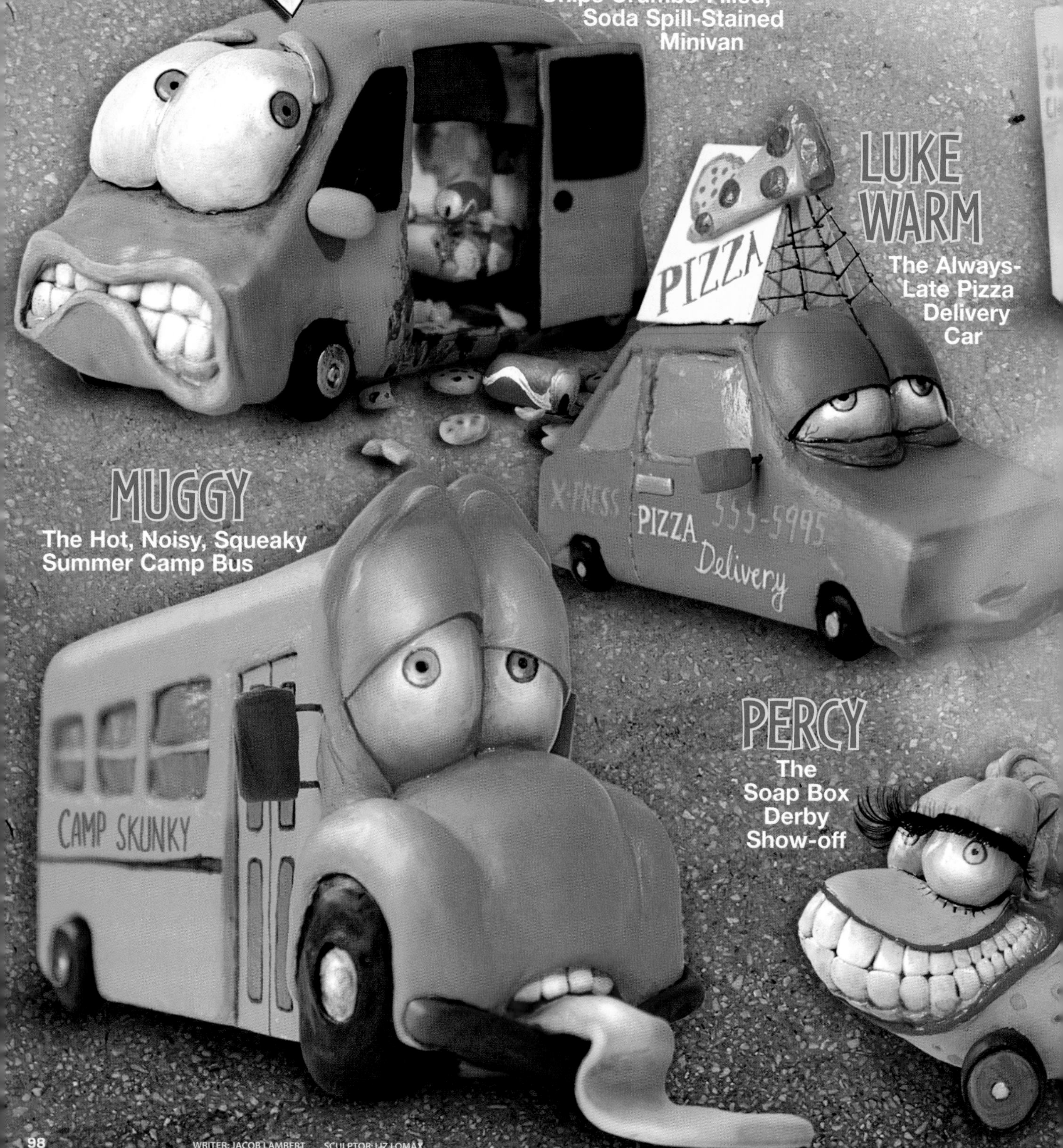
PIZZA
X-PRESS PIZZA 555-5995 Delivery
CAMP SKUNKY

CRUSTY

The Cookie and Chips Crumbs-Filled, Soda Spill-Stained Minivan

LUKE WARM

The Always-Late Pizza Delivery Car

MUGGY

The Hot, Noisy, Squeaky Summer Camp Bus

PERCY

The Soap Box Derby Show-off

WRITER: JACOB LAMBERT SCULPTOR: LIZ LOMAX

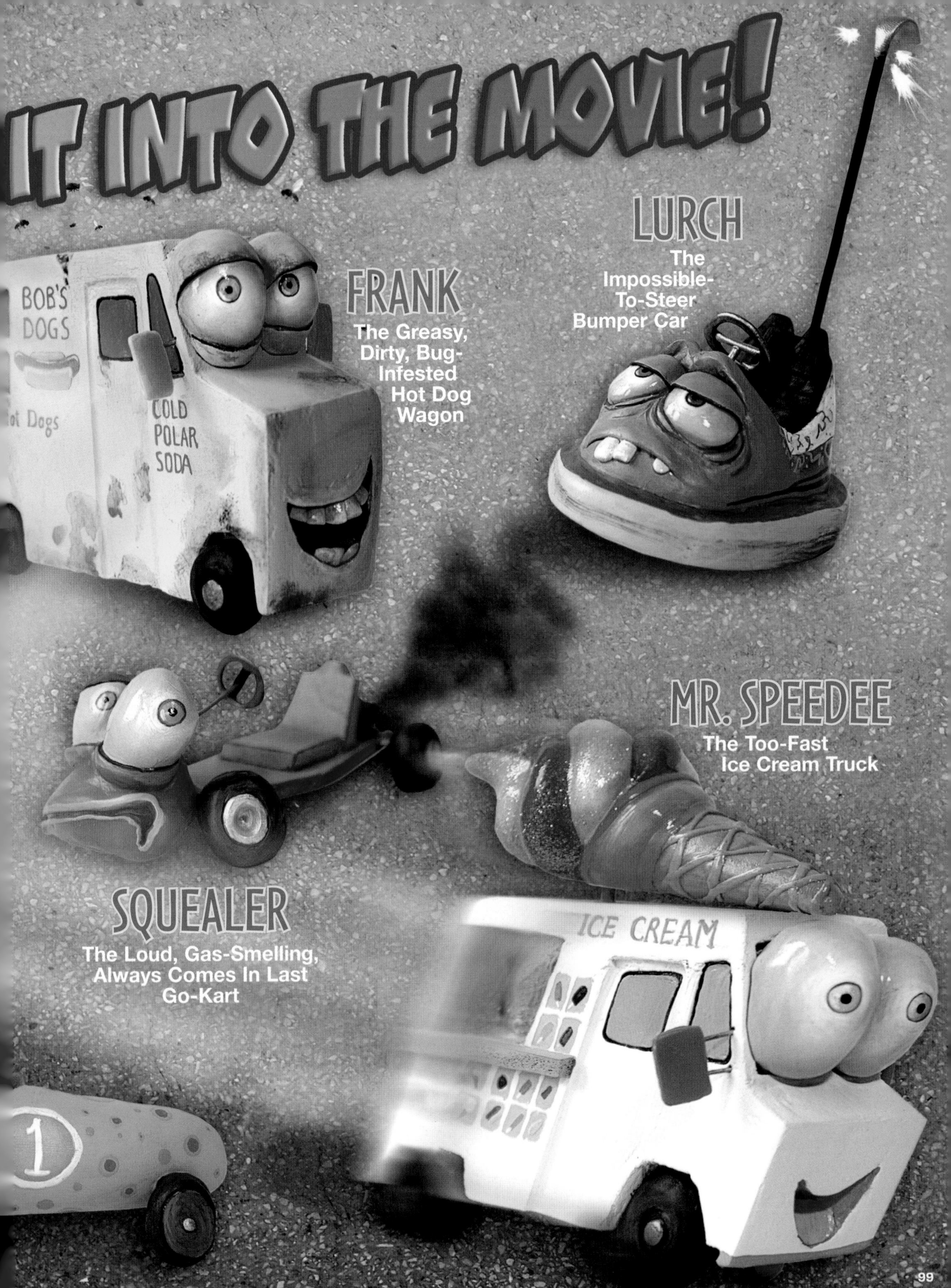
IT INTO THE MOVIE!
LURCH
The Impossible-To-Steer Bumper Car
FRANK
The Greasy, Dirty, Bug-Infested Hot Dog Wagon
BOB'S DOGS
ot Dogs
COLD POLAR SODA
MR. SPEEDEE
The Too-Fast Ice Cream Truck
SQUEALER
The Loud, Gas-Smelling, Always Comes In Last Go-Kart
ICE CREAM
1

THE FARCE BE WITH YOU! DEPT.

A couple of years ago, they made a movie called "Star Wars." It was a smash hit, so they announced that they would make a sequel. Everybody thought it would be called "Star Wars II"...but, lo and behold, they called it "Episode V"! Which means that "Star Wars" was actually "Star Wars IV," and "Star Wars VI" through "X" will be made after "V" but before "I" through "III"! In any case, they'd better surpass this sequel, which doesn't compare to the original! In fact...

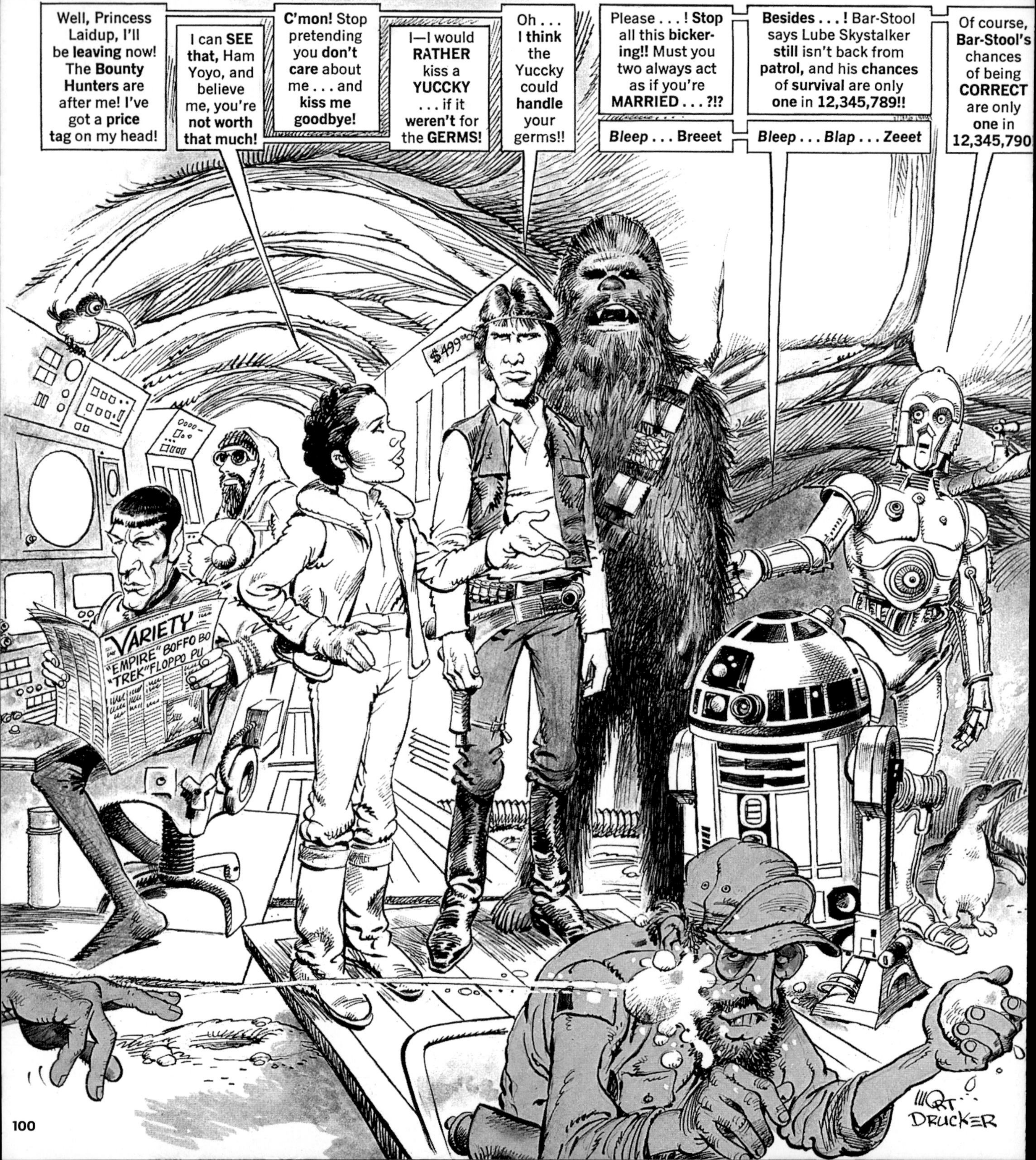
Well, Princess Laidup, I'll be leaving now! The Bounty Hunters are after me! I've got a price tag on my head!
I can SEE that, Ham Yoyo, and believe me, you're not worth that much!
C'mon! Stop pretending you don't care about me . . . and kiss me goodbye!
I—I would RATHER kiss a YUCCKY . . . if it weren't for the GERMS!
Oh . . . I think the Yuccky could handle your germs!!
Please . . . ! Stop all this bicker-ing!! Must you two always act as if you're MARRIED . . . ?!?
Bleep . . . Breeet
Besides . . . ! Bar-Stool says Lube Skystalker still isn't back from patrol, and his chances of survival are only one in 12,345,789!!
Bleep . . . Blap . . . Zeeet
Of course, Bar-Stool's chances of being CORRECT are only one in 12,345,790
$499.99
VARIETY
"EMPIRE" BOFFO BO
"TREK" FLOPPO PU
MORT DRUCKER

THE EMPIRE STRIKES OUT BORES

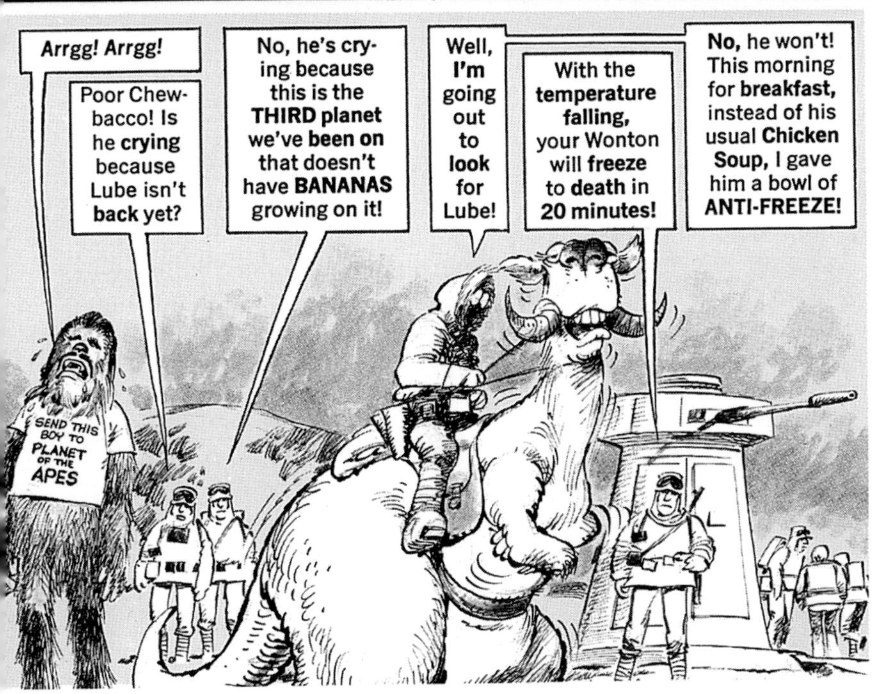
Arrgg! Arrgg!
Poor Chew-bacco! Is he crying because Lube isn't back yet?
No, he's crying because this is the THIRD planet we've been on that doesn't have BANANAS growing on it!
Well, I'm going out to look for Lube!
With the temperature falling, your Wonton will freeze to death in 20 minutes!
No, he won't! This morning for breakfast, instead of his usual Chicken Soup, I gave him a bowl of ANTI-FREEZE!
SEND THIS BOY TO PLANET OF THE APES

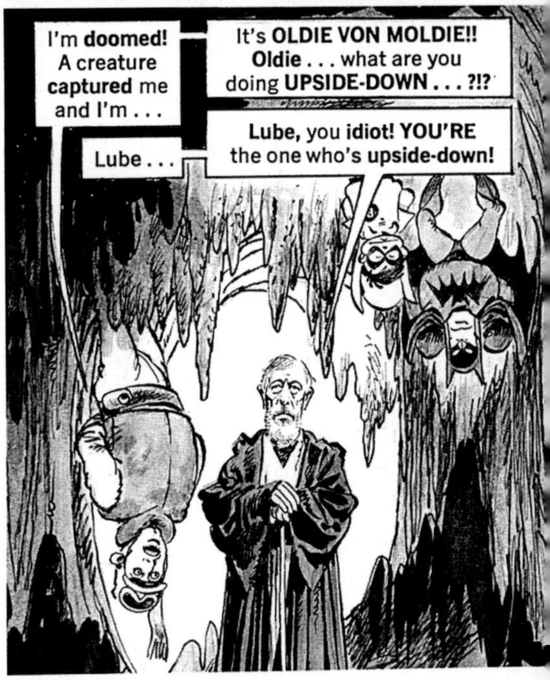
I'm doomed! A creature captured me and I'm . . .
It's OLDIE VON MOLDIE!! Oldie . . . what are you doing UPSIDE-DOWN . . . ?!?
Lube . . .
Lube, you idiot! YOU'RE the one who's upside-down!

ARTIST: MORT DRUCKER WRITER: DICK DE BARTOLO

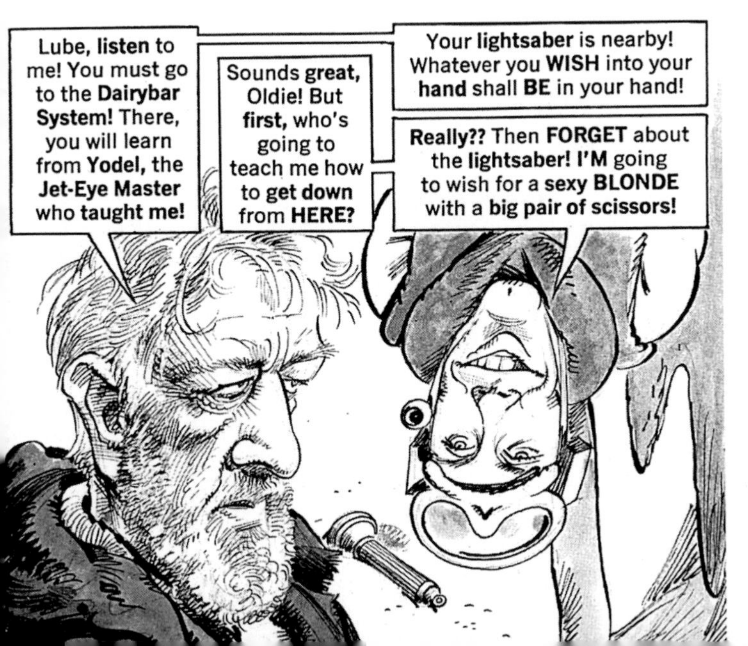
Lube, listen to me! You must go to the Dairybar System! There, you will learn from Yodel, the Jet-Eye Master who taught me!
Sounds great, Oldie! But first, who's going to teach me how to get down from HERE?
Your lightsaber is nearby! Whatever you WISH into your hand shall BE in your hand!
Really?? Then FORGET about the lightsaber! I'M going to wish for a sexy BLONDE with a big pair of scissors!

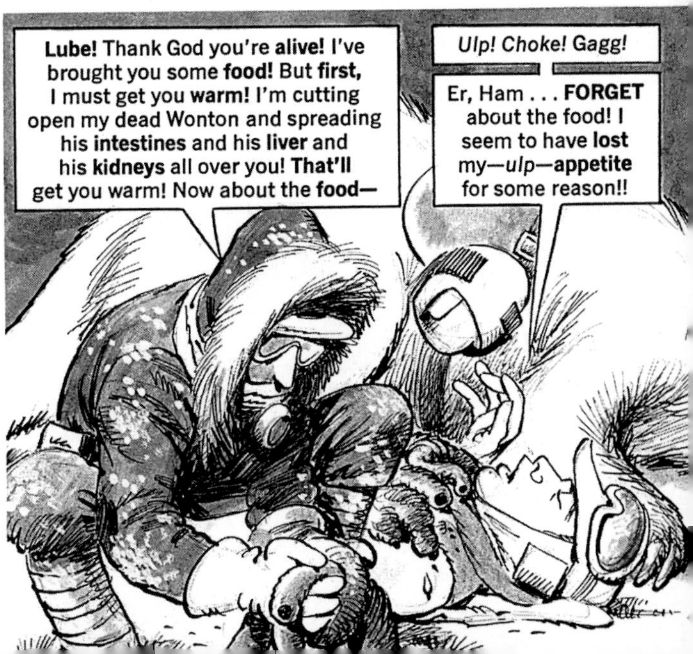
Lube! Thank God you're alive! I've brought you some food! But first, I must get you warm! I'm cutting open my dead Wonton and spreading his intestines and his liver and his kidneys all over you! That'll get you warm! Now about the food—
Ulp! Choke! Gagg!
Er, Ham . . . FORGET about the food! I seem to have lost my—ulp—appetite for some reason!!

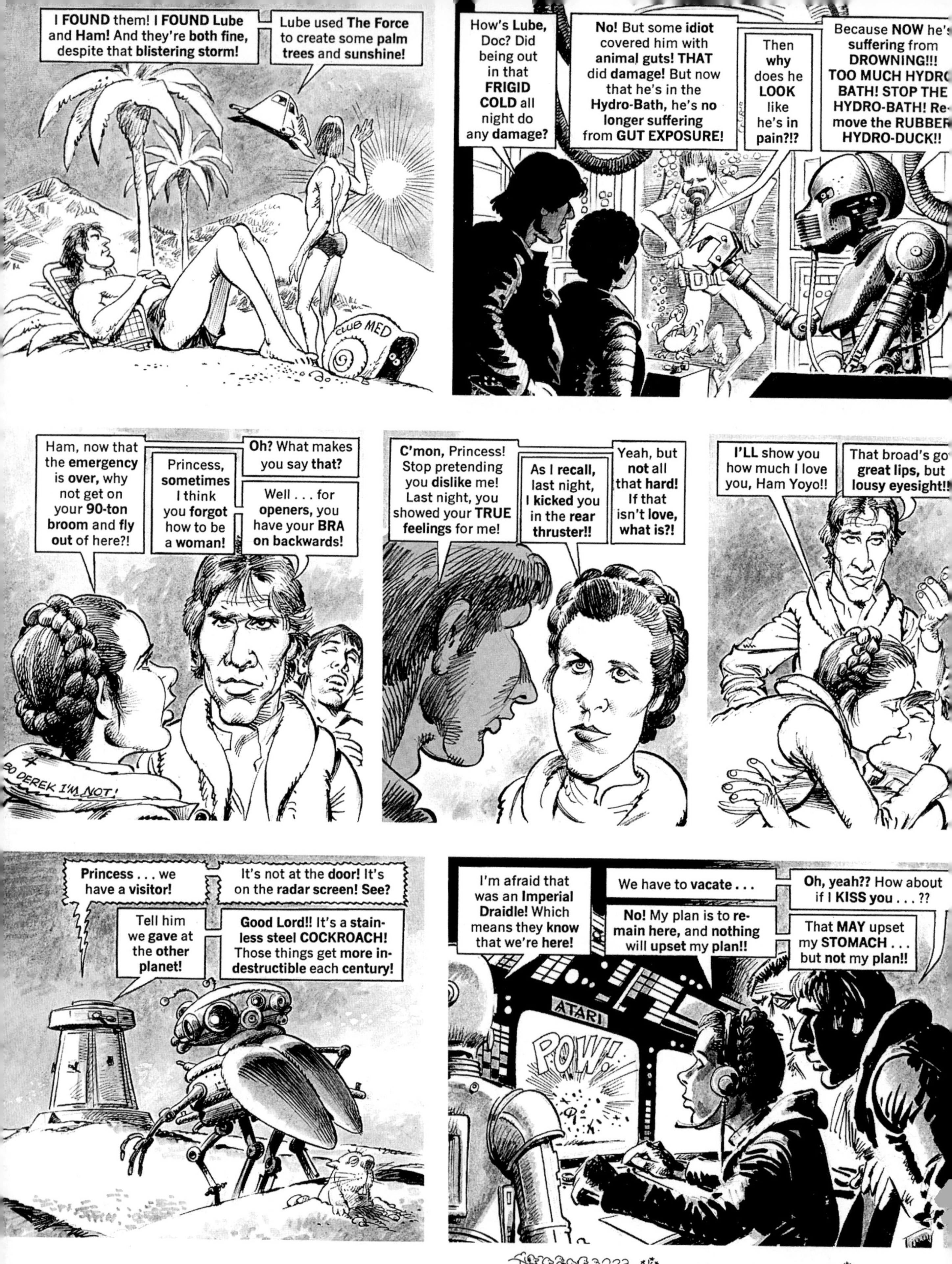
I FOUND them! I FOUND Lube and Ham! And they're both fine, despite that blistering storm!
Lube used The Force to create some palm trees and sunshine!
CLUB MED
How's Lube, Doc? Did being out in that FRIGID COLD all night do any damage?
No! But some idiot covered him with animal guts! THAT did damage! But now that he's in the Hydro-Bath, he's no longer suffering from GUT EXPOSURE!
Then why does he LOOK like he's in pain?!?
Because NOW he's suffering from DROWNING!!! TOO MUCH HYDRO BATH! STOP THE HYDRO-BATH! Remove the RUBBER HYDRO-DUCK!!
Ham, now that the emergency is over, why not get on your 90-ton broom and fly out of here?!
Princess, sometimes I think you forgot how to be a woman!
Oh? What makes you say that?
Well . . . for openers, you have your BRA on backwards!
BO DEREK I'M NOT!
C'mon, Princess! Stop pretending you dislike me! Last night, you showed your TRUE feelings for me!
As I recall, last night, I kicked you in the rear thruster!!
Yeah, but not all that hard! If that isn't love, what is?!
I'LL show you how much I love you, Ham Yoyo!!
That broad's got great lips, but lousy eyesight!!
Princess . . . we have a visitor!
It's not at the door! It's on the radar screen! See?
Tell him we gave at the other planet!
Good Lord!! It's a stainless steel COCKROACH! Those things get more indestructible each century!
I'm afraid that was an Imperial Draidle! Which means they know that we're here!
We have to vacate . . .
No! My plan is to remain here, and nothing will upset my plan!!
Oh, yeah?? How about if I KISS you . . . ??
That MAY upset my STOMACH . . . but not my plan!!
ATARI
POW!
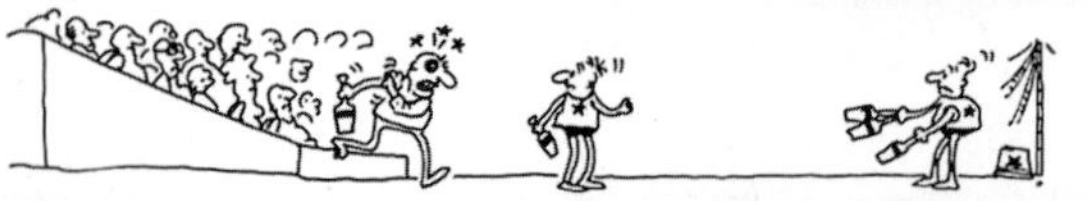

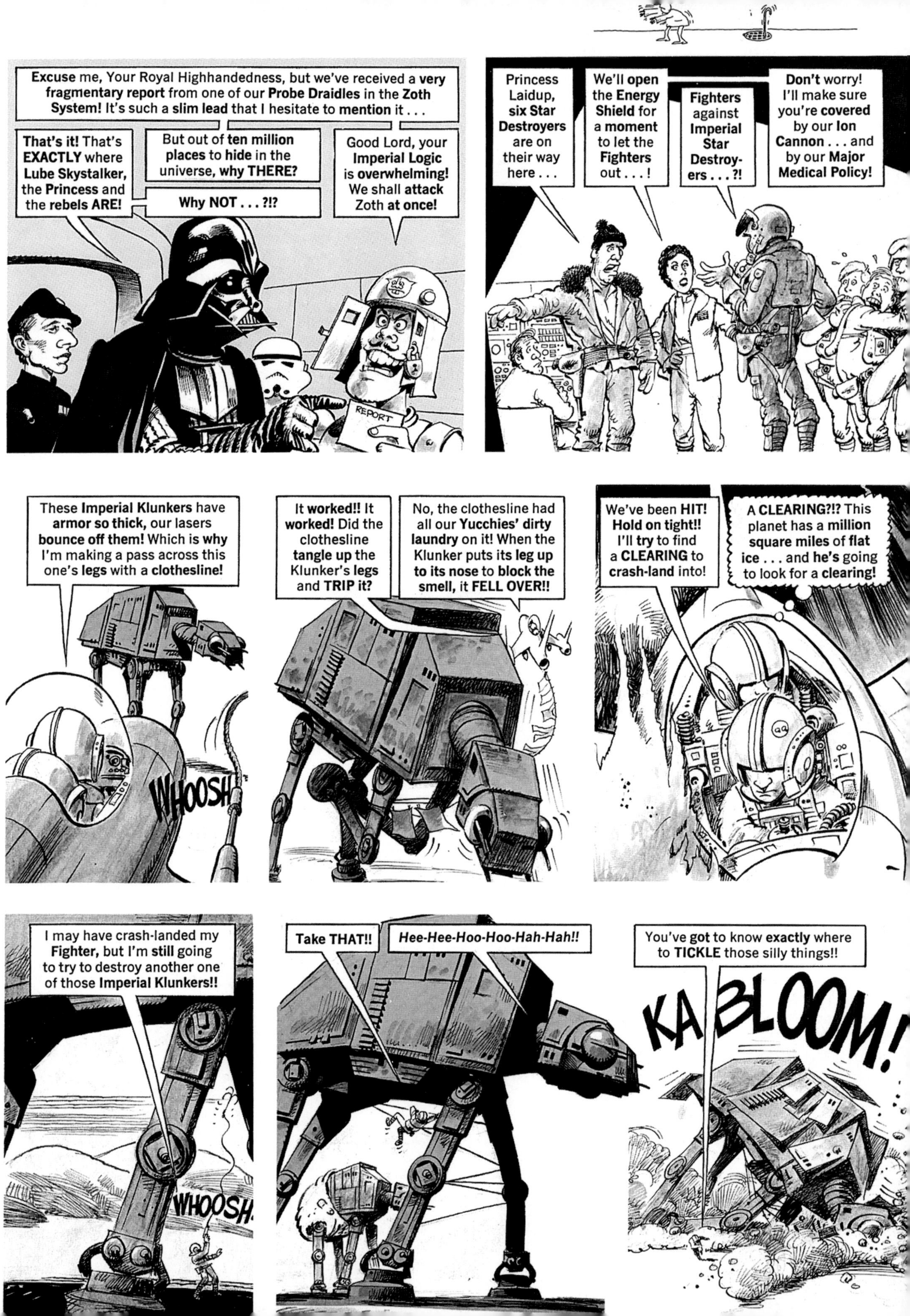
Excuse me, Your Royal Highhandedness, but we've received a very fragmentary report from one of our Probe Draidles in the Zoth System! It's such a slim lead that I hesitate to mention it . . .
That's it! That's EXACTLY where Lube Skystalker, the Princess and the rebels ARE!
But out of ten million places to hide in the universe, why THERE?
Why NOT . . . ?!?
Good Lord, your Imperial Logic is overwhelming! We shall attack Zoth at once!
REPORT
Princess Laidup, six Star Destroyers are on their way here . . .
We'll open the Energy Shield for a moment to let the Fighters out . . . !
Fighters against Imperial Star Destroy-ers . . . ?!
Don't worry! I'll make sure you're covered by our Ion Cannon . . . and by our Major Medical Policy!
These Imperial Klunkers have armor so thick, our lasers bounce off them! Which is why I'm making a pass across this one's legs with a clothesline!
WHOOSH
It worked!! It worked! Did the clothesline tangle up the Klunker's legs and TRIP it?
No, the clothesline had all our Yucchies' dirty laundry on it! When the Klunker puts its leg up to its nose to block the smell, it FELL OVER!!
We've been HIT! Hold on tight!! I'll try to find a CLEARING to crash-land into!
A CLEARING?!? This planet has a million square miles of flat ice . . . and he's going to look for a clearing!
I may have crash-landed my Fighter, but I'm still going to try to destroy another one of those Imperial Klunkers!!
WHOOSH
Take THAT!!
Hee-Hee-Hoo-Hoo-Hah-Hah!!
You've got to know exactly where to TICKLE those silly things!!
KABLOOM!

Hold on, Princess! It's time to leave!
Hah!! Do you really think this bucket of bolts will get us OUT of here?!?
Hey, this is the Aluminum Falcon! This baby's still got a lot of surprises left in her!!
Sir! The entire control panel just shorted out!
See? There's ONE SURPRISE already! And there should be plenty more!!
Well, Princess, I DID manage to get us out of one very tight jam . . .
Look! We're entering an ASTEROID BELT!!
And into another very tight jam! Creepio . . . what do you recommend for ASTEROIDS?
May I suggest you try Preparation H?
Mets
Well, Bar-Stool! Here we are on the planet Dairybar!
Oh, I'm sure it's perfectly safe for Draidles! What I'm worried about is: Is it safe for HUMANS?! But after seeing snow and ice for so long, it's nice to have a change of scene . . . Slime, muck, quicksand, snakes, bats, mist . . .
Bleep Blap Boop Beeep
Beep Bapp Boop! Bleep Screeeep!
Yeah . . . I'M beginning to miss the snow and ice, too!
Welcome to Dairybar! May I help you?
Why . . . yes! I'm looking for a great warrior and Jet-Eye Master named Yodel! I KNOW it seems strange to be looking for a person like that in a slimy mudhole like this, but—
SLIMY MUDHOLE?!? This is my HOME!
Well, I don't exactly consider YOU to be MR. CLEAN!
I am Yodel! I can teach you everything! How to levitate objects, how to fight with a lightsaber, how to transmute metals, how to catch flies on your tongue! I also give an advanced course in "Cute"!
Good! Let's get started!
The FIRST thing you must learn is patience!
Don't talk to me about patience! I've got tons of patience! Now—let's get going, you slimy twit!!
MISS PIGGY FAN CLUB
There's something STRANGE about this asteroid cave we've landed in!
Y-Y-You mean the way the rocks are shaped? That one looks like a giant liver . . . and that one looks like a giant stomach . . .
The one that worries ME is the one that looks like a giant HEART . . . mainly because it's BEATING!
Let's get out of here!

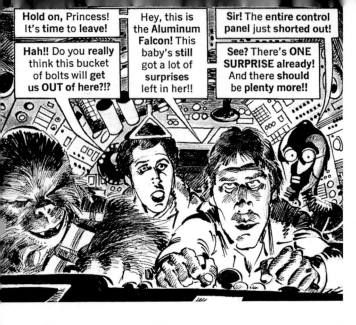

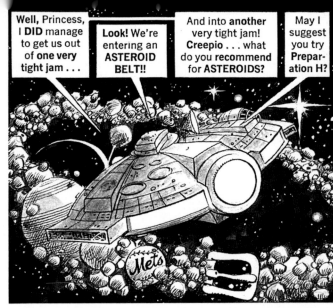

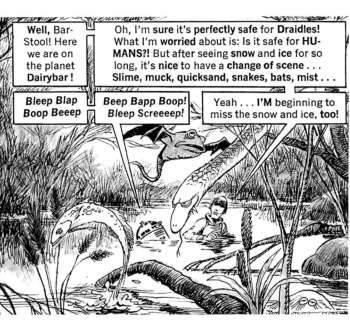

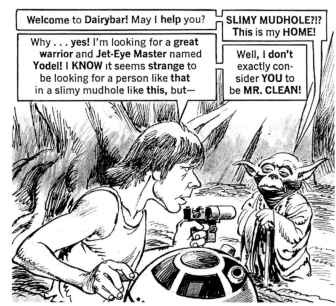

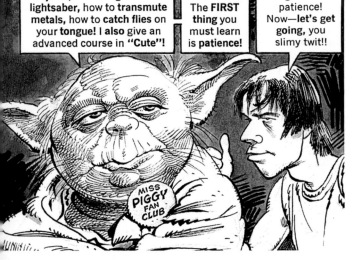

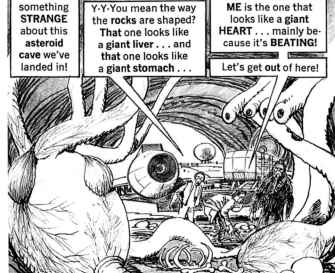

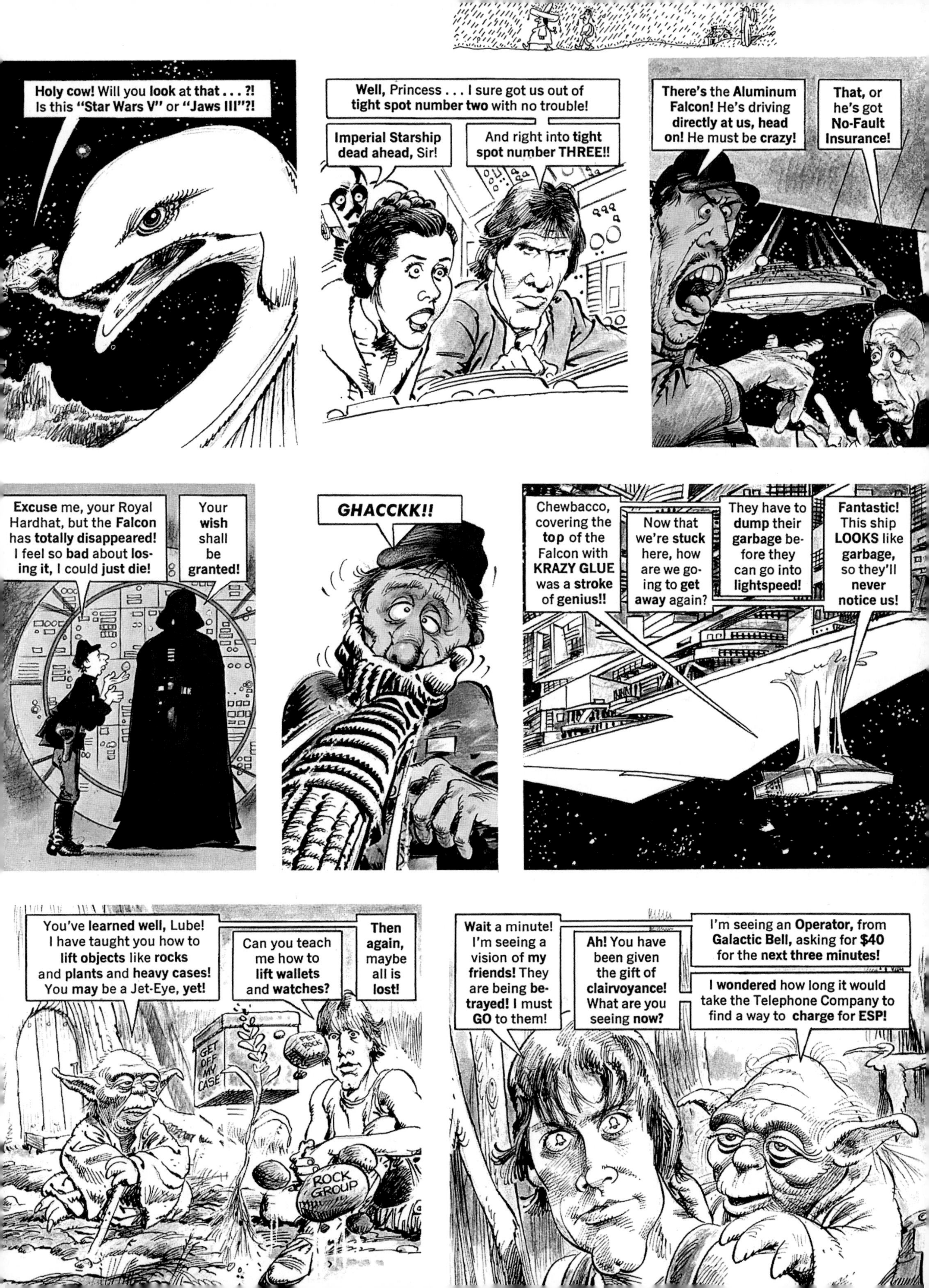
Holy cow! Will you look at that . . . ?! Is this "Star Wars V" or "Jaws III"?!
Well, Princess . . . I sure got us out of tight spot number two with no trouble!
Imperial Starship dead ahead, Sir!
And right into tight spot number THREE!!
There's the Aluminum Falcon! He's driving directly at us, head on! He must be crazy!
That, or he's got No-Fault Insurance!
Excuse me, your Royal Hardhat, but the Falcon has totally disappeared! I feel so bad about losing it, I could just die!
Your wish shall be granted!
GHACCKK!!
Chewbacco, covering the top of the Falcon with KRAZY GLUE was a stroke of genius!!
Now that we're stuck here, how are we going to get away again?
They have to dump their garbage before they can go into lightspeed!
Fantastic! This ship LOOKS like garbage, so they'll never notice us!
You've learned well, Lube! I have taught you how to lift objects like rocks and plants and heavy cases! You may be a Jet-Eye, yet!
Can you teach me how to lift wallets and watches?
Then again, maybe all is lost!
GET OFF MY CASE
PET ROCK
ROCK GROUP
Wait a minute! I'm seeing a vision of my friends! They are being betrayed! I must GO to them!
Ah! You have been given the gift of clairvoyance! What are you seeing now?
I'm seeing an Operator, from Galactic Bell, asking for $40 for the next three minutes!
I wondered how long it would take the Telephone Company to find a way to charge for ESP!

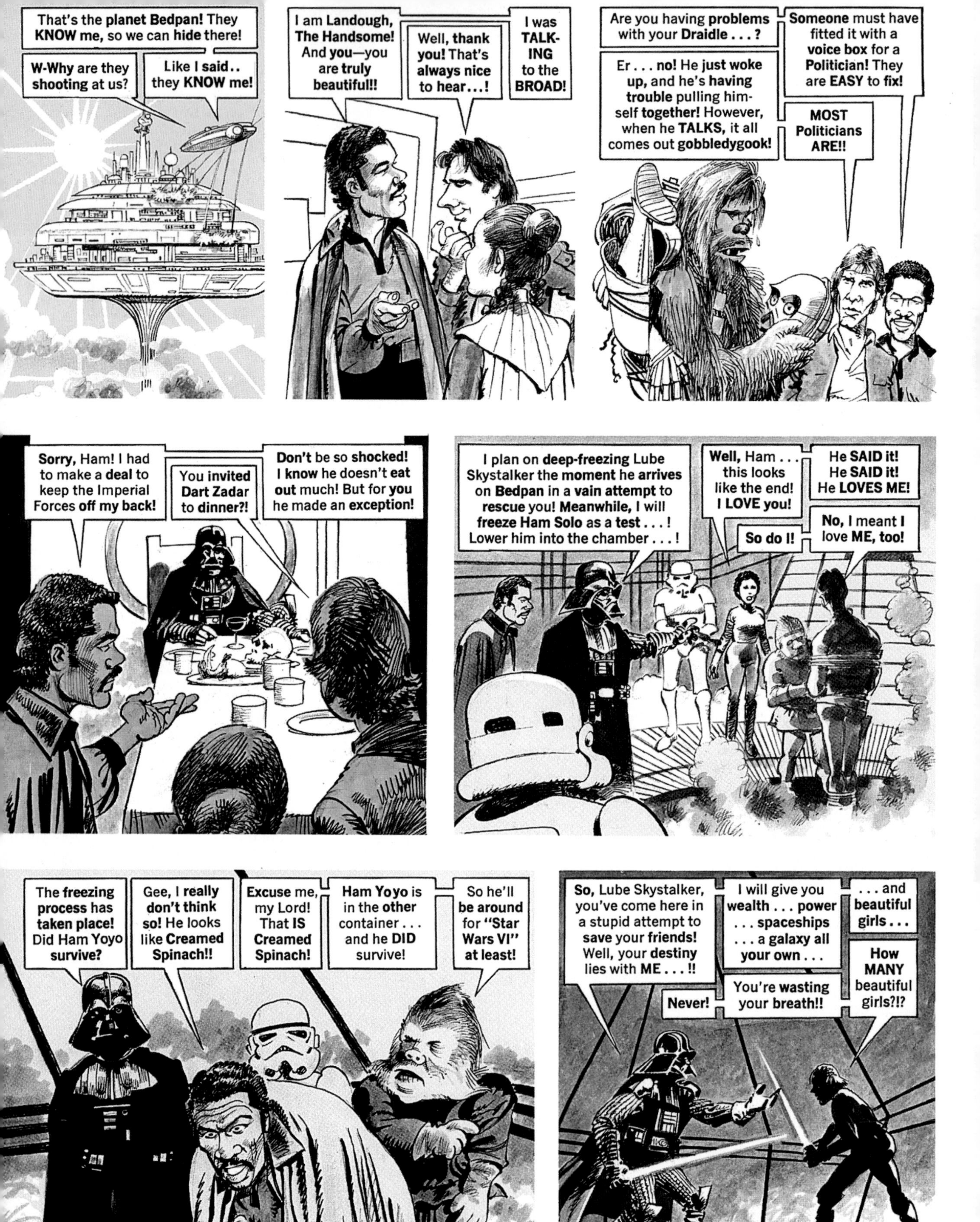

That's the planet Bedpan! They KNOW me, so we can hide there!
W-Why are they shooting at us?
Like I said.. they KNOW me!
I am Landough, The Handsome! And you—you are truly beautiful!!
Well, thank you! That's always nice to hear...!
I was TALKING to the BROAD!
Are you having problems with your Draidle...?
Er... no! He just woke up, and he's having trouble pulling himself together! However, when he TALKS, it all comes out gobbledygook!
Someone must have fitted it with a voice box for a Politician! They are EASY to fix!
MOST Politicians ARE!!
Sorry, Ham! I had to make a deal to keep the Imperial Forces off my back!
You invited Dart Zadar to dinner?!
Don't be so shocked! I know he doesn't eat out much! But for you he made an exception!
I plan on deep-freezing Lube Skystalker the moment he arrives on Bedpan in a vain attempt to rescue you! Meanwhile, I will freeze Ham Solo as a test...! Lower him into the chamber...!
Well, Ham... this looks like the end! I LOVE you!
So do I!
He SAID it! He SAID it! He LOVES ME!
No, I meant I love ME, too!
The freezing process has taken place! Did Ham Yoyo survive?
Gee, I really don't think so! He looks like Creamed Spinach!!
Excuse me, my Lord! That IS Creamed Spinach!
Ham Yoyo is in the other container... and he DID survive!
So he'll be around for "Star Wars VI" at least!
So, Lube Skystalker, you've come here in a stupid attempt to save your friends! Well, your destiny lies with ME...!!
I will give you wealth... power ...spaceships ...a galaxy all your own...
...and beautiful girls...
Never!
You're wasting your breath!!
How MANY beautiful girls?!?

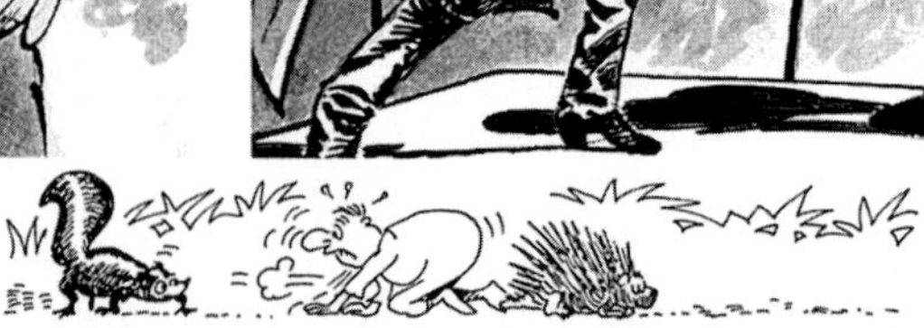

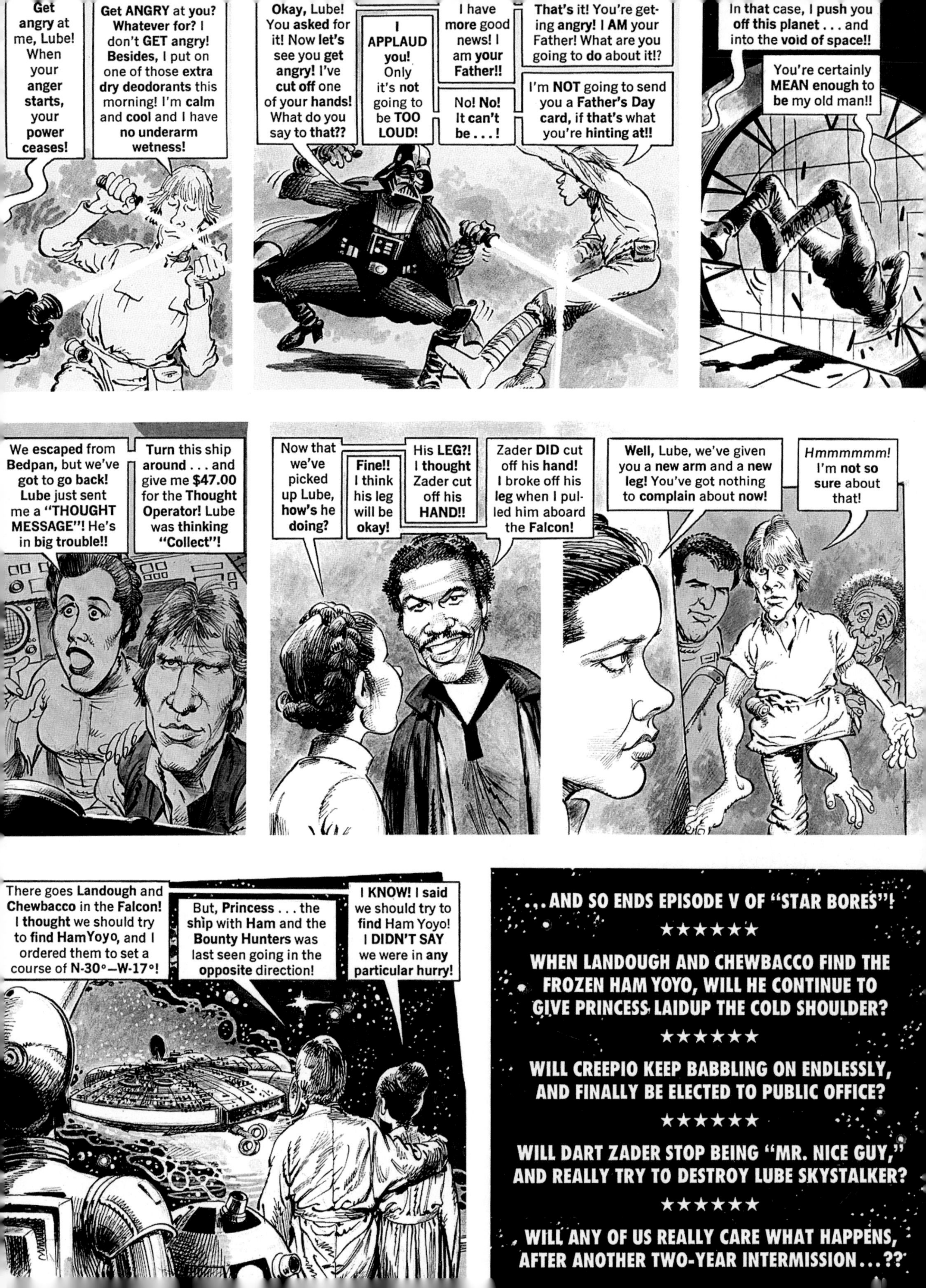
Get angry at me, Lube! When your anger starts, your power ceases!
Get ANGRY at you? Whatever for? I don't GET angry! Besides, I put on one of those extra dry deodorants this morning! I'm calm and cool and I have no underarm wetness!
Okay, Lube! You asked for it! Now let's see you get angry! I've cut off one of your hands! What do you say to that??
I APPLAUD you! Only it's not going to be TOO LOUD!
I have more good news! I am your Father!!
No! No! It can't be . . . !
That's it! You're getting angry! I AM your Father! What are you going to do about it!?
I'm NOT going to send you a Father's Day card, if that's what you're hinting at!!
In that case, I push you off this planet . . . and into the void of space!!
You're certainly MEAN enough to be my old man!!
We escaped from Bedpan, but we've got to go back! Lube just sent me a "THOUGHT MESSAGE"! He's in big trouble!!
Turn this ship around . . . and give me $47.00 for the Thought Operator! Lube was thinking "Collect"!
Now that we've picked up Lube, how's he doing?
Fine!! I think his leg will be okay!
His LEG?! I thought Zader cut off his HAND!!
Zader DID cut off his hand! I broke off his leg when I pulled him aboard the Falcon!
Well, Lube, we've given you a new arm and a new leg! You've got nothing to complain about now!
Hmmmmmm! I'm not so sure about that!
There goes Landough and Chewbacco in the Falcon! I thought we should try to find HamYoyo, and I ordered them to set a course of N-30°—W-17°!
But, Princess . . . the ship with Ham and the Bounty Hunters was last seen going in the opposite direction!
I KNOW! I said we should try to find Ham Yoyo! I DIDN'T SAY we were in any particular hurry!
. . . AND SO ENDS EPISODE V OF "STAR BORES"!
★★★★★★
WHEN LANDOUGH AND CHEWBACCO FIND THE FROZEN HAM YOYO, WILL HE CONTINUE TO GIVE PRINCESS LAIDUP THE COLD SHOULDER?
★★★★★★
WILL CREEPIO KEEP BABBLING ON ENDLESSLY, AND FINALLY BE ELECTED TO PUBLIC OFFICE?
★★★★★★
WILL DART ZADER STOP BEING "MR. NICE GUY," AND REALLY TRY TO DESTROY LUBE SKYSTALKER?
★★★★★★
WILL ANY OF US REALLY CARE WHAT HAPPENS, AFTER ANOTHER TWO-YEAR INTERMISSION . . . ??

You thought you could just skate right through the school year, that you'd be able to do a minimal amount of work and the teachers would pass you on to the next grade — boy, were you wrong, moron! Now it's time to pay the price! So say goodbye to fun in the sun and hello to long days in hot classrooms. It's going to be bad — *really* bad — as you will see in...

JOHN CALDWELL'S

13 THINGS YOU REALLY LEARN I

1

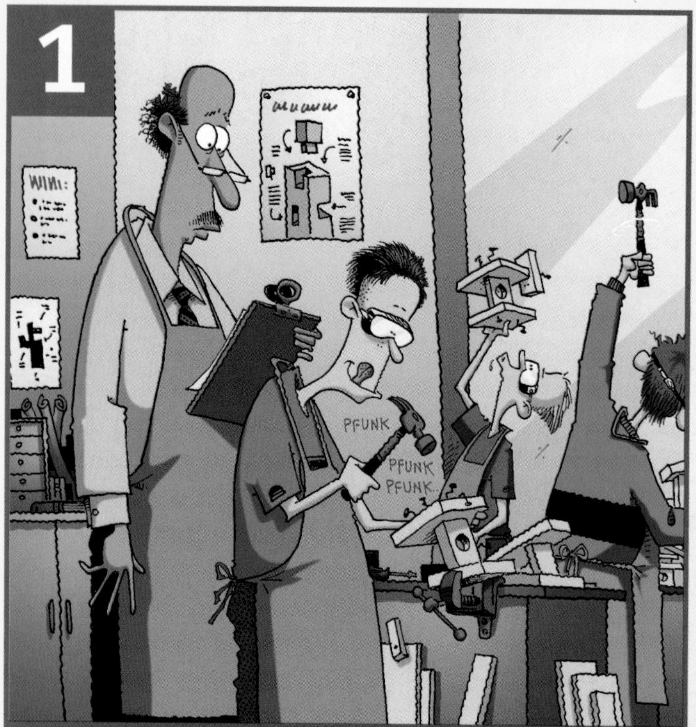
PFUNK
PFUNK
PFUNK

Anybody can suck at math, but it takes a real dipwad to be taking shop class over.

2

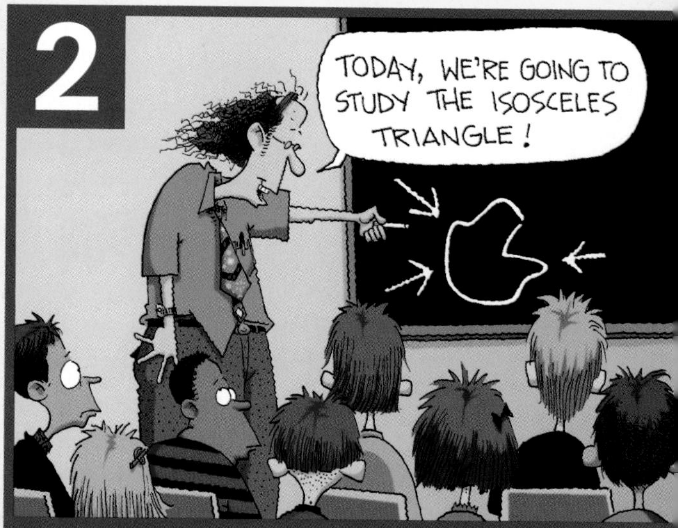
TODAY, WE'RE GOING TO STUDY THE ISOSCELES TRIANGLE!

The really good teachers, like the really good students, don't end up in summer school.

3

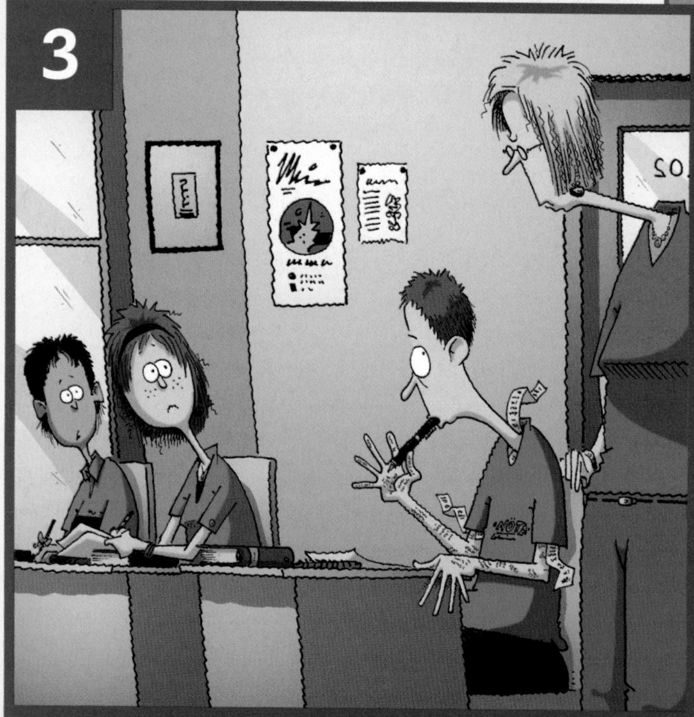

Crib notes, cheat sheets and ballpoint answer tattoos are harder to hide under light summer clothing.

4

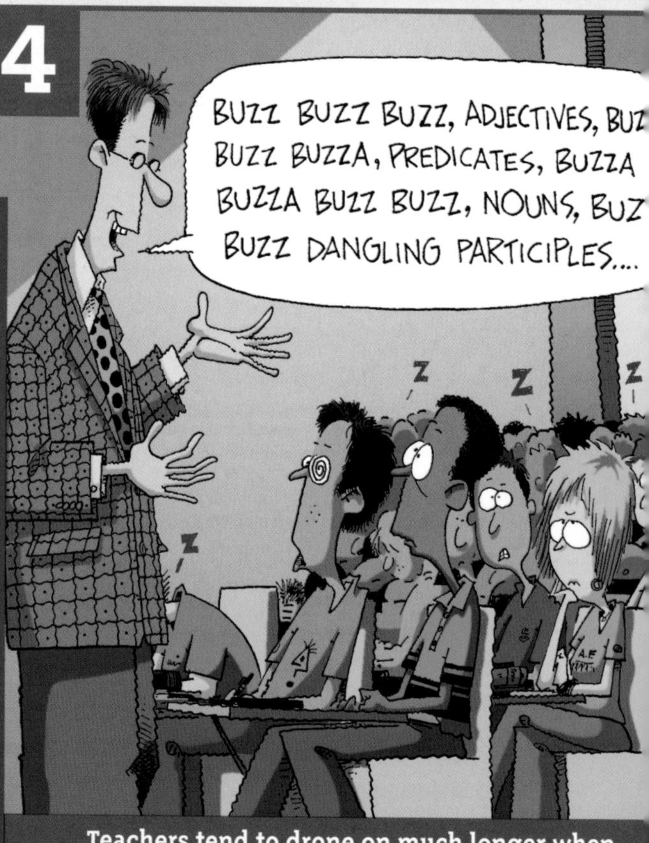
BUZZ BUZZ BUZZ, ADJECTIVES, BUZ
BUZZ BUZZA, PREDICATES, BUZZA
BUZZA BUZZ BUZZ, NOUNS, BUZ
BUZZ DANGLING PARTICIPLES....
Z
Z
Z
Z

Teachers tend to drone on much longer when there aren't any wiseguy know-it-alls there to raise their hands every ten seconds.

ARTIST AND WRITER: JOHN CALDWELL COLORIST: CARRIE STRACHA

SUMMER SCHOOL

5

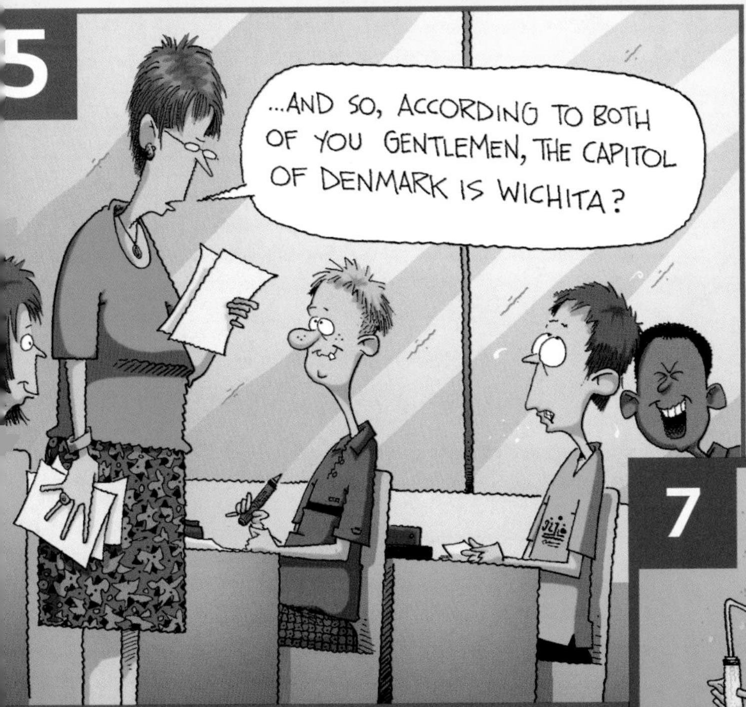

...AND SO, ACCORDING TO BOTH OF YOU GENTLEMEN, THE CAPITOL OF DENMARK IS WICHITA?

When it comes to copying answers on tests, the pickings can be quite slim.

6

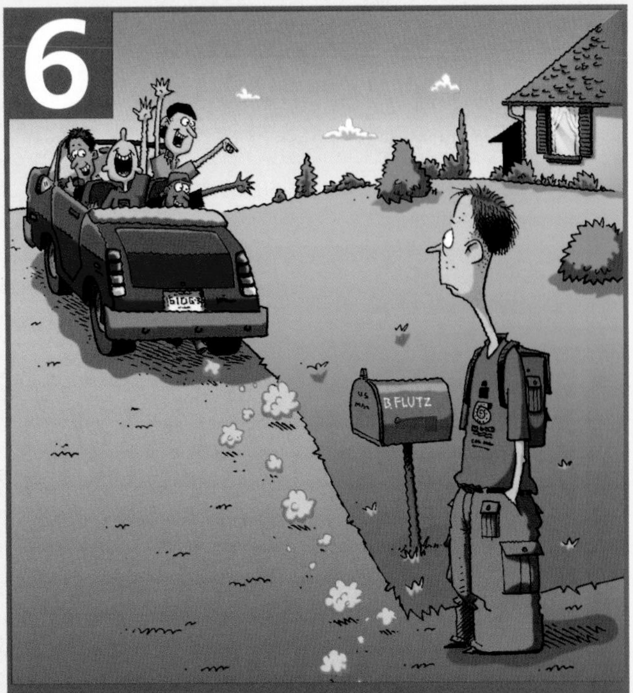

B.FLUTZ

Nothing says "numbskull" like a dork waiting for a school bus as a carload of his friends blows by on the way to the beach.

7

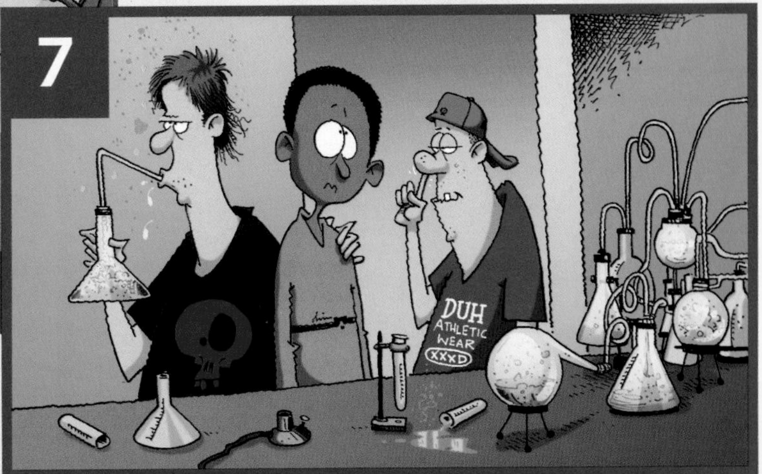

DUH ATHLETIC WEAR XXXD

Unlike the rest of the year, breaking up into teams for a science project doesn't mean there'll be at least one smart kid there to help jackup your grades.

8

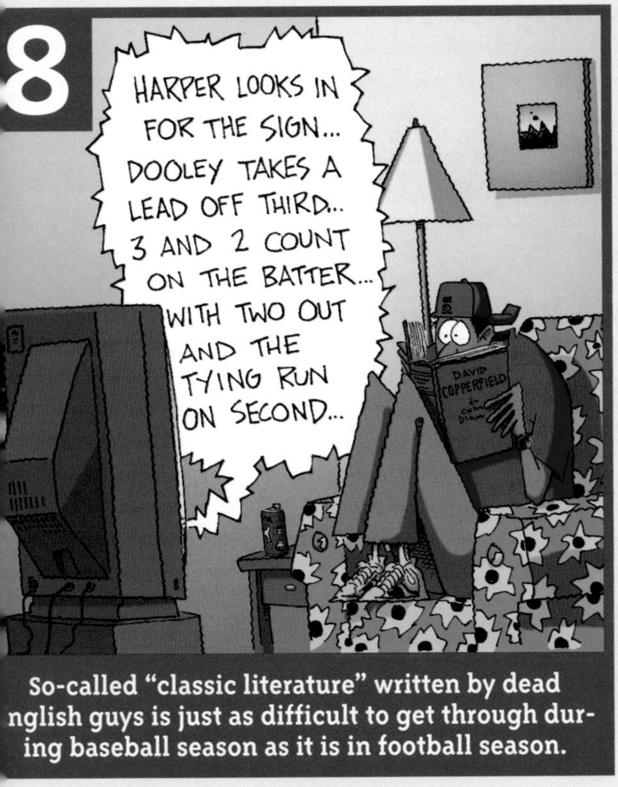

HARPER LOOKS IN FOR THE SIGN... DOOLEY TAKES A LEAD OFF THIRD.. 3 AND 2 COUNT ON THE BATTER... WITH TWO OUT AND THE TYING RUN ON SECOND...
DAVID COPPERFIELD

So-called "classic literature" written by dead nglish guys is just as difficult to get through during baseball season as it is in football season.

9

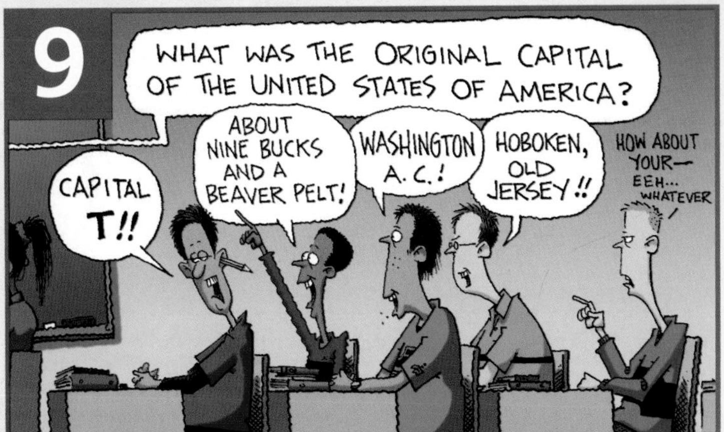

WHAT WAS THE ORIGINAL CAPITAL OF THE UNITED STATES OF AMERICA?
CAPITAL T!!
ABOUT NINE BUCKS AND A BEAVER PELT!
WASHINGTON A.C.!
HOBOKEN, OLD JERSEY!!
HOW ABOUT YOUR— EEH... WHATEVER

Trying to be the class clown in a roomful of other slacker jokesters is just not worth the effort.

10

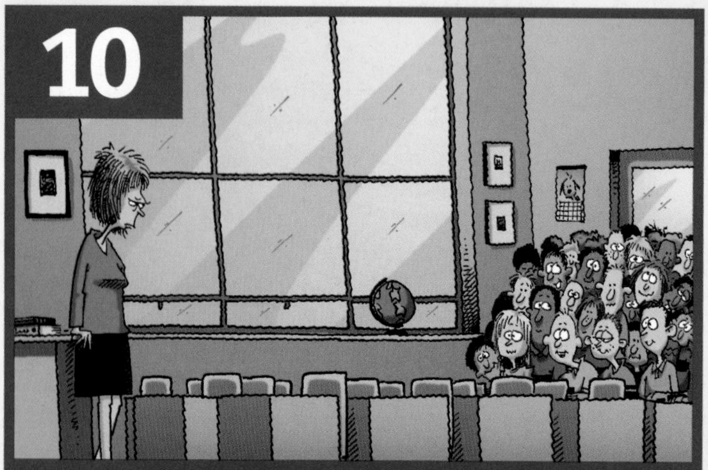

Everybody can't sit in the last row.

11

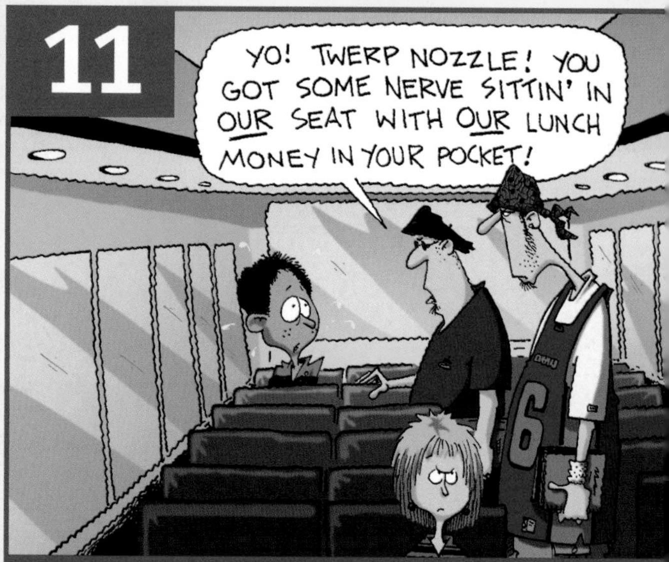
YO! TWERP NOZZLE! YOU GOT SOME NERVE SITTIN' IN OUR SEAT WITH OUR LUNCH MONEY IN YOUR POCKET!

Fewer students on the bus means that it's harder to avoid the bullies.

12

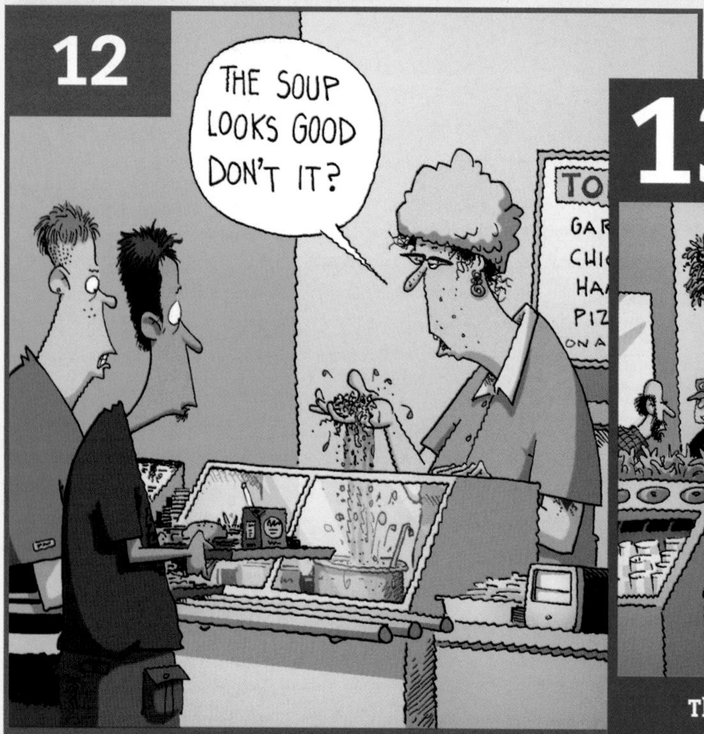
THE SOUP LOOKS GOOD DON'T IT?

There's nothing lower on the culinary ladder than substitute summer lunch ladies.

13

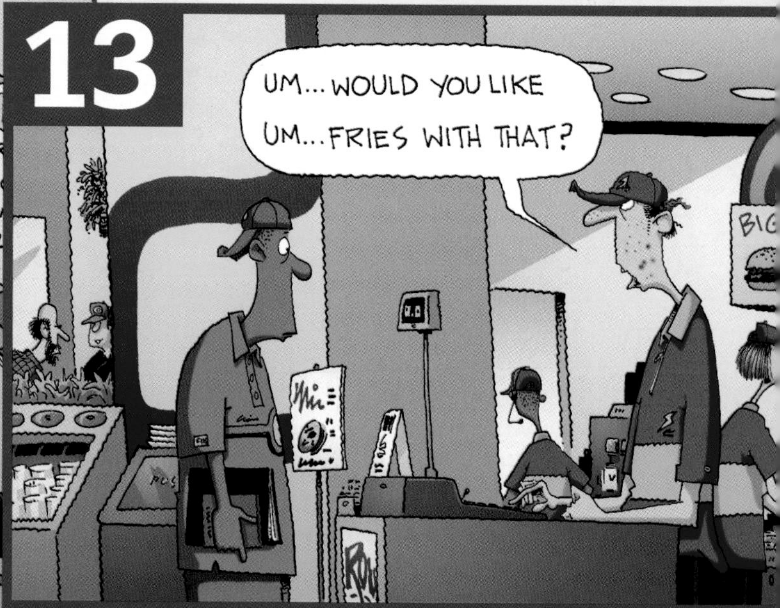
UM... WOULD YOU LIKE UM... FRIES WITH THAT?

The upside of the whole thing is that it means one less menial and humiliating minimum wage summer job that you have to put on your resumé.

ESSAY TOPICS GUARANTEED TO LAND YOU IN SUMMER SCHOOL

- RING AND RUN: A SCIENTIFIC STUDY OF DOORBELLS
- CAPS I HAVE WORN BACKWARDS (A SHOW AND TELL PROJECT)
- GROWING GYM SOCK FUNGUS: A FIELD GUIDE TO SUCCESS
- KLINGON GRAFFITI AN UNRECOGNIZED CAREER OPPORTUNITY
- CHUGGING SLURPEES AND ITS EFFECT ONNNNNN TTHHHHE BRAAAAININININ

TALES FROM the DUCK SIDE

SLITHERING HEIGHTS

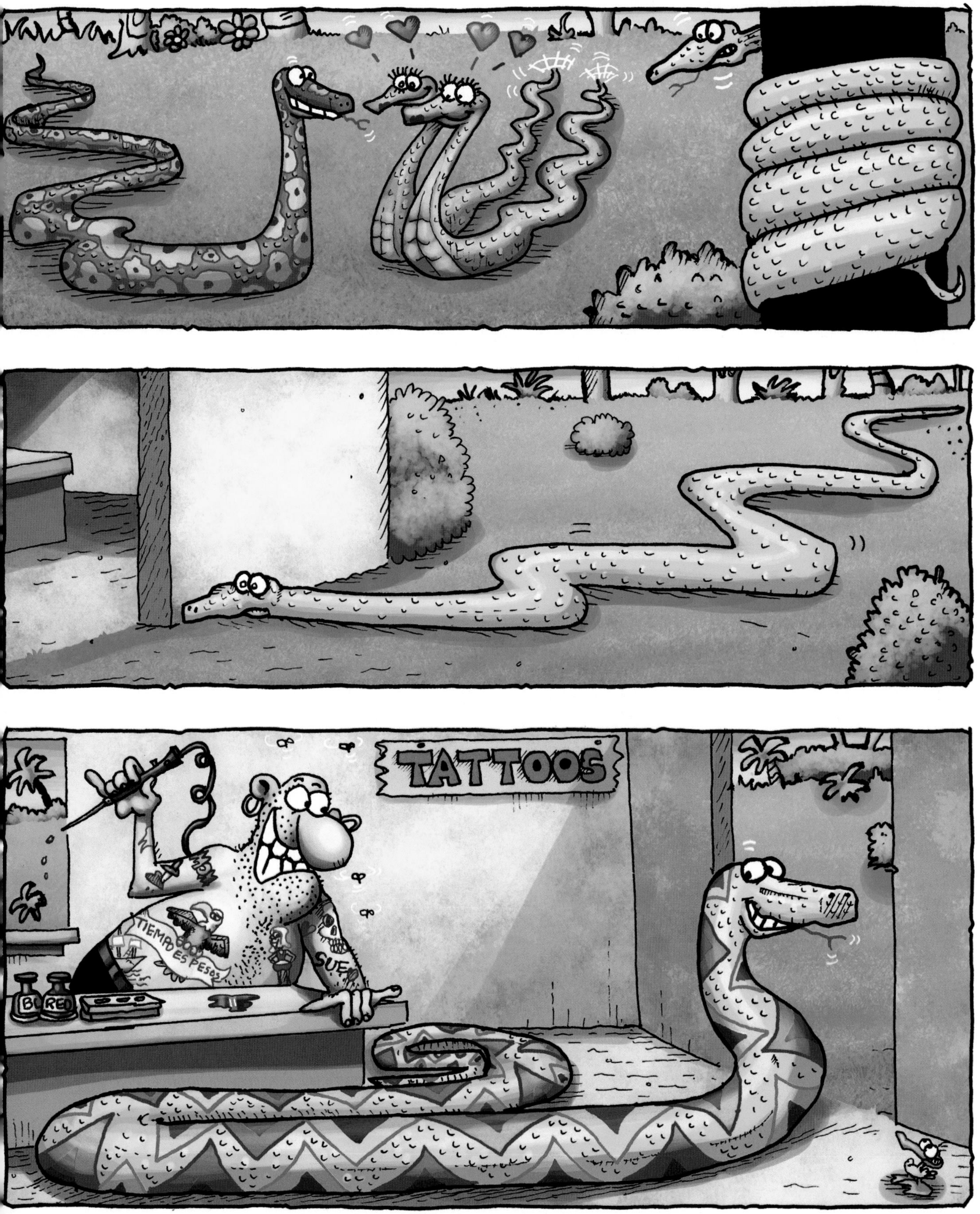
TATTOOS
TIEMPO ES PESOS
SUE
RED

ARTIST AND WRITER: DUCK EDWING COLORIST: CARRIE STRACHAN

IN BLOG WE TRUST DEPT.

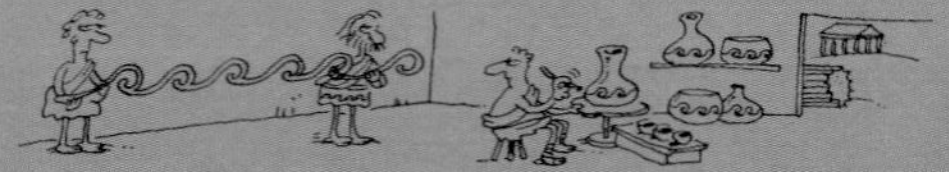

Planet TAD!!!!!

http://www.galaxyo'blogs.com/planettad

Search

Planet TAD!!!!!

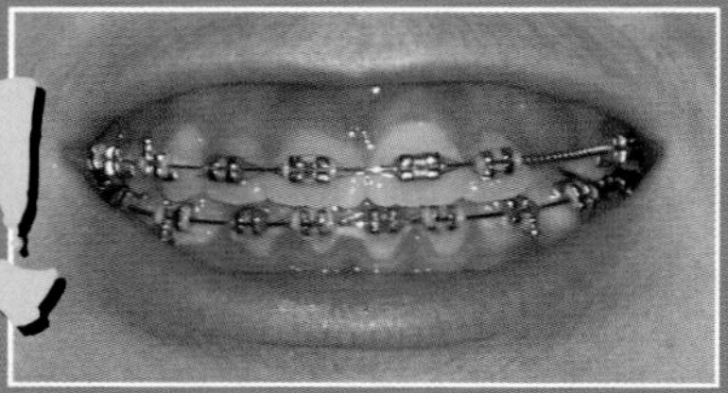

[**About Me**]

[**Name**|Tad]
[**Grade**|9]
[**Monkeys or Apes?**|Monkeys]

[15 February|**03:19pm**]

[**mood**| bored]

In my biology textbook, I read that even blind chameleons change color to match their surroundings. I asked my dad how they figured that out, and he said, "Well, I guess they did a study where they blinded some chameleons and then saw what happened."

I think it's weird that somewhere out there in the world, there's a guy whose job title is: Chameleon Blinder.

I wonder how you know when you've successfully blinded a chameleon. Do you ask it how many fingers you're holding up? Or what?

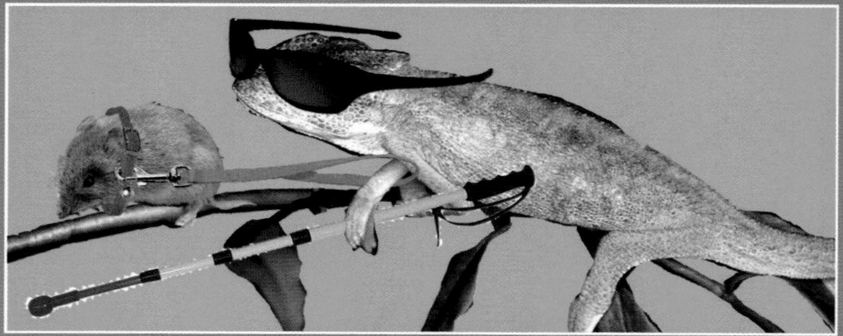

[15 February|**06:41pm**]

I've been thinking about it, and if I ever have a band, it will be called Blind Chameleon.

[16 February|**05:50pm**]

[**mood**| impatient]

My birthday is now six days away. The number of days until I can drive can now be measured in mere hundreds. I pointed that out to my mom today, and she said, "I'll savor every one of them."

Mom's sarcastic sometimes.

[17 February|**03:36pm**]

Chuck Wiggins brought his Nintendo DS to school today. He let me see it. That's all he let me do, though — see it. He wouldn't let me hold it, because, he said, "My mom said I can't let people play with it, because they might break it. Plus, it's flu season, so it's better not to touch things other people have touched." (Chuck's a nice guy, but his mom's super-nervous about everything, and as a result, so's he. Until he was in sixth grade, she made Chuck wear a helmet on the school bus.)

The Nintendo DS is pretty cool — it's got a program that makes it look like it's got a puppy inside it, and you can make it fetch and stay and stuff. Chuck really likes it because his mom won't let him have a dog, because she's afraid it might one day go crazy and kill him just like this dog she saw on the news. I really want a Nintendo DS for my birthday — I've already asked Mom and Dad. I told

[mood| hungry]

If you think about it, "tater tot" is a bad name for a food, because it suggests that you're eating potato babies.

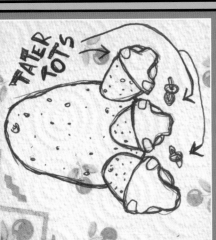

[mood| envious]

I really need a Nintendo DS. In study hall today, Chuck and my friend Darren were sitting on opposite sides of the room, racing against each other on Mario Kart on their DS-es. I had nothing to do but draw baby potato angels.

[21 February|03:43pm]

[mood| anxious]

At breakfast, I reminded my mom and dad that I want a Nintendo DS for my birthday. And my mom said, "Well, maybe if you're good, you'll get that GameBoy you want." And I got all worried and said, "No! I want a DS! Why did you think I wanted a GameBoy? I have a GameBoy!" And she said, "Oh, a DS? Well, it's probably too late to get you one of those." And then she smiled at my dad. So I think they're just messing with my head.

At least, I really hope that's all they're doing.

[22 February|06:50am]

[mood| birthday]

I got a Nintendo DS! Can't blog now — I'm teaching Chuckbiter to fetch.

[28 February|07:26pm]

[mood| devastated]

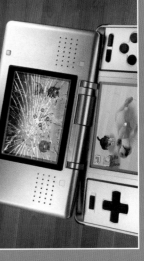

Bad news. I went over to Chuck's today, and Darren came over, and we were all playing with our DS-es. And then I put my DS on the floor and went to the kitchen to get a soda, and then, when I came back, I stepped on it and broke it.

I don't even know what was worse — breaking my DS, or having Chuck's mom come in the room immediately afterward and say, "You see, Chuck? That's why you shouldn't let Tad touch your things."

WRITER: TIM CARVELL   ARTIST: BRIAN DURNIAK

ONE DAY IN THE COUNTRY

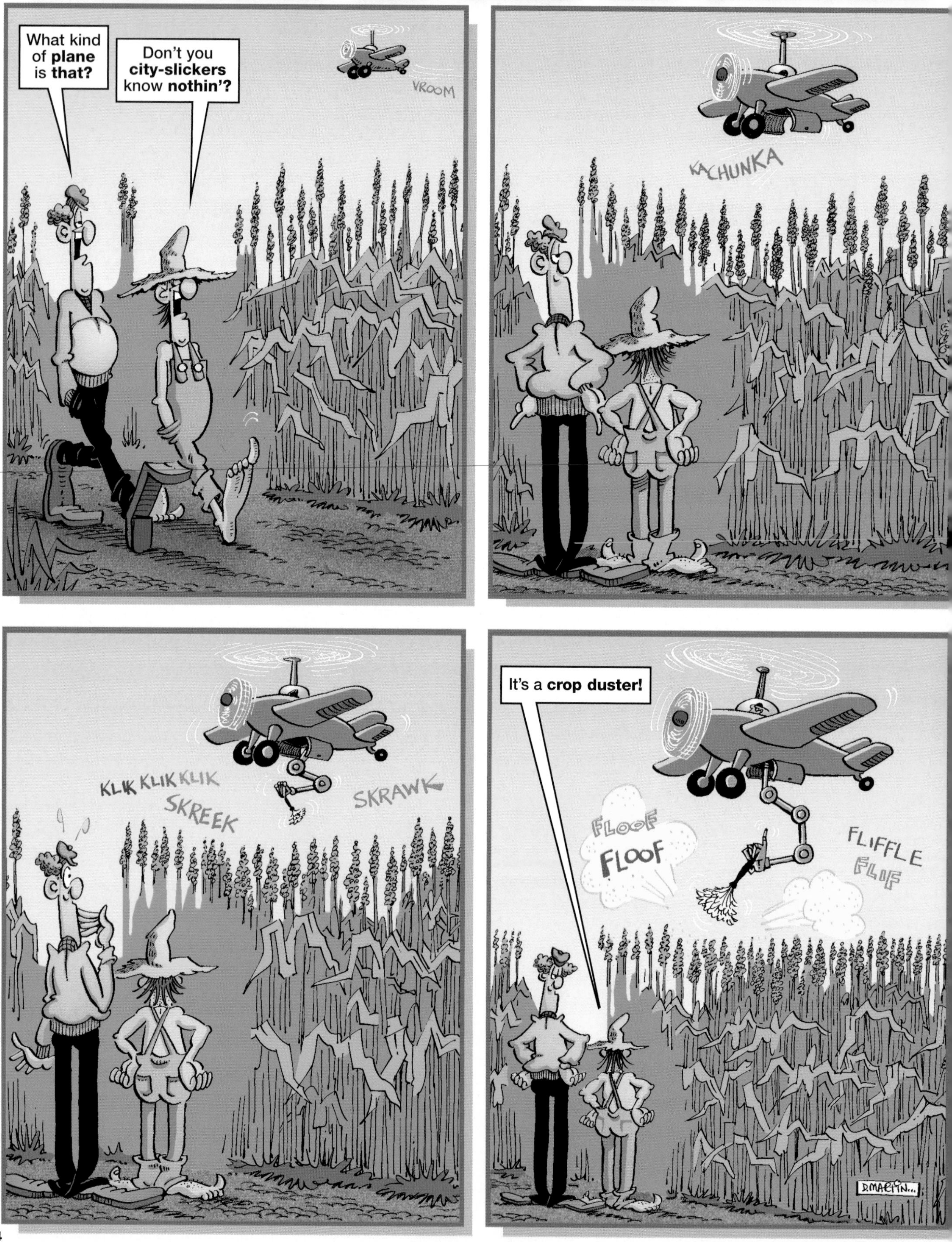

What kind of **plane** is **that?**
Don't you **city-slickers** know **nothin'?**
VROOM
KACHUNKA
KLIK KLIK KLIK
SKREEK
SKRAWK
It's a **crop duster!**
FLOOF
FLOOF
FLIFFLE
FLIF
D.MARTIN...

WRITER: CHARLIE KADAU ARTIST: DON MARTIN

If you like **THIS BOOK,**
a younger reader you know
is sure to like our

DELIGHTFUL ANIMAL BOOKS

shown on the following pages!

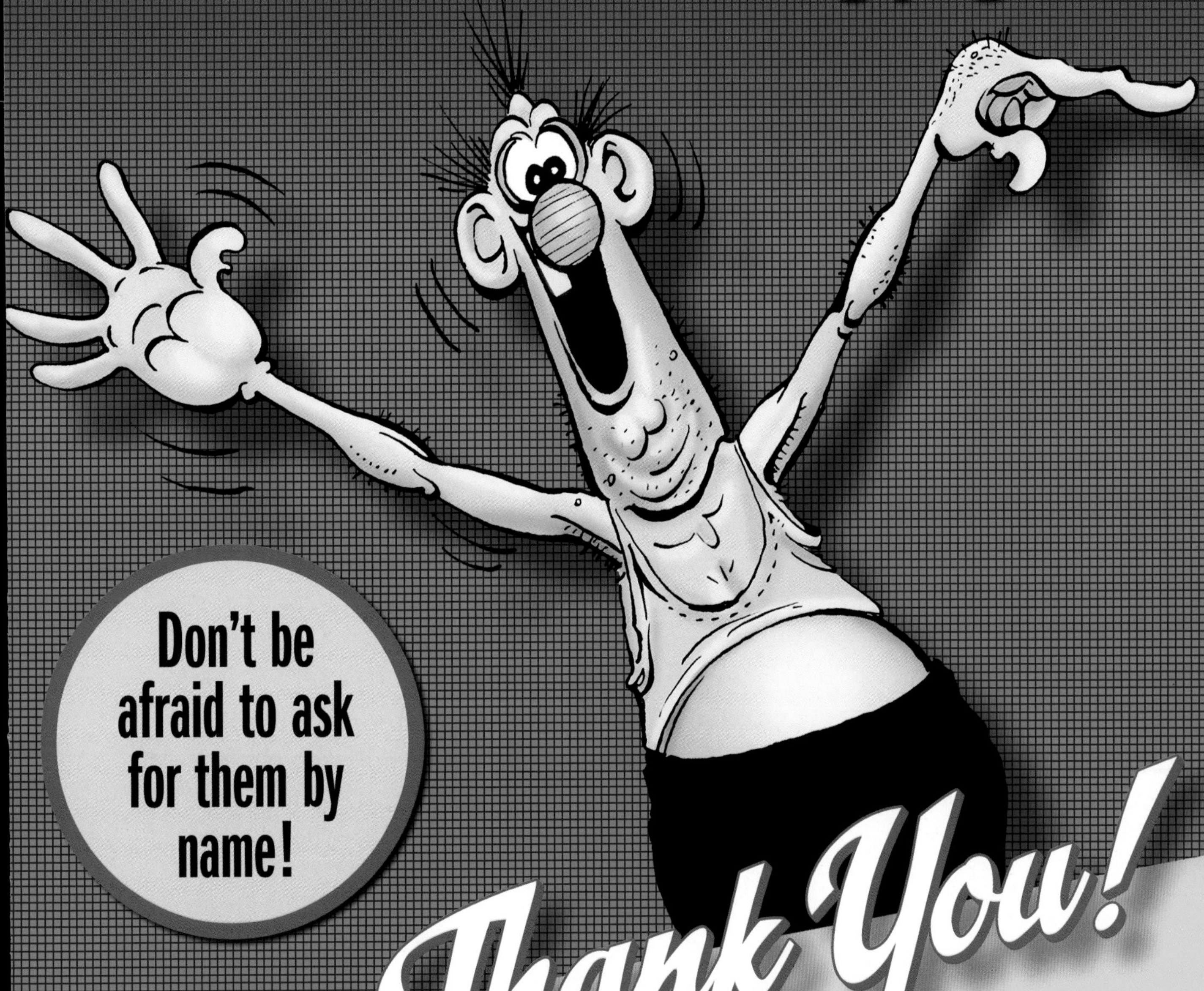

Don't be afraid to ask for them by name!

Thank You!

BAD DOG, CARL

By Alexandra Stray

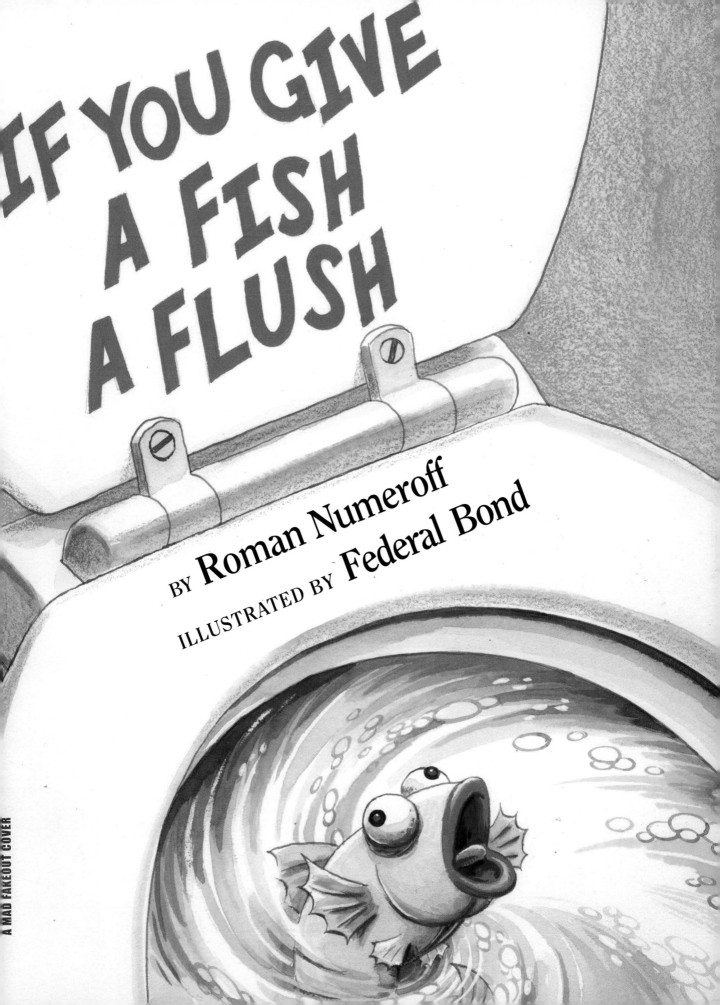

IF YOU GIVE A FISH A FLUSH

BY **Roman Numeroff**

ILLUSTRATED BY **Federal Bond**

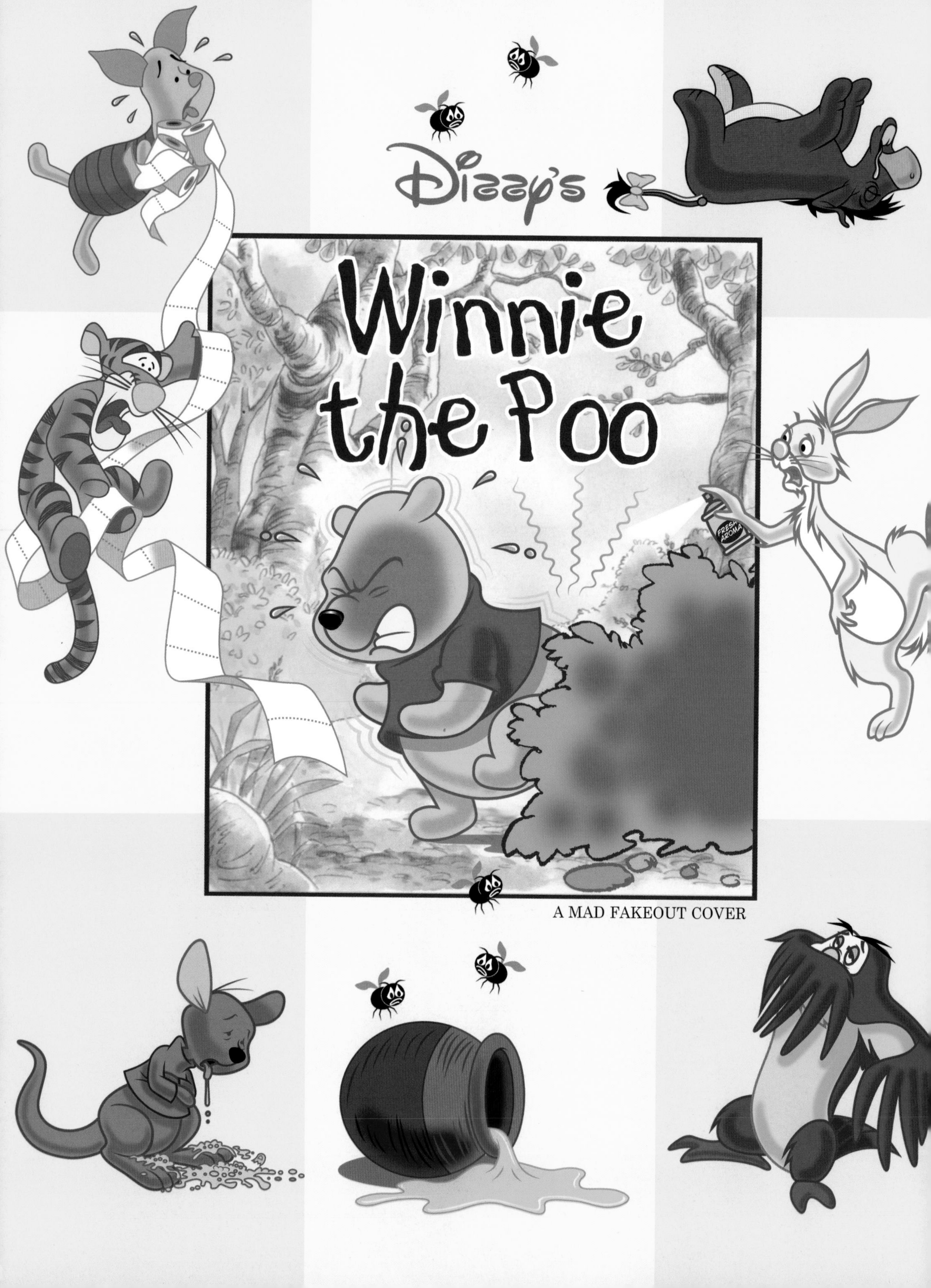
Dizzy's
Winnie the Poo
FRESH AROMA
A MAD FAKEOUT COVER

JOKE AND DAGGER DEPT.

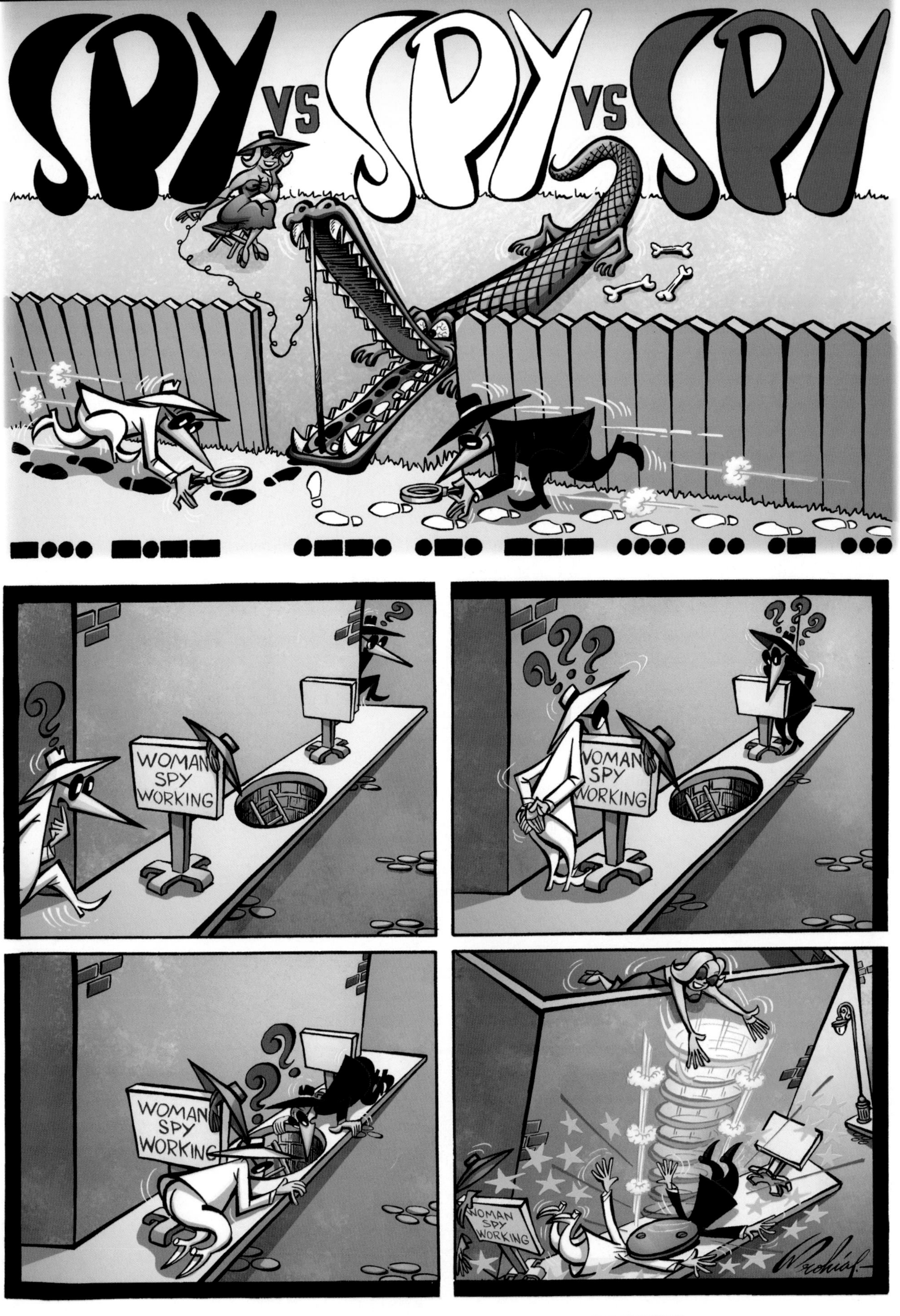
SPY VS SPY VS SPY
WOMAN SPY WORKING
WOMAN SPY WORKING
WOMAN SPY WORKING
WOMAN SPY WORKING
Prohias

WRITER AND ARTIST: ANTONIO PROHIAS COLORIST: CARRIE STRACHAN

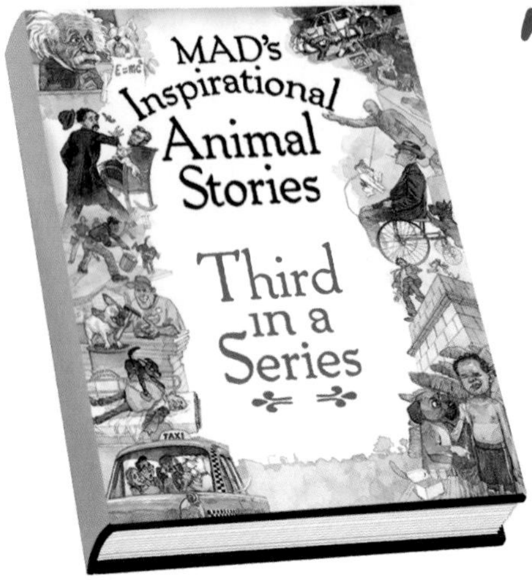
MAD's
Inspirational
Animal
Stories
Third
in a
Series
TAXI

The Eye of a Kitten

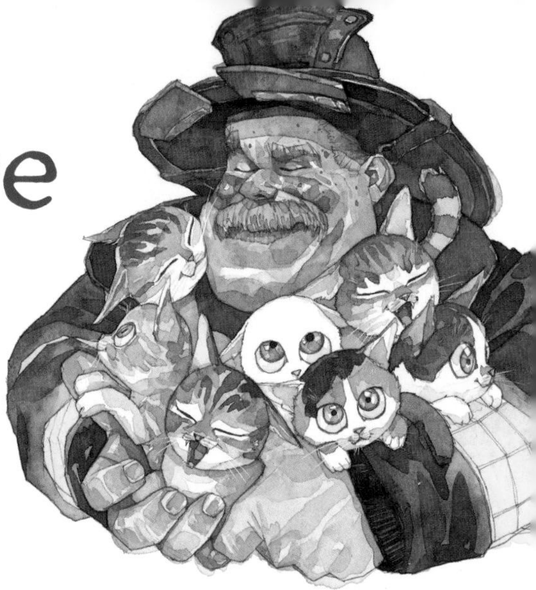

My name is Joe and I've been a Chicago fireman for almost five months now. In that time you could say I've seen it all. I've seen buildings on fire. I've seen buildings NOT on fire. I've seen things on fire I swear I didn't think could even catch on fire. I've seen "safety" matches that, frankly, didn't look all that "safe." But nothing prepared me for seeing an overcrowded nursing home on fire with an adorable litter of kittens, all confused and scared, trapped inside!

There's more to being a fireman than racing through red lights, squirting water into windows and chopping down doors.

It's called saving lives.

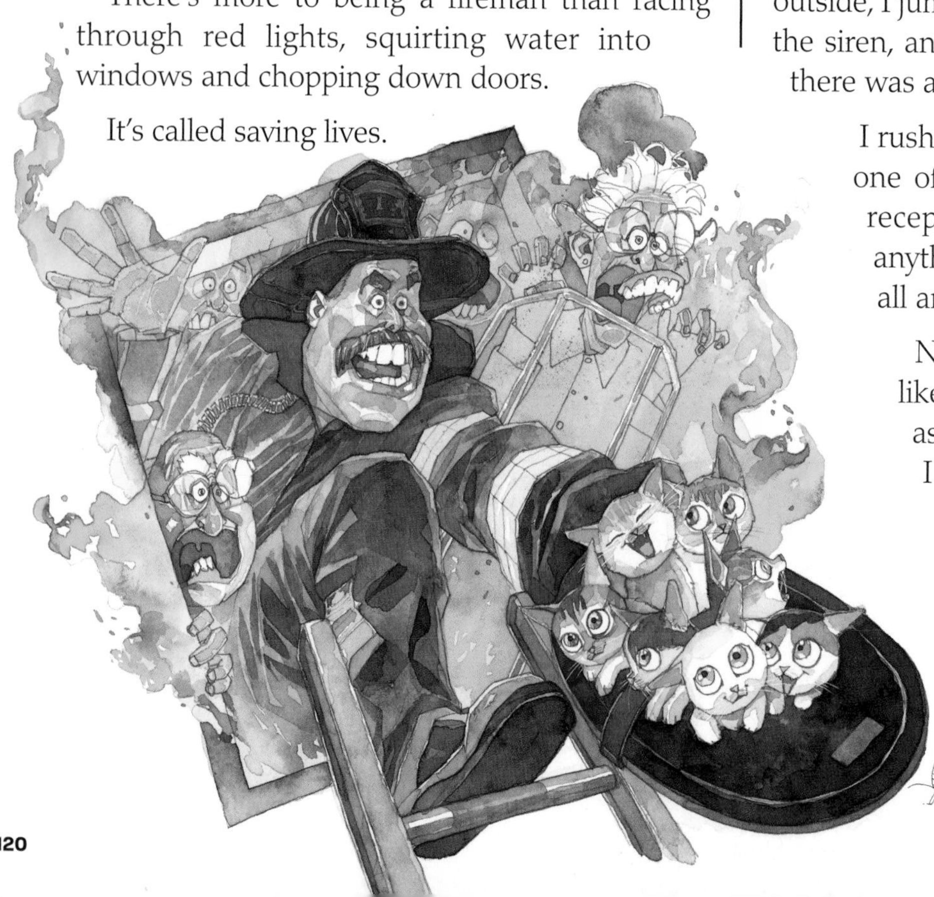

But is a human's life more important than a kitten's? I don't know; that wasn't on the firemen's test. But I know how I felt when I looked in the window and through the smoke saw all those elderly people in a panic, every one of them capable of stepping right on one of those little, defenseless, darling kittens.

I smashed a window, sending glass everywhere. As I went to pick up their cardboard home, it crumbled in my hands. I grabbed a fire helmet from a colleague who had collapsed nearby and I used it as a basket for them. Then outside, I jumped into the closest truck, turned on the siren, and drove north, where I remembered there was a veterinarian's office.

I rushed in and handed over the kittens to one of the several vets sitting around the reception area. I didn't have to say anything; my gear and expression said it all and they sprang into action.

Nervously, I paced for what seemed like hours. Finally, a vet emerged and asked me how I wanted to pay for this. I told him we'd charge it to the county.

"In that case, we better do more testing," he winked and added, "You go home and get some rest; you can't do any good here."

What good could I do at home? I'd just worry myself sick to the point of vomiting. But I did go home for a change of clothes and, sure enough, I vomited on them before I could get into them.

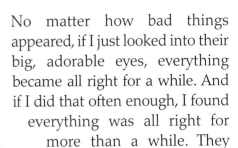

There were a number of messages on my answering machine. Most were from the Chief, who wanted to know where I was and what I did with the hook and ladder. Some folks just aren't cat people and you-know-who, I'm afraid, is one of them. I'd call him later; I didn't want to tie up my phone in case the doctors needed to reach me with some urgent, early test results.

For the next two weeks I practically lived in their reception area, praying for their recovery. At last the test results came: there was a piece of glass in a paw of one kitten, several of them had been dehydrated, and all of them had become addicted to pain killers, but overall, it was good news.

I didn't realize that each of the kittens had been assigned their own night nurse but that sure explained why the bill was almost six figures.

Since their other "home" was burnt to a crisp, I realized I now had 7 new "roommates."

When we got home, I was surprised to learn there was a warrant out for my arrest. It was then I realized that these fuzzy treasures had a special gift to give me.

No matter how bad things appeared, if I just looked into their big, adorable eyes, everything became all right for a while. And if I did that often enough, I found everything was all right for more than a while. They were magical hours that turned into magical days. Then magical weeks soon followed.

Try it and see for yourself. It's what I have come to call the Miracle of the Kittens. But before that, I called it Kitty-time in Blissville. I'd tried Felines in Funtown – that was okay for a while, but then it started to annoy me. Puttie Tats in Wonderland actually angered me, but I used it anyway. Then there's Cutie-Pies from Kremulon, which is a distant planet I travel to when things get weird on Earth and I get the feeling my head is going to start changing shape again.

I'm going to take the kitties with me next time.

— Joe the Fireman
(Temporarily on Indefinite Suspension)

WRITER: BRIAN MCCONNACHIE
ARTIST: LEONARDO RODRIGUEZ

Sergio Aragonés Presents

A MAD LOOK

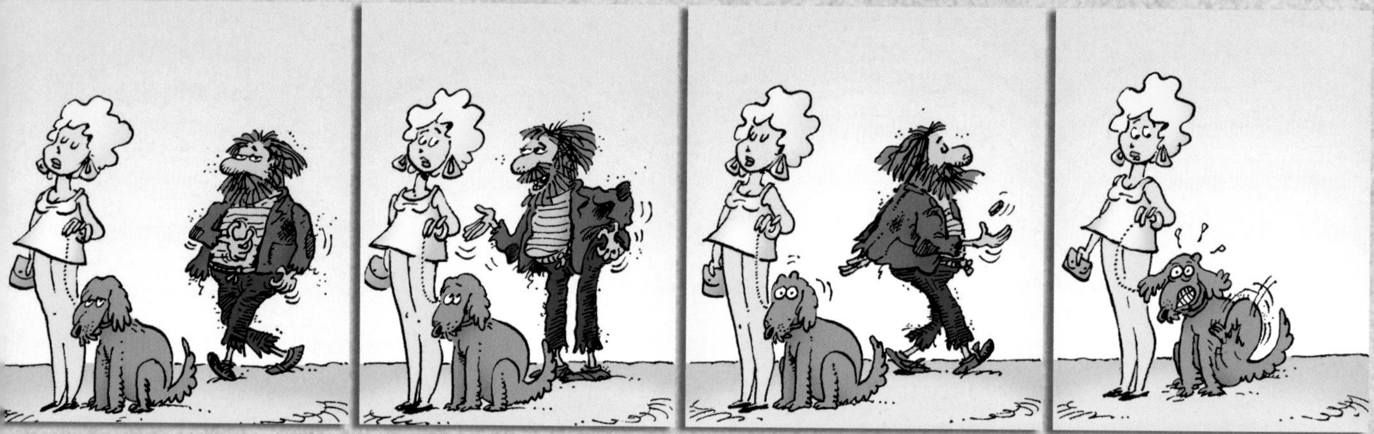

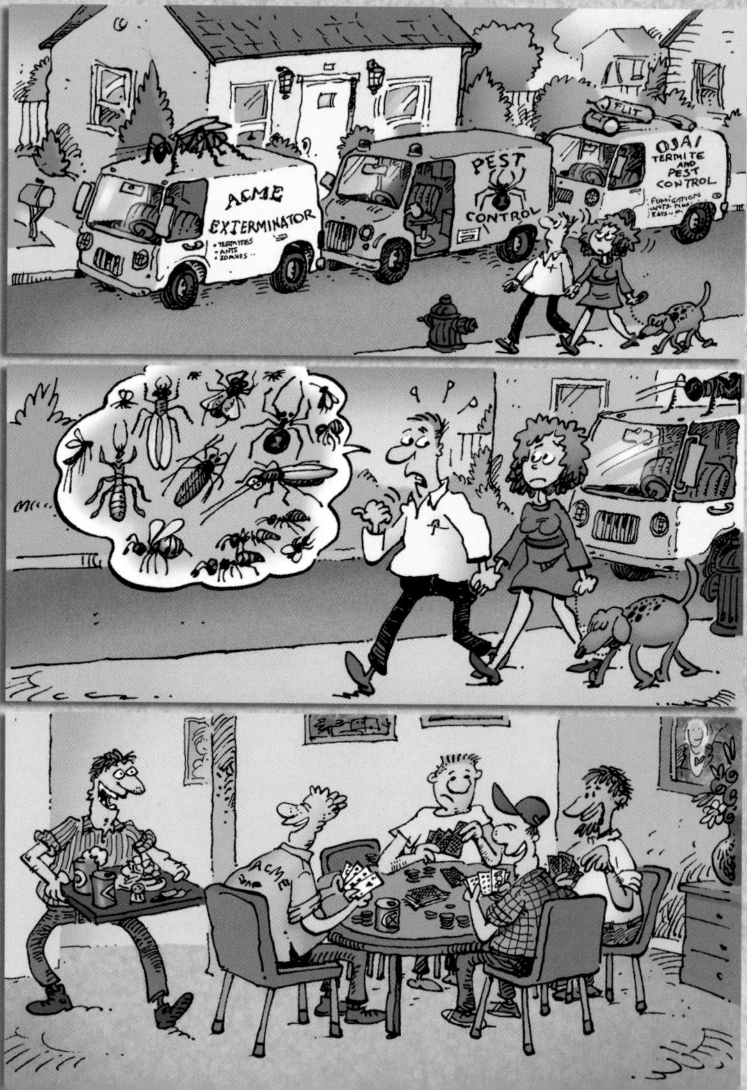
FLIT
ACME
EXTERMINATOR
PEST
CONTROL
OJAI
TERMITE
AND
PEST
CONTROL
FUMIGATION
ACME

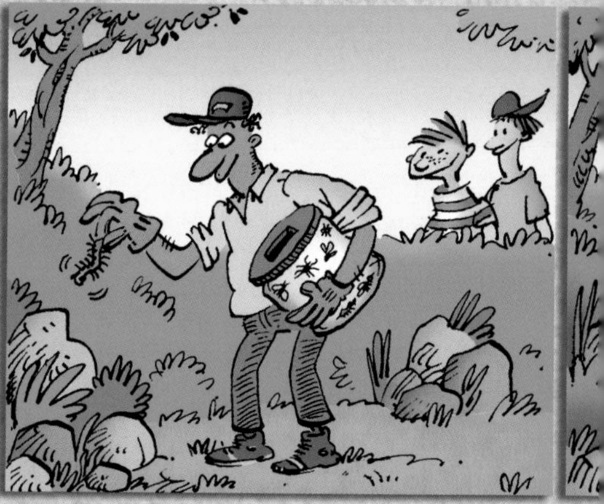

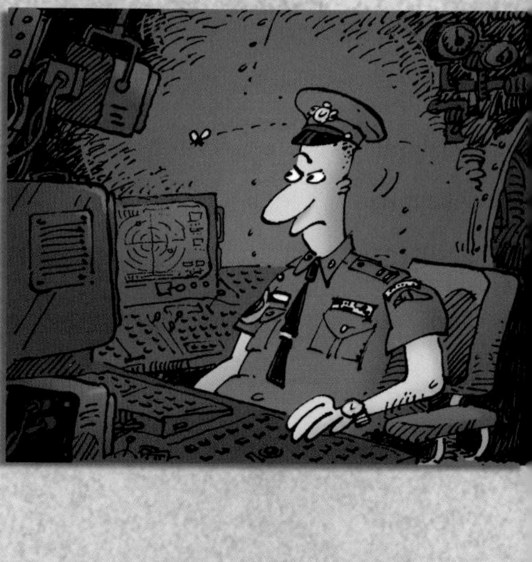

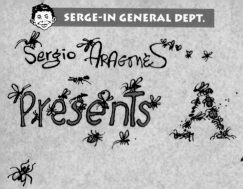

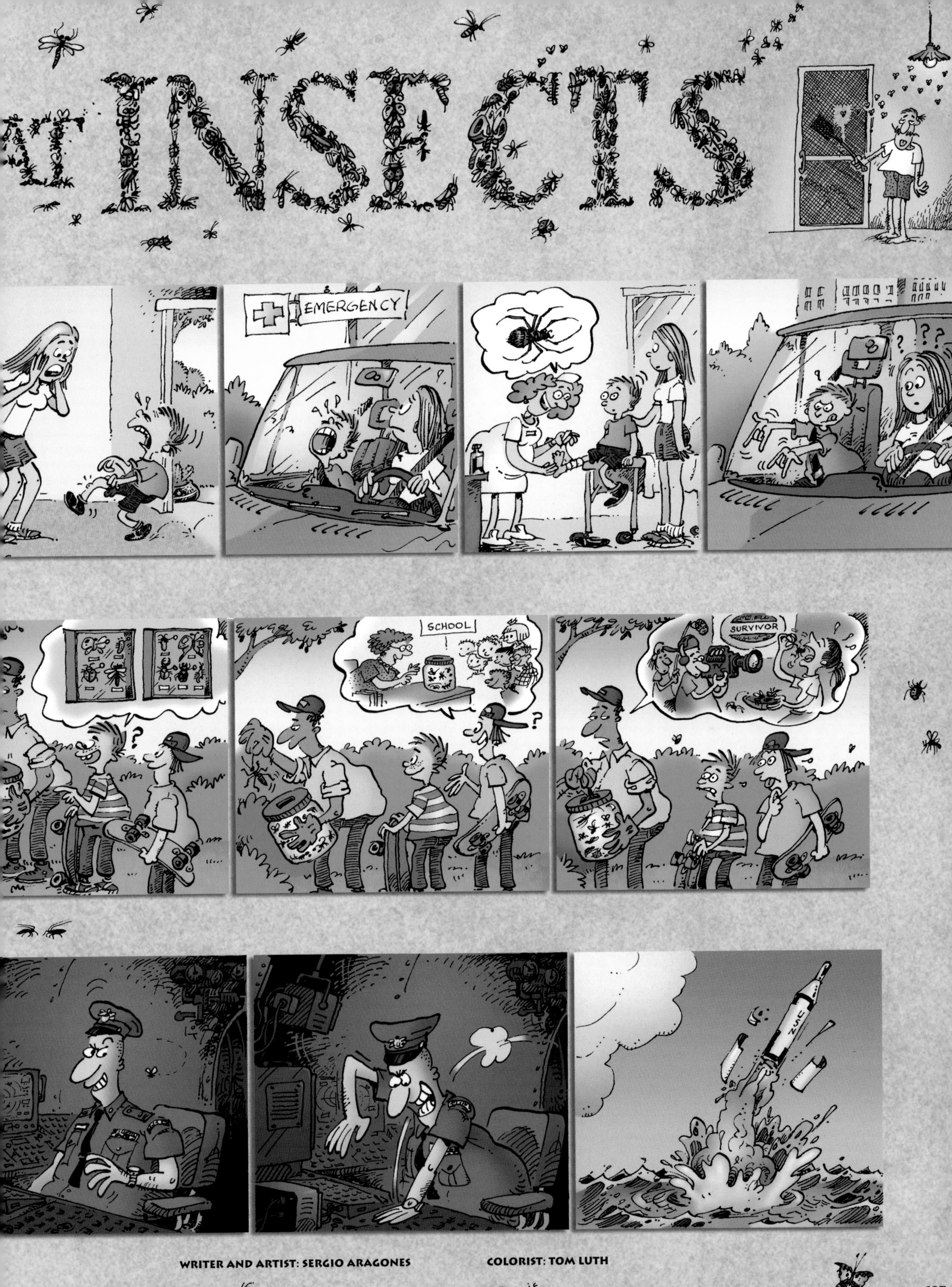
INSECTS
EMERGENCY
SCHOOL
SURVIVOR
USN

WRITER AND ARTIST: SERGIO ARAGONES COLORIST: TOM LUTH

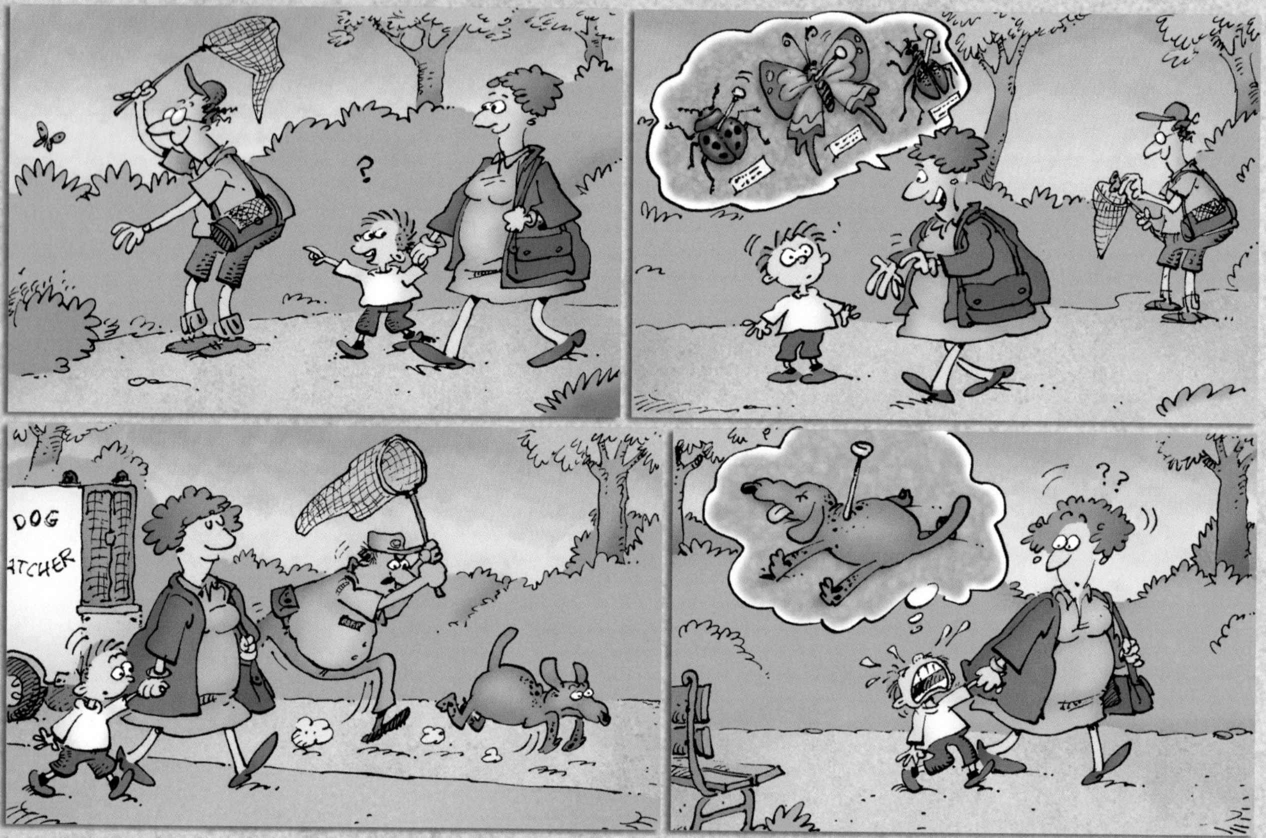
?
DOG
ATCHER
??

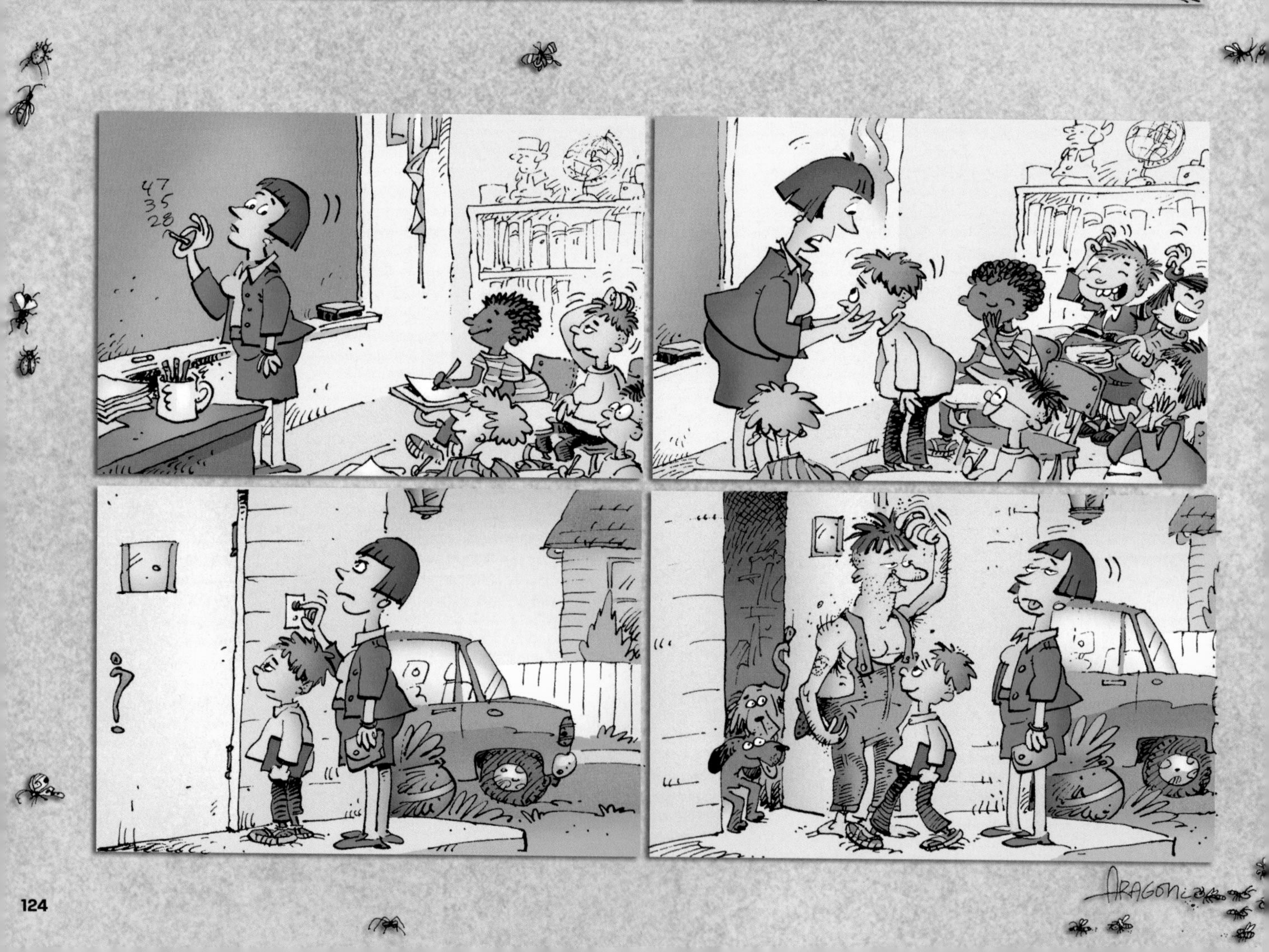
47
35
28
¿

ONE SATURDAY AFTERNOON DOWNTOWN

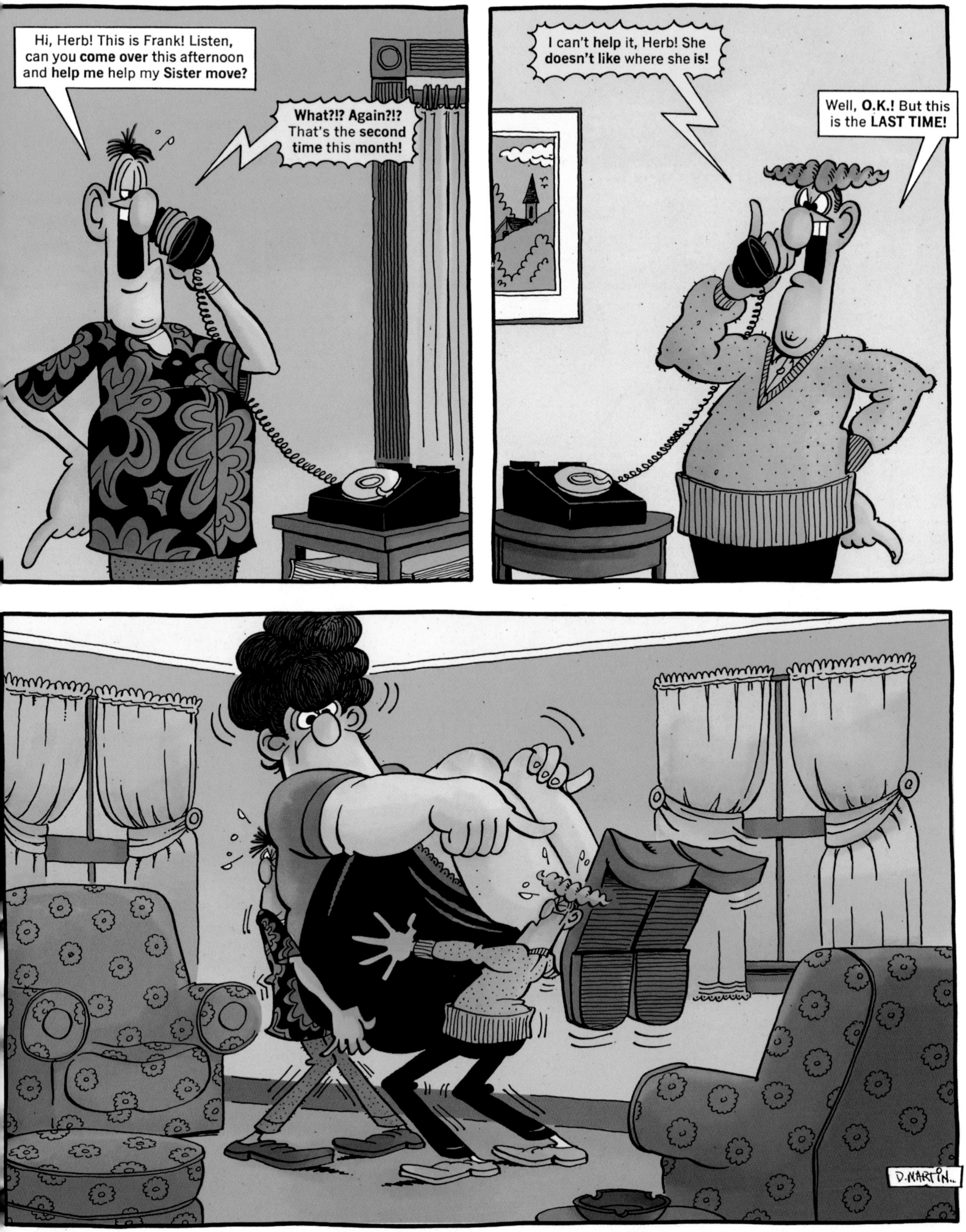
Hi, Herb! This is Frank! Listen, can you **come over** this afternoon and **help me** help my **Sister move?**
What?!? Again?!? That's the **second time** this month!
I can't **help** it, Herb! She **doesn't like** where she **is!**
Well, **O.K.!** But this is the **LAST TIME!**
D. MARTIN

WHEELY PISSED OFF DEPT.

So you're in a vicious battle with your sworn enemies for the fate of the universe, a million miles away from your home planet of Cybertron and facing death at every turn. Sounds tough, right? Well, for the Autobots and Decepticons, all that stuff is child's play compared to these...

Everyday Pet Peeves of TRANSFORMERS

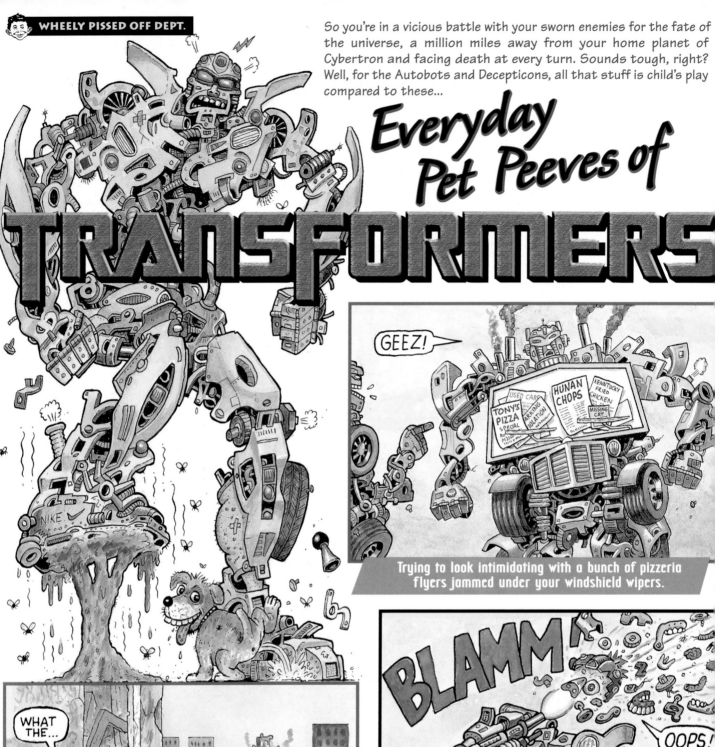

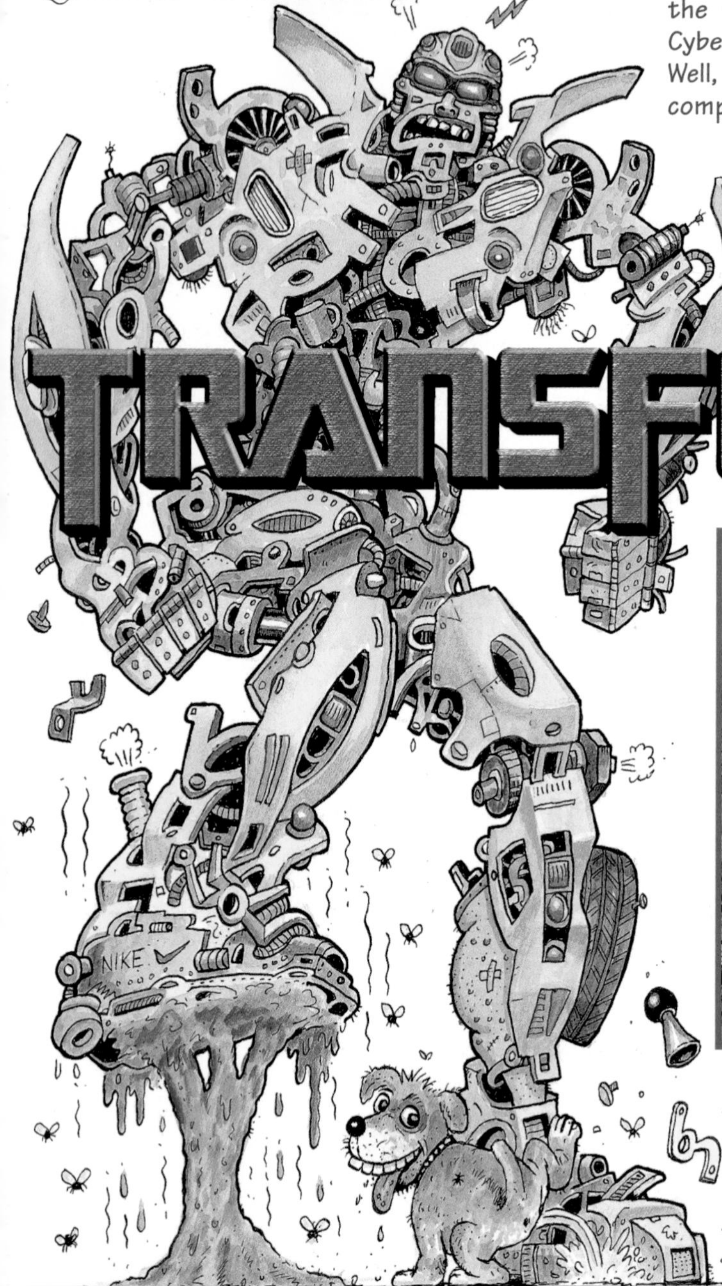
NIKE

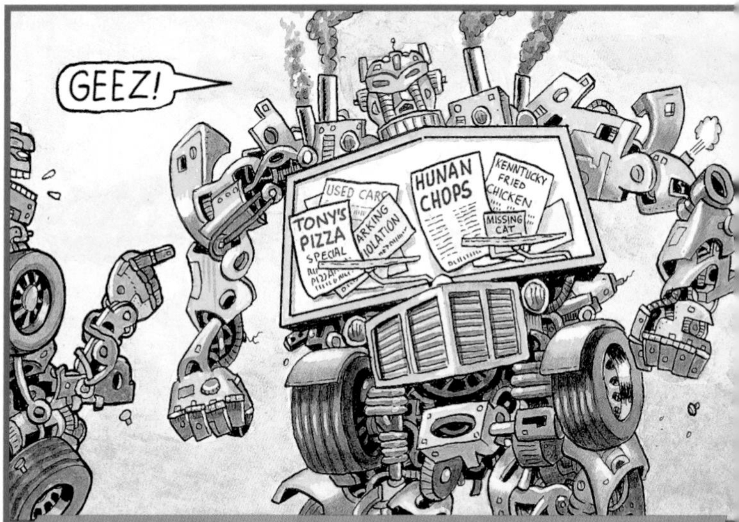
GEEZ!
USED CARS
TONY'S PIZZA SPECIAL
HUNAN CHOPS
KENNTUCKY FRIED CHICKEN
MISSING CAT

Trying to look intimidating with a bunch of pizzeria flyers jammed under your windshield wipers.

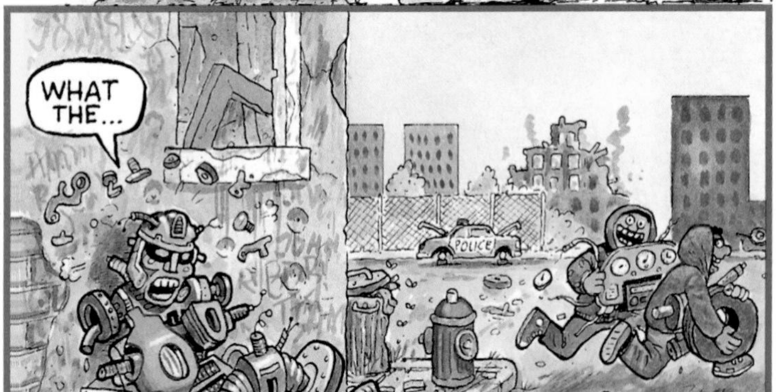
WHAT THE...
POLICE
NO RADIO

Taking a snooze in the "wrong part of town"—and waking up hours later without your arms or legs.

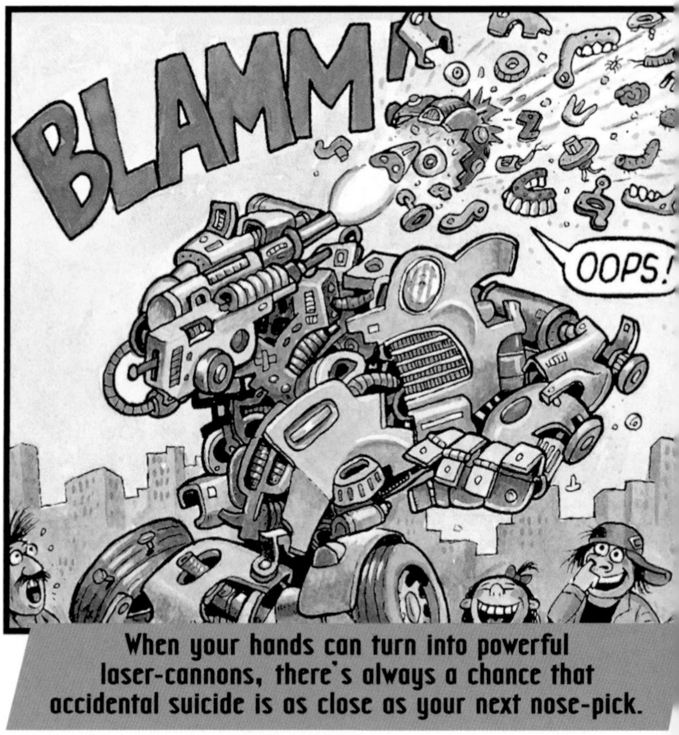
BLAMM!
OOPS!

When your hands can turn into powerful laser-cannons, there's always a chance that accidental suicide is as close as your next nose-pick.

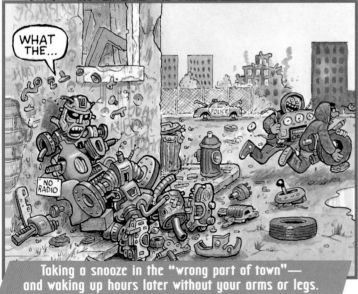

WRITER: JACOB LAMBERT ARTIST: TOM BUNK

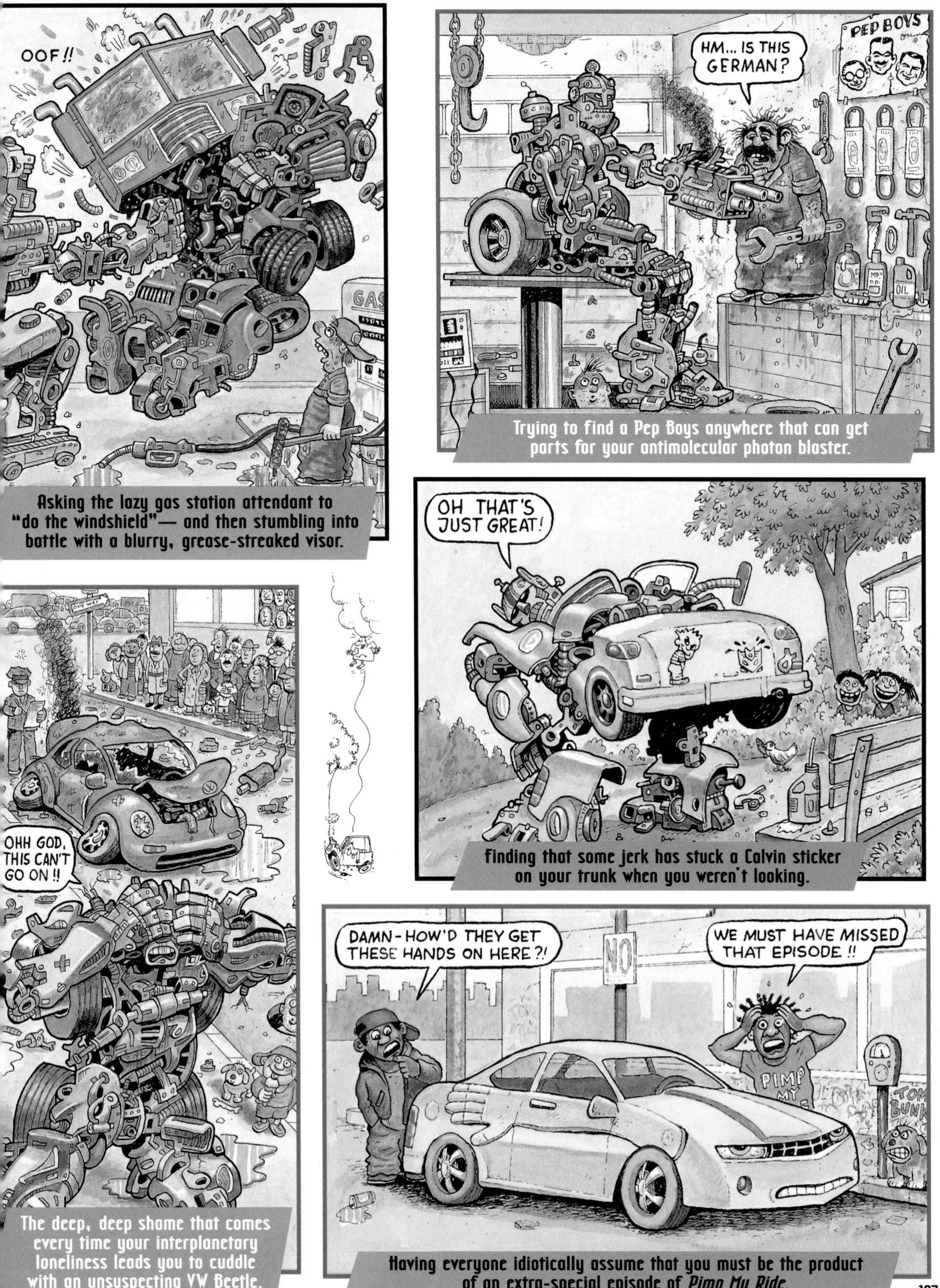
OOF!!
GAS
Asking the lazy gas station attendant to "do the windshield"— and then stumbling into battle with a blurry, grease-streaked visor.
HM... IS THIS GERMAN?
PEP BOYS
OIL
Trying to find a Pep Boys anywhere that can get parts for your antimolecular photon blaster.
OH THAT'S JUST GREAT!
Finding that some jerk has stuck a Calvin sticker on your trunk when you weren't looking.
ONE WAY
OHH GOD, THIS CAN'T GO ON!!
The deep, deep shame that comes every time your interplanetary loneliness leads you to cuddle with an unsuspecting VW Beetle.
DAMN-HOW'D THEY GET THESE HANDS ON HERE?!
WE MUST HAVE MISSED THAT EPISODE!!
NO
PIMP MY
Having everyone idiotically assume that you must be the product of an extra-special episode of Pimp My Ride.

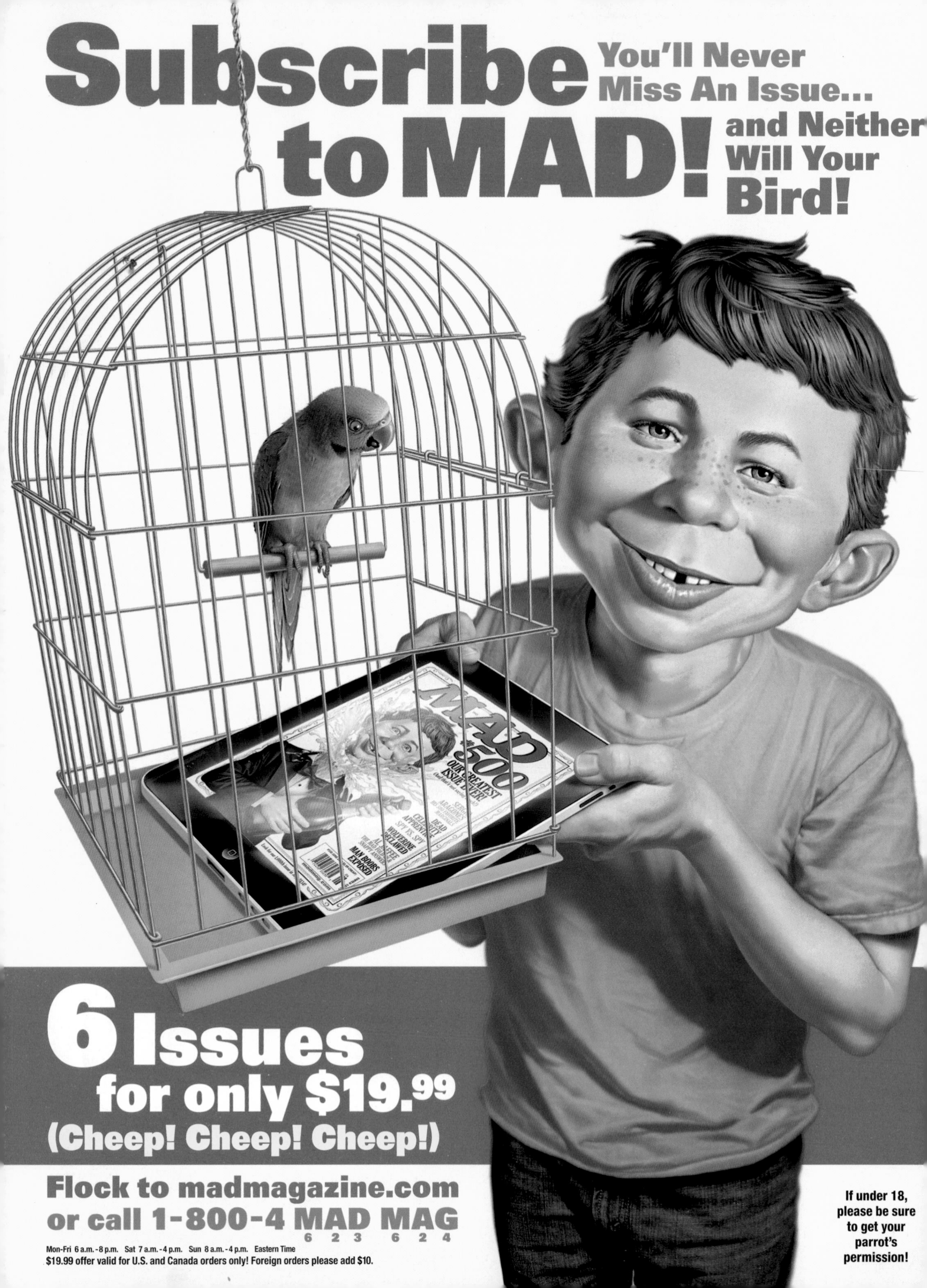
Subscribe to MAD!
You'll Never Miss An Issue... and Neither Will Your Bird!
6 Issues for only $19.99
(Cheep! Cheep! Cheep!)
Flock to madmagazine.com
or call 1-800-4 MAD MAG
6 2 3 6 2 4
Mon-Fri 6 a.m.-8 p.m. Sat 7 a.m.-4 p.m. Sun 8 a.m.-4 p.m. Eastern Time
$19.99 offer valid for U.S. and Canada orders only! Foreign orders please add $10.
If under 18, please be sure to get your parrot's permission!